Urban Development
in Southeast Asia

Urban Development in Southeast Asia

Regional Cities and Local Government

Jürgen Rüland

Westview Press

BOULDER • SAN FRANCISCO • OXFORD

Copyright © 1992 by Westview Press, Inc.

Published in 1992 in the United States of America by Westview Press, Inc., 5500 Central Avenue, Boulder, Colorado 80301-2847, and in the United Kingdom by Westview Press, 36 Lonsdale Road, Summertown, Oxford OX2 7EW

Library of Congress Cataloging-in-Publication Data
Rüland, Jürgen, 1953–
   Urban development in Southeast Asia : regional cities and local
government / by Jürgen Rüland.
      p. cm.
   Includes bibliographical references.
   ISBN 0-8133-0104-1
   1. Urbanization—Asia, Southeastern—Cross-cultural studies.
2. Urbanization—Thailand—Chiang Mai—Cross-cultural studies.
3. Urbanization—Philippines—Iloilo—Cross-cultural studies.
4. Urbanization—Malaysia—Pinang—Cross-cultural studies.
5. Municipal government—Thailand—Chiang Mai—Cross-cultural
studies.   6. Municipal government—Philippines—Iloilo—Cross-
cultural studies.   7. Municipal government—Malaysia—Pinang—Cross-
cultural studies.   I. Title.
HT384.A786R85   1992
307.1'416'0959—dc20
                                                                    92-1335
                                                                    CIP

Printed and bound in the United States of America

The paper used in this publication meets the requirements
of the American National Standard for Permanence of Paper
for Printed Library Materials Z39.48-1984.

10   9   8   7   6   5   4   3   2   1

For Dorothea, Angkana, and Anchalee

Contents

Tables and Diagrams

Diagrams

Acknowledgments

The subsequent study grew out of a research project entitled "Local Government and Urban Development in Malaysia, Thailand, and the Philippines", sponsored by the Foundation Volkswagenwerk, Hannover, Federal Republic of Germany from 1984 to 1987. I am greatly indebted to the foundation as without its generous financial support it would have been impossible to carry out this project. I am particularly grateful to the late Dr. Wolfgang Wittwer, who was in charge of the foundation's Southeast Asia program and who guided the project through its various stages.

The support I received from the Arnold Bergstraesser Institute in Freiburg was just great. My particular gratitude goes to the institute's director, Prof. Dr. Dieter Oberndörfer. He was my academic mentor, and he untiringly encouraged me to carry on with the project. I greatly appreciate his and my colleagues' advice and valuable suggestions provided in various seminars, lengthy discussions, and many casual conversations. Another person who deserves my sincere gratitude is Prof. Donald McCloud, who read an earlier version of this study. His scholarly comments helped me a lot in revising the study for publication.

Quite a few persons and institutions were kind enough to help me in the crucial preparatory stage of the project. Among them were the Centre for Administrative Promotion of the German Foundation for International Development headed by Mr. Joachim Krell and Prof. Michael Faltas of the Institute of Social Studies, The Hague. Also gratefully acknowledged is the friendly cooperation of Prof. Dr. Hans-Dieter Evers, Centre for Sociology of Development, University of Bielefeld.

Without reliable and knowledgeable counterparts in the region, a broadly designed comparative study like this could hardly be carried out. Hence, I feel greatly obliged to these counterparts who hosted me during field research, provided access to their research infrastructure, and shared with me their intimate knowledge about the land and people. My two main counterparts, Dr. M.L. Bhansoon Ladavalya, who was the director of the Social Research Institute of Chiang Mai University, and Atty. Tomas A. Sajo, the dean of the School of Development Management of the University of the Philippines in the Visayas, Iloilo City, introduced me to many of my interviewees and helped me in conducting the surveys. Special thanks also go to Dr. Goh Ban Lee of the Centre for Policy Research, Universiti Sains Malaysia, Penang; Dr. Phang Siew Nooi, Faculty of Economics and Administration, University of Malaya, Kuala Lumpur; Dr. Philip Mawhood and Dr. Malcolm Norris, both senior faculty members of the Institute of Local Government Studies, United Kingdom. I greatly benefited from their scholarship, the discussions with them, and the facilitation of numerous contacts.

Many others have lent me their support, most notably some leading officials in the studied cities. In particular, I would like to mention the kind cooperation of Chiang Mai's permanent city clerk, Khun Wanchai Boonyasuratna, and the former city mayor of Iloilo, Madame Rosa Caram. Also, the support I got from Dr. Gaudioso Sosmeña, the director of the Bureau of Local Government Supervision in Manila; Ms. Ludy Momongan, former director of the Philippine State Accounting and Auditing Center; Dr. Phiraphol Tritasavit, the chief of the Office for Urban Development in Bangkok; and Mr. Veloo, the director of Malaysia's Department of Local Government went far beyond the usual. I also wish to express my sincerest thanks to Mr. Phaisit Rodsawaeng (Chiang Mai), Ms. Bella Grace Legayada, and Ms. Glecy Villareal (Iloilo City) for their dedicated and most capable research assistance. Ms. Margaret Rae and Mr. John Richardson reviewed the English text, and Dr. Rainer Hampel and Mrs. Margarete Panter spent countless hours on formatting the manuscript. Without their selfless and competent assistance, their patience and expertise, I hardly could have managed the technical intricacies of typesetting.

Last but not least I wish to thank my family, especially my wife, for their patience and continuous encouragement throughout this project.

Jürgen Rüland
Arnold Bergstraesser Institute
Freiburg, Germany

1

Theory and Methodology

Local Government Theory

Local government is a stepchild in development research. The overwhelming number of development studies concentrates on political, administrative, and economic processes at the national level. Where local government has been a topic of research, the focus lay on metropolitan areas. The high degree of *urban primacy* in many Third World countries is thus reflected even in academic research. As the primate city is the seat of the national government and due to its strategic importance for regime stability, research on the governance of metropolitan areas was hardly more than an appendage to studies dealing with national politics and development.

The negligence of local government research stands in stark contrast to the importance of subnational government units for national development. Preoccupation with national politics reveals an interest in only a thin layer of a polity, ignoring the fact that national power must rest on a local foundation. As formulated by Pertierra, the "economic, political or cultural macro-structures are ultimately constituted by local actors" and "any explanation of macro-structures depends on an understanding of local actions" (Pertierra 1987:115). Thus, in their cumulative effects local governments have a real impact on the course of national politics (Ashford 1975). The groups controlling the greatest number of local authorities, the most populous local units or localities well-endowed with resources are likely to play a key role in national decision-making.

But local government does not only serve as a power base determining the relative strength of national power contenders, it is also a vital link in the implementation of development strategies. Without cooperation from local leaders, and without a certain administrative and coordinative capacity at the subnational government level, even the best development strategy is bound to fail.

A thorough review of the literature reveals three concepts central to any discussion on local government: *local autonomy, political participation,* and *socioeconomic development.*

Based on the perception of the community as a natural human grouping, concepts such as local autonomy and participation came to be elevated to ends in themselves. Derived from the works of Madison, de Tocqueville, Mill, and Laski autonomous local government is regarded as an essential institutional device for building or preserving a participatory and pluralistic society. Local government is viewed as an integral part of constitutional checks and balances, adding a vertical or areal dimension (Maass 1959) to the doctrine of the division of power. As Ylvisaker pointed out, there are three basic values associated with the areal division of power: liberty, equality, and welfare (Ylvisaker 1959:30).

The aspect of liberty was most powerfully stressed by de Tocqueville. Without municipal governments a nation cannot have the spirit of liberty (de Tocqueville 1976:68). Local governments with a high degree of local autonomy are held to be a check on an all-powerful central government and the abuse of power (Byrne 1981:23). By creating a plurality of power centers in society, local government was seen as a "bulwark against tyranny, an insurance against dictatorship" (Muttalib and Khan 1982:15), and a device to protect minorities. The dispersal of political power through areal division and the existence of strong, self-reliant local governments would thus guarantee a societal development pattern that rests on the principle of diversity in unity.

The aspect of equality aimed at the participatory dimension of local government (Ylvisaker 1959:32). Through encouraging citizens' political participation, local government, it was argued, would constitute a barrier against the concentration of social, economic, and political power.

In the same context, local government was frequently described as a school of democracy. Due to the proximity of rulers and ruled, electors and elected, the less complex nature of issues and the immediate personal concern of government actions at the local level, the local arena was seen as an ideal ground for political education and socialization.

Finally, the welfare aspect was related to the accountability of local government. Through the proximity of local decision-makers to their constituency, the areal division of power is considered an additional assurance that demands will be heard and, accordingly, public services provided in line with people's needs. The welfare aspect thus emphasizes the need for effective, efficient, and performance-oriented governmental action (Ylvisaker 1959:32).

In the 1950s and 1960s, during and shortly after decolonization, the emerging development literature adopted most of these arguments. This held particularly true for the early *decentralization* literature, under which heading a good part of local government studies in newly independent countries may be classified. Decentralization was defined as the "allocation of decision-making powers to autonomous or semiautonomous subsystems and as a devolution of authority on corporate entities" (Lehner 1984:112). Hence, local autonomy must be regarded as a constituting element of decentralization (Faltas 1982:1).[1]

Decentralization with its focus on local government twice became a major theme in development research (Faltas 1982; Conyers 1983, 1984). The first decentralization debate took place in the 1950s and early 1960s. Most studies appearing in that period strongly stressed the normative character of local government.

Hence, decentralization and, as a corollary, local autonomy were seen as a positive contribution to increased political participation, which would eventually lead to socioeconomic development. In other words, democracy (expressed in terms of local autonomy and political participation) would herald socioeconomic development and an improvement in living conditions.[2] As indicated in Diagram 1.1, participation would act as intervening variable between local autonomy and socioeconomic development.

In the wake of disappointing developmental performances in the years following independence -- sluggish economic growth and endemic political instability -- centralist development theories replaced decentralization strategies in the 1960s. The rise of Third-World socialism based on the organizational principles of democratic centralism and central economic planning further strengthened the trend towards centralization of governmental authority. Yet, by the early 1970s it had become clear that authoritarian, centralist regimes were likewise unable to solve the ever increasing social and economic problems of newly independent nations.

As a result, development theory rediscovered decentralization (Maw-

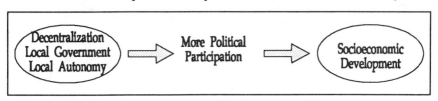

DIAGRAM 1.1 Causal Relations Between Local Autonomy, Political Participation, and Socioeconomic Development

hood 1983:7). In the mid-1970s, concomitant with new development strategies emphasizing basic human needs, "growth with equity", and the "small is beautiful" topos (Schumacher 1977), decentralization was again accorded top priority by development theorists and practitioners. This decentralization debate continues.

However, in the present discussion there is a trend to modify some of the premises of the earlier debate. Although normative justification still plays a certain role, the value connotations are now overarched by a strong emphasis on efficiency. The debate has become more development-oriented, stressing the instrumental character of decentralization, local autonomy, and local government for national development (Faltas 1982:3). Especially among scholars from the Third World there is a trend to view decentralization -- and as a corollary, local autonomy -- as having a direct impact on socioeconomic development (see Diagram 1.2). Unlike in the earlier debate, participation is only a side effect of decentralization and the granting of greater powers to local governments (i.e. more local autonomy).[3]

The instrumental character of decentralization and local government for national development is shown in the following arguments, which Kasfir has somewhat derogatorily called the "standard litany" of development theorists (Kasfir 1983:26): decentralization facilitates the division of labor within the government, thus contributing to a decongestion of the central government from minor issues. It accelerates decision-making and enables government to respond better to local differences. On the premise that "local people know best", local expertise and human resources can be used more efficiently. The delegation of authority is thus seen as a means to increasing the capacity of local units to mobilize local resources for development. On the other hand, the proximity of government and population enables the former to give local people a better understanding of government plans and projects, thus securing the support of the target groups in the implementation of de-

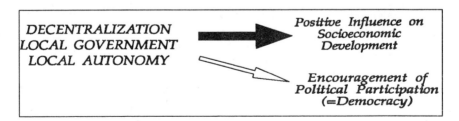

DIAGRAM 1.2 Causal Relations Between Local Autonomy, Socioeconomic Development, and Political Participation

velopment projects (Allen 1990:19). Alderfer's early statement that "local government is one of the keys to sound administration" (Alderfer 1964:175) appears to have become the predominant theme in the present decentralization debate.

Nevertheless, normative elements still persist. Decentralization -- often characterized as an integral part of the *"development from below"* strategy -- refers to the principle of subsidiarity by regarding the smallest possible territorial jurisdiction as the best foundation for economic development. Development from below is *"development from within"* (i.e. based on people's own resources), development by the people, egalitarian and self-reliant development. It rests on the basic needs approach and protects human dignity (Stöhr and Taylor 1981: 454).

From this review of the decentralization debates it is apparent what was central to previous local government research: the interrelation between local autonomy as the ideal and generally most valued form of decentralization, political participation, and socioeconomic development. Explicitly or implicitly, with slight variations and taking into account the terminology of different authors, their view of this interrelationship may be summarized as follows: the more decentralized a governmental structure (i.e. the greater the scope of local autonomy) and/or the greater popular participation in a given political system, the better are the chances for socioeconomic development. These relationships are presented in Diagram 1.3.

However, it is assumed here that this pattern of interrelations is hardly able to explain the complex processes of political and socioeconomic development in Southeast Asian municipalities. It is based mainly on western experiences and does not take into account the historically evolved values that shape the indigenous political culture in the countries of the region. Moreover, the relationships described in Di-

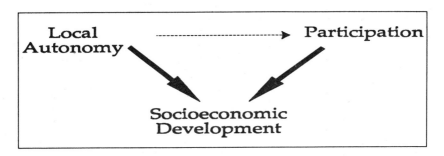

DIAGRAM 1.3 Interrelations Between Local Autonomy, Participation, and Socioeconomic Development

agram 1.3 likewise do not take into account the dynamics of socioeconomic development. In other words, scholars working on local government have rarely paid attention to the *feed-back* relations in this model,[4] thereby neglecting important questions such as how socioeconomic development affects both local autonomy as well as political participation and what is the impact of political participation on local autonomy.

It is, for instance, conceivable that socioeconomic development produces feed-back effects on both autonomy and participation.[5] Rapid socioeconomic development may broaden the social base of the decision-making elite. In the process of development, new social and economic interests may emerge that eventually seek adequate representation in decision-making. At the same time, development creates new and more complex problems and priorities which require additional expertise and technical know-how not available among the established leadership. In this case, changes in the socioeconomic structure of a community also produce changes in leadership composition with possible consequences for the legitimacy of the entire local political subsystem.

In the case of autonomy, these effects can be either direct or indirect. More socioeconomic development may directly induce a greater degree of autonomy, as it enhances the local resources considerably (via greater tax revenues, service fees, licenses, and other income). This, in turn, may make the locality more attractive to qualified government personnel, giving the municipality greater discretion in the delivery of services as well as more opportunities for capital investment and the hiring of more qualified personnel. Indirectly, it may influence autonomy, as socioeconomic development (especially if it has broad spread effects within the community) may draw more people into the political arena. More people will find that they have a stake in local decision-making, as many local functions directly or indirectly affect economic opportunities. Greater participation (provided that it does not violate the rules of the game by creating decision-making deadlocks, violence, or other anomic forms of political activity), may lead to pressure on central authorities to grant communities greater autonomy.

Furthermore, it could be argued that a precondition for more local autonomy is the interest of the public in local affairs and the existence of channels to transform this interest into popular participation. If there is no citizens' participation in municipal affairs, more local autonomy may degenerate into a device for serving the vested interests of a privileged few. The analysis of participatory mechanisms, the forms of participation, and the recruitment of leaders as well as information on their social background, the groups they represent, their values, and their attitudes towards modernization may thus not only explain the developmental path of a local unit, but also illuminate its scope of local autonomy from a different angle.

So far, local government has primarily been analyzed from a top-down perspective. Urban government has always been seen only as a dependent variable of national politics, the national administrative system, and the national and international economy. Little attention, however, has been devoted to the cumulative impact that local governments exert on the national political arena, whether they influence national politics at all and, if so, to what extent, how, and with what effects (Ashford 1975). To find some preliminary answers to these questions should be an objective of this study. These relationships and hypothetical links between autonomy, participation, and socioeconomic development are illustrated in Diagram 1.4, which will also serve as the framework of analysis. The objectives of this study can be summarized as follows:

1. Based on the model as outlined in Diagram 1.4, the study attempts to explain the differences in socioeconomic development in Southeast Asian regional cities. In the analysis I distinguish between:
   - factors specifically relating to the urban political arena (local political culture, local resources, etc.), and
   - external factors influencing urban socioeconomic development

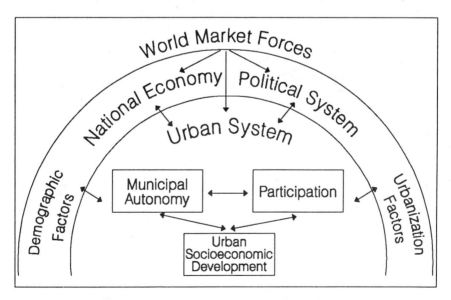

DIAGRAM 1.4 Framework of Analysis

(demographic factors, urbanization, world market forces, national economy, political system, etc.).

2. An analysis of the functions of urban -- and more precisely -- local government for the national political system and the impact of these functions on the national polity.

3. A re-examination of the interrelationships between local autonomy, political participation, and socioeconomic development.[6] This includes:
   - a detailed analysis of central-local relations (local autonomy);
   - an examination of participatory processes within the urban arena; and
   - an analysis of the trends of socioeconomic development at the local level.

Conceptual Premises

Local Autonomy

There is scarcely a study on local government which does not in some way refer to the concept of local autonomy when dealing with local level decision-making, participation, and service delivery. Yet, there is a striking disparity between the frequency with which the concept has been used and the efforts which have been made to clarify its meaning. As a result, the vagueness of the concept considerably reduces its explanatory value.

In the majority of cases, local autonomy was basically equated with freedom of the citizens' immediate living environment -- i.e. the community -- from external (i.e. central government) control and with a minimum of state intervention in local affairs.[7] However, in this connotation the local autonomy concept is an anachronism that has its roots in nineteenth century liberal theory. In America, the origins of local autonomy are two-fold. First, the quest for local autonomy was part of the search of European immigrants for religious freedom. The right of religious minorities to establish and administer their own communities and live there without state interference in accordance with their religious principles was viewed as a precondition for exercising their belief. The second source was the frontier experience of the white settlers in the colonization of the west. Due to the lack of infrastructure, geographical barriers, and the isolation of settlements, many settlers had no alternative but to fend for themselves. Liberal theory later transformed local self-government and the rejection of state intervention in community affairs into a natural right.

In Germany, local autonomy was employed in its puristic sense as an ideological tool in the struggle between the emerging bourgeoisie and attempts by the state to restore its absolute power in the post-Napoleonic era. Local self-government granted by the *Prussian Municipal Order* of the Freiherr vom Stein was not a grand democratic opening, but part of pragmatic reformist legislation (together with peasant liberation and commercial freedom) that aimed at an organizational and economic modernization of the Prussian state after its defeat by Napoleon. Accordingly, the prime objective of the *Municipal Order* was not to increase the participatory rights of the fledgling bourgeoisie, but to enlist the participation of urban commerce and industry in the rehabilitation of the desolate state finances. The rationale for this policy was more taxation in exchange for greater rights of self-government. Local self-government was thus originally a device to stimulate the growth of commerce and trade and to promote the emerging capitalist mode of production. It was only in the *Vormärz* era when the liberal bourgeoisie tried to defend the idea of local self-government against resurgent absolutism and the restoration of the old order, that the concept of local self-government developed into an institution sanctioned by natural right (Rodenstein 1974:40-57; Naßmacher and Naßmacher 1979:19-22). The autonomous community was thus interpreted as an institution that provided the citizen with protection against arbitrary central government (Faltas 1981:6). In the process, the concept of local autonomy was loaded with values such as democracy, liberty, and freedom that still beset the concept in present local government research.

However, under the conditions of rapid socioeconomic and technological change -- as is the case in most newly industrializing countries -- the idea of a largely self-reliant community free from external influences is a myth. Neither in industrialized nor in newly industrializing countries are communities entirely self-sufficient entities. No community is completely autonomous (Clark 1973:5). Total autonomy would require "the withering away of the state" (Fesler 1968:371). On the contrary, as developmental decisions become increasingly specialized, communities are embedded into a network of vertical and horizontal linkages between superior and lower echelons of the politico-administrative system. Bearing in mind the relatively weak and little-diversified private sector the state tends to assume a much greater role in late development, even under the auspices of a capitalist development strategy, than was the case during the modernization phase of the West (Senghaas 1982:57). Autonomy in the afore-mentioned sense would be tantamount to outright isolation. Accordingly, for the purposes of this study another concept of autonomy must be applied that takes into account of communities as part of an interdependent system. Contrary to the numerous scholars who maintain that greater interdependence and the rapid advance of communication and information technologies lead to a centralization of decision-making (Fesler 1968:459; Hsueh 1969:47; Humes and Martin 1969:31; Friedman 1973; Schulz 1979:16; Subramaniam 1980:589), the hypothesis here is that interdependence also entails opportunities for greater local autonomy. Local autonomy, in fact, depends upon:

1. the extent to which the above-mentioned linkages are two-dimensional (top-down and bottom-up);
2. how complex, diversified, and frequent these interrelations are; and
3. to what extent they include not only vertical, but also horizontal linkages.[8]

The more these conditions are present, the greater are the options and bargaining leverages of local authorities, decision-makers, and the participating public to influence policies in favor of perceived local priorities, local values, and local attitudes toward development. More linkages may be equivalent to more communication and more information, and thus provide a more rational basis for decision-making (Naßmacher and Naßmacher 1979:144; Williams 1981:100). The more such two-way linkages exist, the more there are checks and balances against the dominance of particularistic interests and central authorities.

Autonomy, however, is a relative concept and difficult to operationalize. It is not very helpful to measure local autonomy, as frequently proposed, merely on the basis of the allocation of powers between national and local units and the control of the national government over the local bodies (Alderfer 1964:95; Soriano 1966:2; Savelsberg 1980, 1982; Illy 1982:9). Instead, a meaningful concept of local autonomy must include at least three dimensions around which various sets of indicators are grouped: first, a legal constitutional dimension, second, a resource dimension, which is further subdivided into financial and managerial resources; and, third, a linkage dimension which circumscribes the extent to which a local unit is integrated into a network of communicative and organizational linkages. These three sets of indicators are shown in detail in Diagram 1.5.

Political Participation

Political participation is not a single homogeneous variable. As an *"umbrella concept"* (Huntington and Nelson 1976:159), it is one of "those terms that can have so many meanings that it ultimately loses its use-

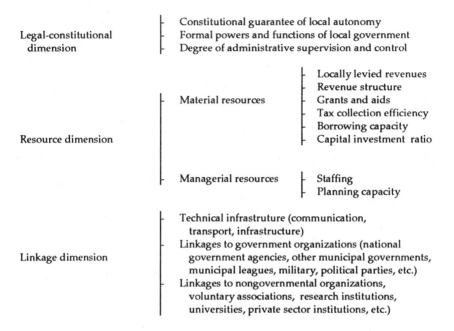

Legal-constitutional dimension		Constitutional guarantee of local autonomy
		Formal powers and functions of local government
		Degree of administrative supervision and control

DIAGRAM 1.5 Dimensions of Local Autonomy

fulness" (Nie and Verba 1975:1). Hence, there is a need for greater conceptual clarity.

In the past, the definition and operationalization of political participation focussed mainly on electoral processes. Due to the fact that electoral data were readily available, voter turnout was utilized as an indicator of participation especially in crosslocal and crossnational research and longitudinal studies (Nie and Verba 1975:2,5). The argument put forward was simple: the greater the voter turnout, the higher the degree of political participation.

Yet, voting is only one form of participation (Huntington and Nelson 1976:14). Political participation neither takes place only at election time nor is election-related participation necessarily the most effective means of citizen influence.

Moreover, the concentration on election behavior as an indicator of political participation contains an ethnocentric bias. It is derived exclusively from the experience of western democracies where making use of one's suffrage was seen as an act of political maturity and responsiveness. Hence, high voter turnout and the existence of a *"participant political culture"* (Almond and Verba 1963) were regarded as two sides of the same coin. The application of the hypothesis that "the greater the voter turnout, the greater the degree of political participation" encounters serious difficulties when applied in a Third-World context. Here, seemingly paradoxically, voter turnout is frequently much higher in rural areas than in urban areas. Such a finding contradicts all previous assumptions on political participation -- for instance, that political participation increases with the level of education, the level of information, and the level of socioeconomic development. All these conditions are fulfilled to a much greater extent in urban than in rural areas. Yet, nonvoting may well be interpreted as a conscious act of political participation. Even if it is not part of an organized election boycott it may still be an implied rejection, a protest against the ruling elite.

On the other hand, high voter turnout may be the result of mobilization by the political leadership -- either through material inducements, or by outright coercion, or both. Except for dogmatic Marxists, nobody would take the regular 99 percent voter turnout in Soviet bloc countries as an indicator of a *"participant political culture"*. Yet, the mere fact that there were regular elections, high voter turnout, and a certain degree of elite circulation has seduced many political analysts into portraying the pre-martial law Philippines as the model democracy of Asia (Day 1974). Hence, I share Nie and Verba's conclusion that electoral activity is an inadequate criterion for citizen participation (Nie and Verba 1975:5). For the individual or for particular groups of citizens the most important political activities may indeed be those between elections, when citizens try to influence government decisions in relation to specific issues that are of concern to them (Nie and Verba 1975:2).

However, it would be wrong to completely disregard acts of *leadership recruitment* as an indicator of political participation. First of all, in the highly stratified developing world the gap between leadership and mass is much wider than in western democracies and, due to a lack of control mechanisms political contests work in a way in which the winner takes all (Faltas 1981:11). As a consequence, leaders must be assumed to have a much more pervasive influence on political decision-making than in western democracies. In contrast to Nie and Verba and Huntington and Nelson, I deliberately extend the participation concept to include leaders such as professional politicians, lobbyists, and government and party officials. A participation concept that is confined to "activity of private citizens", as proposed by Verba and Nie and later by Huntington and Nelson, excludes participatory processes within governmental bodies, though they tend to be much more influential in decision-making than the interaction between private citizens and government. Hence, the distinction drawn between political participants and political professionals is artificial.

Leadership recruitment is a more complex process than mere participation in voting. It must not even necessarily take place in the form of elections. In authoritarian regimes, local leaders are often recruited through appointment, which may be preceded by informal maneuverings. And even if there are formal elections, one must look at the processes of candidate nomination, the candidates' socioeconomic background, their attitudes towards politics and development, their organizational affiliation, the style of campaigning, equality of election chances, and the mobilization techniques rather than at voter turnout in order to gauge how meaningful the election exercise is as an indicator of political participation.

Another indicator of political participation are the *participatory channels* in everyday politics. This involves mainly the organizational infrastructure of the local arena, such as political parties, voluntary associations and interest groups, the media, and religious institutions. Therefore, it is necessary to assess the role of these organizations in interest aggregation, consensus-building, and decision-making as well as their leader- and membership structure, their resources, their accessibility to the individual citizen, and their sensitivity towards local needs.

A third major indicator of participatory behavior within the local arena is the *forms* of political participation, both within formal decision-making bodies and within the local arena at large. This includes questions such as to what extent influence on government actions (or nonactions) is exerted informally or openly in public forums, whether influence is exerted individually (via patron-client ties, through personal contacting) or collectively (in organized form through demonstrations, strikes, etc.), by violent or nonviolent means, or whether participation is autonomous -- in other words, voluntary in nature (i.e. "activity that is designed by the author himself") or mobilized (i.e. "activity that is designed by someone other than the actor to influence governmental decision-making") (Huntington and Nelson 1976:7). Furthermore, in contrast to Nie and Verba both legal and illegal forms of participation are included. The limitation of the participation concept to "legal activities by private citizens" (Nie and Verba 1975:1) is tantamount to legal positivism. To narrow the concept in such a way overlooks the fact that authoritarian and semiauthoritarian regimes usually tend to declare illegal any form of participation implying criticism of the government. What in western democracies would be recognized as truly legitimate forms of participation such as free assembly, critical media reporting, demonstrations, and strikes is stigmatized as conspiracy, sedition, or subversion by authoritarian regimes.

The fourth dimension of political participation is the *issues* of local politics. Issue analysis should provide insights into what is at stake and thus furnish some explanation for the level of competitiveness in local politics.

Finally, participatory patterns are linked to development performance -- i.e. how the prevalent political culture influences the developmental path of a local unit. The four dimensions of the participation concept are outlined in Diagram 1.6.

Socioeconomic Development

The development concept used here deviates from the mainstream growth-oriented concept of neoclassical economic theory that dominated development thinking throughout the 1950s and 1960s and has experienced a revival with the recent rise of conservatism in western countries. This concept is derived from the experiences of the West during its industrialization in the nineteenth and early twentieth centuries. It views development primarily from a macroeconomic perspective, as something which can be stimulated by capital formation, infrastructure development, modern production technologies, a modern educational system, and the transfer of western management techniques. However, three development decades have amply demonstrated that development strategies based on this concept have not achieved their objective of "sustained economic growth" (Rostow 1960). In many cases they stimulated little more than a modernization of enclaves. As it primarily benefited a few favorably located regions (mostly urban or metropolitan) and the middle and upper social strata, modernization helped worsen social and spatial imbalances.

Therefore, socioeconomic development needs to be defined in much broader terms. Here I follow Nohlen and Nuscheler, who defined socioeconomic development as "the formation of productive forces in order to provide all sectors of society with essential material and cultural goods and services". A major precondition for such a process is "a social and political order that offers equal chances to all members of society and provides for participation in decision-making processes and in the benefit of material gains" (Nohlen and Nuscheler 1983:69).

Again, the operationalization of this development concept is not an easy undertaking in comparative urban research. The data base frequently does not allow an empirical analysis in the strict sense. Data relevant to services output and distribution, economic growth patterns, and social change are highly scattered, sometimes deficient, contradictory or even false, aggregated at supralocal levels or incompatible. This has forced me to resort to extrapolations and "guesstimates", which

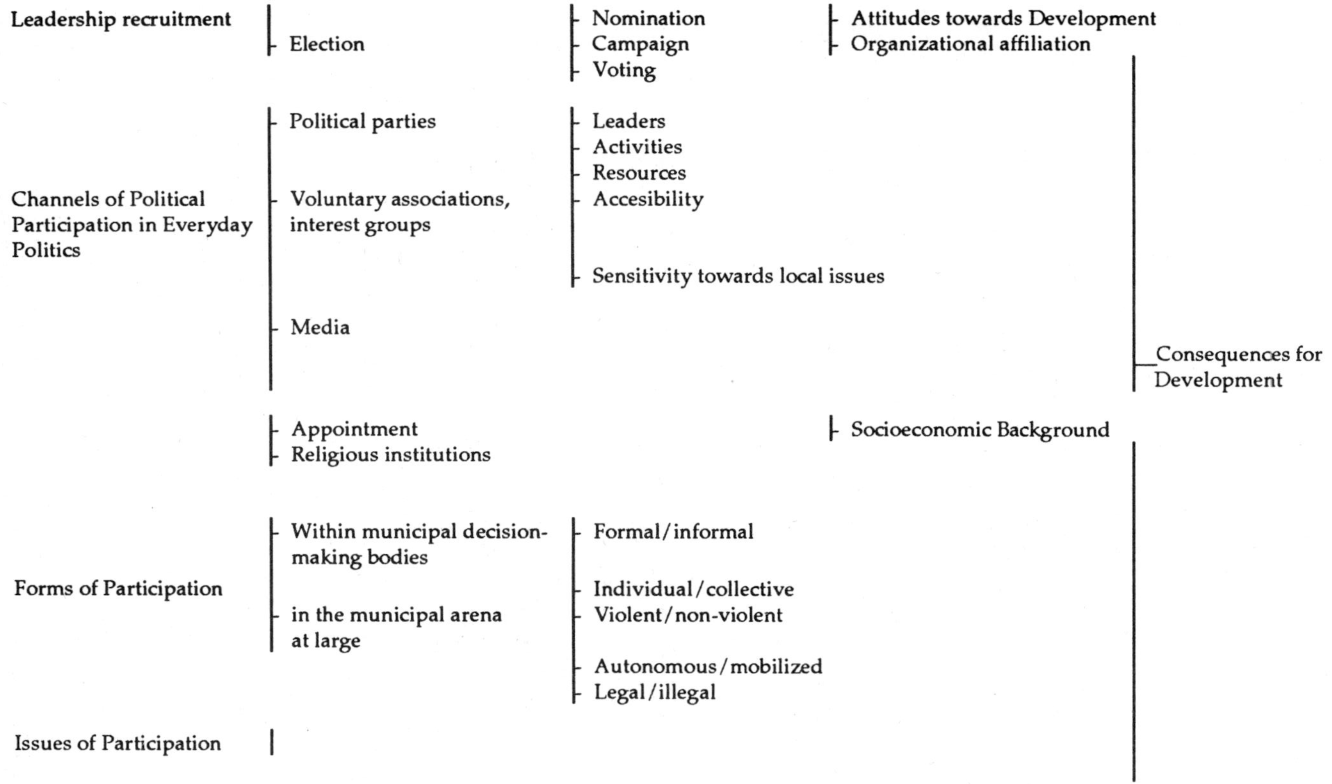

DIAGRAM 1.6 Dimensions of Political Participation

nevertheless should permit the discernment of broad developmental trends.

Diagram 1.7 shows the indicators that are used in the study to measure development. The first major group of indicators deals with the *public services* available in regional cities. While it was impossible to collect data on every service sector, I have attempted to identify trends in a number of key sectors such as public works, health, education, transport, housing, sanitation, garbage disposal, and water and electricity supplies and analyze them on a longitudinal basis -- usually covering the past twenty to thirty years.

Economic development is measured in terms of urban GDP growth, changes in the structure of business establishments, and informal sector development. Individual household incomes, income distribution, poverty incidence, and unemployment rates were selected as indicators of social development trends. Finally, I looked at the *growth potentials* of regional cities, because they were accorded prime roles in spatial decentralization policies and the socioeconomic development of large rural hinterland areas.

Methodology

A detailed review of local government literature on Southeast Asia has been published elsewhere by the author.[9] It distinguishes six major approaches to the study of local government: the *legal-institutional* approach, *normative* approaches, the *model of circular causation, community power* approaches, *"penetrated system"* approaches and *comparative* approaches. For the purpose of this study an attempt has been made to combine three of these approaches: the *comparative* approach, the *legal-institutional* approach, and the *"penetrated system"* approach.

"Comparison has not been one of the major concerns of local government studies". This statement Douglas Ashford made in 1975 is still valid (Ashford 1975:98). Local government research stands in marked contrast to other subdisciplines of political science in which much headway has been made in *comparative* methodology and theory. Yet, in the absence of grand theories, comparative research could well serve as a pacemaker on the way to more acceptable generalizations on local government in developing countries (Friedman 1973:2).

The dearth of comparative local government studies may in large part be attributed to the methodological intricacies involved. A great problem, for instance, is the notorious lack of reliable data. In most cases local government information systems in developing countries are substandard and existing data are rarely disaggregated to the municipal

Services Delivery	Municipal services	Public works Infrastructure develop ment Health Education Housing
	Non-municipal services	Transport Water supply Electricity supply Sanitation
	Services provided by the private sector	Garbage disposal

Economic Development	GDP-growth	GDP-growth in municipal
		  area
		
		GDP-growth by economic
		  sector

	Changes in structure of business establishments	Sector-wise distribution Size Employment generation
	Informal sector develop ment	Income generation Employment generation
Social Development	Household income	
	Distribution of incomes	
	Poverty incidence	
	Unemployment rates	
Socioeconomic Growth Po- tentials	Impact of Regional Cities Development Project	
	Industrial estate develop ment	

DIAGRAM 1.7 Indicators for Socioeconomic Development

or local level. Equally complicated are problems related to the compa-
rability of local government data -- not only on a crossnational level, but
very frequently even between local governments of the same country.

Inconsistencies in the data base are further aggravated by the high degree of ethnic, linguistic, and religious fragmentation of many Third-World societies. This heterogeneity may result in a plurality of local political cultures that make comparisons and generalizations an extremely risky affair.

This volume presents studies of three Southeast Asian regional cities: Chiang Mai in Thailand, Iloilo City in the Philippines, and Penang in Malaysia. Although all three city studies were arranged case-wise, comparisons were made in at least two respects: crossnational and between regional cities of the same country. Chiang Mai was compared with other Thai regional cities such as Nakhon Ratchasima, Khon Kaen, Hat Yai, and Songkhla, developments in Iloilo were compared with those in Davao, Cebu, Bacolod, and Cagayan de Oro and the Penang case was contrasted with Klang, Ipoh, Johore Bahru, and Petaling Jaya.

The *legal-institutional* approach is the approach used most frequently for the study of local governments in the developing world. This approach is popular with, in particular, jurists and scholars of public administration.

Authors using the legal-institutional approach focussed almost exclusively on the "form and structure" (Alderfer 1964:v) of local government. The performance of local governments is primarily seen as a function of their legal and constitutional foundations. Attention is concentrated on the powers granted to local authorities, the functions they perform and how their administrative structure relates to these functions. Other themes include the optimal size of local units (Leemans 1970; Cochrane 1983), local finance (Hicks 1961; International Union of Local Authorities 1979; Davey 1983), and personnel management (Cochrane 1983).

The analytical value of this approach is limited by its legal formalism. Most studies are highly descriptive and unable to provide satisfactory answers to crucial questions such as who governs, when, how, and with what effects. In most cases where the approach is applied on its own it produces a distorted picture of municipal government because the described formal-legal set-up rarely coincides with the actual power structure. Humes and Martin's concern that there may be a "hiatus between the structure of local governments as they exist on paper and as they function in practice" is warranted (Humes and Martin 1969:21).

If I nevertheless utilize the legal-institutional approach in this study, it is primarily for the purpose of describing and analyzing intra-administrative relationships, in particular the central-local dimension. Despite its serious shortcomings, the use of the legal-institutional approach is indispensible, as without information on the organizational, institutional, and legal set-up the peculiarities of local government in Southeast Asian countries can hardly be understood. The legal-institutional approach is useful for examining the following topics: the constitutional provisions for local government, the functions of municipal governments, the supervisory powers of the central government, the resource base of local authorities, planning procedures, and personnel management.

Whereas the legal-institutional approach is largely restricted to the description of administrative structures, and presents central-local relations in a rather static way, the "penetrated system" approach[10] gives a better grasp of the vertical dimension of local government. The penetrated system approach is action and process-oriented, it looks at both the input and the output side of local government.

The *penetrated system* approach seeks to analyze the influence of supralocal forces on local government. Supralocal actors may be the national government, the state governments in federal systems, as in India and Malaysia, and the provincial administration in nations with a unitarian order, as in Thailand, the Philippines, and Indonesia. But higher level bodies of political parties, the headquarters of big companies and transnational corporations, and the board of directors of nationally organized interest groups or other voluntary associations may also be supralocal actors. Their superior financial and legal resources give them an edge in their interaction with local governments. The relationships between these two policy levels are principally unequal. Analysis follows a top-down direction, addressing questions such as how and under what circumstances are local decisions influenced by which supralocal actors. Nonlocal actors are the independent, local decisions the dependent variable. While the majority of studies subsumed under the penetrated system approach operate with clientelist models (Hollnsteiner 1963; Landé 1965; Scott 1969, 1972; Benson 1970; Machado (1972a, 1972b, 1973/74; Wolters 1983), a few are implicitly influenced by theories of authoritarianism (Anthony 1971; Aquino 1977; Rüland 1982a, 1986a; Phang 1985). Relying mainly on empirical evidence from the Ibero-American world, they seek to explain the historical and societal conditions conducive to the rise of authoritarianism in developing countries (Linz 1970, 1975; Schmitter 1973; O'Donnell 1973; Illy, Sielaff, and Werz 1980). Viewed from this theoretical angle, local governments are interpreted as institutional devices for regime stabilization and an integral part of an all-encompassing national security doctrine. In view of the authoritarian legacy of political systems and the importance of patron-client ties as a constituting principle of the social order in Southeast Asia (Scott 1969, 1972), the penetrated system approach promises analytical perspectives that go far beyond those obtained with the legal-institutional approach.

Data collection was organized in two steps. After a preparatory visit to the region from November 1984 to February 1985, field research was conducted between May 1985 and January 1987. Several techniques were used to gather data:

1. During field research in Chiang Mai and Iloilo a survey was made of leading local politicians and senior municipal administrators. However, restrictive research conditions prevented a similar survey in Penang.

For the purpose of the survey a questionnaire was prepared. The Iloilo version differed slightly from the questionnaire used in Chiang Mai; so as to take into account of the different sociopolitical setting. The questionnaire was written in English. The original version was used in Iloilo, and a Thai translation in Chiang Mai.[11] Questions were arranged in three parts covering the following aspects:

- attitudes of the respondents towards the socioeconomic development of their city;
- their opinions on and perceptions of local government in their city; and
- the social background of the respondents.

2. The survey of local decision-makers was complemented by nearly 200 structured expert interviews with officials from various local, provincial, regional, and national government agencies. In addition, interviews were conducted with representatives of public enterprises, the private sector, and local government experts from the academic sector. These interviews were designed to collect additional information on municipal government and urban development patterns and to clarify points that the survey could not adequately deal with.

3. Other sources of information included the analysis of relevant literature, official documents, press reports, statistical files, and participant observation.

All three cities in the study are regional urban centers. I have chosen them in order to counter the metropolitan bias in local government research. For local politics in lower-order urban centers constitutes a much more representative paradigm of the subnational political culture(s) than political processes in the capital regions (Hardoy and Satterthwaite 1986:7).

In the mid-1970s, the Thai and the Philippine government embarked on spatial decentralization programs. Various regional cities were selected for infrastructural development in order to disperse migratory streams and economic growth that had concentrated on the countries' metropolitan areas. By improving investment conditions in provincial cities, it was hoped that economic growth would spread from these urban centers into the rural hinterland. Whether these *Regional City Development Projects (RCDP)*, as they have become known, will ultimately attain these objectives depends to a great extent on the administrative capacities and political culture of these cities. Regional cities play a crucial role not only in demographic and economic decentralization, but also in political and administrative decentralization. It is for these reasons that, at least for the time being, local governments of regional cities deserve special attention.

The study is divided into five sections. The introductory chapter is followed by case studies on local government and development in Chiang Mai, Thailand (chapter two), Iloilo City, Philippines (chapter three), and Penang, Malaysia (chapter four). The arrangement of data is basically the same for all three case studies. Finally, in an attempt to provide answers from a strictly comparative perspective, chapter five returns to the questions outlined in the introductory chapter.

Notes

1. For an excellent discussion of the decentralization theme, see B.C. Smith, *Decentralization. The Territorial Dimension of the State* (London, Boston and Sydney: George Allen & Unwin, 1985).

2. For an illustrative example, see Richard F. Behrendt, *Soziale Strategie für Entwicklungsländer* (Frankfurt: Verlag Fischer, 1965), p. 520.

3. For typical examples, see G. Shabbir Cheema and Dennis A. Rondinelli, eds., *Decentralization and Development. Policy Implementation in Developing Countries* (Beverly Hills, New Delhi and London: Sage Publications, 1983), pp. 18-25.

4. One of the few exceptions is A. Hauck Walsh, *The Urban Challenge to Government. An International Comparison of Thirteen Cities* (New York: Praeger)

5. For a detailed study on the impact of socio-economic development on participation see Samuel P. Huntington and Joan Nelson, *No Easy Choice. Political Participation in Developing Countries* (Cambridge, Massachusetts, and London: Harvard University Press, 1976), pp. 49-78.

6. For earlier attempts see Douglas Ashford, "Theories of Local Government. Some Comparative Considerations", in *Comparative Politics*, Vol. 8, No. 1, pp. 90-107 and Arthur R. Williams, Center, Bureaucracy, and Locality: Central-Local Relations in the Philippines (Ph.D. Thesis, Cornell University, Ithaca, 1981).

7. Dahl and Lindblohm, for instance, defined autonomy as "the absence of immediate and direct control," Muttalib and Khan as "freedom from outside interference." See Robert A. Dahl and Charles E. Lindblohm, *Politics, Economics*

and Welfare. Planning and Politico-Economic Systems Resolved into Basic Social Processes (New York, Evanston, and London: Harper & Row Publishers, 1953), p. 96 and M.A. Muttalib and M.A.A. Khan, *Theory of Local Government* (New Delhi: Sterling, 1982), p. 234. For a critique see Arthur R. Williams, Center, Bureaucracy, and Locality: Central-Local Relations in the Philippines, Ph.D. Thesis, Cornell University, Ithaca, 1981, pp. 96, 104.

8. The linkage concept is derived from economic theory. For studies of local institution-building in rural areas it has been fruitfully applied by Cornell University's Rural Development Committee. See Norman Uphoff and Milton J. Esman, *Local Organization for Rural Development: Analysis of Asian Experience* (Ithaca: Rural Development Committee, Cornell University, 1974); Milton J. Esman and Norman Uphoff, *Local Organizations: Intermediaries in Rural Development* (Ithaca: Cornell University Press, 1984); and Norman Uphoff, *Local Institutional Development: An Analytical Sourcebook with Cases* (West Hartford: Kumarian Press, 1986).

9. See Jürgen Rüland, A Critical Review of Theoretical Approaches to Urban Government in Southeast Asia, in *Urban Government and Development in Asia. Readings in Subnational Development*, ed. Jürgen Rüland (Munich, Cologne and London: Weltforum Verlag, 1988), pp. 12-53.

10. For the term "penetrated system" see Rodney W. Jones, *Urban Politics in India. Area, Power and Policy in a Penetrated System* (Delhi: Vikas, 1975).

11. For reasons of space the questionnaires cannot be reprinted in this volume. Interested persons may write to the author for obtaining a copy.

2

Municipal Government and Development in Chiang Mai

Introduction

Urbanization in Thailand started later than other Southeast Asian countries such as Malaysia and the Philippines. Then it proceeded rapidly, reaching annual growth rates of around 5 percent in the 1950s and 1960s. Initially it went hand in hand with a high national population growth of 3 percent. Cityward migration also increased as a result of a vigorous modernization and industrialization program launched under the regime of Fieldmarshal Sarit Thanarat (1958-1963).

Planners anticipate similarly rapid urban growth in the coming years. The World Bank has estimated that, as a result of a diminishing supply of cultivatable land, an accelerated capitalist penetration of the countryside, increasing ecological problems, industrial growth, and improved transport and communication, urban areas will have to accommodate another ten to twelve million people by the year 2001 (World Bank 1985:1). Thus, by the turn of the century, nearly 30 percent of the Thais will live in cities.

Although urbanization in Thailand has not reached the same pathological dimensions as in many other Third World countries, its polarized nature creates headaches for planners. Thailand has the highest primacy rate in Southeast Asia. 58 percent of the urban population are concentrated in the Bangkok Metropolitan Area. At 37 percent, the Central Region (including Bangkok) is the most urbanized part of the Kingdom, a multiple of the levels of urbanization in the Northeast (5.8 percent), the North (7.9 percent) and the South (12.1 percent). Less than 7.5 percent of the Thais live in municipalities outside the capital. In 1986, only fifteen municipalities had a population of more than 50,000. Bangkok is twenty-six times the size of Nakhon Ratchasima and thirty-three times larger than Chiang Mai (see Table 2.1).

TABLE 2.1 Population of Regional Cities in Thailand

City	Population 1986
Chiang Mai	157,843
Nakhon Ratchasima	206,758
Khon Kaen	130,773
Hat Yai	131,302
Songkhla	84,738

Source: National Statistical Office, Office of the Prime Minister, *Statistical Yearbook Thailand, 1987-1988* (Bangkok: National Census Office, 1988), pp. 23-32.

Thailand's urban growth pattern has resulted in grave regional imbalances. In its early stages the growth of Bangkok was primarily a consequence of the centralist ideology inherent in the Siamese absolute monarchy and the pressure exerted on Siam by European colonialism in the late nineteenth century. The imperialist threat was the immediate reason for King Chulalongkorn's comprehensive reorganization of the government system along strictly centralist lines, thereby gradually bringing the periphery completely under the control of the central authorities and making Bangkok the sole center of power in the Kingdom. London has shown how in a situation of limited resources this policy, that made national security its overriding priority, has benefited exclusively the capital city and a small Bangkok-based ruling elite (London 1979:510). In time this urban-biased policy created vested interests with a built-in tendency to perpetuate the dominant position of the country's metropolitan center. Thus, ironically, the forces of colonialism which have been a major cause of the unbalanced settlement structure in many Third World countries, have indirectly shaped the regional disparities in Thailand too -- the only country in Southeast Asia that was never colonized.

Sarit's industrialization program launched in the late 1950s accentuated Bangkok's dominance. Due to its locational advantages, industrial investment went exclusively to Bangkok. Only much later did it gradually spill over into adjacent provinces. Industrial growth, for its part, stimulated other sectors such as construction, real estate, finance, and business services. This, too, widened regional imbalances, despite cautious spatial decentralization policies in the 1980s. While per capita income in Bangkok is estimated to exceed US $ 2,500, it stagnates at about US $ 300 in the Northeast. Outside the country's core region problems such as deteriorating terms-of-trade, brain drain, and rural poverty persist.

But even Bangkok has been affected by the negative consequences of imbalanced growth. They have long begun to turn the capital's comparative advantages into diseconomies of scale: traffic congestion, ribbon development, slums, and environmental problems such as flooding and land subsidence, water and air pollution are now severely hampering economic and social life in the metropolis.

These problems have long been recognized by the Thai government, academic institutions, and individual scholars alike. Notwithstanding earlier piecemeal attempts, there was no real commitment to tackle urban growth-related problems until the mid-1970s. In the Fourth National and Economic and Social Development Plan (1977-1981) the Thai government outlined a comprehensive national urbanization policy for the first time. Its three-pronged strategy had the following objectives:

1. creating a polycentric Bangkok and decentralizing economic and industrial activities to the suburbs of the capital;
2. developing the Eastern Seaboard (as an alternative location for heavy industries);
3. developing initially five (Chiang Mai, Khon Kaen, Nakhon Ratchasima, Hat Yai, Songkhla) and, later, another five regional urban centers (Phitsanulok, Chonburi, Phuket, Udon Thani, Ubon Ratchathani).

Whereas the national government has taken the lead in designing and guiding the national urbanization program, local authorities must play a pivotal role in its implemention. Successful implementation will depend to a great extent on the management capabilities of urban governments, cooperation on the part of the residents and, in particular, the local elites. It is at the urban level that broad national policy guidelines have to be transformed into decisions adapted to specific local conditions and the routine work has to be carried out. After all, smooth implementation of such a complex program depends not so much on project design per se, but on reconciling the various components of the plan with the intricacies of a changing local microcosm.

To what extent Thai municipalities are able to perform these functions will be discussed in this chapter. The data were obtained from a survey[2] of forty-five municipal decision-makers in Chiang Mai and fifty-eight structured interviews with officals from national agencies, the provincial administration, and the municipal government, managers of public enterprises, representatives of the private sector, and academics. Other sources of information included official documents, newspaper reports, statistics, the relevant literature, and participant observation. The survey covered thirty-six local politicians and nine municipal administrators. The thirty-six local politicians were chosen from the forty-nine candidates who contested the municipal elections of 28 July 1985. Twenty-two of the local politicians interviewed belonged to the *Glum* Ananthaphum, the strongest political group in the city hall and thirteen to *Glum* Prachasanti, the current opposition, whereas one respondent ran as an independent. All nine municipal administrators interviewed were senior civil servants, including the city clerk, six department and division chiefs, the local government inspector, and his assistant.

Local Autonomy

Central-Local Relations: Structures and Functions

The Constitutional and Institutional Framework. Since the abolition of the absolute monarchy in 1932, Thailand had nine constitutions. But only two of them devote a section to local government (Wenk 1964). The 1978 Constitution explicitly upheld the "principle of self-government according to the will of the people in the locality" (Chapter IX, Section 180). But the phrasing "members of the local assembly should be basically elected" indicates that there is no unconditional commitment to elective local government and, hence, the devolution of authority to lower echelons of the government system. The wording "basically" still expresses reservation on the part of the central authorities towards the effectiveness and capabilities of elected local representatives. Thus, "in case of necessity" (Section 182), the law still reserves the central government the right to appoint members of the municipal assemblies, thereby ensuring maximum control over local authorities.

Moreover, there is no exact and binding definition of the powers and duties of local authorities. The statement that "the powers and duties of a local assembly, local administrative committee or local administrator shall be in accordance with the provision of law" endows the central government with additional powers to regulate the role of local governments in line with central interests and priorities.

These precautions against the principle of local self-determination and elective local government are well reflected in the institutional and legal framework of the Thai government system. There is unanimity in the literature about the strong dependence of Thai municipalities on the central government. They are tightly controlled by the Ministry of the Interior's Department of Local Administration (DOLA) and the provincial governor, who is a powerful bureaucrat representing the Interior Ministry at the local level. As a generalist administrator he (a) coordinates and supervises all national government offices operating at the provincial level and (b) supervises, advises, and guides local governments within his jurisdiction. The Ministry of the Interior is the ultimate decision-making center concerning all legal, personnel, financial, and procedural issues within a municipality as well as issues between the municipality and higher government levels. There is neither a court of appeal nor an ombudsman to which municipalities can resort if a central government decision is questionable on legal and procedural grounds (Karnjanaprakorn 1962:54,109). The Ministry of the Interior has the prerogative of dissolving the whole municipal assembly or dismissing individual assemblymen, the executive committee or any member thereof. In times of martial law the Ministry of the Interior can do this even without having to justify its action.

However, except at the introduction of municipal government, there have been few cases in which the whole assembly, the executive committee, or individual assemblymen were dismissed. In his pioneering study of Thai municipal government, Karnjanaprakorn mentioned only three cases of dissolved municipal assemblies in the 1953-1958 period (Karnjanaprakorn 1962:111). In Chiang Mai there have been no dismissals in the last fifteen years. Undoubtedly, the city most affected by suspensions was Bangkok, usually after coups d'etat and the declaration of martial law (Thai University Research Association 1976:336,359). Thus, when the Thanin government took over after the October coup in 1976, the elected Bangkok Metropolitan Government was dissolved in April 1977, but not so the municipal assemblies outside the capital. The latter were permitted to carry on with their functions until the end of their term in December 1979. Their term was extended to June 1980, when, although a semiauthoritarian government was still in power, fresh municipal elections were held.

The governor, too, has broad powers of control and supervision over municipalities. Subject to approval of the Ministry of the Interior he can dismiss the whole assembly, individual assemblymen and the executive committee of a municipality within his jurisdiction. He has suspending veto power in respect of draft ordinances of the municipal assembly and any other action of the municipal government. Apart from this, he can call on any councillor or municipal officer to explain their actions. Furthermore, he appoints the mayor and the members of the executive committee, although usually in consultation with the assembly's majority faction because these appointments must be ratified by the assembly. Normally the governor adheres to the wishes of the majority faction, but there have been cases of governors attempting to manipulate or reverse the assembly's choice (Krannich 1978a:51). Moreover, the entire communication between the municipality and central government agencies must be channeled through the governor's office.

One major reason for this tight control over local authorities has been the "security syndrome" (Dhiravegin 1983:55), a crucial element in Thai politics since the encounter with European imperialism in the late nineteenth century. Ever since, centralism has been viewed by many Thais as a "sine qua non" for territorial integrity, national independence, and nation-building (Dhiravegin 1983:53). After the colonial threat it was Japanese imperialism, and after World War II the communist take-overs in mainland China (1949) and on the Indochinese peninsula (1975), local insurgencies and minority problems which kept alive fears of internal instability and external interference (London 1979). In this light, decentralization and greater local autonomy are regarded as forms of political organization that run counter to the security objective.

Another reason is the managerial problems encountered by many municipalities after their inception in the 1930s. Municipal assemblymen unfamiliar with the spirit of democracy and parliamentarian procedures were deeply involved in factional feuds, thereby exacerbating problems of municipal governance rather than solving them. Therefore, central intervention and control initially aimed at minimizing local corruption and mismanagement and ensuring some continuity in municipal administration. However, after consolidating their strong position vis-à-vis local governments, central authorities never relinquished it. This is not surprising because, unlike in Western political thinking, Thai political culture does not know a subsidiary principle. As a result, the prescriptive element in municipal laws became more and more accentuated. But since there was no public protest against increasing central interference, the center felt no pressure to relax its tight control over local authorities (Karnjanaprakorn 1962).

Furthermore, Thai society is characterized by a pronounced hierarchical structure (Mulder 1985:93). Despite increased opportunities for vertical and horizontal mobility as a result of rapid socioeconomic change during the last three decades, the highly stratified nature of Thai society still determines people's values, attitudes, and actions. The higher a civil servant, who in traditional Thai society was viewed as a direct representative of a divine king, the higher his status. Interaction with superior government officials thus commands deference and affirmative behavior. It is evident that such value patterns conflict with the idea of local autonomy and tend to subdue the emergence of popular demands for greater self-determination in municipal affairs.

However, conventional local government literature tends to overstate legal-institutional aspects in the assessment of local autonomy. That Thailand is not the highly centralized state often depicted in the literature is demonstrated by the fact that municipal decision-makers often successfully circumvent the official line of authority by establishing informal contacts with officials of superior government agencies (Krannich 1982:321). 93 percent of the interviewed local politicians and municipal administrators in Chiang Mai agreed that the use of personal connections is a better way to accomplish an important task than going through the formal channels. Almost 70 percent of the local politicians and 71 percent of the municipal administrators stated that they entertain personal or friendly relations with either the provincial governor, senior officials in regional offices, high-ranking bureaucrats of national government agencies or national politicians. Such informal relationships usually rest on long periods of personal acquaintance: kinship, "old boy" ties between former classmates, service in the same government agency or military unit and membership in the same elite clubs such as the Rotary, Lions or Jaycees.

Chiang Mai was always well represented in the national parliament, political parties, the cabinet, and the government bureaucracy. Moreover, high-ranking civil servants, cabinet ministers, military officers, and businessmen maintain a second residence in Chiang Mai, and are therefore interested in the city's progress. The informal links between municipal decision-makers and senior officials of the national government explain why the municipality has been able to attract a considerable amount of public funds for infrastructure projects that far exceeded the municipality's means. The radial roads, the ring road system, the international airport, the university, Suan Dok hospital, and a variety of other large-scale, capital-intensive projects were mainly financed by the central government.

Among the politicians who stated that they have personal or friendly relations with officials at higher echelons of the government system, 93 percent said that they assisted them when approached for help in getting a project implemented in Chiang Mai. All municipal administrators interviewed confirmed this. Assistance was provided in various forms. Most frequently cited was "advice and counseling", help in "coordination with other agencies", "budgetary assistance", support in "data collection" and "fact finding", and the provision of other "relevant information".

The circumvention of formal channels of authority and a heavy workload explain why -- despite his broad powers vis-à-vis the municipalities -- the governor in fact exerts his influence over municipalities less directly than might be expected by judging purely from the legal point of view. Apart from exerting formal authority, his role usually consists of counseling, guiding, and advising municipal politicians. In their study of gubernatorial functions in six northern provinces, Thomas and Noranitipadungkarn (1975:337) found that the governor of Chiang Mai devotes only 2.5 percent of his working time to supervision of municipal government. In the adjoining provinces the situation was almost the same. Governors spent only a fraction of their working time on municipal affairs: 1 percent in Chiang Rai, 5 percent in Lampang, 2 percent in Lamphun, 5 percent in Nan, and 5 percent in Mae Hong Son. Due to the complex organizational problems involved in the Regional Cities Development Program (RCDP), and the resulting need for efficient interagency coordination, there are, however, indications in the implementation phase of this project that the governor has been influencing municipal affairs more directly in Chiang Mai and the other regional cities.

The details of supervisory work (field inspection, budget review, checks on financial reports, and scrutinizing draft ordinances) are delegated to the local government inspector, a middle-ranking official attached to the provincial administration. But in regional cities such as Chiang Mai his influence on decision-making is limited. His office is severely understaffed and he is junior in civil service ranking to the city clerk, the deputy city clerks, and even some of the department heads, his main counterparts in the municipal government. Moreover, he has to deal with an astute political leadership, which prefers to communicate directly with the governor on important policy matters (Mawhood 1981:11; Multiman, Vol. 1, 1982:57).

Municipal Functions. The definition of municipal functions is an exclusive prerogative of the central government. Thai municipalities are prohibited from adopting and carrying out functions not specified by central law or ordered by the Ministry of the Interior, even if such functions are in accordance with local needs and priorities.

Municipal functions were laid down by the central government in the *Municipal Act of 1953* which, despite some amendments, is still the basic law guiding municipal government. They are divided into compulsory and optional functions. As specified by the Act, the number and scope of functions vary according to the classification of the municipality. Municipalities are divided into three categories on the basis of population, density, and revenue qualifications: *tesaban nakorn, tesaban muang,* and *tesaban tambon* There are eighty-four *tesaban muang,* and thirty-eight *tesaban tambon.* Chiang Mai is the only *tesaban nakorn.* Their functions, and those actually performed by Chiang Mai, are shown in Table 2.2.

A close look at Table 2.2 reveals that Chiang Mai performs nearly all compulsory and many discretionary functions. However, there are only a few (minor) functions such as secondary and tertiary roads, drainage, refuse disposal, markets and slaughterhouses, parks and recreational

TABLE 2.2 Functions of Thai Municipal Governments

| Functions | Tesaban/Municipality | | | |
X obilagtory 0 discretionary	Nakorn	Muang	Tambon	Chiang Mai
Maintain peace and order	X	X	X	X[a]
Provide and maintain roads and water-ways	X	X	X	X
Keep roads, sidewalks, and public places clean including refuse and garbage disposal	X	X	X	X
Prevent and suppress communicable diseases	X	X	X	X
Provide people's education	X	X	X	X
Provide fire fighting equipments	X	X	X	X
Provide clean water supply	X	X	O	X[b]
Provide slaughterhouse	X	X	O	X
Provide and maintain electricity or other lighting	X	X	O	X[c]
Provide and maintain drainage system	X	X	O	X
Provide and maintain medical centres	X	X	O	X
Provide and maintain public lavatories	X	X	---	X
Provide and maintain maternal and child welfare	X	O	---	X
Provide other services necessary to preserve public health	X	O	---	X
Provide markets, ferry, and harbor facilities	O	O	O	X
Provide cemeteries and crematoria	O	O	O	X
Promote occupations for local inhabitants	O	O	O	---
Engage in commercial enterprises including pawnshops	O	O	O	X
Provide and maintain public parks, zoos, and recreation, places	O	O	---	X
Providing for public utilities	O	O	---	X
Provide and maintain hospitals	O	O	---	X
Establish and maintain vocational schools	O	O	---	X
Provide and maintain sports stadia	O	O	---	X
Improve slums and keep city clean	O	O	---	---
Other activities as ordered by the Ministry of the Interior or as stated by law	X	X	X	X

[a]Excluding police services.
[b]Only operation of a sewage collection system, no sewage treatment facilities operated.
[c]In practice confined to street and public area lighting.

Source: Adapted from W. Tanrattanakoon, Linkage Pattern in Small-Scale Industries in Chiang Mai Province, (MA Thesis, Asian Institute of Technology, Bangkok), 1984, p. 44 and interview information provided by the Department of Local Administration, Ministry of the Interior and the municipal government of Chiang Mai.

facilities, fire protection and cemeteries for which the municipality has exclusive responsibility. All other functions are either shared with superior government agencies or performed by public enterprises. In other words, there is little functional autonomy and considerable fragmentation of responsibility.

Moreover, some functions such as policing have been allocated to municipalities which, however, lack the authority to perform them. Although "maintenance of peace and order" is listed as a top priority by the municipal law, municipalities neither have their own police forces nor authority over those operating within their jurisdiction. The enforcement of local regulations and ordinances is performed by a special unit of the provincial police. Although the police are under the formal authority of the Ministry of the Interior and thus theoretically under the supervision of the provincial governor, as a result of an informal alignment with the military the police enjoy relatively wide autonomy (Krannich 1978a:124). Except for good informal relations between local officials, on the one hand, and the police on the other, there are few mechanisms to ensure that the police have the same enforcement priorities as the municipal government. In Chiang Mai, as well as in other regional centers, these problems have been addressed through the assignment to the municipality of a number of police officers by the National Police Department. Their duty is to deal with traffic problems and to enforce local ordinances in cooperation with municipal officials (Multiman, Vol. 1, 1982:32).

While in the past water and electricity supply were genuine municipal functions, they have now been transferred to state enterprises such as the Provincial Water Authority and the Provincial Electricty Authority. Only a few municipalities still operate their own waterworks. Today, Chiang Mai -- like many other municipalities -- is confined to the operation of a sewerage collection system and, with regard to electricity services, to street and public area lighting. This transfer of functions to public and private enterprises -- a trend which can be observed in Malaysia and the Philippines as well -- not only deprives local governments of their traditional functions, but also seriously undermines the accountability principle in service delivery. These enterprises are not responsible to the voters and the people they are supposed to serve, but only to distant headquarters in the capital or to the central government.

Another optional, yet very important function, namely "to promote occupations for local inhabitants", has not been performed by the municipalities at all, except indirectly in connection with public works projects. In fact, it has been left to superior government levels (Ministry of

Industry, Ministry of Commerce, Board of Investment, etc.) and especially to the private sector.

In contrast to Malaysian cities, Chiang Mai and all other Thai municipalities outside Bangkok did not have slum improvement schemes until recently. The provision of low-cost housing was exclusively in the hands of the National Housing Authority (NHA) and the private sector. With the beginning of the Regional Cities Development Project and encouragement from international organizations such as UNESCO, Chiang Mai was the first Thai municipality to start upgrading slum areas.

The Resource Dimension

The resources of a municipality are crucial for the degree of local autonomy. Yet, it is of paramount importance where these resources come from. Are they locally levied or provided by external sources such as the central government? And, to what extent have local authorities discretion in the use of these resources? These questions center primarily on the issue of control over local resources.

In the following sections I distinguish between two forms of local resources: financial resources and managerial resources. As financial resources usually take the form of taxes, license and service fees, etc. they are an indirect reflection of the municipality's economic structure or, more precisely, the extent to which the economy can be tapped for public purposes. The availability of managerial resources, on the other hand, is a decisive factor in ensuring that the financial resources will be utilized effectively.

Financial Resources. Thai municipalities are financially weak. They suffer from an inadequate, inelastic, and underutilized resource base. To a large extent, this is the result of outdated legislation and rigid central control. The legal framework for fiscal management is the *Municipal Revenue Act, 1954* which has remained basically unchanged. The Act determines the municipal revenue sources, establishes the rates of taxation, prescribes the procedures for obtaining loans, and fixes ceilings for fees, duties, licenses, and municipal surcharges (see Table 2.3). Only where income from municipal property is concerned, is some discretion left to local authorities. But as revenues from municipal property accounted for only 3.19 percent of the total revenues of Chiang Mai in 1982, they have no significant impact on the financial maneuverability of the municipality.

Growing at an annual rate of 15.2 percent between 1977 and 1982, Chiang Mai's revenues increased substantially in nominal terms. Among the five major regional cities only Hat Yai (1,012 Baht) had a higher per

TABLE 2.3 Revenue Sources of Thai Regional Cities

Tax Category	Tax
Locally levied taxes	House and rent tax
	Land development tax
	Slaughtering tax
	Signboard tax
Locally levied nontax revenues	Permits
	Fees
	Fines
	Revenues from municipal property
Surcharges of up to 10 percent	Business tax
	Liquor and beverage tax
	Entertainment tax
	Petroleum and petroleum products tax
	Gambling tax
	Cement tax
Shared taxes	Export duty on paddy and rice
	Vehicle tax
Central government grants	
Other resources	Reserves
	Loans

Source: Department of Local Administration, Ministry of the Interior.

capita income than Chiang Mai (948 Baht).[4] At 16.3 percent, per capita revenues increased faster than in any other regional city except for Nakhon Ratchasima (19.9 percent) (see Tables 2.4 and 2.5).

Although revenues of Thai regional cities grew rapidly, the revenue structure worked against greater fiscal autonomy. Only four of the eleven taxes enumerated in the *Municipal Revenue Act* are collected by the municipalities: the house and rent tax, the land development tax, the slaughterhouse tax, and the signboard tax. Only the house and rent tax -- about 10 percent of the total -- makes a major contribution to municipal revenue. All other taxes are either surcharges on national taxes or shared taxes.

By comparison, Thai municipalities had a considerably lower share of locally levied revenues than their Philippine and Malaysian counterparts. Even more worrying is the sharp decline of locally levied revenues. In Chiang Mai they declined by 6 percent from 36 percent in 1977 to 30 percent in 1982. In other cities the decline was even more dramatic: from 52 percent to 27 percent in Nakhon Ratchasima and from 27.4 percent to 20.2 percent in Khon Kaen. By 1982 only Songkhla (33.3 percent) had a higher share of locally levied revenues than Chiang Mai.[5]

TABLE 2.4 Municipal Finance in Thailand

City	Total revenues, 1982, in million Baht	Average per capita revenues, 1982, in Baht	Average increase in per capita revenues, 1977-1982, in percent	Tax collection efficiency, 1982, in percent	Percentage of locally levied revenues, 1982
Chiang Mai	98,743	948	16.28	67	29.98
Nakhon Ratchasima	63,336	710	19.92	96	27.12
Khon Kaen	51,724	477	9.43	85	20.72
Songkhla	38,309	462	9.54	79	33.34
Hat Yai	115,377	1,012	8.28	88	n.d.

Source: Computation based on Multiman, *Municipal Management and Finance Study, Concept Report* (Bangkok: Multiman, Royal Government of Thailand, Ministry of Interior, United Nations Development Programme, 1982), and World Bank, *Thailand. Regional Cities Development Project* (Washington, D.C.: World Bank, 1985), pp. 68-71.

TABLE 2.5 Revenue Sources, Chiang Mai Municipality, in Percent

Tax Category	1977	1978	1979	1980	1981	1982
Locally levied taxes	16.36	18.96	17.91	15.01	12.32	14.45
Local non-tax revenues	19.61	16.10	15.77	16.87	15.91	15.53
Surcharge taxes	11.10	19.43	15.64	15.49	17.78	15.67
Shared taxes	31.92	23.12	22.42	24.58	27.88	22.31
Grants	21.02	22.04	25.26	20.89	25.43	20.57
Other resources	---	---	---	7.16	0.69	11.47
Total locally levied revenues in percent	35.97	35.07	33.67	31.88	28.23	29.98
Per capita revenues in Baht	447	519	644	717	764	948

Source: Computed from World Bank, Thailand. Regional Cities Development Project (Washington, D.C.: The World Bank, 1985), p. 68.

The financial bottlenecks of Thai municipalities are due to an obsolete legal framework and numerous exemptions granted to tax payers. For many years the municipal tax base has not been adjusted to the rapidly changing socioeconomic conditions in urban areas. For example, fees for garbage collection, parking, and building permits are extremely low. The sharing formula for the increasingly important motor vehicle tax benefits small municipalities more than larger ones, while the surcharge on the business tax subsidizes Bangkok at the expense of hinterland cities (Multiman, Vol. 2, 1982).

The house and rent tax is confined to buildings rented out by the owners, in which case a rate of 12.5 percent of the annual rental value is imposed on the dwelling. This is only slightly above the 10 percent threshold, below which the tax becomes uneconomical (Hamer, Steer, and Williams 1985:66). At 55 percent, Chiang Mai had one of the highest shares of owner-occupied dwellings (World Bank 1978:25), but only 13.6 percent of the houses were taxed in 1980. In the other regional cities this percentage was even lower: 11.1 percent in Hat Yai, 9.9 percent in Nakhon Ratchasima, and 8.6 percent in Khon Kaen. Only Songkhla (25.5 percent) had a significantly higher ratio of taxed houses. In addition, property values are seldom reassessed and therefore, in many instances, buildings are grossly undervalued. Yukobol found that in the central area of Nakhon Ratchasima the assessment level is equivalent to only 24.5 percent of the actual annual value of properties (Yukobol 1984:64-65). Data of the Department of Local Administration indicated similar underassessments. In the cities surveyed by the department, the house and rent tax was usually based on 40 to 60 percent of the market values (Department of Local Administration 1988:22). Although the introduction of a standardized real property tax has been under debate for a long time, there is a stalemate between the Ministry of the Interior and the Ministry of Finance over how to collect and administer the tax (Southeast Asia Development Advisory Group 1976:9).

Not surprisingly, tax evasion and relatively high delinquency rates plague most Thai municipalities. The delinquency rate of 33 percent in Chiang Mai is the highest among the five regional cities (see Table 2.4). Nevertheless, the municipal government is optimistic that it will soon succeed in reducing this rate considerably with the help of a tax mapping system established in recent years.

The decline in fiscal autonomy has increased the dependence on central government funds. While the percentage of central government grants changed only slightly in regional cities, there is a marked increase in surcharge taxes. Surcharge taxes increased from 11 percent to nearly 16 percent in Chiang Mai and even more in Nakhon Ratchasima, and

Songkhla. Municipal governments are entitled to add a surcharge of up to 10 percent to certain national taxes. They are collected by the local representatives of the Revenue and Excise Department of the Ministry of Finance (Yukobol 1984:57). The decline in shared taxes observed in Chiang Mai, Nakhon Ratchasima and Khon Kaen, however, is more than matched by considerable contributions from other sources -- in almost all cases disbursements from the municipalities' accumulated reserves. As disclosed by one study, cash reserves were substantial in all regional cities, ranging from 10 million Baht in Nakhon Ratchasima to 30 million Baht in Chiang Mai (Multiman, Vol. 2, 1982:30).

Reserves are created through a legal provision that municipal expenditure may not exceed 97 percent of the estimated income. 90 percent of this surplus goes into the municipality's reserve, from which it can borrow without interest with the consent of either the mayor, the governor or the Minister of the Interior, depending on the amount borrowed. The remaining 10 percent of the budget surplus must be paid into the centrally administered Municipal Development Fund. Membership of the fund, which operates like a savings bank, is compulsory. Deposits yield an interest rate of 4 percent per annum, and are available for loans to municipalities at interest rates between 4 and 8 percent, depending on the purpose. While Chiang Mai, like other regional cities, has made extensive use of reserves in recent years, the fund has not been tapped so far because of the complicated administrative procedures involved (World Bank 1985:23).

Over the years, central government grants have become an increasingly important source of funding for Thai municipalities. Between 1956 and 1982 the percentage of central government grants to municipalities rose from 27.2 percent[6] to 35.6 percent (Yukobol 1984:156). Although the percentage of grants decreases with increasing city size, they nevertheless play a major role in the finances of regional cities. However, at an average 22.5 percent (1975-1982) Chiang Mai seems to be less dependent on this source of revenue than other regional cities. Only Hat Yai's share (14.5 percent) is smaller, whereas the figures for Khon Kaen (36.6 percent) and Songkhla (37.6 percent) suggest a heavy reliance on grants. The average percentage of grants for all five regional cities was 27 percent for the eight years between 1975 and 1982.[7]

The inelastic structure of grants seriously restricts financial decision-making. There are three categories of grants: (a) grants for educational purposes, (b) general grants, and (c) specific grants. Educational grants must be spent exclusively on municipal teachers' salaries and operating costs of municipal primary schools. They make up the lion's share of grants, amounting to 70 percent in Chiang Mai and between 64 and 74 percent in the other regional cities (Multiman, Vol. 2, 1982:25). General grants are given for general operating purposes on a per capita basis (60 Baht per head in 1987), while specific grants are based on project proposals from municipalities. There is, however, an upper limit of 600,000 Baht for cities with revenues exceeding 15 million Baht. In Chiang Mai this grant has been used mainly for public works and cleanliness projects. Unfortunately, the procedures for the release of specific grants are rather cumbersome. The project proposals are thoroughly screened by several agencies ranging from the provincial government to the Ministry of the Interior and the Budget Bureau. Even worse, in many cases the fiscal year was almost over before approval for the grants was forthcoming.

A limited revenue base and the inefficient resource utilization of municipalities were major causes of inadequate investment performance. At 4 percent, the share of local governments in total public expenditure was very low, especially if compared to industrial countries, where local governments account for between 25 and 30 percent of public expenditure (International Union of Local Authorities 1978:42; Statistisches Bundesamt 1985:217)).

The financial maneuverability of Thai municipalities is further limited by constantly rising costs for general administration and personnel. In Chiang Mai, the municipality spent an average of 44 percent for these items between 1977 and 1982. This was a higher percentage than for all other Thai municipalities, where these costs averaged 40.1 percent in the early 1980s (Mawhood 1981).[8] Yet, with operational expenditures rising faster than locally levied revenues,[9] it is difficult to stop this trend. As a result, compared to Malaysian cities, capital investment ratios were rather low. On the average, Thai regional cities set aside 26.2 percent of their expenditure for capital investment. While Hat Yai (40.3 percent) performed well above the average, Khon Kaen's investment ratio (8.7 percent) was as low as those in the Philippines. With 23.3 percent, capital investment in Chiang Mai was below the average, too (Multiman, Vol. 2, 1982:5). Disturbing is the declining trend in capital investment ratios. While capital expenditure of Thai local governments still averaged 0.89 percent of GDP during the fourth plan period (1977-1981), by 1985 it had dwindled to 0.54 percent (World Bank 1986:67).

New burden sharing formulas for capital investment have been proposed under the sixth plan. These assign a greater role to local authorities in the physical development of the areas under their jurisdiction. These policy changes might have been the reason why even the status-quo-oriented Ministry of the Interior came up with plans to strengthen the fiscal capabilities of municipalities. Apart from proposing additional measures to improve local governments' tax collecting by better training of tax officers, updating the tax rolls, tax mapping, and the computerization of tax administration, the ministry also suggested additional revenues for municipalities, such as a 10 percent surcharge on the tobacco tax and a fee for the use of public parks. Moreover, a general increase in surcharge taxes from 10 to 12 percent and a share in lottery fees and the registration fees for land transactions is under discussion at present (Department of Local Administration 1988:21). However, most of these suggestions do not relieve municipalities' fiscal dependence. Moreover, there is a surprising coincidence between DOLA's proposals and the fiscal policy preferences of local administrators in Chiang Mai, who opted for more central government subsidies, too, when asked how the municipality's finances could be improved. Although four-fifths of the interviewed local politicians and administrators were in favor of greater local policy-making powers, their ideas about municipal finances do not foster greater local autonomy. Respondents were asked to check those two items they thought most likely to improve Chiang Mai's revenue base. Responses were weighted according to the priority given to them. Over 51 percent of all preferences were given to two items: "the increase of local resources through a greater share in national taxes" and "more central government subsidies".

Municipal Management Resources. Personnel is an important resource factor influencing the degree of local autonomy. The more qualified a municipality's staff, the better its management capabilities, the greater its service output, and the more efficient its resource utilization. Moreover, qualified administrators may be less inclined to follow every whim of their superiors when their directives are ill-founded. They may be expected to act in a way that is more in accordance with local realities, and they may have greater resources in circumventing the formal, usually top-down, flows of authority. Hence, the assumption that there is a direct correlation between a competent staff and socioeconomic development.

Personnel administration is highly centralized in Thai municipal government. Everything, including position classification, the determination of staff size, recruitment, transfers, promotion, training, disciplinary action, and retirement is in the hands of the Municipal Personnel Committee or the Local Government Affairs Division of the Ministry of the Interior. While the Municipal Personnel Committee acts as the policy and decision-making body, the Division of Local Affairs carries out the day-to-day operations of the committee (Krannich 1978a; Multiman, Vol. 1, 1982).

By contrast, the mayor, the local chief executive, has little power in personnel affairs. Nominally he is the appointing authority for municipal staff, but actually his recruitment powers do not go beyond grade four positions in the eleven grade Thai civil service system. His major subordinates, the city clerk, the deputy city clerks, the department heads, and division chiefs are recruited and selected by central government bodies (Krannich 1975:94; Multiman, Vol. 1, 1982:36; Multiman, Vol. 2, 1982:204).

Moreover, since the Municipal Personnel Committee is composed of representatives from several important central government agencies whose interests sometimes conflict, even informal influence is difficult to exert. Thus, appointments of key personnel are often made with little or no prior consultation of the municipality (Multiman, Vol. 2, 1982:213).

The dominant role of the central government in personnel affairs divides the loyalty of municipal officers between the central government and the local authority. Loyalties towards the municipality are often weaker than towards the Ministry of the Interior, which is the decisive agency in the career advancement of municipal officers. Loyalty towards the municipality is likewise impaired by the frequent transfers of senior municipal officers, although Chiang Mai, which has a permanent city clerk and several long-serving department heads has been less affected than other cities.

Chiang Mai has more employees than any other regional city in Thailand. Its staff of 1,268 employees (Multiman, Vol. 2, 1982:200) has now risen to over 1,500 (see Table 2.6) However, at 1:118, Chiang Mai's staff-to-population ratio is less favorable than Hat Yai's (1:96), but much better than that of Songkhla (1:137), Khon Kaen (1:165), and Nakhon Ratchasima (1:250).

Chiang Mai also employs the greatest number of professionals such as physicians, nurses, engineers, and architects -- positions which many city governments have great difficulties filling. The relatively high percentage of nonpermanent municipal employees is also remarkable, especially in Chiang Mai and Hat Yai. The data seem to suggest that the bigger the municipality, the larger is the share of the nonpermanent staff (see Table 2.6).

Recruitment of qualified personnel is constrained by a number of factors. First, municipal service is a career which offers few opportunities for lateral entry into higher level government positions. Second, due to the limited scope of authority, municipal service appears to be less attractive than a career in the central government. And third, there is a high turnover rate even among senior municipal officers, primarily be-

TABLE 2.6 Municipal Staff, by Personnel Category

Personnel Category	CM	HY	KK	NR	Song-khla
Classified municipal personnel	194	151	69	144	74
Unclassified municipal personnel	54	35	10	72	14
Municipal teaching personnel	207	237	320	157	209
Regular employees	266	232	164	95	115
Temporary employees	547	537	134	296	167
Total	1,268	1,192	697	764	579
Percentage of nonregular employees and workers	43.1	45.1	19.2	38.7	28.8

Source: Calculated from Multiman, *Municipal Management and Finance Study, Concept Report* (Bangkok: Multiman, Royal Government of Thailand, Ministry of Interior, United Nations Development Programme, July 1982), Vol. 2, Exhibit 9-A.

cause of the ambiguity of their position. City clerks and department heads, for instance, are not only under close central and provincial government supervision, but also quite often under political pressure from the mayor and the executive committee (Krannich 1978a:43).

Nevertheless, in terms of staff competence Chiang Mai appears to be better off than most other municipalities in Thailand. Due to its high quality of life, Chiang Mai is one of the favorite places in a municipal official's career. As a transfer to Chiang Mai is a reward for qualified officials, the municipality has no problem in maintaining high staffing standards.

Planning capacities are another important managerial resource factor. Surprisingly, however, planning is not mentioned among the twenty-five mandatory and optional functions enumerated by the *Municipal Law*. The reason is that physical as well as socioeconomic planning is a rather fragmented process strongly dominated by central agencies. According to the *Town Planning Act of 1975*, land-use planning (or the preparation of a general plan as it is termed in the nomenclature of the Act) has been assigned to the Bangkok-based Office of Town Planning, although local authorities are granted the right to prepare general and specific plans[11] themselves (Town Planning Act, 1975, Sect. 18). But in such a case, prior consent is required from the Board of Town Planning, a high-powered interagency committee at the central government level. The board is the major decision-making body concerned with all technical aspects of land-use planning in Thailand. Moreoever, once a general plan has been prepared by a local authority it must be forwarded to the Office of Town Planning for consideration (Town Planning Act, 1975, Sect. 20). Thus, although municipal governments are formally empowered to plan for their own localities, this power is tightly controlled by the center. Not surprisingly, no municipality has ever prepared its own land-use plan.[12]

So far, seventy-one land-use plans[13] have been completed, among them at least nine[14] which have been signed into law. All of them were prepared by the Office of Town Planning. The office sent out expert teams to the respective municipalities -- usually for fifteen to forty-five days, and around ninety days to a big municipality like Chiang Mai -- in order to collect relevant data and information. The plan was then prepared in the head office in Bangkok. Although the Town Planning Act provides for local participation through public hearings, a public display of the draft plan, and regular consultation between the Office of Town Planning and municipal authorities, the completed draft plan often deviates considerably from local preferences (Suthandhan 1979:2). Thus, the observation that the legal basis for land-use planning "treats the activity as one where central leadership is required, where the central interest is paramount, and where central government alone is competent" (Multiman, Vol. 2, 1982:47) comes close to reality.

While municipal participation in urban land-use planning is limited at best, the local authorities are not well equipped to enforce the regulations laid down in the plan. In 1985, Chiang Mai had only four inspectors for each of its four administrative districts. These officials were hopelessly overburdened and hardly able to enforce the regulations laid down in the city's general plan.

The military is another factor that complicates local planning. In his speech delivered during the seminar on the "Development of Regional Centers in Northern Thailand", a high-ranking military officer outlined five vital concerns of the military in city planning:

First, there should be enough bridges in cities located along rivers (such as Chiang Mai);

Second, a ring road system circumventing the city center should be constructed in order to ensure troop mobility and swift military operations. Thus, what at a first glance appeared as far-sighted city planning, has been the work of military strategists. This is particularly true of the ring roads that have been systematically built around most urban centers in northern and northeastern Thailand, including Chiang Mai.

Third, all public offices should be concentrated in one compound so that their defense can be organized at low cost and with little logistic effort. Chiang Mai's new provincial government complex fits this concept perfectly: some 7 km outside the city center, on an open space, along the Mae Rim road, it is located adjacent to a military camp.

Fourth, urban planning should create sufficient open space that can be utilized by the military for possible assault or retreat operations.

And fifth, public installations (electricity lines, water mains, etc.) should be constructed in such a way that they can easily be guarded against sabotage.

Socioeconomic planning is centralized and fragmented, too. In 1979 the Department of Local Administration started a pilot project with medium-term planning to identify local capital and service needs for a five-year period. Chiang Mai was one of the first municipalities to experiment with five-year planning, which is now compulsory for all municipalities. Although municipalities seem to have a greater role in the preparation of five-year plans, their influence is strongly circumscribed by central project priorities and policy guidelines. After completion the draft plan is again subject to tight controls from the provincial government, the Department of Local Administration, and the Budget Bureau under the Office of the Prime Minister.

While five-year planning is a deliberate attempt to coordinate the sectoral plans, particularly those of agencies involved in infrastructure development, it is an extremely cumbersome process. Plan enforcement is very weak and the agencies involved often place higher priority on directives from their Bangkok headquarters than on complying with local priorities. Municipalities are thus hardly able to fulfill major economic functions such as "promoting employment for local residents".

Interestingly, however, and in contrast to another study where local officials pleaded for greater planning competencies (Suthandhan 1979:73), respondents in Chiang Mai were divided in their assessment of the vertical dimension in planning. When asked whether they feel sufficiently consulted during the preparatory stage of long-range plans affecting Chiang Mai drawn up by national planning authorities, 47 percent said that they are not consulted sufficiently, while 38 percent were satisfied with the extent of consultation. Almost 16 percent did not know or gave no answer.

Local means of influencing central agency decision-making seem to be limited, too. When respondents were asked how they can influence national plans affecting Chiang Mai, the most popular reply (30.2 percent) was "the collection of alternative data for presentation to the respective authorities". However, more than 16 percent claimed that the municipality had no influence, citing the high value and the legitimizing effect of seniority and superiority in Thai culture. Around 14 percent opted for the creation of interagency committees or for organizing meetings with the respective agency. 9 percent preferred the use of informal contacts and another 9 percent opted for applying political pressure through the mass media, collective forms of protest, and petitioning.

Not only is municipal planning impaired by legal-institutional and financial constraints, the administrative fragmentation of urban areas is another obstacle. Urban areas are narrowly defined and do not cover the substantial suburban development in recent years. Chiang Mai's built-up area, for instance, has lately expanded at a rate of 7 to 8 percent per year (Prabudhanitisarn 1985:26). This has repercussions on urban planning in various ways:

1. In Chiang Mai urban planning and service delivery are fragmented among several local entities with varying resource capacities: the province, the municipal district *(amphoe muang)*, and a sanitary district *(sukhaphiban)* adjacent to the municipality. This results in a spatially inequitable pattern of services.

2. A narrowly defined municipal jurisdiction deprives the city of substantial revenues (Kammeier 1986).

3. Especially on the urban fringe haphazard growth occurs that is difficult to remedy even after the area comes under municipal land-use plans. This means that there is little scope for urban planners to direct future urban growth patterns. Plans are thus hardly more than a description of developments that have already taken place (Hennings and Kammeier 1978:74; Technische Universität Berlin 1983/84:40).

Hence, most municipalities have been trying to expand their boundaries. Yet, in Nakhon Ratchasima it took more than twenty-three years before the municipal boundaries were finally extended in 1983. In Hat Yai and Chiang Mai the decision-making process took somewhat less time; but here, too, eight respectively six years passed before the municipal area was enlarged (Mawhood 1981:12). Fortunately, due to rapid suburban growth (Pongquan 1980; Kammeier 1986), the central government has accelerated decision-making on municipal boundary extension in recent years.

Two reasons contributed to the time-consuming nature of boundary extensions: the complicated legal procedures, and they affected the power structure in the annexed areas. The provinces and districts, but -- to a greater extent -- the adjoining sanitary districts stood to lose revenues and territory, the village heads *(phu yai baan)* and tambon chiefs *(kamnan)* their position. Not surprisingly, opposition to boundary extension was mainly orchestrated by these grassroots leaders, who played on fears of tax increases, higher service fees, and the loss of eligibility for rural development projects. The majority of residents, however, seemed to be in favor of the boundary extension, expecting better services (Rungvisai 1985). Nevertheless, it took the municipal officials an intensive house-to-house campaign, lengthy deliberations with the village leadership, promises to improve service delivery, and pledges not to increase taxes for a transitional period of ten years, before full agreement over the annexation of adjoining suburban areas could be reached. With the boundary extension in 1983, Chiang Mai's municipal area almost tripled from 17.5 km2 to 45 km2.

The Municipality and the Societal Linkage Pattern

As has been pointed out in chapter one, a community's linkage pattern is important for its degree of local autonomy. These linkages will be examined in the subsequent sections on the basis of three major criteria: direction of communication, intensity of information flow, and frequency of contacts.

The Communication Infrastructure. A major precondition for the development of linkages between the municipality and other governmental and nongovernmental institutions is the existence of a communication infrastructure that facilitates cheap and fast exchange of information. Such an infrastructure includes above all transport and the telecommunication systems.

In recent years the communicative distance between Chiang Mai and external centers of know-how has been tremendously reduced. Chiang Mai has got an International Airport, which directly links the city with Bangkok and other capitals of the region, like Singapore and Hong Kong. There are at least six flights a day to and from Bangkok; the flight takes one hour. Moreover, Chiang Mai airport links the city with other urban centers in the North such as Chiang Rai, Mae Hong Son, Phrae, Nan, and Phitsanulok.

The short travel time and frequent flights to Bangkok have a direct impact on the frequency and mode of communication between central government agencies and the municipality. In general, it seems that officials at both government levels travel more often in either direction than hitherto. Direct contacts have increased, at the expense of mediation by the provincial government. While this may lead to more direct control by the central government, it also enables municipal officials to present their cases to their superiors. Moreover, representatives from central authorities may get a better understanding of the local situation by first-hand insights and on-the-spot inspection.

Road and rail transport between Bangkok and Chiang Mai are also fairly well developed. Travel time to Bangkok by private car is approximately nine to ten hours, eleven hours by bus, and fourteen hours by train. Though in a physically good condition, the road network is not yet very dense in the Northern Region. Only the area around Chiang Mai and the settlements along the Lampang-Chiang Mai-Chiang Rai axis are well served. Other towns such as Nan, Phrae, Phayao, and Mae

Hong Son can only be reached via considerable detours. Moreover, there is no railway line between Chiang Mai and the Northeast.

Chiang Mai's telecommunication network was inadequate in the past. Recently, however, the system has been substantially upgraded, though it still does not fully satisfy demand. In 1974 there was only one exchange with a capacity of 2,000 lines. There were three in 1981 and four in 1985 (with 7,200 lines). By 1989, the number of lines had increased to 22,680, equivalent to one telephone for every ten persons in *amphoe muang* (Chiang Mai Chamber of Commerce 1990:117).

While the ratio of telephones per person in Chiang Mai province is more favorable than in other Northern provinces, it is still a far cry from the ratio in Bangkok. Moreover, long-distance calls are comparatively expensive in Thailand, so that only urgent calls are made (Chiang Mai Municipality 1990).

As of 1986 the municipality had no direct access to electronic data processing. Accordingly, information management was rather unsystematic and slow. Data must be calculated by hand and were unsystematically stored. However, in the 1986 budget the municipality set aside 3 million Baht for the purchase of a computer to facilitate household registration, tax collection, and access to land-use information. Computerization started in 1987 under the guidance of the Department of Local Administration, and one year later, more than twenty municipalities had computerized tax administration (Department of Local Administration 1988:27).

Linkages between the Municipality and Other Government Units. The overwhelming majority of municipal contacts are vertically structured. They extend mainly to the Ministry of the Interior and the provincial government, and to a lesser extent to the Ministry of Finance and the Budget Bureau. In most cases, it is the center which determines the communication flow.

Only a few municipal administrators and local politicians engage directly in communication with higher government echelons. The frequency of contacts between actors at the municipal level and superior government agencies decreases rapidly, the more one descends in the administrative and political hierarchy. Thus, it is the city clerk (twelve times a year) and the mayor (ten times a year) who travel most frequently, followed by the department heads (two to ten times) and the members of the executive committee. The same officials also receive visitors more frequently. The city clerk and the mayor, for instance, receive visitors from central government agencies five to ten times a month. This also shows that central officials tend to come more often to Chiang Mai than local officials go to Bangkok. Not only do top administrators and politicians make and receive more visits, contact by mail and telephone, which is the normal means of communication, also concentrates on this group of persons.

Chiang Mai's horizontal linkages, i.e. links to other municipalities, were little developed. An effective means of horizontal linkages are municipal associations, which may act as a pressure group vis-à-vis the center. Although there is a Municipal League in Thailand, of which Chiang Mai is a member, its role as a spokesman for the municipalities is only nominal. The league has no independent organizational infrastructure, and is more or less an integral part of the Ministry of the Interior. Its leadership is recruited from among high-ranking officials of the Department of Local Administration, and the day-to-day work is also done by DOLA staff. Even as a source of information, the Municipal League is limited. Regular annual conventions are not sufficient to foster meaningful intermunicipal cooperation, and the training courses offered by the league for senior municipal administrators are often shaped by the priorities of the center rather than of the local units (Mawhood 1981:6; Multiman, Vol. 1, 1982:39). The mayor of a regional center in the Lower North even went so far as to state that the league serves little more than organizing exposure trips abroad for local officials.

Horizontal bonds can also be established through single-purpose or multi-purpose committees with members from various municipalities. Although the Municipal Law permits municipalities to band together in a cooperative association, there are no cases known of such forms of cooperation. The legal hurdles and tight central government controls discourage municipalities (Multiman, Vol. 1, 1982:23).

Although the impact of political parties on the municipal arena will be analyzed in greater detail in section three, political parties must nevertheless be considered a part of the vertical and horizontal linkage pattern into which Chiang Mai is integrated. Depending on their internal structure, political parties may either strengthen or weaken local autonomy; they may provide sources of information, act as mediators and brokers, or even as a pressure group on behalf of the city.

Political parties in Thailand are weak in terms of organization. Except for the Democrat Party, most parties lack grassroots organization (Thongdhamachart 1982). Although virtually all major parties have set up local chapters in Chiang Mai, only the Democrats and the Social Action Party (SAP) have a well established organizational network. Activated only at election times for the mobilization of voters, the other parties rather resemble political clubs. Because the Thai parties are "loosely structured", highly personalized, and particularistic in nature, they do provide for a certain degree of "localism". Compared to the bureaucracy, the cohesive power of their central bodies is weak. Unlike in other Southeast Asian countries, the party system is not a limiting factor for local autonomy.

Linkages to Semi- and Nongovernmental Institutions. A well developed, locally-based network of interest groups providing information and voluntary services to the community may be another counterbalancing force against central dominance in municipal politics. In fact, Chiang Mai as the largest city in the North is the location of a broad range of interest groups. The most important of these operate in the economic sphere, such as the Chiang Mai Chamber of Commerce, the provincial branch of the Thai Federation of Industries, the Thai Hotel Association, the Tourist Business Association, various associations of the construction and real estate industry, the Chiang Mai Banker's Club, and the Committee on Tourism Promotion of Chiang Mai Province, to name a few.

Although membership of interest groups and of the municipal assembly overlaps, it seems that interest groups in Chiang Mai have established relatively few connections with the municipal government. In most cases, such contacts are rather informal, based on personal ties, and activated only when the need arises. Moreover, if there are interactions between the municipality and local interest groups, they are initiated by the latter and are preoccupied with the protection of specific interests of the membership. The issues at stake usually revolve around local taxes, land use and deficient public utilities.

Many local interest groups find it more beneficial to maintain close links with the provincial government and, to a lesser extent, central government agencies based in Bangkok. Yet, there are exceptions such as the Committee for Tourism Promotion of Chiang Mai Province, of which the mayor is a member. In the past, the committee has addressed demands to the municipal government concerning market regulations (especially Chiang Mai's major tourist market, the night bazaar), informal sector policies, the organization of festivals, and the general im-provement of Chiang Mai's tourism infrastructure (cleanliness, beautification, reconstruction of historic sites, building permits for tourism-re-lated businesses, etc.) (Wahnschafft 1984:218).

Civic clubs, such as Chiang Mai's various Rotary and Lions Clubs and the Jaycees, also entertain close relationships with the municipality and, in addition, have developed an impressive network of links to other groups, institutions, and individuals both within Thailand and abroad. In the last decade, a number of nongovernmental development organizations (NGDOs) have emerged, too. However, the majority of them is preoccupied with issues of rural development. Nevertheless, rapid changes in the cityscape have given rise to urban groups that attempt to present alternative development scenarios for the city. Although their relationships with the authorities are sometimes strained, their impact on urban decision-making is increasing.

As the biggest educational center outside Bangkok, Chiang Mai has a vast pool of knowledge and skills relevant to urban development in, for instance, the fields of land-use planning, social science, environmental sanitation, and engineering. There are Chiang Mai and Payap Universities, the Mae-Jo College of Agriculture, the Rajamangala Northern Technical College, and the Teacher's Training College. However, it seems that in the past this resource potential, which could give Chiang Mai more independence from the center, was not fully utilized. Communication flow between Chiang Mai University and the municipality has so far been one-way, with the university as the initiator. It was the university which offered studies and know-how. Yet, these offers were ignored or only marginally utilized by the municipality. The city government elected in July 1985, under the banner of the Ananthaphum group, recognized this situation and announced its willingness of improving relationships with the academic sector. In its election platform Ananthaphum expressed its intention of inviting locally-based experts, academics, and others to contribute to urban development in Chiang Mai. Although several studies were commissioned by the municipality to university institutes, communication between the two is still far from optimal.

The structure of organizations and enterprises in the private sector may also influence the scope of municipal government. Empirical studies in industrialized countries have demonstrated that policy options of local authorities tend to decrease when the economic structure of a city is dominated by absentee-owned organizations. These are branches of large companies operating on a national or even global scale. Given the centralized internal organization of such companies, the probability increases that company decisions made in the headquarters conflict with priorities set by the local government. There may be pressures for tax holidays, certain infrastructure investments, reductions in environmental standards, and changes in land-use and zoning regulations that, if ignored, may result in the relocation of the plant. In case of conflicts between a company and local government, the chance that company demands prevail increases in proportion to the firm's capacity to withdraw vital resources such as jobs, tax income, and donations for social institutions or cultural activities in the locality. Due to their supralocal organization and greater flexibility in locational decisions, absentee-owned corporations are in a much more favorable bargaining position vis-à-vis the local authority than locally-based entrepreneurs. Supralocally organized enterprises are thus well able to get the most out of the competition between local units to attract investments.

Chiang Mai's economic structure is characterized by small-scale local firms. This is particularly true of the manufacturing sector. Yet, as Wahnschafft has shown, especially in the tourist industry -- a key sector of Chiang Mai's economy -- there is an increasing participation of Bangkok- and foreign-based investors (Wahnschafft 1984:157-164). Since urban policies relating to the tourism sector, such as land-use, informal sector regulations, beautification, infrastructure development, and restoration of historical sites, occupy a high priority among Chiang Mai's decision-makers, and institutional links between the tourist industry and the local authority exist, it must be assumed that the influence of external economic actors on Chiang Mai's decision-making is growing. Cases in point are the controversies over the Doi Suthep cable car project and the mushrooming high-rise buildings, which will be analyzed below.

Political Participation

Whereas previously the vertical dimension in municipal government was examined, in the following sections, policy-making will be analyzed at the level of the municipal arena. The questions addressed are who participates, how, when, and why under the conditions of limited local autonomy.

Leadership Recruitment through Municipal Elections

Municipal elections in their present form are quite a recent phenomenon in Thailand, although local elections were held as early as the 1930s. After the 1932 Revolution municipalities were created under the *Municipal Law of 1933*. This was an attempt by a western-educated faction among the coup leaders to instill ideas of western liberal democracy into a polity that had hitherto been autocratically ruled by a divinely sanctioned monarchy. Elective municipal government was considered the local foundation of parliamentary democracy, which, as stipulated by the 1932 Constitution, was to be the form of government of modern Thailand. The idea behind the creation of a western-type elective municipal government was to foster political participation and to promote the development of a democratic value system at the grassroots level (Karnjanaprakorn 1962:37).

Local elections to fully elective municipal councils have been held regularly since 1974. In Chiang Mai the voters elect twenty-four assemblymen. The municipal assembly approves the budget, local by-laws, ordinances, and regulations. Smaller municipalities, the *tesaban muang* and *tesaban tambon*, have eighteen and twelve assemblymen, respectively. Once elected, the assemblymen elect from among themselves a mayor and the four members of the executive committee, all of whom need formal appointment by the governor. The mayor, as the head of the executive committee, formulates policy, exercises supervisory and ceremonial functions, and plays a minor role in personnel management. The other members of the executive committee assist him by directing and supervising the operations in major service sectors such as public health, finance, education, and public works.

Unlike in Philippine cities, political competitiveness and mobilization and participation levels in Chiang Mai and other Thai cities are rather low (Murashima 1987:364-365). Although four groups ran for municipal posts in the 1974 and 1980 elections, the strength of these groups was so uneven that one can hardly speak of a serious electoral contest. At that time local politics in Chiang Mai was firmly controlled by a group of local leaders who had formed a political organization called Prachasanti.

A sizeable number of independent candidates and the formation of loose election alliances were major reasons for the number of candidates per seat to rise from 2.88 in 1974 to more than 4.08 in 1980. Yet, the sheer number of candidates had little influence on the level of competitiveness. Most candidates lacked the organization and finance to mobilize voters, and thus were unable to run a proper election campaign.

Changes from this customary pattern of leadership recruitment occurred in the July 1985 elections. This time only two groups contested the seats for the municipal assembly: the Ananthaphum group had emerged as a serious rival for Prachasanti. As a result, political activity, competitiveness and mobilization increased markedly in Chiang Mai (Rüland and Ladavalya 1986:441), although they were still low compared to local elections in the Philippines.

Preparations began about six months before the election. Right at the beginning of the election year, both groups began to evaluate their chances, raise funds, and screen suitable candidates. At the time of the election, Prachasanti and Ananthaphum were both well entrenched in the local political scene. Prachasanti had been the dominant force in municipal politics for more than twenty years, controlling the city hall with overwhelming majorities. Ananthaphum, on the other hand, was of more recent origin, although its core members such as the Tantranondhs, Wiboonsantis, Osathaphans, and Chutimas, all economically successful families with a Sino-Thai background, had close business relationships with each other that can be traced back to the 1950s (Chananan 1987:118,119). Formed in 1979, Ananthaphum contested municipal elections for the first time in 1980, though with modest success. The group won only two out of the twenty-four seats. Some of its leaders, however, had already run unsuccessfully in 1974 under the banner of the Phalang Chiang Mai group. Both Prachasanti and Ananthaphum had a well established network of supporters in the city, with Prachasanti claiming about 3,000 members against Ananthaphum's 1,000. Whereas in the Philippines national party juntas nominate the party slates for local elections, the nomination process in Chiang Mai is essentially a local affair, although national politicians such as the city's MPs or cabinet ministers from Chiang Mai may exert some informal influence.

Candidates were selected by an executive committee composed of the groups' major leaders. Similar to national parties, recruitment of candidates was a two-way process. Persons vying for public office approached the groups, seeking nomination on their tickets, while there were also cases in which the group leaders themselves asked "strategic" personalities in the community to run under their group's banner. Each group could choose from among approximately sixty candidates. From these sixty applicants, twenty-four were shortlisted. In general, the nominating committees used three criteria to make their choice:

1. *Popularity in the community.* A Candidate must be a wellknown and respected personality who, by nature of his profession or social activities, has influence on a considerable number of people. Teachers, lawyers, and physicians in particular meet this criterion. They build up a following through free legal aid and free medical services, while teachers benefit from the great respect that traditional values accord them.

To be well-known among voters also depends on long-time residence within the community. Like in Iloilo, local people seem to have greater electoral chances. No less than 75 percent of the interviewed local politicians were born in Chiang Mai or had lived in the city for a long period. 8.3 percent were born in other northern provinces, while another 8.3 percent had migrated to Chiang Mai from Bangkok.

In seven out of ten cases the parents of candidates were also born in Chiang Mai and vicinity which suggests that, on the one hand, geographical mobility among candidates and their families is relatively low and, on the other hand, that family ties of candidates in Chiang Mai reach back to former generations. Yet, there was also a remarkable 11 percent of fathers and 6 percent of mothers who migrated to Chiang

Mai from China. If grandparents were included, the proportion of candidates of Chinese descent would rise well above the 20 percent margin.

2. *The resources of a candidate.* Election campaigns are very expensive. The competing groups must also use their limited funds to support less wealthy, yet popular contestants. As a result, the ticket must include as many wealthy candidates and good fund raisers as possible.

3. *Political experience.* Because election campaigns require tactical and political skills, groups prefer to select candidates who have already contested elections before. In the 1980 and 1985 municipal elections, 62.5 percent of Prachasanti candidates had prior electoral experience. In 1980, the first time that Ananthaphum contested local elections, 20.8 percent of its candidates had prior electoral experience compared with 50 percent in 1985.

Campaign activity began in earnest about four weeks before the elections. Both groups started putting up posters advertising their candidates. A novelty in the 1985 election in Chiang Mai was the creation of four voting zones. These voting zones corresponded to the four administrative districts delineated after the extension of the city boundaries in 1983. In each zone the contesting groups were permitted to nominate a slate of six candidates. Because much of zone 4, covering the western and the northern parts of Chiang Mai, was newly incorporated into the municipal area and this was a controversial issue, campaign strategists anticipated that the outcome of the elections would be decided here. Hence, the priority given to that zone during the campaign.

Whereas Prachasanti started campaigning earlier, Ananthaphum concentrated on the week immediately preceding the elections. The closer election day came, the more aggressive and intensive became Ananthaphum's campaign, while Prachasanti's efforts appeared rather lacklustre. The number of posters throughout the city increased rapidly, as did the output of leaflets and other campaign materials. One of the Ananthaphums's shrewdest moves was the nomination of a leading representative of Chiang Mai's samlor (bicycle rickshaw) drivers -- not only because he was able to mobilize a substantial voter block from among the city's more than 3,000 samlor drivers, but also because samlor drivers advertised Ananthaphum by carrying posters on the back of their pedicabs.

The poster and leaflet campaign was complemented by advertisements on radio and in local newspapers. A content analysis of Thai News, the leading Thai language daily in the North, showed that only Ananthaphum made use of this medium. In the four weeks before the election, Ananthaphum placed five advertisements, and Prachasanti none. This contrasts starkly with former elections, when Prachasanti's advertisements dominated the local press. There were thirty advertisements for Prachasanti's candidates in 1974, and seven in the four weeks preceding the 1980 elections. In addition, loudspeaker trucks of both groups toured the city.

There was an array of other tactics employed to mobilize voters. Almost all candidates engaged in door-to-door campaigning within their voting zone, although this was done more intensively by Ananthaphum. Ananthaphum had set up a headquarters in every zone, where campaign strategies were carefully reviewed and outlined from day to day and street to street.

Ananthaphum canvassers also visited schools and temples. Both institutions were regarded as important multipliers. Although, according to interviewees, religious leaders rarely exerted their influence openly, they nevertheless gave hints to the voters about what characteristics a good candidate should possess. Similar observations were made by Murashima in Nakhon Sawan. Although the Sangha authorities and orthodox interpretations of the Vinaya, the monastic code of discipline, require monks to refrain from secular politics (Suksamran 1982:52), Murashima reported that candidates made donations to temples, hoping that their abbots might influence voting behavior (Murashima 1987:382).

Rallies were held in densely populated public places such as markets and business centers, especially in the last week. However, they seem to have little impact on voting behavior. Many bystanders were more interested in the entertainment provided, as both groups fielded popular actors and singers to support their campaign. Rallies usually did not draw large crowds. In an opinion poll conducted by political science students of Chiang Mai University, only 36 percent of the respondents said they had attended rallies or listened to campaign speeches. A discussion between candidates of both groups organized on the university campus was attended by just sixteen people. The debate, that was expected to be a highlight of the campaign, had to be canceled.

In contrast to Prachasanti, Ananthaphum produced an election platform consisting of twelve major points, including a more open, participatory, and management-oriented style of municipal administration. Mechanisms were outlined to encourage people's participation and to pursue a style of administration that would be more responsive to people's needs. Moreover, the platform promised to preserve ancient local traditions and to improve the city's cleanliness. The program is a reflection of the socioeconomic background of Ananthaphum's leaders. As young, dynamic businessmen they pleaded for the application of the same modern management techniques in municipal administration that they use to run their businesses. Economic considerations also explain their concern for the conservation of historical movements and old customs. This policy was fueled by a strong interest in promoting tourism -- the number one income earner in Chiang Mai: more tourists would improve economic opportunities in the city which, in turn, would attract new investors.

Prachasanti attempted to counter Ananthaphum's aggressive campaign style by emphasizing its administrative experience. Its major theme was "performance". Public works projects such as road repair, street lighting, and antilitter programs, were stepped up to underscore the group's service and performance orientation.

During the campaign there were frequent allegations of vote buying by both camps. Although these claims could not be verified by personal observation, interviews and newspaper reports seem to confirm that voters were actually bought.[21] Vote buying, a common phenomenon in Thai electoral politics, also seems to have taken place in the contest studied by Murashima. According to him, canvassers in Nakhon Sawan paid 20 Baht for a vote -- a rather small amount compared to the amounts distributed during national elections (Murashima 1987:382). While Prachasanti accused its opponents of money dumping and vote buying, Ananthaphum supporters often suspected the incumbent Prachasanti-led municipal administration of tampering with household registration documents in order to bring in "ghost voters" from adjacent rural areas. Such accusations, too, are not uncommon in Thai municipal elections, as newspaper analyses suggest.[22]

Although in the days prior to the election it seemed that the outcome would be a close race, Ananthaphum's victory came as a surprise for many pundits. With 51.46 percent of the vote, Ananthaphum won fourteen seats, while Prachasanti polled 48.05 percent of the vote and won ten seats. Zones 1 and 2 were won by Ananthaphum with comfortable majorities, in zone 3 the race ended with a slight advantage for Ananthaphum. Zone 4 was the stronghold of Prachasanti, where it polled nearly 62 percent of the vote. The sole independent candidate obtained only 1.7 percent of the votes, thus confirming a nationwide trend in municipal elections towards clearly recognizable group affiliations.

At 37.5 percent, turnout was higher than in previous elections.[23] Nevertheless, despite a vigorous information campaign conducted by the municipal administration, the targeted 50 percent turnout was not reached in Chiang Mai. Voter turnout in Chiang Mai remained well below the national average in local elections and even further below that of parliamentary elections.[24] With 14 percent in 1983 and 17 percent in 1984, it had been even lower in municipal by-elections. The low participation clearly reflects the low level of mobilization in Chiang Mai's municipal politics.

Four reasons may be advanced to explain the unexpected defeat of Prachasanti, after controlling city hall for more than twenty years.

1. Ananthaphum's campaign strategy was obviously better planned, staffed, financed, and organized, and conducted in a more professional style. Ananthaphum successfully portrayed its candidates as young, dynamic, performance-oriented managers, able to instill municipal government with fresh ideas, at the same time depicting Prachasanti as a group of ageing and conservative politicians clinging to their posts and blocking progress in the municipality. The sole exception to this was zone 4, where Prachasanti organized a well-orchestrated campaign and scored accordingly.

In fact, Ananthaphum candidates were considerably younger than their rivals. On average, they were 44.8 years old, i.e., almost nine years younger than their opponents (53.75 years). For too long Prachasanti had controlled the municipal government without rejuvenating its leadership. Ananthaphum, on the other hand, represented the challenge of a group of local "Young Turks" who saw no prospect of influencing municipal policies as long as Prachasanti held the reins of power.

2. The novelty of dividing the municipality into four voting zones suited Ananthaphum's campaign strategy, which was built on close contact with the voters. Election teams could thus approach neighborhoods more frequently and intensively than if the entire municipality were just one constituency as previously.

3. A comparison of the 1985 election with the elections of 1974 and 1980 shows that there was no landslide against Prachasanti, neither in absolute nor in relative terms. Between 1974 and 1985, Prachasanti's proprotion of votes decreased by 8.9 percent -- a margin not unusual given the rapid socioeconomic change in the city and the natural erosion of electoral appeal affecting most long-serving political parties. In 1985, however, the polarization of the contest between only two groups evidently worked to the disadvantage of Prachasanti. The two preceding municipal elections were contested by four groups and opposition votes slit among the three challengers.

Moreover, in former elections Prachasanti benefited from a low turnout. Prachasanti was always uccessful when turnout was low. Among the groups competing for municipal posts, Prachasanti had the best organized machine with the largest clientele, which it could successfully mobilize. In the 1985 election, Prachasanti was again able to mobilize this traditional clientele, although to a somewhat lesser extent than in previous elections. With the higher turnout this was not sufficient to win the election. Ananthaphum must have successfully mobilized previous nonvoters and first-time voters.

Ananthaphum's support did not come from the newly annexed municipal areas, but -- perhaps not surprisingly, given the socioeconomic background of Ananthaphum candidates -- from the inner-city where businesses are concentrated. In zone 4, the annexed area, Prachasanti was able to make a clean sweep, winning all six seats. The annexation of these areas, which took place under the Prachasanti administration, was thus not a decisive issue in the election.

4. The organizational affiliation of Ananthaphum candidates allowed a better mobilization of voters. The organizational membership profile of Ananthaphum was fairly homogeneous, although with an average of 2.86 memberships they were less frequently affiliated to voluntary associations than Prachasanti candidates (3.54 memberships). Most Ananthaphum candidates were members of at least one, and more often even two or three, of the following organizations: the Jaycees, the Village Scouts, the Thai Territory Defense Volunteers, the Lion's Club, the Buddhist Association of Chiang Mai, and the Youth Group *(Glum Num Sao)*. The organizational profile of Prachasanti candidates, on the other hand, was much more heterogeneous, with participation in a great variety of educational, religious, economic/professional, welfare, and cultural organizations (see Table 2.7).

Another decisive factor for the outcome of the election was Ananthaphum's control over mass organizations. Many Ananthaphum candidates were active in the Village Scouts movements which, since its inception in 1971, has been particularly popular in the north of Thailand (Muecke 1980:410), and had some 20,000 members in amphoe muang alone. In addition, Ananthaphum candidates were leaders in the so-called Youth Group *(Glum Num Sao)*, which likewise had some 8,000 members in amphoe muang. Despite their inauspicious role as a militant, and even violent vanguard of rightest forces in the 1970s, the Village Scouts, enjoying royal patronage, command great prestige among the populace and are treated with deference even by the authorities (Morell and Samudavanija 1981:242-246; Girling 1981:213). They may have won a lot of votes for Ananthaphum. Ananthaphum membership in the Thai Territory Defense Volunteers also had a considerable multiplier effect, especially among military and police personnel, public officials, and voters with a staunchly conservative and patriotic value system. Finally, through the inclusion of the samlor drivers' spokesman, Ananthaphum became attractive to the urban poor and the working class as well.

TABLE 2.7 Membership of Local Decision-Makers in Voluntary Associations, by Type of Association, Chiang Mai Municipality

Type of Organization	Total interviewed local politicians		Anathaphum		Prachasanti		Public Officials		Total Respondents[a]	
	N	%	N	%	N	%	N	%	N	%
Educational	16	14.0	4	6.3	12	26.1	5	50.0	21	16.9
Religious	14	12.3	7	11.1	7	15.2	-	-	14	11.3
Civic	32	28.1	22	34.9	8	17.4	2	20.0	34	27.2
Economic/professional	8	7.0	3	4.8	5	10.9	2	20.0	10	8.1
Para-military	20	17.5	17	27.0	3	6.5	-	-	20	16.1
Youth	8	7.0	7	11.1	1	2.2	-	-	8	6.5
Sports	3	2.6	2	3.2	-	-	-	-	3	2.4
Welfare	9	7.9	1	1.6	6	13.0	-	-	9	7.3
Cultural	4	3.5	-	-	4	8.7	1	10.0	5	4.0
Total	114	99.9	63	100.0	46	100.0	10	100.0	124	100.0

[a]Includes one independent

Source: Survey of local decision-makers, Chiang Mai, 1985.

Participatory Patterns in Everyday Politics

In its role as the political forum between elections the municipal assembly plays a rather limited role in decision-making. Some respondents went so far as to describe it as a body that merely ratifies decisions taken elsewhere.

The assembly meets infrequently. The law prescribes just two regular sessions per year of fifteen days each -- one in February and one in August. Additional sessions may be called, if a supplementary budget has to be approved or other urgent issues arise.

There were usually few discussions in the assembly. If there were any, like, for instance, when the budget or major public works projects were deliberated, they were rather short, often lasting no longer than half an hour. In the past this was mainly a consequence of Prachasanti's overwhelming majority. There was no effective opposition able to exert some control and to question decisions made by the ruling group. Most decisions were made informally in small circles and were no longer a topic of discussion when they reached the assembly. No wonder a majority of local politicians (63.8 percent) felt that the municipal assembly was either "not so active" or "inactive". However, the majority of critics came from the Ananthaphum group. By contrast, Prachasanti candidates took a more positive view of the role of the municipal assembly. Almost 70 percent of the Prachasanti candidates interviewed concluded that the assembly was either "very active" or "active".

But changes in the political culture of Chiang Mai's municipal assembly must be anticipated. Now that municipal politics has turned from a "dominant group" into a "two group"-type of arena, conflicts will intensify and become more open, making municipal politics in Chiang Mai more competitive. Apart from that, there are indications that national political parties such as the Democrats or Bangkok Governor Chamlong Srimuang's Phalang Dharma Party (PDP) will also intensify their mobilization efforts and may contest municipal elections in the future.

Since few sessions are held, the local legislature is rarely in a position to exert meaningful control over the local bureaucracy. Top ranking municipal administrators thus enjoy a strong position in local decision-making, especially if the mayor is weak (Krannich 1975, 1978a). This situation is reinforced in cases where a strong and experienced administrative leadership exists, as in the person of Chiang Mai's permanent city clerk who has served in the city for more than ten years. Senior municipal civil servants like him have a near monopoly of expertise about of how to reconcile political decisions made by the municipal assembly or the executive committee with the complex web of rules and regulations of Thai bureaucracy. This legal, administrative, and procedural know-how makes the city clerk a key figure not only in decision-making per se, but also as a counselor in the preparatory phase and a modifier and implementer in the postdecision stage. Accordingly, if decisions are made without prior consultation and approval of the city clerk, he can easily obstruct them.

As a result, municipal conflicts usually involved the same individuals. This was corroborated by the interviews with Chiang Mai's decision-makers: more than 64 percent of the interviewed politicians and almost 67 percent of municipal administrators made statements to this effect. In its election platform, Ananthaphum announced it would replace this elitist style of municipal decision-making by a team-work approach. After assuming office, the group institutionalized weekly meetings of its assemblymen and another regular meeting with the group's grassroots leaders to facilitate communication between the elected representatives, the organization, and supporters. Yet, it is questionable whether these meetings have brought about more than cosmetic changes, because Ananthaphum too has an inner leadership dominating policy formulation within the group.

In the past, the general public did not participate much in municipal affairs. Most participation took place informally during social events such as receptions, parties, inaugurations, ceremonies, and cultural events which were attended by local politicians and administrators. Another forum for lobbying was the weekly meetings of civic clubs like the Rotary and Lions Clubs or the Jaycees. The exclusive nature of these clubs, however, restricted meaningful participation to a relatively small group of well-to-do and prominent personalities.

While it is true that, except at election time, municipal decision-makers make little effort to establish closer links with the public, it is also true that ordinary citizens rarely approach their representatives with demands or complaints. If they do so, they strongly rely on personal ties and usually approach a representative residing within their neighborhood. The issues forwarded to the assemblymen are often rather particularistic and personal in nature and seldom affect a larger section of the public. Until the mid-1980s, forms of broad solidarity or public protest such as demonstrations were virtually unknown in Chiang Mai municipal politics.

Broad strata of the public are thus only marginally politicized. They show little interest in municipal politics and often have quite hazy ideas about the municipal institutions and their functions. Although sessions of the municipal assembly are open to the public, few people attend. Even when important decisions with far-reaching consequences for future urban development and the living conditions of each individual citizen are at stake, there is little public participation. Less than 100 persons, for instance, attended the hearings on the Chiang Mai general plan in 1983, which regulates future urban land use. Most of them were real estate brokers, representatives of the construction industry, professionals, and academics.

The most active sections of the public, sometimes openly criticizing municipal authorities and frequently trying to influence their decisions, are the merchants, businessmen, and hawkers. Their motivation for participation, however, is less democratic ideals than economic interests, which are frequently affected by actions of the municipal administration. This is the case, for instance, with local taxes, the distribution of licenses and franchises, land-use policy, building permits, and antihawking legislation.

An important instrument to facilitate popular feed-back to the municipal administration is the mass media, especially the press. While a majority of respondents (77.8 percent) named the press as a major critic of municipal politics in Chiang Mai and felt that newspapers frequently report municipal affairs, this assessment was not corroborated by a content analysis of *Thai News*. However, a change occurred in the late 1980s with the inauguration of the *Kao Sayam* newspaper, which as a mouthpiece of Prachasanti, critically covered the policies of the municipal government.

A noteworthy deviation from this "low-level participatory political culture" was the movement that was formed by concerned citizens in 1985 to protest the construction by a consortium of Bangkok businessmen of a cable car system linking Chiang Mai with Wat Prathat, a famous Buddhist monastery located on top of nearby Doi Suthep mountain. The businessmen argued that -- by improving access to Wat Prathat -- the cable car project would considerably enhance the city's attractiveness for tourists. In their view, the road leading to the sanctuary was dangerous and unable to handle the increasing tourist traffic.[25]

The project's critics countered that the existing road was totally adequate and stressed the environmental dangers of the project: it would intensify hillside deforestation, soil erosion, and flooding. The rich wildlife on Doi Suthep, a national park with many rare species, would be seriously endangered.[26] Fears were also expressed that the cable car project was only the first stage of a long-range development plan for Doi Suthep, to be followed by subdivision and hotel development on the lower reaches and shopping arcades, restaurants and Disneyland-like amusement parks at the top. What, however, politicized the issue were fears of religious-minded Thais and the Sangha that the anticipated invasion of more than 10,000 visitors per day would tarnish the sacredness of Wat Prathat, where a much revered relic of the Buddha is preserved.

Criticism against the 113 million Baht project was first aired in a series of letters to the editor of major English and Thai-language dailies. Then, in May and June 1986, amid intense lobbying with the provincial authorities against the project, several peaceful demonstrations were staged in Chiang Mai and a petition signed by 30,000 persons was submitted to the government.[27]

The controversy was, however, not a municipal issue in the strict sense. Since the project site lay just outside the municipal boundaries, protests were mainly addressed to the provincial and central authorities.[28] Despite the large number of petitioners, the movement could mobilize only a minor portion of Chiang Mai's population, as demonstrated by the poor attendance of demonstrations and rallies. Most of the activists were academics, students, workers of nongovernmental development organizations (NGDOs), ecologically concerned foreigners, and Buddhist monks. The Sangha's determined support was crucial, as it gave the protest movement prestige and legitimacy. Initially the drivers and owners of minibuses plying the Doi Suthep route also joined the protest, but they were lured away with the argument that the loss of the Doi Suthep route would easily be compensated by a tremendous increase of tourists attracted by the cable car system.[29]

Soon afterwards the provincial authorities announced that, for the time being, they would not give the "go-ahead" for the project. This decision, however, was less a success of the protest movement, than the result of political circumstances. In June 1986, coinciding with the protest activities in Chiang Mai, a mass demonstration against the construction of a tantalum plant in Phuket turned into a riot, in the course of which the plant was totally destroyed. Another popular uprising against a major government-supported modernization project a few weeks before the general elections on 27 July 1986 would have harmed the electoral prospects of the coalition parties. Although at present the project seems to be cancelled, observers in Chiang Mai still suspect that under changed conditions it might be revitalized and eventually pushed through.

Nevertheless, the protest movement against the Doi Suthep cable car project had a lasting impact on ecological awareness and political participation in Chiang Mai. Under the leadership of a retired senior government official and academics of Chiang Mai University, the movement did not disband after the cable car project was shelved, but soon developed into a major voice in Chiang Mai's local politics. Known as the

"Club for Chiang Mai" (*Chomrom Pua Chiang Mai*), the group and its
supporters organized public meetings, discussions, and exhibitions to
make authorities and the public aware of the environmental hazards of
unrestrained economic growth. Such dangers have increased as the city
has been flooded by a wave of investments during Thailand's breathtak-
ing economic growth in the late 1980s. Its most visible effect was an unprecedented urban construction boom. As of mid-1989, foreign and
Bangkok-based real estate firms, partly in collusion with local businessmen and municipal politicians and strongly supported by Chiang
Mai's provincial Chamber of Commerce, had initiated some thirty-six
high-rise condominium, hotel, and shopping center projects with a investment of some 2.985 billion Baht.[30]

Unfortunately, as their rationale was the quick realization of profit in
a competitive market, many of these projects were poorly planned and
hastily implemented. There was no municipal regulation that required
the projects to conform with existing city plans and as a result of legal
loopholes, the builders were able to start construction whereever a project promised maximum rates of return. Many of the condominiums
were built in areas where there are inadequate services and utilities.
Especially in Chiang Mai's western parts, at the foot of Doi Suthep, water shortages are a serious problem, forcing some projects to use water
from a nearby irrigation canal, while others drilled artesian wells,
thereby aggravating soil subsidence. The unresolved discharge of waste
water and garbage disposal were related problems. Moreover, safety
aspects remained unattended too: there is no effective protection against
fire hazards or earthquakes. On top of this, many projects violate avia-
tion regulations as they lie in the flight path of Chiang Mai airport.

It was at this point that the Club for Chiang Mai orchestrated the
protest of the environmentalists, cultural conservationists, and other
people adversely affected by these projects. High-rise buildings, the
protestors complained, turn Chiang Mai into an ugly concrete jungle,
depriving the city of its natural charm and unique cultural features. Particularly resented was the construction of condominiums in close proximity to Buddhist temples, dwarfing these sacred places -- an act considered highly demeaning and disrespectful of the Buddhist religion.

Although the Group for Chiang Mai has not markedly expanded its
active support over the years -- still mainly relying on elements of
Chiang Mai's educated urban middle-class -- it has been able to mobilize
public attention through a variety of strategies: (a) organizing rallies,
some of which were attended by more than 1,000 people; (b) sending
petitions to government representatives such as the mayor, the governor, and even the prime minister; (c) confronting the cabinet with the is-

sue during the *"Mobile Cabinet"* meeting in Chiang Mai in May 1989;[31] (d) registering the support of prominent figures of public life such as former prime minister Kukrit Pramoj; (e) establishing good relations with especially the liberal English-language press, although *Kao Sayam,* a newly founded Thai-language local daily also reported frequently and symphathically on the anti-condominium campaign; and (f) performing religious ceremonies, including the cursing of the condominium industry.

The protest had two main targets: first, the business community led by the provincial Chamber of Commerce was accused of pursuing an exclusively profit-oriented model of development irrespective of irreparable environmental damage and a decreasing quality of life in the city, and second, the municipal government was seen as colluding with the housing investors by issuing building permits.

Initially, the group demanded an immediate freeze of all high-rise construction and the creation of a task force for drafting an ordinance that would regulate the construction of condominiums and other high-rise structures. These demands were later toned down, although the group remained adamant in advocating the introduction of zoning regulations for high-rises. By August 1989 the group had exerted so much pressure on the Ministry of the Interior, the provincial government, and the municipal administration that a zoning regulation was announced that marked out four high-rise free zones: a first zone located within the inner-city walls imposes a maximum height of 12 m on buildings; a second zone ranging from the western part of the city moat to the foot of Doi Suthep provides for a maximum height of 20 m and not more than five storeys; a third zone along both sides of the Ping river, restricts building heights to a maximum of 12 m; and, finally, a fourth zone covers a radius of 50 m from temples, schools, official buildings, archaelogical sites, and hospitals and stipulates a maximum height of 16 m.

Undoubtedly, the drafting of this zoning regulation was a major success for the anti-condominium movement. However, construction of new condominiums continued unabated as it took the Ministry of the Interior until April 1990 to finally approve the slightly modified ordinance.[32] Some observers regarded this as a deliberate delaying tactic, enabling a businessmen-dominated central government to stifle local protest on the one hand, and buy time for investors to push through their projects, one the other.

Apart from this incipient formation of popular protest, in recent years gradual changes in the relationship between local officials and the public can be observed that seem to facilitate greater people's involvement in local government. After its election victory, Ananthaphum began to build up a street-level organizational network in each of to the four electoral zones in the municipality. Each zone had its own head-quarters. Here the issues, complaints, and demands reported by the street-level representatives of the group are collected, discussed, and, if necessary, forwarded to the municipal assembly.

Although this is undoubtedly a device to build up a political machine for mobilizing voters in forthcoming elections and to perpetuate Ananthaphum's grip on the city hall, it seems that this feed-back mechanism has actually produced participatory results.

Moreover, once a week a group of municipal assemblymen, the city clerk, and department heads visited the city's neighborhoods in order to listen to the complaints and suggestions of the residents. The group was accompanied by a garbage truck and municipal workers. If, for instance, garbage in the area visited has not been properly collected, it was removed on the spot. The same held true for minor repairs that were likewise carried out at once.[33]

All this seems to indicate that -- at least for a while -- Ananthaphum has kept its campaign promises. When they were asked what would be the best way to keep in touch with the local people's needs and demands, 54 percent of Ananthaphum respondents opted for a decentralized administrative structure which would extend from the city hall down to street-level. Many Prachasanti respondents, too, preferred regular inspection trips by municipal decision-makers in the city's neighborhoods (47.4 percent). The politicians' opinions, however, contrasted with the more passive attitude of local bureaucrats -- a majority of whom felt that people themselves must take the initiative and air their complaints to the authorities. Moreover, public officials also had greater belief in "scientific" methods, such as regular surveys and opinion polls, which received only little support from politicians.

Obstacles to Mobilization and Participation

Although the Thai municipal government system provides formal channels and mechanisms for citizens' participation, the actual level of participation is low in Chiang Mai. Participation in municipal politics is little more than voting in local elections, but even this most basic political right is exercised only by a minority of the population.

On a general level, Thai cultural values determining human interactions provide a key to understanding nonparticipant behavior. Despite greater social mobility, increasing functional diversification of society, and a more pronounced division of labor, traditional value patterns have long remained intact in Chiang Mai and other Thai cities. This traditional value system implies forms of social organization that rest on hierarchical sets of interactions. In his study *"Everyday Life in Thailand"* the Dutch anthropologist Niels Mulder (1985) brilliantly described the attitudes internalized by Thais at an early stage in their socialization[34] that inhibit political action.

At the center of the Thai socialization process are the attitudes of *krengcaj* (inhibition), *kreng klua* (respectful fear) and *waangaj* (acceptance of the wisdom of the elders). Respect, fear, and deference towards elders and superiors such as father, mother, and teacher are among the earliest lessons Thais learn. While the power of superiors may be benevolent -- as in the case of the parents or the teacher -- it also arouses awe because, if disturbed, it may become vengeful and and dangerous. Mulder thus concludes that "soon one learns . . . to accommodate with power and keep the social process pleasant and superficial" (Mulder 1985:64). This holds even more true for interactions with persons who are not close:

> People perceive each other as potentially harmful, because real intentions remain unknown. Consequently such persons meet with each other as with potentially harmful forces that need to be subdued by nice, polite and pleasant behavior (Mulder 1985:71).

This behavioral predisposition explains the high value Thai society places on smooth interaction and avoidance of open conflict. When everybody knows his place and behaves accordingly, these ideals can be easily achieved in everyday life. These observations lead Mulder to conclude that

> Thailand is a society of rather conservative people who appreciate the predictability and quietness of their social life to which they readily conform and in which they feel secure (Mulder 1985:70).

The consequences of these value patterns for political participation are evident. Forms of political participation other than individual contacts or filing petitions will be adopted only with great reluctance. Open criticism of the state and its representatives and face-to-face confrontation are avoided whenever possible out of fear of retribution from these powerful forces. Thai cultural values thus militate against the emergence of more radical forms of political participation. The frequency of participation is likewise determined in large part by these values. As participation implies incalculable personal risks, people resort to political action only sporadically, when much is at stake and all other means of solving the problem have proved futile.

Another reason is the weakness of political parties. Of the two rival groups in Chiang Mai's municipal arena, neither Prachasanti nor Ananthaphum are political parties in the strict sense; their organization is exclusively local in nature. In Chiang Mai, as in most other municipalities, no national political party fielded its own ticket. Political parties in Thailand are still mainly Bangkok-centered personal followings with little or no nationwide grassroots organization and mass base. The Democrat Party, for instance, the oldest and best organized party, has only 113 branches nationwide. They cover fifty of the country's seventy-four provinces, but only 102 of 719 districts. Of 14,719 registered members, 4,986 or 34 percent live in Bangkok (Samudavanija 1987:10). The majority of other parties barely exceed the 5,000 member margin, the legally prescribed minimum for official registration as a party with the Ministry of the Interior.

Since political parties have no or only very poorly organized party branches in the provinces, the local arena is not very important for mobilizing electoral support in national elections. As a consequence, much less is at stake in local elections than, for instance, in the Philippines. Hence, the low levels of competitiveness and the rather lacklustre efforts at voter mobilization.

In Chiang Mai, neither Prachasanti nor Ananthaphum have nurtured close ties with national political parties. Only a few candidates (13.9 percent) said that they were members of a national political party. Prachasanti had a greater share of political party members (23.1 percent) than Ananthaphum (9.1 percent). Interestingly, however, there is no homogeneity as far as membership is concerned. Candidates of the Ananthaphum group were members of the Social Action Party (SAP) and Prachakorn Thai, while Prachasanti candidates were affiliated with the New Force Party, SAP, and Chart Thai. Some other candidates disclosed that -- as sympathizers -- they entertain close, though informal, links with a political party. Conversely, by establishing links with at least some candidates, parties try to compensate for their organizational weakness. Hence, they do not seek ties with one faction only, but strive to establish connections with all major local groups.

Another explanation for the low level of political participation in Chiang Mai's municipal politics must be sought in the power equation that has determined the local arena for almost two decades. The dominance of the Prachasanti machine and its widely recognized leadership had a constraining effect on political participation in municipal politics. However, the loss of this dominant position and the ensuing polarization of the political process may result in more participation in the future. This process will almost certainly be reinforced by the city's recent rapid modernization which, in the long run, will produce new interest configurations and an upwardly mobile and increasingly vocal urban middle-class with aspirations in the municipal political arena.

As stated earlier, there are numerous interest groups and voluntary associations in Chiang Mai. However, their involvement in municipal politics is limited to recruitment and mobilization during election time. As the personality factor is crucial in Thai politics, personal popularity is a major precondition for a successful election campaign. Therefore, like occupation, membership in voluntary organizations has important multiplier effects on a candidate's popularity -- especially if he occupies executive positions in such organizations.

Eight out of ten candidates were members of at least one voluntary association. More candidates of Prachasanti were members of such organizations than their rivals from Ananthaphum, although the Ananthaphum figure must be adjusted upward, because four candidates, who were known to be affiliated with voluntary associations, failed to answer this question in the questionnaire. With an average of 2.86 memberships, Ananthaphum candidates were also less frequently affiliated than Prachasanti candidates (3.54). Affiliated candidates seemed to have a preference for civic clubs like the Rotary, the Lions Club, and the Jaycees. At 28.1 percent, membership in this type of association topped the list. Paramilitary organizations such as the Thai Territory Defense Volunteers or the Village Scouts (17.5 percent), educational associations (14.0 percent) and religious organizations (12.3 percent) were also very popular (see Table 2.7).

The limited role of interest groups and voluntary organizations in municipal politics must mainly be attributed to the fact that they are a new phenomenon in Thai politics. Many of them emerged during the so-called "democratic interregnum" (1973-1976) or -- as concomitants of the gradual liberalization process that characterized the Thai polity since 1978 -- are of even more recent origin. Yet, even today interest groups and voluntary associations are distrusted by the state. They are tightly controlled by the central government through numerous legal provisions designed to prevent them from gaining political influencethrough financing politicians' campaigns or otherwise supporting political parties (Chenvidyakarn 1977). Another tactic of the state to keep them organizationally weak was to prohibit the formation of provincial branches. Although provincial business and professional organizations, clubs, and other voluntary associations have proliferated in recent years, the majority of them are still based in Bangkok. Of the 276 trade associations registered in 1990, 206 (= 74.6 percent) were located in the capital. Similarly, ninety-nine or 73 percent of the 136 nongovernmental development organizations (NGDOs) listed in the Directory of the Thai Volunteer Service had their headquarters in Bangkok.[35] Hence, local elites were frequently not members of organizations or interest groups operating in their municipality, but of associations based in Bangkok (Noranitipadungkarn 1981:38-39).

The picture is quite similar for lower-class organizations such as labor unions (Mabry 1977:937). In 1976, 90 percent of all trade unions were registered in Bangkok (62 percent) or in seven provinces within a 50 mile radius of the capital (28 percent). None was located in Chiang Mai. Nine years later the situation had not changed much. Of a total of 436 registered labor unions in the whole kingdom, only one was registered in Chiang Mai. The overwhelming majority were still concentrated in Bangkok (50 percent) and adjacent provinces (40 percent).

The internal structure and the activities of these voluntary organizations further explain their limited effect on mobilization and participation in Chiang Mai. While civic clubs such as the Rotarians, Lions, and the Jaycees are places where opinion is formed and decisions are prepared, they are open only to a small urban elite of wealthy businessmen and prominent personalities. By contrast, organizations open to ordinary citizens tend to be hierarchically organized -- often under the same leadership that holds key positions in the exclusive civic clubs. Most of these "mass organizations" such as the Village Scouts, the Thai Territorial Defense Volunteers, the Youth Group and the Buddhist Association rarely deal with municipal issues, except for the mobilization of voters during elections. They pursue very general objectives such as the promotion of nationalism, patriotism, religion, and militant anticommunism. One can even go so far as to assert that some of them, such as the Village Scouts, have a distinctly antiparticipatory history and ideology. Created in the early 1970s, they were used by the military and other right wing forces to crush leftist and militant lower-class social movements during the 1973-76 period. While today the Village Scouts and other paramilitary organizations seem to have scaled down their political activities, they nevertheless serve as a kind of "stand-by mobilization force" of the military and other conservative elements in Thai politics that can be activated at short notice.

Apart from a few occupational organizations (vendors, samlor drivers), there were virtually no organizations fostering horizontal solidarity among the lower-classes. Until recently, there was no organization representing the interests of slum dwellers and squatters. In Chiang Mai, self-help organizations of the urban poor were created on initiative of UNESCO, which sponsored a program to upgrade living conditions in two of Chiang Mai's largest slum areas. Similar community organizations were later formed in other slums of the city, but can hardly be considered independent representatives of the interests of the poor, because they operate under close supervision of the municipal authorities. Unlike in Malaysia, political parties have made no effort to mobilize the poor on a permanent basis and to represent their interests, although voter turnout among the poor is higher than among the better-off strata of urban society. In most cases this is only "mobilized" participation -- stimulated by material or symbolic rewards distributed by the canvassers of the candidates.

The low mobilization level in Chiang Mai municipal politics, as exemplified by the notoriously low turnout, raises the question to what extent clientelist ties are still the dominant form of social organization in Thai society. Or, going even further, in view of equally low levels of voter participation in previous elections, one may ask whether -- at least in urban areas -- patron-client ties have ever had such a pervasive influence on social relations as is suggested by the anthropological literature.

Indeed, much speaks for the conclusion that -- as far as political behavior is concerned -- patron-client relationships in urban Chiang Mai are weaker and less cohesive than usually assumed in the literature, and also less cohesive than in Philippine urban centers. Apart from the fact that in a less politicized society there is not much need for high-geared mobilization, the apparent lack of cohesiveness of the patron-client ties may be attributed to two factors. First, there is the growing participation in municipal politics of candidates with middle-class backgrounds, whose appeal does not rest on age-honored traditional legitimacy (as the former Northern nobility, who in the 1960s still wielded considerable influence in Chiang Mai's politics),[36] but more on economic and educational achievements. However, although many of these candidates are wealthy, with a few exceptions they have neither the financial resources nor the coercive means to launch a powerful and pervasive mobilization drive (such as Philippine local politicians). Second, clientelist networks are strongest where wealth is distributed in a highly inegalitarian manner. However, in Chiang Mai and other Thai regional cities a fairly broad urban middle-income strata has emerged during the last two decades, and is increasingly less dependent on material benefits or other favors allocated by patrons. Accordingly, this middle-class displays a more independent political behavior, including the decision not to vote, than the impoverished urban population in the Philippines. As a result, the clientelist networks commanded by Chiang Mai's local politicians are fairly small, neither cohesive nor affective, but predominantly instrumental (votes for money) and temporary. Moreover, the low turnout and the low mobilization capacity of local politicians seems to

confirm the weak interlinkages between political parties, voluntary associations, interest groups, and the population at the municipal level.[37]

Chiang Mai's Political Culture:
Impact on Socioeconomic Development

Chiang Mai's political culture is more conducive to socioeconomic
development than that of Iloilo City. Political competitiveness in Chiang
Mai is low, mainly because the political linkages between the local and
the national level are weak. Hence, local political machines play a much
less important role in the mobilization of voters during national
elections than in the Philippines. The low level of mobilization and
competitiveness explains why in Chiang Mai municipal politicians need
fewer patronage resources to maintain their political position in the local arena. In fact, sizeable patronage resources for vote buying and
campaigning are needed only every five years when local elections take
place. Yet, it seems that a sizeable portion of these patronage funds
comes from the candidates' own pockets, rather than from public resources. Moreover, in a rapidly expanding economy (like Chiang Mai)
the waste of resources through patronage has a less adverse effect on
the developmental capacities of the municipal government than in a
stagnating or even shrinking economy such as in Iloilo.

Patronage politics is further hampered by the existence of a strong,
comparatively independent bureaucracy. Although the municipal administration is formally under the direction of local politicians (mayor,
executive committee), de facto the administrative wing under the leadership of the city clerk plays an important role in the running of municipal government. It is in fact the city clerk who, due to his vast experience in bureaucratic procedures and closeness to the Ministry of the
Interior, directs and decides a great deal of the day-to-day business in
the municipality. The municipal bureaucracy is strong enough to ward
off political intervention that seeks to manipulate resource distribution
and to strengthen the bailiwick of individual politicians. While the
bureaucracy may use its patronage to play its own power games, there
are limits to this. The municipal administrative personnel are part of a
national service and hence under close disciplinary supervision by the
center. Furthermore, since a transfer to Chiang Mai is a reward for top
performers, administrative personnel in the city is well qualified. It is
therefore quite difficult to manipulate Chiang Mai's administrative staff,
which is fairly independent of political actors, conscious of its profes-
sionalism, and has developed its own esprit de corps. In addition, while
the practice of consensual committee-type decision-making and the
screening of decisions by numerous officials may considerably slow

TABLE 2.8 Occupational Background of Local Decision-Makers, Chiang Mai[a]

Profession	Total interviewed local politicians[b]		Ananthaphum		Prachasanti	
	N	%	N	%	N	%
Merchant/business-man	34	69.4	17	70.8	17	70.8
Teacher	6	12.2	2	8.3	4	16.7
Medical doctor	1	2.0	-	-	1	4.2
Lawyer	1	2.0	1	4.2	-	-
Civil servant (retired)	1	2.0	-	-	1	4.2
Employee	5	10.2	3	12.5	1	4.2
Housewife	1	2.0	1	4.2	-	-
Total	49	99.8	24	100.0	24	100.0

[a]Data available for all 49 candidates of municipal elections in Chiang Mai, July 1985.
[b]Includes one independent candidate

Source: Survey of local decision-makers, Chiang Mai, 1985.

down administrative action, it is an effective check against politically motivated corruption.

Chiang Mai's political culture is less elitist than that of Philippine cities. This applies both to the socioeconomic background of local leaders as well as their value pattern and belief system. As shown by Table 2.8, the overwhelming majority of local decision-makers in Chiang Mai come from upper-middle and upper-class backgrounds. Almost 70 percent of the forty-nine election candidates were businessmen or merchants, followed by teachers (12.2 percent), and employees (10.2 percent). Among the businessmen, there was the son of a leading local business tycoon and several other candidates who themselves or whose families operated major business enterprises in northern Thailand and in Bangkok. However, unlike in Iloilo, decision-makers in Chiang Mai did not come from long-entrenched local dynasties, but mainly from upwardly mobile social strata. Today's decision-makers differ profoundly from the elite of the early 1970s, when Noranitipadungkarn and Hagensick (1973) carried out their community power study. Noranitipadungkarn and Hagensick had identified a closely knit power elite composed of members of the former northern nobility and other traditional elite families. The interlocking nature of this elite has changed. Since the early 1980s a dualistic leadership structure grouped around Ananthaphum and Prachasanti has emerged. Moreover, middle-class elements with business interests and/or professional background have entered the municipal arena.

Yet, there was a conspicuous absence of lower-class representatives among Chiang Mai's decision-makers. Only one of the interviewed candidates could be considered a spokesman of the urban poor. His candidacy -- and subsequent election -- was facilitated by his ability to balance his lack financial resources with a big clientele. As a leader of the local samlor drivers, he controlled a potential of 2,000-3,000 votes.

Another indicator suggesting greater middle-class involvement in Chiang Mai politics than in Iloilo and Penang is the educational qualifications of local decision-makers. More than two-thirds of the interviewed local politicians have not gone beyond secondary school.[38] The proportion of local politicians with university education is much lower than in Iloilo and other Philippine cities. Of the two rival groups, Prachasanti had a higher educational level than Ananthaphum. More Prachasanti candidates had a university education (46.2 percent) than Ananthaphum (22.7 percent) and fewer had only primary education (7.7 percent as against 13.6 percent). Remarkable, however, was the high educational standard of public officials, the direct outcome of the consistent professionalization policy of the Thai government with respect to its municipal civil servants (Krannich 1975). All municipal administrators interviewed in Chiang Mai had a university degree -- at least a BA, some even a MA.

Chiang Mai's local leaders share a conservative political and socioeconomic value system. When they were asked to identify development agents that should play a leading role in the development of the city, agents representing the economic sphere received by far the highest score (43.9 percent). While this predominance of "economic agents" hardly comes as a surprise given the background of the respondents, Chiang Mai's municipal decision-makers obviously had strong reservations about developmental agents reputed to advocate radical socioeconomic change. As a result, intellectuals (sixth), social workers (eighth), and trade unionists (eleventh) obtained low ratings as preferred developmental agents (see Table 2.9). The aversion to more radical participatory demands and to the formation of autonomous lower-class social movements coincides with the organizational affiliation profile of local politicians analyzed above. Many local leaders -- especially those affiliated with Ananthaphum -- were members of organizations with close connections to the military and other right wing forces. About one-fourth of Ananthaphum candidates were members of the Village Scouts and the Thai Territorial Defense Volunteers. A look at the political party membership pattern of local politicians confirms this assessment: of the five councillors with party membership only the one affiliated with

TABLE 2.9 Opinions of Local Decision-Makers Towards Developmental Agents, Chiang Mai

	Total interviewed local politicians		Anathaphum		Prachasanti		Public Officials		Total Respondents[a]	
	Score	% of Score	Score	% of Score	Score	% of Score	Score	% of Score	Score	% of Score
Civil servants	36	16.4	26	19.3	10	12.8	12	23.5	48	17.8
Politicians	26	11.9	6	4.4	17	21.8	12	23.5	38	14.1
Religious leaders	11	5.0	8	5.9	3	3.8	-	-	11	4.1
Intellectuals	21	9.6	16	11.9	5	6.4	1	2.0	22	8.2
Businessmen/entrepreneurs	31	14.2	15	11.1	16	20.5	10	19.6	41	14.2
Social workers	14	6.4	11	8.1	1	1.3	-	-	14	5.2
Landlords	7	3.2	2	1.5	5	6.4	3	5.9	10	3.7
Trade unionists	1	0.5	1	0.7	-	-	-	-	1	0.4
Managerial executives	31	14.2	19	14.1	11	14.1	-	-	31	11.5
Foreign experts	14	6.4	10	7.4	4	5.1	7	13.7	21	7.8
Professionals	27	12.3	21	15.6	6	7.7	6	11.8	33	12.2
Total	219	100.1	135	100.0	78	99.9	51	100.0	270	100.2

[a]Includes one independent

Source: Survey of local decision-makers, Chiang Mai 1985.

the New Force Party belonged to a more progressive, albeit powerless, party.

Though conservative, Chiang Mai's leaders nevertheless seem to have a better understanding of the socioeconomic problems confronting their city than their counterparts in Iloilo. Although, in general, local laders in Chiang Mai opted for a dynamic expansion of the modern economic sector, they exhibited some scepticism as regards the applicability of fashionable, foreign-inspired development strategies. Neither the industrial estate concept nor foreign investment were seen as a panacea for economic development, as often suggested by economic theorists and international development agencies.

Only four out of ten respondents were in favor of setting up an industrial estate in Chiang Mai. 50 percent of those who opposed the estate cited pollution as a major reason for their negative response. Due to Chiang Mai's location in the Ping River Valley, which is surrounded by mountains of more than 1,600 metres, air pollution and other environmental problems were seen as great dangers emanating from such an estate. An additional 9 percent maintained that industrialization was incompatible with Chiang Mai's role as a tourist center, while others said that the newly inaugurated industrial estate near Lamphun (about 30 km from Chiang Mai) is sufficient to meet the needs of the entire Northern Region.

The picture was slightly different with regard to foreign investment. A majority of respondents (64.4 percent) was in favor of more foreign investment in Chiang Mai, but opinions were divided between Ananthaphum and Prachasanti candidates. While almost seven out of ten Ananthaphum candidates favored the promotion of foreign investment, more than half (53.8 percent) of the Prachasanti candidates were against it. As one Prachasanti candidate put it, there should be a "Thai first" investment policy in Chiang Mai. The divergent opinions may be explained by the fact that a number of Ananthaphum respondents are involved in economic activities that depend on foreign counterparts: in the tourist sector, trade, commerce, and banking. Moreoever, the greater inclination of Ananthaphum candidates for outward-looking economic strategies correlates with changes in the composition of Thai political elites. The 1980s saw the rise of upwardly mobile business groups into positions of political power. They are proponents of an export-oriented industrialization, which contrasts with the more inward-looking import-substitution model favored by the traditional military and bureaucratic elites.

But even those who favored an increased influx of foreign investment, did not do so unconditionally. Almost 70 percent of the respon-

dents in favor of foreign investment opted for a qualifying "yes, but",
advocating that foreign investors should, for instance, locate their plants
outside the municipal boundaries, avoid pollution, or concentrate their
investment only on tertiary sector activities (such as supermarkets,
department stores, hotels, etc.).

Though it is a much less urgent problem in Chiang Mai than in Iloilo
and other Philippine regional cities, unemployment was identified as
one of the major problems confronting the city and, especially the lower
income strata. Among fifteen major problems confronting the city, unemployment was ranked second. The reasons most frequently cited for
the perceived increase in unemployment were economic recession,[39] the
fact that the labor market is unable to absorb the vast increase in
university graduates,[40] the reluctance of well educated persons to ac-
cept work below their educational standard and rural-urban migration.
Social inequality was ranked seventh; housing (ninth) and overcrowding (twelfth) received low priorities as developmental problems in
Chiang Mai (see Table 2.10). Yet, this does not signify a disregard for
the problems of the urban poor, since substandard housing is indeed
only a minor problem in the city.

Although 50 percent of the respondents opted for "relocation to prepared lots on the urban fringe" as the best strategy to solve the squatter
problem, many of them had strong reservations about this approach.
There was a sizeable number of interviewees who explicitly opposed the
resettlement approach, because they felt it would create more problems
than it would solve. The key reason cited for this was that relocation
would substantially increase the cost of living for the resettled households. As in the resettlement sites employment opportunities usually do
not exist and the social infrastructure is undeveloped, transport costs
for communting to the city rise sharply. Two respondents, both from
Ananthaphum, even called for the expropriation of big landlords
(against compensation) in order to get enough land to implement low-
cost housing projects -- a rather radical approach by Thai standards.
Finally, one candidate from the same group argued that the key to the
solution of the slum and squatter problem is the improvement of income generating opportunities for the urban poor. Eviction should be
avoided whenever possible; rather the homeless should be permitted to
stay on public land.

Commenting on the other solutions suggested in the questionnaire,
the majority of respondents argued against social high-rise housing. In
their opinion, living in walk-up apartment blocks is neither in accordance with Thai cultural values, nor does it permit subsistence food
production by low-income groups. Furthermore, it would considerably

TABLE 2.10 Opinions of Local Decision-Makers Towards Major Urban Problems in Chiang Mai

	Total interviewed local politicians		Anathaphum		Prachasanti		Public Officials		Total Respondents[a]	
	Score	% of Score	Score	% of Score	Score	% of Score	Score	% of Score	Score	% of Score
Inadequate food supply	-	-	-	-	-	-	-	-	-	-
Unemployment	37	18.4	29	24.8	8	10.3	6	11.1	43	16.9
Too little industrial development	14	7.0	9	7.7	5	6.4	7	13.0	21	8.2
Inadequate housing	7	3.5	5	4.3	-	-	5	9.3	12	4.7
Overcrowding	1	0.5	-	-	1	1.3	-	-	1	0.4
Social inequality	13	6.5	4	3.4	9	11.5	-	-	13	5.1
Poor infrastructure	32	15.9	24	20.5	5	6.4	9	16.7	41	16.1
Poor planning	23	11.4	9	7.7	13	16.7	7	13.0	30	11.8
Inadequate public transportation	-	-	-	-	-	-	3	5.6	3	1.2
Pollution/environmental problems	4	2.0	2	1.7	2	2.6	7	4.3	11	4.3
Inadequate garbage disposal	16	8.0	12	10.3	4	5.1	1	1.9	17	6.7
Flooding	-	-	-	-	-	-	-	-	-	-
Poor health conditions	6	3.0	3	2.6	3	3.8	-	-	6	2.4
Inadequate financial resources	39	14.4	14	12.0	25	32.1	9	16.7	48	18.8
High crime rate	9	4.5	6	5.1	3	3.8	-	-	9	3.5
Total	201	100.1	117	100.1	78	100.0	54	100.3	255	100.1

[a]Includes one independent

Source: Survey of local decision-makers, Chiang Mai, 1985.

increase the "pull-effect" of Chiang Mai, thus causing more rural-urban migration. Ironically, however, only three years after these opinions were aired, Chiang Mai's municipal decision-makers gave their blessing to the construction of numerous high-rise condominium and hotel complexes in the city.

While Chiang Mai's local politicians saw development in a broader perspective than Iloilo's local elite, enabling them to formulate more sophisticated and more balanced municipal policies, it cannot be denied that their assessments of social problems were a typical reflection of the businessman's view of urban development. Social problems were mainly defined as a dependent variable of economic development. Economic growth, it was argued, would generate employment which, in turn, would increase income. More income would stimulate consumption and, hence, business activities, thereby indirectly augmenting the tax income of the municipality. The latter would eventually translate into improved services.

The strong representation of businessmen in the municipal bodies and their bias towards economic and infrastructural development prevented the formulation of programs to improve the lot of the poor. But this was also due to the fact that there were almost no organized efforts by the poor themselves to articulate their demands. Consequently, there was no pressure on the municipal government to design and implement social action programs. It was only through RCDP that, to a limited extent, social programs were initiated at the municipal level and a government-controlled organization of slum dwellers was encouraged. The lack of strong pressure groups among the poor is perhaps the most important reason why approximately one-fifth of Chiang Mai's population still lives below the poverty line.

Socioeconomic Development

In the following paragraphs the output side of municipal government in Chiang Mai will be examined. This will include questions such as how and to what extent the municipality has been able to influence processes of urban development, who benefits, and why. Unfortunately, the data do not always allow an empirical analysis in the strict sense. Data with regard to service output, distributional, and social effects are highly scattered, sometimes deficient, contradictory or even false, or aggregated at the provincial level. I am thus forced to resort to extrapolations and estimates, which nevertheless permit me to roughly outline broad developmental trends.

Urban development in Chiang Mai compares favorably with other regional cities in Southeast Asia. Despite frequent interference in municipal government by central agencies, financial bottlenecks, and the lack of long-term perspectives in urban planning, public services improved considerably. These improvements were the result of careful cost-benefit analyses and the absence of "white elephants". Due to a resource-conscious development perception, municipal decision-makers valued routine maintenance work more highly than expensive, yet uncertain, show-case projects. Until recently, they saw themselves more as "housekeepers"[41] than aggressive developmentalists. This helped to utilize scarce resources efficiently and to secure a comparatively high level of collective consumption. In Chiang Mai social inequalities that usually go hand in hand with rapid urban growth are less glaring than in most other cities of the region. However, under the impact of the country's recent economic boom, development perceptions are beginning to change. Although the municipal government continued to pursue rather cautious fiscal policies, it did little to check the wild proliferation of ill-planned large-scale housing and tourism projects of the private sector.

Municipal Services

Predominant among municipal activities are small-scale public works projects such as the expansion and repair of roads and bridges, the dredging of rivers and canals, flood prevention measures, and the improvement of street lighting. These projects well reflect the development perceptions of local politicians and municipal administrators, who see the municipality's role primarily in providing and maintaining an infrastructural framework that fosters the growth of the urban economy.

Like many other Third World cities, Chiang Mai has experienced tremendous growth in traffic volume since the 1960s. Between 1970 and 1979 the number of motor vehicles tripled, growing at an average annual rate of 13.4 percent. Although motorcycles accounted for the lion's share of that increase (nearly 70 percent), Chiang Mai was faced with mounting difficulties in accommodating the swelling tide of traffic. With a road network of 147 km, road space is equivalent to only 2.2 percent of the municipal area, which is only a tenth of the space allocated to transport in industrialized countries (Chiang Mai Municipality 1990:7). The central government helped the municipality to ease its traffic problems in the outer areas through the construction of the Super Highway, a ring road system, and the extension of radial roads. However, little space was available to expand the road network in the inner-city. Municipal efforts to cope with traffic congestion therefore focussed primarily on the installation of traffic lights and one-way systems. How-

ever, in the face of the ever-increasing number of vehicles these efforts
have not improved traffic flow. Especially during peak hours, the average speed in these parts of the city is very low.

Despite an increasing traffic volume, Chiang Mai's road network is in
a fairly good condition. The main roads and even many secondary
roads are asphalted. Repairs, especially during the rainy season, are
done reasonably quickly. The proportion of asphalted roads, however,
decreases with increasing distance from the city center. Especially in the
newly annexed areas, only the trunk roads have so far been asphalted.
The secondary roads are still dirt roads that become almost impassable
in the rainy season.

For a secondary city, Chiang Mai offers good educational and health
services. In 1980, 16.2 percent of the municipal expenditure was spent
on education and 34.2 percent on health services (Multiman, Vol. 2,
1982). In 1976, there were ninety-six primary, secondary, and vocational
schools in *amphoe muang*, five colleges, and two universities (Research
Division 1977). By 1985 the number had increased to 122 primary, secondary, and vocational schools, two colleges, and three universities
(Chiang Mai Municipality 1985a). Eleven primary schools with 123
classrooms, 207 teachers, and 3,460 pupils were directly administered
by the municipality. The pupil-teacher ratio in these schools is the lowest among the regional cities, decreasing from 23.2:1 in 1977 to 16.2:1 in
1985. However, compared with the other cities, Chiang Mai has a considerably lower student enrollment in municipal schools and a smaller
teaching staff (Multiman, Vol. 2, 1982). What at a first glance may look
like a deficiency in service standards, is more than offset by an abundance of private schools. This also explains why Chiang Mai does not
have to spend as much on education as the other regional cities and
thus can allocate more resources to services such as public works,
health, clean streets, and environmental sanitation.

Even more impressive are Chiang Mai's health services. Whereas in
1976 there were eleven hospitals in the municipality, four public and
seven private (Research Division 1977), this number had increased to fifteen in 1985 (five public and ten private) (Chiang Mai Municipality
1985a). Furthermore, Chiang Mai is the only regional city which has its
own municipal hospital (with a capacity of thirty beds), providing general medical, maternity, and limited surgical services. Already in 1976
there were 1,960 beds for patients in Chiang Mai municipality, which
was then equivalent to a bed-to-population ratio of 1:50. This compared
with a ratio of 1:781 for the whole of Thailand and approximately 1:500
for Bangkok. Furthermore, the municipality runs six clinics offering
family planning, maternal and child care, immunization in schools, and

general health services on an out-patient basis. Mobile health units cover eleven of the municipality's fourteen *tambons* (subdistricts), giving priority to slums and other low-income communities (Chiang Mai Municipality 1990:19). Chiang Mai is also first among the regional cities in terms of health staffing. The municipality employs sixteen physicians and nurses, compared to eight in Hat Yai, four in Khon Kaen, three in Nakhon Ratchasima, and only one nurse in Songkhla (Multiman, Vol. 2, 1982:20).

The high proportion of municipal expenditure for health services and the large staff working in this sector (36.2 percent of the municipal personnel) are also due to the fact that the municipal health department is responsible for garbage collection, refuse disposal, and environmental sanitation. Street sweeping and garbage collection is done on a daily basis, in some public markets and inner-city areas where garbage output is particularly high even twice a day. The municipal government claims that approximately 93 percent of the garbage is collected. Due to financial constraints, however, acquisition of equipment for garbage collection has not kept pace with other developments. Whereas in 1972 the municipality had twenty-three garbage trucks, by 1982 it had only twenty-five, although, according to DOLA criteria, there should be a minimum of thirty-one trucks. Also in terms of garbage bins the municipality is underequipped. While there should be at least 5,420 garbage bins, the municipality had only 3,340 (Chiang Mai Municipality 1990:17). The garbage dump site in Mae Hia is inadequate and poses environmental hazards as the garbage is dumped and burnt openly. These deficiencies substantiate complaints of citizens that seemed to belie the municipality's own performance evaluation in this sector.

The inspection of food processing and eating establishments is another area in which the municipal administration has made slow progress. Due to shortages in qualified staff, inspections are usually limited to once a year and focus more on the enforcement of physical requirements than on maintaining acceptable health standards. As stated in one report, about 50 percent of the meat entering the city's markets has not undergone veterinary inspection (Multiman, Vol. 2, 1982:22). But despite these shortcomings, Chiang Mai has clearly the best record for health and environmental services among the five regional cities.

During the last decade, fire prevention services improved. Between 1976 and 1988, the number of fire stations rose from two to four and the number of fire trucks from seven to thirteen. This, however, is still short of the eight fire stations and the fourteen fire engines that a city of Chiang Mai's size should have (Chiang Mai Municipality 1990:27).

Moreover, most of the equipment is inadequate for the fire hazards posed by Chiang Mai's mushrooming high-rise buildings. As up-to-date fire equipment is very costly, it is unlikely that the situation will improve noticeably in the immediate future.

Non-Municipal Services

Originally, water and electricity supply were genuine municipal functions. But in Chiang Mai, as in most other municipalities, these services were transferred to parastatal enterprises such as the Provincial Water Authority (PWA) and the Provincial Electricity Authority (PEA). In the past, delivery levels in these service sectors were low in provincial towns and regional centers. According to a World Bank report, only 40 percent of Chiang Mai's households had direct access to piped water in 1974 (World Bank 1978:19). This rate was considerably below that of other regional centers and only half that of Bangkok. By 1982, 76 percent of Chiang Mai's households were served with piped water, but, as a consequence of the extension of the municipal boundaries, declined to 49 percent in 1983. By 1985 it had again increased to 55 percent.

The relatively high proportion of households with regular water supplies in 1982 showed that the extension of services took place almost exclusively in the inner-city areas. These figures, however, do not include upper-class households with their own wells.

While the quantitative expansion of the water supply looks impressive, there are major problems in the quality of the service. During the dry season, pressure is very low and interruptions in supplies occur frequently, especially in the western parts of the city.[42] Also, loss of water due to leakages in the mains and illegal tapping is considerable, amounting to no less than 40-50 percent.

Unfortunately, exact figures for households served with electricity could not be obtained. According to estimates of the Provincial Electricity Authority (PEA), 80-90 percent of households were served in 1985. While these figures seem to indicate rather satisfactory service levels, they conceal two major shortcomings: undersupply in the surrounding semiurban and rural areas and high cost. Although 55-60 percent of Thailand's electricity is produced in the Northern Region, the main beneficiary is Bangkok. Moreover, rates for Bangkok are subsidized to the disadvantage of provincial users. In the mid-1970s, energy costs for commercial and industrial users in northern provinces were between 51 and 105 percent higher than in Bangkok (United Nations, Vol. 3, 1979:7). The negative effect of such rate differentials on comparative locational advantages is evident.

While energy rates for commercial use are high, there is a progressive rate scale for residential use. The greater the energy consumption, the higher the rate per unit. The same principle applies to private water consumption. This indirect subsidization of lower-income households may be one of the major reasons why neither service can meet its operating expenses. On the other hand, low charges have forestalled developments found in other Third World cities, where the lower-classes are virtually priced out of urban services. The picture presented in a World Bank survey investigating the water charges of low-income groups has changed little over the years. According to that survey, the lowest 20 percent of urban dwellers in Thailand spent 0.5 percent of their monthly income on water, whereas in Manila it was 9.3 percent, in Nairobi 6.8 percent, in Lima 5.0 percent, in Sao Paulo 4.7 percent, and in Ahmedabad 4.25 percent (World Bank 1979:269).

Housing problems in Thailand's regional cities are less serious than in the capital. Construction activity has risen constantly over the last few years, and like in most urban areas of Thailand, reached unprecedented levels after 1987. Between 1979 and 1984 the annual number of building permits issued rose from 273 to 615. During the first half of 1989 building permissions for municipal areas increased by 91.7 percent in the Northern Region.[43]

Measured by Third World standards, the percentage of slum dwellers and squatters is low in Thai regional cities. About 10-15 percent of Chiang Mai's population live in substandard conditions. In Nakhon Sawan and Nakhon Ratchasima only 10 percent of the population live in slums and squatter settlements, in Songkhla about 20-25 percent. With a slum and squatter population between 25 and 30 percent, housing problems in Bangkok are more pressing. Housing stock in regional cities is usually better than in the capital, and low-income residential quarters are less congested. Yet, physical conditions are very poor -- slums and squatter settlements are prone to frequent flooding, and suffer from substandard services in respect of water supply, electricity, garbage disposal, drainage, and sewerage.

In connection with the RCDP, and with funding from the UNESCO and the World Bank, Chiang Mai municipality started upgrading two of its largest slum areas in 1984. The projects in the Thipanet and Rakaeng communities benefited nearly 3,000 people. The municipality encouraged the formation of community committees to tap the self-help potentials of the target group, introduced basic health and family planning services, and improved water supplies. In addition, in Rakaeng the houses were reblocked because part of the settlement was located on private land and thus not eligible for upgrading (Chiang Mai Municipality 1985b).

Remarkably the World Bank, which, as a major funding agency, played a pivotal role in project planning and implementation, deviated from its previous cost recovery policies. Nevertheless, it was estimated that the beneficiaries' expenses for housing rose by one-third as a result of increased service charges and taxes. This has increased the danger that the poorest sectors of the population may be displaced and, as in many other low-cost housing projects in Third-World cities, the projects will finally end up benefitting lower-middle-class families. Precisely this is happening in another low-cost housing project in Chiang Mai. In Tambon Nonghoi, where the National Housing Authority implemented a sites-and-services project, an evaluation report commissioned by the World Bank found "that a large number of beneficiaries in the project were investors or middle-income families that apparently understated their income to qualify for the project". Most of these families were in the fortieth to seventieth income percentiles.[44]

Public transport in Chiang Mai is almost entirely provided by the private sector and accounts for 93 percent of all trips made in the city. A World Bank survey found that more than 2,200 mini-buses serve inner-city routes and about 830 mini-buses connect the city with adjacent districts (World Bank 1978:22). Unlike in many other Third World cities, the majority of mini-buses are owner-operated and the sector seems to provide profitable incomes (Pendakur 1984:36). Buses play a much less significant role in public transport. In 1977, there were forty-two buses operating in Chiang Mai, accounting for 7 percent of all trips. Due to break-downs of the bus units the situation is even worse today. They operate only a few routes and most of the vehicles are slow moving, dilapidated units offering little comfort to the passengers. Apart from buses, around 3,000 samlor drivers used to offer their services. While tricycles were the most common means of transport before motorization began in the 1960s, samlor drivers were the losers in the process of modernization of transport. Tricycles have been progressively displaced by the mini-buses and have almost totally disappeared since motorized tricycles, the so-called tuk-tuks, began to appear on Chiang Mai's roads in 1986. Today samlors are little more than a nostalgic attraction for tourists. Samlor drivers belong to the poorest strata of the municipality, usually renting their tricycles and earning about 30-40 Baht a day.

Economic and Social Development

Chiang Mai municipality has experienced sustained economic growth over the past three decades. As elsewhere in urban Thailand, business and commerce are booming. Newly registered businesses in Chiang Mai increased faster than in the other urban centers of the north. At present, the city's economic growth is estimated at almost 10 percent per annum. It is expected that high growth rates around 8 percent will persist for the rest of the century (Kingdom of Thailand 1983:1 B:3).

Tourism was the engine of Chiang Mai's rapid economic growth. Today 30-40 percent of the city's income is directly or indirectly related to tourism (Chiang Mai Chamber of Commerce 1985:17). Tourist arrivals grew by more than 10 percent annually in recent years. By 1986 they had reached a level seven times as high as the one in 1971 (Tourism Authority of Thailand 1987:70). Similarly, the number of hotel rooms increased by nearly 50 percent between 1978 and 1983 and the number of accommodation establishments by 45 percent between 1976 and 1985. By 1992, an additional five large hotel complexes with a total of 1,350 rooms will be in operation (Technische Universität Berlin 1983/84:48).

Manufacturing, construction, trade, transport, and finance also contributed significantly to Chiang Mai's thriving economy. The manufacturing sector, for instance, grew by approximately 10 percent over the last ten to fifteen years. Although data from the various sources are hardly comparable, extrapolations suggest that the number of manufacturing establishments grew by approximately 40 percent between 1966 and 1975 and 37 percent between 1976 and 1985. Growth in industrial employment increased by 73.4 percent over the last ten years.

Despite impressive growth, Chiang Mai's economy is still characterized by a high degree of "tertiarization". As the major administrative center in the North, 33.7 percent of the persons formally employed in Chiang Mai are civil servants or government employees. In the private sector, too, around 80 percent of the employed work in the tertiary sector. Almost 27 percent of private sector employment is in the wholesale and retail trades and commerce, 17.7 percent in community, social, and personal services, 10.9 percent work in hotels and dormitories, 8.7 percent in foodsale and restaurants, and 8.6 percent in finance, insurance, real estate, and business services. On the other hand, only 19.7 percent are employed in the secondary sector. With 15.1 percent of total private sector employment, manufacturing is the greatest source of jobs in the secondary sector (see Table 2.11).

Tertiary sector dominance in Chiang Mai is even more pronounced when one takes the distribution of business establishments. 86.3 percent of business establishments belong to the tertiary sector. Again, the lion's share falls on wholesale and retail trades and commerce (43 percent), followed by community, social, and personal services (20.6 percent), and foodsale and restaurants (10.7 percent) (see Table 2.11). Only 12.5

TABLE 2.11 Number of Employed, by Size of Establishhment, in Amphoe Muang, Chiang Mai Province, 1985[a]

Activities	Number of Employed, by Size of Establishment				In Percent
	1-4	5-19	>20	Total	
Mining	7	57	155	219	0.8
Manufacturing	411	1,037	2,723	4,171	15.9
Electricity, gas, and water	23	37	423	492	1.9
Construction	14	11	936	961	3.7
Wholesale, retail, and commerce	1,702	2,583	2,710	6,995	26.7
Foodsale and restaurant	363	823	1,081	2,267	8.7
Hotel and dormitory	62	176	2,606	2,844	10.9
Transport, storage, and communication	92	343	910	1,345	5.1
Finance, insurance, real estate, and business services	140	485	1,612	2,237	8.6
Community, social, and personal services	801	1,226	2,600	4,627	17.7
Total	3,615	6,778	15,765	26,150	100.0

[a]Figures do not include informal sector workers, self-employed, etc.

Source: Computed from the files of the Department of Labor, Regional Office, Chiang Mai, 1985.

percent of establishments are in manufacturing. Many of them are involved in agro-industry, while the rest produce garments, furniture or handicrafts. But despite its growth, manufacturing still plays a subordinate role in Chiang Mai's economy. Most manufacturing enterprises are "small shop industries" with low productivity, labor-intensive technologies and long working hours.

The majority of economic entities in Chiang Mai are labor-intensive, small-scale enterprises. More than 60 percent of establishments employ less than five workers and more than 90 percent less than twenty. Only 1.4 percent employ 100 and more workers. On average, private sector establishments employed ten people (see Table 2.12).

The proportion of small-scale establishments (less than five employees) was particularly high in wholesale and retail trades and commerce (67.3 percent) and community, social, and personal services (67.4 percent), whereas establishments with twenty and more workers were mainly found in construction (55.5 percent), hotel and dormitories (31.1 percent), and finance, insurance, real estate, and business services (29.1 percent). Hotel and dormitories had the highest percentage of establishments with over 100 workers (13.5 percent).

Chiang Mai's "bazaar type" economy, which can be found in most towns outside Bangkok, is run predominantly with family labor. Almost 64 percent of establishments in services and the wholesale and retail trades employed family members. Moreover, until recently few foreign investors came to Chiang Mai. Most of them were Americans or Japanese and were involved in agro-industrial enterprises. As of 1985, no multinational corporation had located a plant in Chiang Mai.[45] As Tanrattanakoon has shown in her study of Chiang Mai's small-scale industries, the overwhelming majority of entrepreneurs were of Thai nationality. 64.2 percent were natives of Chiang Mai and an additional 10.1 percent came from other northern provinces. Only 17.4 percent came from Bangkok and 7 percent from other regions (Tanrattanakoon 1984:31).

Satisfactory performances by the government in the provision of services and vigorous growth in the private sector have been the main reasons for a marked improvement of living conditions, which have benefited about 70-80 percent of Chiang Mai's population. The city's recent development has given rise to the emergence of a broad strata of middle-income earners. Over 50 percent of Chiang Mai's households had an income of between 4,000 Baht and 13,999 Baht in 1982 (see Table 2.13).

Yet, it seems that income inequalities have declined. Based on data for all northern municipalities, Ikemoto and Limskul found that the Gini coefficient for urban areas decreased from 0.4782 in 1969 to 0.4284 in

TABLE 2.12 Number of Establishments, by Size, in Amphoe Muang, Chiang Mai Province, 1985[a]

Activities	Number of Establishments							
	1-4 workers		5-19 workers		> 20 workers		Total	
	N	%	N	%	N	%	N	%
Mining	2	20	4	40	4	40	10	0.4
Manufacturing	170	51.8	116	35.4	42	12.8	328	12.5
Electricity, gas, and water	8	53.3	5	33.3	2	13.3	15	0.6
Construction	6	33.3	2	11.1	10	55.5	18	0.7
Wholesale, retail, and commerce	761	67.3	319	28.2	50	4.4	1,130	43.0
Foodsale and restaurant	156	55.3	105	37.2	21	7.4	282	10.7
Hotel and dormitory	29	39.2	22	29.7	23	31.4	74	2.8
Transport, storage, and communication	37	42.5	36	41.4	14	16.1	87	3.3
Finance, insurance, real estate, and business services	52	36.9	48	34.0	41	29.1	141	5.4
Community, social, and personal services	364	67.4	140	25.9	36	6.7	540	20.6
Total	1,585	60.4	797	30.4	243	9.2	2,625	100.0

[a]Figures do not include informal sector workers, self-employed, etc.

Source: Computed from the files of the Department of Labor, Regional Office, Chiang Mai, 1985

TABLE 2.13 Household Income Distribution in Thai Regional Cities, 1982

City	Household Income (Baht/Month)				
	< 2,000 Baht	B 2,000-5,999	B 6,000-9,999	B 10,000-13,999	> 14,000 Baht
Chiang Mai	13	51	18	8	5
Khon Kaen	28	49	12	10	1
Nakhon Ratchasima	11	48	24	8	9
Songkhla	33	59	5	3	--
Hat Yai	22	70	7	1	--
All munici palitiesa	12	51	23	8	6
Bangkok	4	44	30	12	10

aExcluding Central Region and Bangkok.

Source: Kingdom of Thailand, Ministry of the Interior, United Nations Development Programme, Feasibility Studies for Regional Cities Development. Final Report, April 1983 (Bangkok: Ministry of the Interior, United Nations Development Programme, 1983), Vol. 1.

1981. Over the same period, the percentage of households in the top 20 percent income bracket decreased from 54.73 percent to 48.99 percent, while the share of the bottom quintile increased slightly from 4.25 percent to 4.59 percent (Ikemoto and Limskul 1987:256).

At 18 percent Chiang Mai's poverty incidence is lower than in other Thai regional cities, except for Nakhon Ratchasima (11 percent), and considerably lower than in Philippine and Indonesian cities (Table 2.14). The median monthly household income is 4,220 Baht (1982) which is about two-thirds that of Bangkok and about 10 percent less than the average for Thailand's municipalities (Kingdom of Thailand, Vol. 2, 1983:2C-6). Among regional cities it is second only to Nakhon Ratchasima, but considerably higher than in Khon Kaen, Hat Yai, and Songkhla.

Urban poverty in Thailand declined during the past twenty years. In this respect, too, the country differs from other Southeast Asian countries such as Indonesia and the Philippines (World Bank 1988). The figures, however, conceal an absolute increase in the number of urban poor which, for Thailand as a whole, may amount to 500,000 persons, and for Chiang Mai to about 10,000 persons.

Despite the lack of accurate data on Chiang Mai's income distribution, it must be suspected that income disparities in Chiang Mai are higher than in other regional cities. However, distributional indicators may be distorted by the wealth of Chiang Mai's upper 5 percent of households, many of which are newcomers to the municipality. Due to

TABLE 2.14 Proportion of Households below the Poverty Threshold and Median Monthly Household Income in Thai Regional Cities, 1982

Municipality	Proportion of Households below the Poverty Threshold[a], in percent	Median Monthly Household Income, in Baht
Chiang Mai	18	4,200
Khon Kaen	28	3,500
Nakhon Ratchasima	11	4,900
Songkhla	33	2,600
Hat Yai	22	2,800
Bangkok	9	6,270

[a]The poverty level for Bangkok is B 2,500 per month, for provincial cities the poverty level is B 2,000 per month.

Source: Kingdom of Thailand, Ministry of the Interior, United Nations Development Programme, *Feasibility Studies for Regional Cities Development, Final Report* (Bangkok: Ministry of the Interior and United Nations Development Programme, 1983), Vols. 1 and 4.

its natural beauty and its favorable climate, Chiang Mai has become a second residence for rich Bangkokians and foreigners. Chiang Mai thus does not only exert "pull effects" on the rural poor but also on the metropolitan upper-class. This trend may increase the more Chiang Mai modernizes, offering amenities which hitherto were available only in the capital. The immigration of affluent households will have negative effects on the social fabric of the municipality. It will increase the cost of living and the pressure on land prices, which already rose by 2,200 percent between 1975 and 1982 (Janssen 1982:6), and by another ten times in the late 1980s, dislocating the lower social strata living in the semiurban peripheral areas.[46] The growth of slums and squatter settlements will intensify and may lead to a vicious circle already well known in Bangkok and other Asian metropolises: the demolition of slums and squatter settlements to make way for new investments, relocation to remote urban fringe areas, and -- due to the lack of employment opportunities and the rising cost of living -- remigration to other or newly emerging inner-city slums and squatter settlements. This sequence of events will repeat itself many times and create a strata of "urban refugees" (Boonyabancha 1983:254).

Whereas excessive immigration of well-to-do families to Chiang Mai may create serious equity problems in the future, the following sections attempt to explain why in the past a rather broad range of the population has benefited from urban development.

Urban development in Chiang Mai was more influenced by exogenous factors than by the performance of the municipal government.

Nevertheless, the municipal government supported rapid urban development through its consistent "housekeeping" approach. In addition, through a well-developed network of informal linkages to higher political echelons and the central bureaucracy, Chiang Mai's local leaders were able to attract enormous government and private sector resources for the continuous expansion of services and the city's physical infrastructure.

Although the municipal government did not have a specific economic development strategy, its tourism promotion policy created a favorable climate for the two-fifths of Chiang Mai's trades and businesses that are directly or indirectly linked to the tourism sector. Such measures pursued the objective of making Chiang Mai more attractive for visitors through the renovation and reconstruction of the old city gates, the earthern city wall, and the ancient part of the moated city. Although not entirely successful, building regulations have been issued prohibiting the construction of high-rise concrete buildings inside the moated city in order to preserve the traditional and historical character of this area. Drives to clean up the city and beautification projects were designed to consolidate Chiang Mai's image as a "flower city". Moreover, the municipal government was actively involved in the organization of annual festivals such as the *loi krathong* (light festival) in November, the flower festival in February or *songkhran* (the Thai New Year) in mid-April. During the festival season hotels and other tourist accommodation have their highest occupancy rates; restaurants, the retail sector, souvenir shops, and informal sector businesses record peak profits.

Another positive contribution of the municipal government to the city's socioeconomic progress is its undogmatic informal sector policy. Except for a few instances and a few strategic locations in which the informal sector competed directly with formal sector ventures, informal sector activities were tolerated. Contrary to the practice of many other local governments in Southeast Asia, Chiang Mai municipality essentially abstained from large-scale punitive drives against the informal sector.[47] The municipality's flourishing informal sector is thus in a position to cushion urban poverty. The sector is well diversified and closely linked to formal small-scale enterprises. About 20-30 percent of Chiang Mai's labor force works as peddlers, hawkers or vendors, guards in parking lots, mobile eatery operators, domestic workers, or home industry laborers (lacquer-ware, bag-making, etc.). Many of them are women and children. They do not appear in labor statistics, though they may contribute between 600 and 2,000 Baht per month to household incomes.

While the provision of services by the municipality and other governmental agencies improved gradually and at low investment costs, basic services were affordable even for the lower-income groups, as a cost recovery approach was not used and service fees were cross-subsidized in favor of the less affluent. This was true of water and electricity charges; the flat fee for garbage disposal was very low, too.

However, due to the low service fees, the municipality and other agencies provided services below actual costs. As a consequence, they were hardly able to expand services and to make the necessary investments for new facilities and equipment. While, contrary to a proposal in a recent NIDA study (National Institute of Development Administration 1983), I believe that charges for most basic services should be kept at a low level or subsidized for the poorer sections of urban society, there are some areas in which revenues could be increased and the resulting revenues translated into new investments. One issue that has been intensively discussed is the introduction of a real property tax or at least a more efficient assessment and collection of the house and rent as well as the land development taxes. In addition, an increase in parking fees would also yield significant additional income. At the time of the field research, parking fees were very low, ranging from 1 to 2 Baht in inner-city areas. A more efficient collection of property taxes and a more vigorous "taxation" of private motorists would draw the additional revenues largely from the more affluent urban groups.

But Chiang Mai's socioeconomic gains, the large-scale modernization of its infrastructure and social facilities, are unthinkable without the persistent economic expansion that has produced national average growth rates of 7 percent between the early 1960s and the mid-1980s. This growth has opened up economic opportunities for a wide range of small and medium-scale entrepreneurs and, lately, began to attract domestic and foreign big business as well. Moreover, since the 1960s Chiang Mai has become the headquarters of numerous foreign and international development organizations implementing development projects in northern Thailand. This has increased the influx of resources into the city's economy (Vatikiotis 1984b:145). Moreover, as has been demonstrated in Vatikiotis' brilliant study, Chiang Mai's strategic location in the border triangle between Burma, Thailand, and Laos, the growing influx of tourists, and the isolationist policies of Burma have intensified a lucrative, yet illegal cross-border trade. By virtue of its geographical location, Chiang Mai has become the center of this trade: "imports" to Thailand of gems, handicrafts, antiques, forest products (bamboo, teak), and narcotics and "exports" of virtually all kinds of consumer goods, pharmaceuticals, cosmetics, and other luxury items.

As a result, a lot of "hidden" wealth has been generated in the city (Vatikiotis 1984a:18).

Chiang Mai's economy, with its high proportion of small-scale enterprises and a great demand for unskilled or semiskilled labor, created a flexible labor market with many niches and a high absorption capacity. Until recently, prolonged unemployment was relatively rare in the city. Although no exact data were available, the economic recession of the mid-1980s led to a rise in unemployment in Chiang Mai, but at a much slower pace than in Iloilo and other Philippine cities. Unemployment data for municipal areas in the north indicate an increase from 0.4 percent in 1971 to 3.4 percent in May 1985, with a climax of 5.4 percent in May 1984. This performance compares reasonably well with the national trend. According to official sources, unemployment fluctuated between 1.5 and 4 percent in the 1970s, before rising to 6.2 percent in 1985. After this peak, unemployment fell again to a low level of 3.6 percent in 1989.[48] In Chiang Mai's slums, such as Thipanet and Rakaeng, however, this figure may have been as high as 11-15 percent.

The groups most affected by unemployment were the new entrants into the labor market: the age groups between fifteen and twenty-four and, increasingly, university graduates. The latter face difficulties in being absorbed into Chiang Mai's economy and, because of the centralized structure of the bureaucracy (which traditionally absorbed university graduates) and the big private sector enterprises (such as banks), are forced to apply to the Bangkok-based head offices. In Chiang Mai, as well as in most other Northern and Northeastern municipalities, the unemployment problem is compounded by seasonal rural-urban migration in the dry season, when labor demand in the agricultural sector decreases by some 25 percent.

There is a less pronounced influx of impoverished rural migrants into Chiang Mai. This is in large part due to a well developed road network linking Chiang Mai with the adjacent districts, cheap public transport ("minibus revolution"), and a booming construction sector. Since most construction companies use labor-intensive technologies, the building industry is able to absorb a large proportion of low-skilled rural workers. The well-developed transport network, on the one hand, and flexible recruitment practices, on the other, allow these workers to participate in the urban labor market without being forced to migrate to Chiang Mai on a permanent base. This explains why there is not the same immense demand for "lowest-cost" accommodation that, together with spiralling land prices, is a major reason for the rapid sprawl of slums and squatter settlements in other cities. As commuters are able to maintain a foothold in their village economy, this diversifies their employment options. Singhanetra thus rightfully observes that "the nature of farm work and construction work complemented each other in the way that labor inputs can be adjusted from day to day" (Singhanetra 1982a:18).

Chiang Mai's modernization produced social change without, however, fully destroying traditional subsistence mechanisms. Thai culture has a remarkable capacity to selectively adapt external influences to traditional values and belief systems (Mulder 1985:179). For example, family networks, classmate and, nowadays to a lesser extent, patron-client relationships still play a role in the provision of labor and the exchange of goods and services at favorable conditions. Similarly, traditional redistributive mechanisms such as festivals, religious rites, and charities still provide effective barriers against destitution.

As shown in Vatikiotis' study of Chiang Mai's impoverished Rakaeng community, the temple provides subsistence-level services in at least four respects. The temple school provides cheap access to primary education, while the institution of temporary novicehood helps to cushion unemployment among adolescents. Furthermore, the temple provides inexpensive housing by renting out parcels of temple-owned land for less than 20 Baht per month and allows the poor to tap the temple's well free of charge (Vatikiotis 1984b:303-304). Traditional value patterns also find their expression in the morphology of the city. Though gradually disappearing under the onslaught of the current construction boom, the village-like "muban-style" of settlement is -- except for the central business district -- still very common and leaves room for subsistence food production.

The Development Potential of Chiang Mai

Chiang Mai was one of four regional cities chosen by the central government for the first stage of its Regional Cities Development Project (RCDP). RCDP is part of a comprehensive national urbanization strategy outlined in the fifth development plan (1982-1986) with the objective of mitigating regional development imbalances. Planners hope that through the infusion of massive infrastructure investments the selected regional cities will become dynamic growth centres, stimulating economic growth in the surrounding rural areas. Such a scenario would enable regional cities to absorb Bangkok-bound migration, divert urban and economic growth, and contribute to administrative decentralization (Rüland and Ladavalya 1986:445). Whether Chiang Mai has the potential to actually perform such functions will be the main theme of the following paragraphs.

The Regional Cities Development Project. Until recently, efforts to redress the primacy of Bangkok and to promote the growth of regional urban centers have been rather sporadic, although such plans can be traced back to the days of Fieldmarshal Sarit Thanarat (Noranitipadungkarn and Hagensick 1973:1). For the first time, the idea of developing major regional urban centers was elaborated more systematically in the Fourth Economic and Social Development Plan (1977-1981). During the plan period, the World Bank surveyed the service levels of the country's major regional cities. As a result, the Fifth Plan (1982-1986) presented a regionalization strategy based on advanced regional planning theories by combining a bundle of complementary policies.

1. measures to discourage further growth of Bangkok;
2. development of the Eastern Seabord as an alternative location for heavy industries;
3. development of regional urban centers in order to build up a close network of linkages extending from the regional centers to the rural areas;
4. promotion of lower-order urban centers in order to build up a close network of linkages extending from the regional centers to the rural areas;
5. supporting economic measures such as more investment incentives, an improvement of credit facilities and marketing systems, the encouragement of commerce, small-scale industries, and agricultural production and the promotion of technical advisory and extension services.

During the early 1980s, a number of feasibility and project identification studies were carried out by foreign consultants. At the same time an Office for Urban Development was created in the Ministry of the Interior to coordinate and implement the project in cooperation with the respective municipal governments. When implementation of the project finally started in 1985,[49] three major project components had been singled out by planners: infrastucture development, the improvement of local management capacities, and poverty alleviation (World Bank 1985:2).

The Chiang Mai part of RCDP provides for 13.53 km of drainage improvements, 9.11 km of road improvement, the construction of a new bridge across the Ping River and the widening of Nakorn Ping bridge, riverfront development, restoration of historic sites, and slum improvement in two communities (Kingdom of Thailand, Vol. 2, 1983).

Costs for Chiang Mai amount to Baht 329.8 million or 23.8 percent of the total project costs of Baht 1.38 billion (= US $ 50.9 million) (World Bank 1985:1).

Demographic Impact. One of the major goals of the project was the diversion of population growth away from Bangkok and the development of a more balanced urban system. A closer look at the underlying population projections, however, shows that the project's impact on Bangkok-bound migration is low -- especially as long as the first project stage is not backed up by the development of lower order centers. Regional cities alone are not able to divert migratory streams significantly.[50]

Based on population growth estimates which are lower than actual growth rates for the period between 1970 and 1981, the four cities have to accommodate 500,000 additional inhabitants by the year 2001. Assuming that 50 percent of this growth will be due to natural growth and 50 percent to migration, there will be a migratory gain of approximately 250,000 people over a twenty year period (1981-2001). Given an average annual immigration into Bangkok of roughly 75,000 persons (Angel 1985), this constitutes only 15 percent of the capital's expected migration-fed growth until the year 2001.

In Chiang Mai the chances of absorbing Bangkok-bound migrants are even less favorable. Rough estimates show that migration accounts for less than 40 percent of Chiang Mai's growth. This is less than what has been assumed in the calculation above. Apart from that, studies have shown that Chiang Mai offers little attraction for interregional migrants. The migratory pattern of Chiang Mai is characterized by a dominance of short-distance moves (Singhanetra-Renard 1982a). According to one survey, 90.6 percent of Chiang Mai's migrants came from the Northern Region and 67.3 percent were born in Chiang Mai province (Prachid na Bangchang 1981:10). Moreover, almost 50 percent of Chiang Mai's provincial population is concentrated in the municipality and the six surrounding districts. These districts are connected with the city through a well developed road and transport network, so that for many workers commuting provides a viable alternative to migration (Singhanetra-Renard 1982a). The more remote parts of Chiang Mai province and the three adjacent provinces of Chiang Rai, Mae Hong Son, and Lamphun are thinly populated and thus have rather limited migratory potential. Migrants from other provinces in the Upper North (Lampang, Phrae, Phayao, and Nan) prefer Lampang which is more industrialized than Chiang Mai, while Bangkok is the destination of migrants from the Lower North.

Economic Impact. During the conceptualization stage it was believed that the main impetus of urban growth would come from the industrial sector. The Fifth National Economic and Social Development Plan (1982-1986), for instance, named the "strengthening of the industrial base" as a priority for regional city development.[51] However, such a view overlooked major obstacles to up-country industrialization. Moreover, at least in Chiang Mai, local elites aired strong reservations about industrialization. Most of the interviewed decision-makers neither desired industrial development nor held it economically viable. They cited the environmental hazards of industrialization and the lack of markets and raw materials as the major reasons for their disapproval.

These are not the only obstacles to industrialization in Chiang Mai. Due to higher transport and energy charges, production costs are higher than in Bangkok. Moreover, wage differentials between Bangkok and Chiang Mai are not attractive enough for investors and are more than offset by the capital's abundance of skilled labor and well-trained management personnel. In 1987 minimum wages for industrial workers stood at 73 Baht in Bangkok, 67 Baht in Chiang Mai, and 61 Baht in the Northern Industrial Estate near Lamphun.

Although the banking system in Chiang Mai province expanded from fourteen branches in 1968 to sixty branches twenty years later (Chiang Mai Chamber of Commerce 1990:120), lack of credit facilities is another major obstacle to industrial development. It has been argued "that provincial banks tend to operate as deposit institutions rather than as full service banks, and permission often has to be secured from Bangkok to make loan commitments" (World Bank 1978:43). Reportedly more than 60 percent of the deposits made in the provinces were channeled back to Bangkok (World Bank 1978:43). Decisions on loans were frequently delayed because private sector institutions adhere to the same centralist ideology as the government. Local bank managers have little autonomy in decision-making, and must submit loan applications to the headquarters in Bangkok for final approval. Due to these drawbacks and the fact that the network of public and private finance institutions was not yet well-developed, nearly 80 percent of manufacturing establishments in the Northern Region paid cash for their raw materials in the 1970s (United Nations, Vol. 3, 1979:2). In 1984, despite improvements, 51 percent of the surveyed entrepreneurs still paid their bills completely in cash (Tanrattanakoon 1984:37).

Any change in Thailand's Bangkok-centered industrial investment patterns will take a long time. Between 1960 and 1986 nearly 83 percent of firms promoted by the Board of Investments (BOI) located their plants in Bangkok or the Central Region. Only 5 percent went to the north, 9 percent to the south and 3 percent to the northeast. Even in recent years this trend has not been decisively reversed, although the radius in which firms locate plants in the Central Region is wider around Bangkok than hitherto. Not surprisingly, the Industrial Estate Authority of Thailand (IEAT) had enormous difficulties in finding investors for its newly opened industrial estate near Lamphun (Rüland and Ladavalya 1986:446). The estate was one of four Investment Promotion Zones, created by the Board of Investment (BOI) in the late 1970s, and offered a broad range of incentives to investors. As of late 1986, nearly two years after its inauguration, only seven investors had agreed to locate their plants in the estate.[52]

If at all, the industrial estate will be attractive primarily to foreign investors or large Bangkok-based companies. However, an industrial structure which mainly consists of branch factories is not likely to contribute meaningfully to the socioeconomic development of Chiang Mai and the surrounding region. Operations of such firms entail a high proportion of intracompany transactions and thus establish few linkages with the regional economy. Salaries and wages constitute the only spread effect of the estate, which is thus barely more than an industrial enclave in an otherwise agricultural, artisan, and service-oriented economic environment.

More recent studies, however, were more careful in assessing the industrial growth potential. The initially vague industrialization strategy for regional cities was modified by laying greater emphasis on resource-based, small-scale enterprises.

In Chiang Mai agro-industries and semiindustrial cottage industries provide the best opportunities in the manufacturing sector. There is a wide range of agricultural products in Chiang Mai's hinterland such as vegetables, onion, garlic, fruit (strawberries, longan, lychees, apples), tea, tobacco, and coffee which could be processed in the city. All of them have good export potentials to East Asian and European countries. A major precondition for a viable agro-industry, however, is the attraction of canning and processing industries to Chiang Mai as well as the improvement of cold storage facilities.

A better utilization of the province's resources for agro-industrial development may well contribute to a diversification of Chiang Mai's industrial structure. 81.1 percent of all industrial establishments in the province can presently be categorized as agro-industrial enterprises, of which 61.5 percent are rice mills. As Boonchorntarakul (1976:60) has shown in her study of Chiang Mai municipality's impact on its rural surroundings, agro-industries could produce the greatest linkage effects between the urban center and the rural hinterland. Such linkages would encourage crop diversification, farm intensification, and higher productivity in the rural areas.

Although promotion of agro-industries seems to be the most promising approach for expanding Chiang Mai's industrial base, not too much should be expected of it. Much depends on the framework in which the strategy is implemented. The dominance of a few big monopolist companies, for example, may thwart crop diversification and transform the whole region into a monoculture. The highly negative social effects of TNC-led agro-industrial modernization in the southern Philippine island of Mindanao should serve as a warning for decision-makers in Chiang Mai in their negotiations with transnational corporations intending to invest in the province. Furthermore, agro-industries are vulnerable to changing world-market prices, protectionism, changes of taste in industrialized countries, weather conditions, and competition from other developing countries with a similar product structure.

Handicrafts and trades such as silk and cotton weaving, silversmith working, umbrella making, and lacquerware and other souvenir production may provide some additional growth potential. These products can either be exported or find an outlet in the local tourist markets. Most local economic sectors, however, be it small-scale industries or the service sector, are strongly dependent on the growth of the tourist industry. While the growth of tourism seemed to slow down in the mid-1980s, with actual growth rates reaching just half of the targeted 8 percent, the industry's growth appreciated to double-digit figures after 1986. Foreign tourist arrivals grew by 17 percent in 1988 and another 13 percent in 1989. In 1988 some 570,000 foreign tourists visited Chiang Mai.[53] Tourism became the engine of Chiang Mai's economic growth and will remain it for quite some time.

A major precondition for the success of RCDP is the extent to which linkages with the surrounding rural areas can be fostered through the project. While surveys show that there are substantial backward linkages within the city, only few linkages have been established with the rural hinterland. This finding clearly supports the reservations aired against the spread effect concept that sees socioeconomic development radiating unilinearly from the urban center to the rural areas. In fact, up to 1987 RCDP has not gone beyond the traditional "growth pole" concept or, to use Douglass' term, "concentrated decentralization" (Douglass 1981:183). What is needed to overcome spatial imbalances and socioeconomic disparities, is a two-way development strategy: one that induces equitable development within the urban center, thereby penetrating the settlement hierarchy from the top, while at the same time stimulating bottom-up effects from the rural areas to the urban centers and leading to an upgrading of income levels and purchasing power in the agricultural sector (Hackenberg 1980).

In the past, surrounding rural areas have benefited little in terms of spread effects emanating from urban Chiang Mai. About 90 percent of all newly registered companies in Chiang Mai province were located in *amphoe muang*. Currently Chiang Mai's linkage pattern is characterized more by backward than forward linkages. According to Tanrattanakoon, who surveyed 109 establishments in Chiang Mai, backward linkages are primarily created through the purchase of raw materials. Almost 80 percent of the surveyed enterprises bought their raw materials locally (Tanrattanakoon 1984:42). To a lesser degree, backward linkages were established through the purchase of machines. Forward linkages were created by only 11 percent of sample firms and constituted only 8.3 percent of sales (Tanrattanakoon 1984:74).

Small firms had higher linkage effects than bigger enterprises. Nine out of ten bought their raw materials from local sources (Tanrattanakoon 1984:75). The larger the establishments were, the less important was the local economy for the purchase of inputs and the marketing of the products. On the other hand, large establishments seemed to have greater spread effects in terms of wages and salaries.

The urban bias in economic transactions is illustrated by Boonchorntarakul, who examined the spending pattern of factories in Chiang Mai. According to her survey, 40 percent of factory spending for raw materials remained in urban Chiang Mai, while 18 percent went to Bangkok and 18 percent to rural areas immediately surrounding Chiang Mai. Linkage effects through factory spending decreased with increasing distance from the urban center. The picture was somewhat different for wages and salaries, constituting 33.5 percent of total factory spending. About 41 percent of wages and salaries went to the rural areas adjacent to the city center, but 56 percent still remained in urban Chiang Mai (Boonchorntarakul 1976:38). In other words, the main spread effect came in the form of salaries and wages. Thus, it is not surprising that multiplier effects through factory spending were almost eight times higher in urban Chiang Mai than in the rural areas. 1 Baht spent by Chiang Mai factories created another 0.84 Baht in urban Chiang Mai, but only 0.11 Baht in rural areas. An even more negative picture emerges when the spending of urban residents is investigated. While 1 Baht spent by urban residents of Chiang Mai created another 2.23 Baht in urban Chiang Mai, no money was created in rural areas (Boonchorntarakul 1976:60). A recent replication of Boonchorntarakul's study con-firmed the her previous findings: urban infrastructure development primarily stimulates economic growth in urban Chiang

Mai, while the "trickle down" to the rural surroundings is modest (Ladavalya et al. 1987).

After 1987 a new source of urban-generated income spread to the suburban and rural surroundings. As a result of the on-going construction boom, many farmers sold their land to urban-based land speculators and subdivision developers. While the amount of funds flowing into the countryside through these transactions may be huge indeed, their developmental impact is at best doubtful. Many farmers are unable to reinvest these revenues productively and tend to spend them for consumption purposes. Others open up a business, but, lacking the expertise to run it, they falter after a short period, leaving them ruined as they have lost not only their land, but their money as well. According to estimates of the NESDB, almost one-third of cultivatable land in the Chiang Mai valley has been bought by land speculators in recent years.[54] The socioeconomic impact of these land transactions is an important area for future studies in urban-rural relations.

Social Impact. As Phisit Pakkasem put it, regional city development is incomplete if housing and social services are not provided simultaneously with the other project components. Otherwise, uncontrolled and improperly serviced settlements are likely to emerge. Consequently, a slum improvement component has been incorporated into RCDP (Pakkasem 1981:196).

Unfortunately, however, slum improvement measures constitute less than 3.1 percent of total project costs. This figure illustrates the primarily economic rationale and growth-oriented conception underlying the project. Even in the slum upgrading component, the project provides mainly physical improvements, while neglecting social services. The child and youth programs, vocational education, and child care programs are not well integrated into the project design and are little more than an appendage to infrastructure development. Moreover, as a consequence of the infrastructural improvements, beneficiaries will have to spend more for public services such as water and street lighting, because the maintenance costs will be recovered from them.

Negative social impacts may also arise due to the rapid expansion of the tourist industry. Although Thais possess a deeply rooted cultural identity, tourism may change values, tastes, and consumption patterns and exert inflationary pressures on the local economy. An example of the undesirable effects of tourism is the rapid increase in prostitution and AIDS in Chiang Mai, where, in 1985, no less than 121 brothels were counted.[55]

Notes

1. Calculated from National Statistical, Office, Office of the Prime Minister, *Statistical Yearbook of Thailand, 1987-1988* (Bangkok: National Statistical Office, 1988), pp. 23-32.

2. The survey was conducted by the author between 25 July 1985 and 4 October 1985 in collaboration with the Social Research Institute of Chiang Mai University.

3. A *tesaban nakorn* must have "sizeable revenues", a population of at least 50,000, and a density of more than 3,000 people per sqkm. A *tesaban muang* must have the same qualifications except that the population must not be less than 10,000. In addition, all provincial capitals are given the status of a tesaban muang. A *tesaban tambon* is set up "where it is deemed appropriate regardless of other prerequisites". Lately, however, the DOLA pursues a policy of abandoning these distinctions among municipalities. Interview information.

4. By 1988 Chiang Mai's municipal revenues had increased to Baht 231.9 million. This is equivalent to a further annual revenue increase of 15.4 percent since 1982 and translates into a per capita revenue of Baht 1,460 or nearly 61 US$. Information obtained from Chiang Mai municipality.

5. Calculated from World Bank, *Thailand. Regional Cities Development Project. Staff Appraisal Report* (Washington, D.C.: World Bank, 1985), pp. 68-71.

6. Calculated from Choop Karnjanaprakorn, *Municipal Government in Thailand as an Institution and Process of Self-Government* (Bangkok: Institute of Public Administration, Thammasat University, 1962), p. 207.

7. Calculated from World Bank, *Thailand. Regional Cities Development Project.*, pp. 68-71 and National Statistical Office, Office of the Prime Minister, *Statistical Reports of Changwat* (Bangkok: National Statistical Office).

8. In 1956 expenditure on general administration and personnel amounted to only 28.7 percent of total municipal expenditure. Calculated from Choop Karnjanaprakorn, *Municipal Government*, p. 208.

9. In Chiang Mai, expenditure for salaries, wages, and general administration increased by about 19 percent per year, whereas locally levied revenues only grew by about 7 percent. See World Bank, *Thailand*, p.24.

10. The Municipal Personnel Committee is chaired by the Minister of the Interior and is composed of seven other high-ranking government officials.

11. A plan limited to an area or function within a city.

12. Interview information.

13. *Prachachart Turakid*, Bangkok, 29 July-1 August 1990.

14. In Chiang Mai, Khon Kaen, Hat Yai, Lampang, Nakhon Sawan, Phuket, Rayong, Surat Thani, and Nakhon Ratchasima. *The Nation Review*, Bangkok, 16 May 1986, p. 3.

15. Organized by the *Social Research Institute* of Chiang Mai University on 4-5 April 1986.

16 Two members in a *tesaban muang* and *tesaban tambon*.

17. For Nakhon Sawan, Murashima came to a similar conclusion. See Eiji Murashima, "Local Elections and Leadership in Thailand: A Case Study of

Nakhon Sawan Province," in *The Developing Economies*, Vol. XXV, No. 4, December 1987, p. 374.

18. In Nakhon Sawan, too, almost 71 percent of the candidates were born in that city. Murashima, *"Local Elections ,"* pp. 366-367

19. In Nakhon Sawan, nearly 80 percent of the candidates held a political office prior to the 1980 municipal election. Murashima, *"Local Elections ,"* pp. 366-367.

20. *Thai News*, Chiang Mai, 27 July 1985, p. 1.

21. Prior to the September 1990 municipal elections *Kao Sayam*, a local daily, expected candidates to spend between 20 and 30 million Baht for campaign purposes. See *Kao Sayam*, Chiang Mai, 4 August 1990, p. 10.

22. *Thai News*, Chiang Mai, 20 July 1990, p. 12 and *Bangkok Post*, 25 August 1990, p. 3.

23. Voter turnout was 28.45 percent in 1974, 22.63 percent in 1980, and 42.22 percent in 1990.

24. In local elections national voter turnout was 54 percent in 1974, 40.89 percent in 1980, 46.53 percent in 1985, and 48.80 percent in 1990. In general elections, national voter turnout was even higher: 47.17 percent in 1975, 43.99 percent in 1976, 43.90 percent in 1979, 50.76 percent in 1983, 61.43 percent in 1986, and 63.56 percent in 1988.

25. *The Nation Review*, Bangkok, 21 August 1987, p. 8.

26. For details see Hans Bänziger, "How Wildlife Is Helping to Save Doi Suthep: Buddhist Sanctuary and National Park of Thailand," in I. Hedberg (ed.), *Proceedings of the Symposium "Systematic Botany. A Key Science for Tropical Research and Documentation"*, Stockholm, 14-17 September 1987, pp. 255-267.

27. *The Nation Review*, Bangkok, 21 August 1987, p. 18.

28. Nevertheless, the mayor of Chiang Mai too was a member of the *National Park Committee* which approved the project in principle. *The Nation Review*, Bangkok, 12 November 1985, p. 18.

29. Interview information.

30. *Daan Setakit*, Bangkok, 11-17 June 1990, p. 59.

31. In 1989, the cabinet held several meetings outside Bangkok: in Hat Yai, Khon Kaen, and in Chiang Mai. The exercise became henceforth known in the press as the *"Mobile Cabinet."*

32. *Prachachart Turakit*, Bangkok, 22-25 April 1990, p. 22.

33. Information provided by Chamnien Paul Vorratnchaiphan, Asian Institute of Technology. However, by the time of my latest visit to Chiang Mai in 1990, these outreaches had ceased.

34. See also David Morell and Chai-anan Samudavanija, *Political Conflict in Thailand. Reform, Reaction, Revolution* (Cambridge, Massachusetts: Oehlgeschläger und Hein, 1981), pp. 7-39.

35. Thai Volunteer Service, *Directory of Non-Government Development Organizations in Thailand 1987* (Bangkok: Thai Volunteer Service, 1987).

36. Chakrit Noranitipadungkarn and A. Clarke Hagensick, *Modernizing Chiang Mai: A Study of Community Elites in Urban Development* (Bangkok: Research Center National Institute of Development Administration, 1973).

37. Clark Neher and Budsayamat Bunjaipet, who studied clientelism in the rural parts of Chiang Mai province in 1986, came to a similar conclusion: "Patron-client relations are no longer (if they ever were) the explanatory variable for understanding Thai society." Clark Neher and Budsayamat Bunjaipet, "Political Interaction in Northern Thailand" in *Southeast Asian Journal of Social Science*, Vol. 17, No. 1, 1989, p. 66.

38. In Nakhon Sawan, Murashima came to similar findings. Two-thirds of the candidates had secondary education, while the rest had university degrees - either a BA (25 percent) or a MA (8.3 percent). Murashima, *"Local Elections ,"* pp. 366-367.

39. This recession, however, was comparatively mild. While other Southeast Asian economies had to contend with negative growth, Thailand still registered growth rates of 4.5 percent (1985) and 3.6 percent (1986). Asia Yearbook (Hong Kong: Far Eastern Economic Review, 1987 and 1988), p. 6.

40. Unemployment among university graduates and vocational students became a serious social problem in the 80s. Between 1977 and 1985 unemployment among educated persons increased from 36,000 to more than 200,000. *The Nation Review*, Bangkok, 10 March 1986, p. 5 and 22 August 1986, p. 18.

41. For the term "housekeeper", see Ronald L. Krannich, *Mayors and Managers in Thailand. The Struggle for Political Life in Administrative Settings* (Athens: Ohio University Center for International Studies, Southeast Asia Program, 1978), p. 33.

42. *Bangkok World*, 29 May 1985, p. 2.

43. *Bangkok Post*, Economic Review, Year-End, 1989, p. 36.

44. *Urban Edge*, Washington, D.C., November 1985, pp. 5-6.

45. Towards the end of the 80s, and as a consequence of increasing business opportunities, foreign investments are pouring into Thailand and become increasingly felt in Chiang Mai as well. In Chiang Mai major targets for Bangkok-based and foreign firms are hotel, tourism-related, and real estate projects.

46. At the time this study goes to print, these concerns are increasingly becoming reality. Land prices are soaring, construction booming. As a result, in 1988 and 1989, thirty-six high-rise condominium projects were under construction or in the planning stage. Over 50 percent of these 6,000 high-cost living units are sold to buyers from Bangkok, about 10 percent to foreigners, while only 35 percent are purchased by local people. The real estate boom of the late 80s goes hand in hand with the destruction of green space, orchards, and low-income housing. For a detailed documentation of these processes, see *The Nation Review*, Bangkok, 8 May 1989, afternoon edition, p. 1, 9 May 1989, p. 24, 15 May 1989, p. 24, 16 May 1989, p. 16, 3 August 1989, p. 23, 17 August 1989, p. 25 and Matichon, 7 August 1990, p. 18.

47. An exception was an eviction drive against traders in front of Talad Warorot, the city's main market in 1986.

48. *Bangkok Post*, Economic Review, 1991 Mid-Year, July 1991, p. 14.

49. Implementation started in four cities, i.e. Chiang Mai, Nakhon Ratchasima, Khon Kaen, and Songkhla. Hat Yai was dropped from the project at this stage.

50. A second phase of the project - known as RCDP II - has entered planning stage in 1988 and includes the following cities: Hat Yai, Nakhon Sawan, Rajburi, Ubon Ratchathani, Udon Thani, Phitsanulok, Kanchanaburi, and Chonburi.

51. Office of the National Economic and Social Development Board, Office of the Prime Minister, *The Sixth National Economic and Social Development Plan (1987-1991)* (Bangkok: Office of the National Economic and Social Development Board, 1987), p. 155.

52. Until late 1988, twenty-five firms have committed themselves to set up plants in the estate. *Bangkok Post,* 27 February 1989, p. 13.

53. *The Nation Review*, Bangkok, 22 February 1989, p. 22.

54. Interview information obtained from officers of the northern office of the National Economic and Social Development Board, Chiang Mai.

55. *The Nation Review*, Bangkok, 26 December 1985, p. 3.

3

Urban Government and Development in Iloilo City

Introduction

The Philippines is one of the most urbanized countries in Southeast Asia. At present, more than 40 percent of Filipinos live in urban areas. Urban growth averaged 4.4 percent during the 1970s, but rose to more than 6 percent towards the end of the decade. As these high growth rates persisted in the 1980s, continued rapid urbanization must be anticipated into the next century.

Urbanization in the Philippines first gained momentum in the 1920s, setting in much earlier than in neighboring countries. Urban growth was stimulated by both natural population growth and rural-urban migration. Net migratory gains seem to have been greater than natural growth in the initial phase, but the impact of the two factors was reversed after 1960. The sharp upward trend in urbanization after 1975 is suggestive of another wave of cityward migration. While in the 1950s and 1960s both *"pull"* and *"push"* factors were simultaneously responsible for the pace of rural-urban migration, the latest upsurge in migration must be primarily attributed to *"push"*-factors. Rural-rural migration to frontier areas in Mindanao and the Cagayan Valley ceased as the supply of arable land diminished and security deteriorated with the rapid spread of a communist-led insurgency.

Although less skewed than in Thailand, the Philippine settlement pattern nevertheless displays marked regional imbalances. With a population of over six million, the National Capital Region (the offical term designating the Metropolitan Manila Area) contains 33.1 percent of the country's urban population. As indicated by the primacy rate, the dominance of Manila rose constantly, from 3.9 in 1960 to peak at 4.3 in 1975, before dropping slightly to 4.1 in 1980.[1] Since the 1960s the National Capital Region (NCR) has been the most favored destination of Filipino migrants (Stinner/Bacol-Montilla 1981:5). The spatial imbalances are further underscored by the fact that the two regions adjoining the NCR, Central Luzon (41.8 percent) and Southern Tagalog (36.9 percent), likewise display a high level of urbanization. Altogether, almost 57 percent of Philippine city dwellers live in the NCR, Central Luzon, and the Southern Tagalog Region.

Outside this core area urban growth is concentrated on a few regional centers. 30 percent of the urban population lives in the six largest regional cities. With the exception of Iloilo City, these regional urban centers have experienced rapid growth (see Table 3.1). Here, urban growth has become haphazard and increasingly difficult to manage. Urban ills such as high rates of unemployment, sprawling slums and squatter settlements, and uncontrolled land use are now common features of these cities.

Like Thailand, the Philippine government embarked on regional development strategies in order to check the widening regional and intraurban disparities. Bacani (1981) has summarized the major strategies:

- the creation of a Regional Development Council (RDC) in each of the country's thirteen regions, with the task of coordinating development activities within the region;
- a ban on industrial location within a radius of 50 km of Metro Manila;
- a nationwide industrial estate program;
- the promulgation of an *Investment Promotion Act* for less developed areas;
- Integrated Area Development programs; and
- the Regional Cities Development Program (RCDP)

The Regional Cities Development Program was included in the Philippine Development Plan 1977-1982 as a major regional development strategy. The principal objectives of the program, which is financially supported by the World Bank, are the dispersal of economic and industrial growth and the diversion of migratory streams away from the NCR.

Iloilo City has been selected as a case for two major reasons: first, Iloilo was one of the cities chosen by the central government for the RCDP and, second, the city seemed to offer good prospects for a successful implementation of the RCDP. It was the country's leading sugar entrepôt during the first half of the twentieth century, and the enormous wealth generated by this trade provided the city with a physical and institutional infrastructure that was second only to Manila. To what extent Iloilo was able to utilize these assets and to perform the functions of

TABLE 3.1 Population Growth in Philippine Regional Cities

City	Population Growth				Average Annual Growth Rates, in Percent		
	1960	1970	1975	1980	1960-1970	1970-1975	1975-1980
Bacolod City	119,315	187,300	223,392	262,415	4.62	3.58	3.27
Cagayan de Oro City	68,274	128,319	165,220	227,312	6.52	5.19	6.59
Cebu City	251,146	347,116	413,025	490,281	3.29	3.54	3.49
Davao City	225,712	392,473	484,678	610,375	5.69	4.31	4.72
Iloilo City	151,266	209,738	227,027	244,827	3.32	1.60	1.52
Zamboanga City	131,489	199,901	265,023	343,722	4.28	5.80	5.34

Source: Republic of the Philippines, National Economic and Development Authority, National Census and Statistics Office, *Philippine Yearbook 1985* (Manila: National Economic and Development Authority, National Census and Statistics Office, 1986), pp. 133-138.

a regional growth center is one of the major questions discussed in this chapter.

Empirical data were obtained through a survey conducted in Iloilo between 4 May and 5 July 1986. The survey covered thirty-four local politicians and senior city administrators. Among the interviewed politicians were the incumbent city mayor, the vice mayor, and eleven of twelve members of the city council *(Sangguniang Panglungsod)*. Apart from the incumbents ten major local leaders belonging to other political groups were interviewed, among them three former city mayors. Out of a total of twenty-three interviewed local politicians eight were affiliated with the United Nationalist Democratic Party (UNIDO), five with the Kilusang Bagong Lipunan (KBL), and four with other groupings. All of the eleven administrators interviewed were senior civil servants, including eight department heads.

The survey of local decision-makers was completed by structured expert interviews with officials from central government agencies in Manila, regional directors of national government agencies, managers of public enterprises, businessmen, and academics. These interviews were conducted in three stages: from 1 December to 18 December 1984, from 28 January to 6 March 1986, and 4 May to 5 July 1986. Other sources of information included the analysis of relevant literature, official documents, press reports, statistics, and participant observation.

Local Autonomy

Central-Local Relations: Structures and Functions

The Constitutional and Institutional Framework. Three of the four Philippine Constitutions since 1899 contained provisions on local autonomy and local government. The *Malolos Constitution* of 1899 included an article providing for local government according to the principles of the "most ample decentralization and administrative autonomy". Other sections called for more "popular and direct election of local officials and for provincial and municipal taxation" (Ocampo/Panganiban 1985:4; Brillantes 1987:134).

Viewed exclusively in legal terms, the degree of local self-determination was surprisingly high during the initial phase of American colonial rule. Two major reasons may serve to explain this. First, there was the somewhat naive intention on the part of the colonizers to institute a political system in the Philippines based on American principles of democratic government. Second, when Washington became a colonial power, it did so without the willingness to commit substantial resources to this end.

The ability to govern the colony thus essentially depended on the co-operation of the Filipino elite. The creation of elective local government positions open to Filipinos was a move to attain precisely this goal. While the cooptation of Filipino elites allowed the United States to rule the islands with a minimum of American personnel, it politically entrenched the socioeconomic elite that has kept its grip on local institutions up to the present day. American colonial rule legitimized the power of this oligarchy "by supplying it with a strong political identity through the holding of public office" (Cullinane n.d.:26). The *Municipal Code Act No. 82* passed by the Philippine Commission under Taft in January 1901 provided for the election of local officials, authorized municipalities to devise their own public works projects, and vested them with powers in the field of financial and personnel management (Cullinane, n.d.:12).

This initial period of relatively broad local autonomy was shortlived, however. By 1903, intense politicking, the negligence of developmental activities and reports about corruption and "undemocratic activities" had brought to an end American efforts to institute municipal autonomy in the Philippines (Cullinane, n.d.:14). In the following years the colonial government in Manila increasingly strengthened its supervisory authority. The *Jones Law*, promulgated in 1916, further curbed the powers of local government (Cullinane, n.d.:16; Brillantes 1987:134).

While the Americans allowed for an increasing Filipinization of government, they made sure that this was a centralized government system. This became most evident during the *Commonwealth* era (1935-1946). Although under the *Commonwealth Constitution* of 1935 a wide range of government responsibilities was transferred to the Filipinos (including the presidency and the legislature, the Congress), Romani and Thomas concluded that the cities were "little more than extensions of the President's Office" (Romani and Thomas 1954:84). The president appointed the city mayors and the department heads and he could dismiss them at any time. The central government even exercised an item veto on financial matters (Romani and Thomas 1954:84). Not surprisingly, the *Commonwealth Constitution* lacked a commitment to local autonomy. The brief passage on local government only stressed the supervisory powers of the president over local governments (de Guzman 1966:238).

After independence (1946) little changed. City governments were hardly more than spoils in the political game. By appointing local officials, the president repaid political debts to loyal supporters. As a result, local officials were not appointed by virtue of their administrative qualifications or merit -- patronage and political loyalty were more important recruitment criteria (Romani and Thomas 1954:88). In addition, the president exerted far-reaching controls over the administrative process in Philippine cities. In a survey of Philippine city charters, Bernabe found that in thirty-nine cities the president had powers to approve or disapprove even such ordinances, resolutions or motions that were vetoed twice or repassed twice by the city council. In seventeen cities he also had powers to disapprove any ordinance, resolution or motion of the local legislature that he deemed "ultra vires" (Bernabe 1969b:24).

Changes in central-local relations occurred in the mid-1950s, when the Congress passed several bills making the positions of mayor and councillor elective in ten cities -- among them Iloilo. In 1959, Congress approved the *Barrio Charter* (Republic Act 2370), Republic Act (RA) 2259, calling for the election of all city mayors and city councillors, the *Local Autonomy Act* (RA 2264) (Brillantes 1987:135; Padilla 1990:2), and, in 1967, the *Decentralization Law* (RA 5185) (de Guzman 1966:239). Favorable Supreme Court rulings further enlarged the scope of local autonomy (Mariano 1958b:48).

The relaxation of central control over local governments through pro-autonomy congressional legislation reflected gradual changes in the Philippine political system. President Magsaysay's populism successfully increased the center's mobilization capacities at the grassroots (Doronila 1985), while at the same time eroding the intermediary role of local oligarchies as organizers of electoral support for the incumbent administration. Community development and rural infrastructure projects increasingly established the state as an alternative patron -- a trend that became even more pronounced in the Marcos years. As long as presidential appointments for local offices rewarded political loyalties of local elites, the latter were in a strong position to influence such appointments. Hence, there was no majority in Congress for an overhaul of central-local relations. Moves to increase local autonomy were usually initiated by opposition legislators in an attempt to protect their local power base against challenges by rival factions which had presidential backing. As the strength of the central state under Magsaysay and later Marcos increased, legal changes in central-local relations became acceptable to Philippine legislators irrespective of partisan interests. "More local autonomy" became the battle cry of provincial power elites in their attempt to alter the power equation in their favor.

The trend towards greater local autonomy was reinforced by several academic studies recommending greater decision-making powers for local government units. Moreover, influenced by the Anglo-American model of political development, the incipient programs of international development assistance also propagated decentralization as a necessary condition for development. In the process, it was increasingly recognized by Philippine politicians that the introduction of more local autonomy -- if only in legal terms -- would considerably facilitate the influx of bi- and multilateral development aid.

Paradoxically, the legal competence of local authorities was further extended even after the imposition of martial law in 1972. Article II, Section 10 of the Constitution of 1973 explicitly guaranteed local autonomy by stating that "the State shall guarantee and promote the autonomy of local government units, especially the barrio, to ensure their fullest development as self-reliant communities". Provisions for local autonomy were further elaborated in Article XI, which included safeguards against gerrymandering. Under the 1935 Constitution the president was able by virtue of executive order to define the boundary of any political subdivision and increase or diminish the territory comprised therein. Not surprisingly, this legal instrument was frequently utilized either to enhance the electoral prospects of party followers or to curb the chances of the rival faction (Tapales 1970:67-77). Hence, the 1973 Constitution provided that changes of local government boundaries "shall not take effect until ratified by a majority of the votes cast in a public plebiscite called for the purpose" (Section 2). The creation, division, merger, abolition or alteration of boundaries was henceforth subjected "to the approval by a majority of the votes cast in a plebiscite in the unit or units affected" (Section 3), instead of being the prerogative of Congress and the president. Another provision empowered local governments "to create their own sources of revenue and to levy taxes subject to such limitations as may be provided by law" (Section 5). The *Local Government Code (Batas Pambansa Blg. 337)*, enacted on 10 February 1983, largely confirmed the broadened scope of local autonomy as granted by the 1973 Constitution.

However, on closer scrutiny it became evident that the 1973 Constitution contained many safety valves that allowed the president to curtail local autonomy whenever he deemed it necessary. Such a clause could be found in Article VII, Sect. 16, which gave him the powers of the anti-autonomy 1935 Constitution (Sosmeña 1988):

The incumbent President of the Philippines shall be the Prime Minister, and he shall continue to exercise all his powers even after the Interim Batansang Pambansa is organized and ready to discharge its functions, and likewise, he shall continue to exercise his powers and prerogatives under the 1935 Constitution and the powers vested in this Constitution.

In addition, as the latter part of Article XI, Sect. 5 demonstrates, the wording of the constitution also provided ample opportunities to curb local autonomy through the special legislation. Legal provisions designed to increase fiscal autonomy[3] of local governments were neutralized by numerous other laws. Sosmeña is certainly right when he states that the "central government gives the local governments power with its right hand and immediately thereafter is taking it back with its left hand" (Sosmeña 1980:256) . This has given rise to what was called a "dualism of centralism and decentralization" (Sosmeña 1980:255) or "illusory decentralization" (Aquino 1977-78:60), which supports the conclusion that local autonomy was characterized by a high degree of legal formalism (Padilla 1990:1).

Amongst Philippine constitutions, in legal terms, the broadest powers were granted to local governments by the 1987 Constitution. Article X, Section 2 explicitly recognizes "local autonomy". Section 3 calls for a "more responsive and accountable local government instituted through a system of decentralization with effective mechanism of recall, initiative, and referendum" (Sect. 3), complementing decentralization by elements of plebiscitary democracy. Furthermore, "each local government shall have the power to create its own sources of revenues and to levy taxes, fees, and charges", yet "subject to such guidelines and limitations as the Congress may provide", but "consistent with the basic policy of local autonomy" (Sect. 5). Finally, local governments are encouraged to "group themselves, consolidate or coordinate their efforts, services, and resources for purposes commonly beneficial to them in accordance with law" (Sect. 13).

Legal provisions allegedly designed to promote local autonomy always stood in stark contrast to the limited role of local politicians in urban decision-making. Key instruments shaping local politics, such as the appointment of most city department heads and the allocation of national funds, remained largely in the hands of the national government. Thus, the actual degree of local autonomy was primarily a function of national politics.

Prior to martial law, under a political system of dyadic vertical alliances, local autonomy greatly depended on the relationship local officials had with national leaders. City governments closely aligned with the ruling circles in Manila had greater leeway in local affairs than a local leadership supporting the opposition party. In the latter case, the city administration was subject to all kinds of administrative obstructionism and harassment from the center, with the ultimate goal of discrediting the incumbent local leaders, eroding their support base by starving them of vital (national) resources, and eventually unseating them in the next local election. In Iloilo the perhaps most telling incident of this nature occurred during the latter part of the Quirino administration (1949-1953). Following an unsuccessful power struggle over the ruling Liberal Party's (LP) vice presidential slot in the forthcoming 1953 national elections, the Lopez-Ledesma faction, Iloilo's then undisputed provincial leaders, defected from the LP to the Democrata Party and later to the Nacionalista Party (NP). With them went Dominador Jover, Iloilo's city mayor. Soon after Vice-President Fernando Lopez resigned from his post, President Quirino started assaulting the local power base of the Lopez-Ledesma faction. He replaced Jover, a Lopez-protégé, as city mayor with Juan V. Borra, a member of a local rival faction. Jover was ousted, although he had been appointed only three months before and the city charter defined a six-year term for the mayor. The issue was finally resolved by a Supreme Court ruling that reinstated mayor Jover on the grounds that -- given the legally prescribed six year term -- he could not be removed from office without due cause (Romani and Thomas 1954:94; McCoy 1977:512-516). Interference in city government from highest government levels through appointments of personae non gratae or nonprovision of essential national counterpart funds for urban development projects also occurred during the LP-administration of President Diosdado Macapagal (when Iloilo's city government was under NP control) and during the third term of mayor Rodolfo Ganzon (1971-1972), at the time one of the most vocal opponents of President Marcos.

Under Marcos' emergency rule (1972-1981) de facto centralization continued. Perhaps with the exception of the first years of martial law, when the government sought to strengthen its legitimacy through well-publicized development schemes, regime stabilization through grassroots control received higher priority than service delivery (Rüland 1982a). State interest in local government affairs was mainly guided by deliberate attempts of the regime to install its proxies at the subnational level. The political measures to achieve this goal were highly sophisticated. Whereas it was a standard procedure of authoritarian regimes to suspend local elections -- as did Marcos, too, -- it was a shrewd move to replace only the most vocal critics (including Iloilo's city mayor Rodolfo Ganzon), while retaining the majority of local officials. As there was a considerable number of Marcos critics among local officials elected in the 1971 polls, their political power was quietly neutralized by expanding the membership of local councils and filling the new posts with supporters of the regime. These measures were accompanied by occasional purges, allegedly implemented to eliminate "corrupt and nonperforming officials". Institutional changes such as the creation of a Depart-

ment of Local Government and Community Development (1972), the
Metro Manila Commission (1975), and the Ministry of Human Settlements (1978) completed the regime's moves to gain firm control over the
lower layers of the political system. Law and order functions of cities
and municipalities were likewise centralized; control over police forces
was wrested from the mayors' hands and transferred to the Philippine
Constabulary/Integrated National Police (PC/INP). Local governments
thus became instruments in the hands of the ruling circles for the ad hoc
implementation of whatever plans, programs, and policies were handed
down to them (Rüland 1982a:34,107; Rüland 1985a).

Despite constitutional safeguards, gerrymandering did not cease during the Marcos era. Between 1972 and 1986 the number of provinces
was increased from fifty-four to seventy-four and the number of municipalities from 1,410 to 1,520. The latest, well-publicized case, was the
creation of the province of Negros del Norte in late 1985. Negros del
Norte was scraped out of the northern parts of Negros Occidental. That
the constitutional requirements were only some sort of formalism was
shown in the way the plebiscite was organized. With the help of his private army and a mixture of threats, intimidation, plain force, and material rewards Armando Gustilo, a warlord, sugar planter, Marcos ally,
and later governor of Negros del Norte, easily produced the necessary
majority in favor of the boundary alterations. Negros del Norte was created for two reasons: first, to formally separate the fiefdoms of three
important, yet rivalling Marcos allies -- the Gustilos (in the north of Negros), the Montelibanos (in the central part of Negros Occidental) and
the Gatislaos (in the southern parts of the island) -- and, second, to increase the vote-getting capacity of the KBL in the February 1986 presidential elections in Negros.[4]

After the collapse of the Marcos regime even the Aquino government
continued to place national political interests over its declared goal of
strengthening local autonomy. The purge of nearly all local officials,
their replacement with hand-picked Officers-in-Charge (OICs), and the
postponement of the May 1986 local elections was predominantly dictated by considerations of stabilizing the regime by establishing a local
power base. The first two local government ministers of the Aquino
administration, Aquilino Pimentel and Jaime Ferrer, openly admitted
this. According to Pimentel, local officials are "obliged to support and
pledge their loyalty to the Aquino government to which they owe their
position".[5] That the new government considered local authorities primarily "as a machinery to smoothly carry out its policies and programs"
(Minister Ferrer) became particularly evident before and after the referendum on the 1987 Constitution.[6] Already in November 1986 the Min-

istry of Local Government announced that it would impose "harsh measures" on those newly appointed local officials who do not campaign for the ratification of the constitution. What was meant with such allusions became evident soon after the referendum. Within a few weeks, Ferrer ousted twenty-six mayors in towns where the "no"-vote won. Most of them came from the "Solid North" -- the Ilocos Norte and Cagayan Valley provinces -- the strongholds of ex-President Marcos and dismissed Defense Minister Enrile, the main opponent of the new constitution.

Local leaders were well aware of this centralization. In a survey conducted by Gaudioso C. Sosmeña in 1979, 91.2 percent of 352 interviewed local officials considered intergovernmental relations either as "highly centralized" (29.3 percent) or "centralized" (61.9 percent) (Sosmeña 1980:205,213). Sosmeña's findings were confirmed by the survey results of this study. A clear majority of Iloilo's local decision-makers opted for an extension of the authority of local councils as the major decision-making body of local governments. Almost 65 percent of the respondents were in favor of "more authority for the local councils".

The centralized nature of intergovernmental relations also explains why more than 80 percent of the decision-makers interviewed in Iloilo found it essential to establish "close personal or friendly relationships" with national government officials. Although only 32 percent of the respondents admitted that "an important task can best be accomplished by use of personal connections rather than to go through formal channels", 82 percent entertained relationships with regional directors, 68 percent with other senior officials in regional agencies, 82 percent with national politicians (such as former MPs or executives of national political parties), and 74 percent with ministers and other senior officials in the national government.

The fact that informal interactions of Iloilo decision-makers with representatives of superior government agencies concentrated on national politicians and regional directors of national government agencies illustrates the closely interwoven nature of the national and local political arena. Regional directors often serve as brokers between local level decision-makers and the headquarters of national government agencies where no informal links with high-ranking bureaucrats exist. They may act as intermediaries in the formulation and implementation of national projects with impact on the local level. Depending on their personality, resourcefulness, and connections within the headquarters, regional directors may have considerable influence on resource allocation to the city. The other major link with the national political arena are national politicians. They are likewise of strategic importance in terms of resource allocation to the city and are often approached to lobby for projects and funds benefiting it. Moreover, informal ties with national politicians are an important device to consolidate, stabilize or improve one's own power base at the local level. Alliances with national politicians serve the major purpose of checking or reducing the influence of political rivals and their alliances.

However, after the imposition of martial law, local decision-makers were left with a decreasing range of options as far as informal links to national politicians were concerned. The existence of a numerically small inner-ruling circle made it essential for most informal contacts to be geared towards a few powerful kingpins who had ready access to this inner-ruling circle -- such as Roberto S. Benedicto, the Region VI chairman of the regime's Kilusang Bagong Lipunan Party (KBL).

Indeed, as the survey results show, in most cases such informal ties with higher government echelons proved beneficial to local decision-makers. 76 percent of the respondents reported that they were given assistance by politicians and officials from superior government levels when they requested it. Usually such assistance took the form of "facilitating contacts" (32.6 percent), the "provision of data and information" (30.4 percent) and "financial assistance" (23.9 percent).

The Functions of City Government. Unlike in Thailand and Malaysia, there is no explicit enumeration of city government functions in the Philippine constitution or the *Local Government Code*. However, some provisions about the functions of city governments are contained in the city charters, while others must be extracted from various sections of the *Local Government Code*, especially those dealing with the powers and functions of local officials and the local legislature *(Sangguniang Panglungsod)*.

Table 3.2 shows that, like in Thailand, Philippine cities perform few functions that are genuinely local in nature. A closer look at these functions seems to support the widespread notion that local governments only render fairly trivial services, such as street lighting, sanitation, administering cemeteries, parks, libraries, and recreational facilities, or running slaughterhouses. Most other functions one would expect to be performed by city governments are either exclusively carried out by the national government, shared with superior government levels or transferred to public enterprises and the private sector. This observation clearly illustrates the de facto administrative penetration of city government by superior government levels in functional terms. What has been said earlier about Thai municipalities holds true for Philippine cities as well: there is only little functional autonomy of city governments.

A closer examination of the erosion of local government functions in the Philippines reveals two major phenomena: first, that the erosion

TABLE 3.2 Functions of City Governments in the Philippines

Function	City Government	National Government	Public Enterprise	Private Sector
Maintaining peace and order	X	X	---	---
Road construction and maintenance	X	X	---	---
Street lighting	X	---	---	---
Health	X	X	---	X
Public sanitation	X	---	---	---
Refuse collection and disposal, street sweeping	X	---	---	X
Traffic management	X	X	---	---
Sewage disposal	X	X	---	---
Drainage	X	X	---	---
Education	X	X	---	X
Welfare services	X	X	---	X
Family planning	X	X	---	X
Water supply	---	---	X	X
Electricity supply	---	---	X	X
Markets	X	---	---	X
Cemeteries	X	---	---	---
Sports, parks, and recreation	X	---	---	X
Beautification	X	---	---	---
Housing, slum clearance	X	X	---	X
Libraries	X	---	---	---
Fire protection	---	X	---	---
Urban planning	X	X	---	---
Transport	---	---	X	X
Agricultural promotion	X	X	---	X
Slaughterhouse	X	---	---	---
Regulation of land use, building	X	X	---	---
Population registration	X	X	---	---
Environmental protection	X	X	---	---

Legend: X function performed   --- function not performed

Source: Interviews with local officials and officials of the Ministry of Local Government.

process started as early as the 1930s and second that, over time, it took a see-saw course that was primarily dictated by national politics. A case in point are the peace and order functions of city governments.

The nationalization of police forces in 1937 under Commonwealth Act No. 86 was a consequence of the centralization policy of President Manuel Quezon during the *Commonwealth* era. The Act took away policing functions from local governments and created instead a State Police Force under the Ministry of the Interior (Mariano 1958a:365; Soberano/Waldby 1965:337). The *Police Act 1966 (RA 4864)*, on the other hand, reflected the trend towards increasing local autonomy in legal terms that had set in a decade earlier. Under the Act, city mayors were granted the power to appoint the chief of police and his assistant as well as to supervise the police forces in their jurisdiction. The shift from the nominal presidential democracy to authoritarian rule again had an impact on control over police forces. PD 765 removed control over the police from the mayors. The police was then placed under the command of the Philippine Constabulary and the Integrated National Police (PC/INP) and directly supervised by the Ministry of National Defense (Sosmeña 1980:131). This regulation was still in force in 1986, although the Marcos regime had collapsed, and city and municipal mayors were increasingly lobbying for authority over the police to be returned to the local chief executive (Padilla 1990:5).

Complaints of local officials against the centralization of the police also surfaced in the interviews with local decision-makers in Iloilo City. The criticism directed against the INP primarily focussed on the city's obligation to contribute 18 percent of its general fund expenditure to the national government for financing police services without having any noticeable authority over police matters and without getting adequate services in return. Several respondents spoke about demoralized police forces in Iloilo City, due to a long-standing rivalry between the PC and the city police. The PC, which controls the allocation of funds, equipment, and other resources, was reported to be holding back even the items designed intended for use by the city police. In consequence, Iloilo's police is poorly equipped and understaffed, lacking firearms, vehicles, gasoline, and even office supplies.

Before 1955, fifteen out of twenty-eight cities operated their own waterworks (Romani and Thomas 1954:114). The creation of the National Waterworks and Sewerage Authority (NAWASA) through RA 1383 (1955) marked the centralization of the waterworks management (Mariano 1958a:369; de Guzman 1966:240). A slight return to a greater control of local governments over waterworks was the establishment of the Metro Iloilo Water District (MIWD). Apart from the City of Iloilo, MIWD covers the towns of Maasin, Cabatuan, Sta. Barbara, and Pavia. The district is managed by a five man board of directors appointed for a term of six years by the city mayor of Iloilo and subject to confirmation by the city legislature, the *Sangguniang Panglungsod*.[7]

Electricity is usually supplied either by public enterprises, cooperatives or private companies. Since the prewar era Iloilo City has been serviced by the Panay Electric Company (PECO) -- a private enterprise owned by a local prominent family.

Unlike Malaysian cities, but similar to Thai municipalities, Philippine city governments are rarely involved in the provision of housing. In the past, Iloilo's city government was responsible for housing only in a few instances -- mostly in the form of resettling victims of fire disasters. Otherwise, housing is a domain of the private sector and a number of national government agencies such as the defunct Philippine Housing and Homesite Corporation (PHHC), the National Housing Authority (NHA), the Ministry of Human Settlements (MHS),[8] the Social Security System (SSS), and the Government Services Insurance System (GSIS). Lately, as part of RCDP, low-cost housing programs have been initiated by the World Bank. However, so far the city government has had only a limited share in the planning and implementation of the proposed sites-and-services and slum-upgrading projects.

While there are at least some formal provisions in Thailand requesting municipalities "to promote occupations for local inhabitants", there is no similar stipulation in Philippine local government laws. Even worse, social problems stemming from unemployment are usually addressed in a rather negative and punitive way.[9]

The Resource Dimension

Financial Resources. Although the 1973 Constitution seems to grant Philippine cities greater financial freedom than central rules and regulations leave to Thai municipalities, in practice the situation is rather similar (see Table 3.3). For instance, the wording of Article XI, Section 5 of the 1973 Constitution subordinated the power of local governments to raise their own revenue to a specific central law. Such a law has been enacted through PD 231, otherwise known as the *Local Tax Code*. PD 231 not only defines the majority of local revenue sources, but also fixes the upper and lower limits of the respective taxes, fees, and charges. PD 231 is supplemented by the *Real Property Tax Code (PD 464)*, PD 436 (on specific tax allotments), PD 144 (on internal revenue allotments) and PD 752 (on credit financing). A summary of the revenue sources of Philippine cities is presented in Table 3.3.

Fiscal centralization was firmly established through numerous other administrative rules and regulations that in essence run counter to the spirit of local autonomy. Until 1978 budgets prepared by local governments had to be approved by the Department of Finance.[10] Especially in premartial-law days this instrument was frequently utilized by the central government to obstruct locally initiated development programs in places where the opposition party or a rival faction controlled the city administration. In order to keep political opponents off-balance, budget

TABLE 3.3 Financial Resources of Philippine Cities

Tax Category	Tax
Locally levied taxes	- Real property tax (PD 464)
	- Idle land tax (PD 464)
	- Special assessment levy (PD 464)
	- Tax on transfer of real property ownership (PD 231)
	- Tax on business of printing and publication (PD 231)
	- Franchise tax (PD 231)
	- Sand and gravel tax (PD 231)
	- Occupation tax (PD 231)
	- Amusement tax on admission (PD 231)
	- Tax on peddlers (PD 231)
	- Annual fixed tax per delivery truck or van of manufacturers or producers of, or dealers in, certain products (PD 231)
Locally levied non-tax revenues	- Fees for scaling and licensing of weights and measures (PD 231)
	- Rental fee for use of municipal waters, rivers, etc. (PD 231)
	- Fees and charges (PD 231)
	- Fines and penalties (PD 231)
Shared taxes	- Residence tax (PD 231)
	- Special education fund tax (RA 5447)
Central government grants	- Internal revenue allotment (PD 144 as amended)
	- Specific tax allotment (PD 436)
	- National aids
Other resources	- Reserves
	- Loans, borrowings (PD 752)
	- Municipal Development Fund (Presidential Decree 1914)

Sources: RA 5447; PD 144, PD 231, PD436, PD 464, PD 752, PD 1914; and R.B Ocampo and E.M. Panganiban, *The Philippine Local Government System. History, Politics and Finance* (Manila: Local Government Center, 1985).

approval was deliberately withheld (at times for up to one year) or even refused outright. The only option then left for the city government concerned was to govern with the previous year's budget and, as was usually the case, once these resources were insufficient, to pass so-called supplemental budgets. The same obstructive effects were achieved through delays in the remittance of national government grants and aids. The negative effects of such practices on long-term planning are obvious.

Another indicator of increasing fiscal centralization is the declining share of the local government sector in total public expenditure. While national government expenditure increased at an average annual rate of 23.95 pecent between 1971 and 1984, local government expenditure grew less rapidly at an average annual rate of only 16.5 pecent (Paderanga 1984:1). As a result, the percentage of local government expenditure in total public expenditure decreased from 20.7 percent in 1969 (Bahl and Miller 1983:3) to 10.25 percent in 1979, before recovering slightly to 12.0 percent in 1984.[11] Similarly, the ratio of local government expenditure declined from 3.0 percent of the GNP in fiscal year 1967/68 (Caoili 1972:99) to 1.37 percent in 1984.

Although at a first glance Philippine cities appear to have a greater number of revenue sources than Thai municipalities, they are in no way financially better off. The revenue potential of most of these sources is negligible. Thus, not surprisingly, what has been said about municipal finances in Thailand, is even more applicable to Philippine regional cities. They are faced with severe financial constraints and suffer from an inadequate, inelastic, and underutilized resource base.

Despite average annual revenue increases of 13.8 percent between 1980 and 1984, Iloilo was a financially weak city. In terms of revenue increases Iloilo ranked third among the five major regional centers: behind Cebu City (21.4 percent) and Cagayan de Oro City (17.0 percent), but ahead of Davao City (9.9 percent) and Bacolod City (7.3 percent). Iloilo City's revenue growth rate was slightly above that of Philippine cities in general (14.9 percent between 1979 and 1984). It should be noted, however, that these revenue increases were to a large extent caused by a spiraling inflation which, during most of the investigation period, reached double-digit figures.[12] Revenue increases in real terms were thus minimal, if there were any at all (Bahl and Miller 1983:3). Also in terms of per capita annual increases, at first sight Iloilo's performance appears in a favorable light (see Table 3.4). At 11.2 percent, the city displays the second fastest average annual growth rate in per capita revenues, far behind Cebu (33.45 percent), but ahead of Cagayan de Oro (10.9 percent), Davao (5.6 percent) and Bacolod (3.7 percent). This performance, however, must be mainly attributed to Iloilo's sluggish population growth. On the other hand, compared with the per capita revenues of the other regional centers, Iloilo was second from the bottom. In 1984, per capita revenues stood at P 197, while Cebu, Cagayan de Oro, and Bacolod recorded P 294.4, P 217.3, and P 211.3, respectively. At 166.2 Pesos, only Davao had lower per capita revenues (see Table 3.4).

The financial maneuverability of Iloilo's city government is grossly limited by various other factors. Locally levied revenues declined between 1980 and 1984, from 62.8 percent to 59.99 percent. Nevertheless,

TABLE 3.4 Finances of Philippine Regional Cities

City	Total Revenues 1984, in million Pesos	Per Capita Revenues, 1984, in Pesos	Average Increase in Per Capita Revenues, 1980-1984, in Percent	Tax Collection Efficiency, 1984, in Percent	Percentage of Locally Levied Revenues, 1984
Iloilo City	52,723.8	197.0	11.24	53.99	59.99
Davao City	119,624.0	166.2	5.62	55.44	44.07
Cagayan de Oro City	61,131.0	217.5	10.91	64.43	56.20
Bacolod City	62,844.0	211.3	3.68	59.18	60.59
Cebu City	163,808.0	294.4	33.45	39.88	45.32

Source: Republic of the Philippines, Commission on Audit, *Annual Financial Report, Local Governments (Provinces, Cities, Municipalities)* (Manila: Commission on Audit, 1979-1984).

its proportion of locally levied financial resources was higher than that of the other regional cities, except for Bacolod (see Table 3.4).

The decline in locally levied revenues was primarily the result of a decrease in business taxes. Revenues from business taxes contracted by nearly six percent in the 1980-1984 period, reflecting the collapse of the Philippine sugar industry in the early 1980s and the faltering of many businesses in the dramatic economic recession following the assassination of opposition leader Benigno Aquino in 1983.

The decline in locally levied revenues was paralleled by an increasing dependency on national grants and aids which rose from 37.2 percent in 1980 to 40.0 percent in 1984 (see Table 3.5). This was slightly above the national average for Philippine cities. Between 1979 and 1984 nonlocal revenues of the country's sixty-one cities rose from 27.7 percent to 38.1 percent. Philippine cities thus exhibited an even greater dependency upon central government grants than Thai municipalities, although, due to revenues from shared taxes and surcharges, Thai cities had a lower share of locally levied revenues. Moreover, the second half of the 1970s ended a short period of fiscal consolidation which was marked by a declining share of nonlocal revenues (Ocampo and Panganiban 1985:37).

But despite the nominal growth of internal revenue allotments and national aids, the grant system does not provide an adequate source of revenue for Philippine local governments (Bahl and Miller 1983:134). A major reason is that local governments rarely received the full amount of grants due to them. This feature of central-local relations can be traced back to the beginnings of the republic. In Baguio City, for instance, only 14.3 percent of the city's internal revenue allotments were

TABLE 3.5 Revenue Sources of Iloilo City, 1980-1984

Sources of Revenue	1980	1981	1982	1983	1984
Percentage of national aids, assistance to local revenues	37.18	38.06	39.67	39.52	40.01
Real property tax as percentage of total revenue	19.05	23.32	20.50	19.18	18.75
Business tax as percentage of total revenue	24.67	21.61	18.97	18.74	18.51
Receipt from operations and services as percentage of total revenues	13.55	12.19	10.81	11.23	11.08
Locally levied revenues	62.82	61.94	60.33	60.48	59.99

Source: Republic of the Philippines, Commission on Audit, *Annual Financial Report, Local Governments (Provinces, Cities, and Municipalities)* (Manila: Commission on Audit, 1979-1984).

actually remitted by the central government (Bernabe 1969a:47). Under martial law, through PD 144, the internal revenue allotments to local governments were increased to 20 percent. However, subsequent legislation (PDs 937, 1231, and 1741) introduced formulas forestalling the full realization of PD 144. The effect was a drastic decline in real terms (Bahl and Miller 1983:102). In 1980 the actual distribution of the grant was equivalent to only about 7 percent of the national government's entire internal revenue collection, compared to the 20 percent stipulated by PD 144. In other words, only approximately one-third of the actual grant was being distributed (Bahl and Miller 1983:102). As revealed by one interview source, cuts in the grant revenues of cities were particularly pronounced during election years. Although no exact figures were provided by the source, it was already evident in May 1986 that Iloilo City had been deprived of a considerable portion of its grant resources, which had allegedly been spent during the presidential election campaign in January 1986.

At least five major factors account for Iloilo's financial bottlenecks:

First, existing income sources were grossly underutilized. In all major regional cities except Cebu city governments did not levy the maximum real property tax rates of 2 percent of a commercial or industrial property's assessed market value until RCDP was inaugurated. Moreover, certain tax sources were not tapped at all (RCDP Financial Study 1979:11). No Philippine local government has levied the special assessment tax (on land improvements) and the idle land tax both of which have an in-built equity effect and discourage land speculation.

A second factor is wrong assessment[13] or gross underassessment of property values. Since the Second World War there have been only four real property revaluations in Iloilo City, which took place in 1948, 1964, 1974, and 1979. Although the *Real Property Tax Code* (PD 464) stipulated that assessments must be revised every five years, and an amendment to the code (PD 1621) shortened this period to three years, no revaluations took place in 1982 and 1985. The regime suspended property revaluations nationwide until 1988, citing the critical state of the nation's economy as the reason behind this measure. The result of this moratorium was a progressively widening discrepancy between assessment levels and actual market values. Taking into account this irregular pattern of revaluations, the assessment level of commercial and residential properties in inner-city locations represented only 15-20 percent of market values. In addition, real property collections in Iloilo suffered from a presidential edict allowing typhoon victims to defer their property tax payments in 1984. As Iloilo was not among the areas worst hit by the storm, the ordinance was widely interpreted as an invitation to tax delinquency.

Third, numerous exemptions likewise contributed to the erosion of Iloilo's and other Philippine cities' real property tax base. Tax exemptions are granted on government-owned properties, pioneer investments (according to the *Investment Incentives Act*, RA 5185), charitable and religious property, property of low-income households, nonstock, nonprofit educational institutions, and foundations as well as government-owned or -controlled corporations. The latter provision constituted a considerable drain on local government revenues, especially after the Philippine government took over the business empires of a number of Marcos cronies following the *Dewee Dee crisis* in 1981.[14] Almost 26 percent of properties in Iloilo were tax-exempt, compared with 33 percent in Tacloban, 31 percent in Cagayan de Oro, 28 percent in Cebu, 22 percent in Davao, and 9 percent in Bacolod (RCDP Financial Study 1979:12).

Iloilo's land-use pattern and economic structure placed additional limits on the city's tax base. 65.7 percent of land under the city's jurisdiction was agricultural land and open space, which are the least taxed property categories. Even greater fiscal problems for the city were only forestalled by the effects of a nationwide tax mapping project which, according to one interview source, has considerably updated the city's property tax base.

"Soft assessment" and infrequent revaluation must also be seen against the social background of Iloilo's decision-makers. Most members of the city council belonged to the propertied classes and have interests in real estate. Moreover, as the construction and real estate industry was represented by at least one councillor in previous city councils, one is safe in assuming that the industry was able to exert a restraining influence on moves to strengthen the city's property tax base. The strong position of business interests, realtors, and professionals in Philippine local politics became particularly evident after the enactment of the *Local Tax Code* (PD 231) in 1973. When nationwide local treasurers began to draft new tax ordinances, imposing the maximum rates as provided for by the code, the opposition of vested interests became so vocal that after a few months PD 231 had to be suspended and amended by PD 426 (de Guzman et al. 1977:13).

Fourth, collection efficiency is notoriously low in Philippine cities. In Iloilo the collection efficiency averaged 61 percent for the 1978-1985 period. Despite fluctuations, interviews with assessment officials suggest a deteriorating collection performance after 1978. Yet, Iloilo's collections are well within the range of other regional cities' performances. Iloilo's collection efficiency was above the national average for Philippine local governments in 1982 (47.7 percent) and slightly below the national average in 1984 (54.2 percent).

Collection efficiency is even worse for business and amusement taxes. As city governments rarely have the staff and the legal instruments for proper assessment, they must rely on the taxpayer's self-report. Bahl is certainly right stating that this makes the business tax "a voluntary payment where understatement is widespread" (Bahl and Miller 1983:237). Accordingly, a probe by the city government revealed that for years Iloilo's moviehouse owners evaded amusement taxes worth millions of pesos.[15]

In 1983, the top ten tax delinquents alone owed the city government more than 2.4 million pesos. This is equivalent to almost 7 percent of the city's revenues. Since then, however, the situation has worsened dramatically. When the Aquino-appointed city government took over in April 1986, it discovered that tax delinquencies amounted to P 30.5 million or more than 50 percent of the city's annual budget. In part, this was due to the fact that penalties for tax delinquency are rarely enforced in the Philippines, although a few auctions of properties in arrears took place in Iloilo.[16] Moreover, the penalties appear rather mild and do not deter potential delinquents. In fact, considering the high interest rates in the Philippines paying a fine for tax delinquency is more economical than paying the taxes in time.

Fifth, the unsatisfactory financial position of many Philippine cities must also be attributed to the fact that tax administration is one of the most corruption-prone areas in local government. In a case like Iloilo, a city with a shrinking economy, an increasing tax burden,[17] and a poorly remunerated assessment and collection staff, the potential for corrupt practices is great. That such irregularities must have been a major problem in Iloilo became very obvious in the interviews with treasury officials. Moreover, the tax collection was used as a political tool in interfactional disputes. While political opponents were harrassed by the local tax administration, the clientele of the incumbent faction was either completely exempted from taxation or taxed "softly".

The issue of low tax collection efficiency was presented to the survey respondents. They were asked to check those two items out of a list of eight to which they attach highest priority for improving the revenue situation in Iloilo City. But unlike Sosmeña's respondents,[18] Iloilo decision-makers did not feel that they lack adequate taxing powers. Only 2.15 percent of the score went to that item. Neither did they opt for increases in the real property tax (4.3 percent of score) nor in the fees and charges for urban services (2.15 percent). In this respect they shared the views of the majority of Chiang Mai respondents. They differed, however, from Chiang Mai decision-makers in that they did not propose more national grants and aid or more tax sharing between the central government and local governments which, in effect, leads to even greater fiscal dependence upon the center. Instead, they strongly suggested improvements in collection efficiency. Almost 55 percent of the score went to "more efficient tax collection". This view was held by representatives of all three groups interviewed -- i.e. the incumbent local politicians, the city administrators, and the nonincumbent political leaders. "Share of tax revenues" ranked second among the priorities, but mustered only 17.2 percent of the score.

As a result of their limited resource utilization Philippine cities are unable to invest much in urban development. In addition, well over 70 percent of the city's revenues must be earmarked for mandatory purposes.[19] Budgetary options for development projects are thus further narrowed down. Accordingly, capital investment in Iloilo accounted for only 5.2 percent in 1983 and 7.0 percent in 1984. At 13.6 percent, Bacolod City had a somewhat higher capital investment ratio in 1983 (Bacolod City 1985:120). A survey covering twenty-two cities exhibited similar capital investment ratios. Capital investment of these cities averaged 13.1 percent for the 1978-1982 period (Prantilla et al. 1986:161).

Borrowings and the *Municipal Development Fund*[20] have yet to make a meaningful impact on development financing. In the Philippines, borrowing ceilings are much lower than, for instance, in Malaysian cities. In the Philippines borrowings are restricted to 7 percent of the aggregate assessed value of the taxable real properties in a local jurisdiction, less outstanding loans and other long-term indebtedness, whereas Malaysian municipalities may borrow up to five times the annual value of the assessed properties. Thus, in 1984 only 3.3 percent of total city revenues came from borrowings, and the five regional cities did not borrow at all (Republic of the Philippines, Commission on Audit 1985:79-81). Of all sixty-one cities, only sixteen made use of credit facilities. Total public debt of local governments in 1984 stood at P 853 million, which is about 11 percent of their total income. Most loans contracted were used for construction of public markets and the purchase of heavy equipment (Yoingco 1986:71).[21]

Rigid controls over local government disbursements, which require MLG approval for any capital outlay, even if only for the purchase of stationary, had a discouraging effect on capital investment decisions. The announcement of former Local Government Minister Pimentel, himself a former city mayor, of the removal of this red tape remained an unfulfilled promise until October 1988, when the Office of the President and the Department of Budget and Management issued a memorandum circular, authorizing local governments to purchase heavy equipment (Padilla 1990:8). In order to finance large-scale urban infrastructure projects such as RCDP, Philippine cities are highly dependent on central grants or assistance from international donors such the World Bank, the Asian Development Bank (ADB) or the United Nations Development Program (UNDP).

Managerial Resources. Personnel management of Philippine cities is highly centralized. In this respect, the situation is not markedly different from Thailand. The city mayor as the local chief executive does not have a say in the appointment of key positions such as the treasurer, assessor, health officer, city engineer, the police chief, and the city fiscal officer. These officers are either appointed directly by the president or the respective cabinet ministers.

However, in Iloilo City -- as in most other Philippine cities -- the situation is complicated by the fact that department heads are protégés of local and national politicians, who utilize their informal contact network in Manila to get loyal followers appointed to key administrative posts. Control over departments or divisions in the city administration is a particularly important device for politicians who are not part of the incumbent faction to exert influence on local policy issues. In view of the prevalence of *"utang na loob"* (debt of gratitude), which characterizes such patron-client relationships, the politician's "agent" within the city administration can be instrumentalized to dilute, obstruct or delay projects and policies of the incumbent party or faction. The objective of such actions is to undermine the political efficacy, credibility, and eventually the electoral popularity of the rival faction.

Not surprisingly, such patterns of interaction have led to a profound politicization and factionalization of the administrative branch in local government, with loyalties split between the mayor, the appointing authority at the national level, and the recommending politicians. Seemingly trivial administrative issues often develop into protracted battles among local political leaders fought by their bureaucratic proxies. Interdepartmental coordination and cooperation, which is essential for the successful implementation of projects, is thereby thwarted.

Central government dominance in personnel management increased during the martial-law era. Letter of Instruction (LOI) No. 265, for instance, released on 5 April 1975, created a so-called Performance Audit Team composed of twelve senior cabinet ministers for screening the performance of local officials (Sosmeña 1980:11). However, the well-timed creation of this body a few months before of the term of local officials elected in the 1971 local polls expired aroused suspicion that the team was primarily a device for a politically-motivated purge. As the 1971 elections brought into office a substantial number of politicians affiliated with the opposition Liberal Party (LP), the expiry of their term in December 1975 provided a convenient opportunity to get rid of local politicians who still refused to give full support to the martial-law administration. The Performance Audit Team was designed to justify a political move under the pretext of increasing administrative efficiency, though in reality seeking to stabilize the regime at the grassroots level (Rüland 1982a:106).

LOI No. 981 imposed restrictions on filling vacant and creating new positions. It stipulated that no vacant position could be filled and no new position created unless the concerned department could reduce its operational expenses by 10 percent. As it was next to impossible to comply with this provision in the light of double-digit inflation, the ordinance was widely interpreted as a ban on hiring and promoting local government personnel (Regional Cities Development Project 1980:15).

Finally PD 1136, creating the Joint Commission on Local Government Personnel Administration, placed position classification and pay plans of all local governments under national responsibility. Together with the MLG, the commission became the body responsible for the creation of new positions at the local level (Sosmeña 1980:130).

Staffing of Iloilo's city government fluctuated between a low of 1,155 (Sept. 1979) and a peak of 1,637 (June 1980) employees (City of Iloilo 1980:37). In December 1984, the city employed 1,175 persons. Although Iloilo had a smaller staff than the other regional cities, it ranked third in terms of staff-to-population ratio (212:1) (see Table 3.6). What is remarkable, however, is the comparatively low percentage of nonpermanent staff among Iloilo's city employees. While in Iloilo the percentage of temporary and casual workers was only 29.3 percent, it was 41.1 percent in Bacolod, 47.0 percent in Cagayan de Oro and 56.7 percent in Davao (Regional Cities Development Project 1980:21). These nonpermanent positions play a pivotal role in patronage politics. In most Philippine cities, factional or partisan changes go hand in hand with the replacement of many casual employees. The vacancies created in this way enable the new incumbents to reward their rank-and-file supporters with jobs. In Iloilo, not long after her appointment in April 1986, mayor Caram terminated 197 casuals.[22]

However, overstaffing in nonpermanent positions is also a consequence of LOI No. 981 and its de facto ban on hiring personnel. The assessor's offices in Iloilo, Bacolod, and Davao, for instance, were heavily dependent on casual employees for their field operations (RCDP Municipal Management Study 1980:15), which was another reason why collec-

TABLE 3.6 Staffing Pattern of Philippine Regional Cities, by Staff Category

Staff Category	Bacolod City		Cagayan de Oro City		Davao City		Iloilo City	
	N	%	N	%	N	%	N	%
Permanent	852	50.9	684	53.0	1,058	43.3	817	70.7
Temporary	359	21.4	473	36.7	1,384	56.7	138	12.0
Casuals	464	27.7	133	10.3	---	---	200	17.3
Total	1,675	100.0	1,290	100.0	2,442	100.00	1,155	100.0
Population-staff-ratio	157:1		176:1		250:1		212:1	

Source: Regional Cities Development Project, *Municipal Management Study* (Manila: National Economic Development Authority, 1980), p. 21.

tion efficiency was so low in Philippine regional cities (Regional Cities Development Project 1980:15).

Like cities in Malaysia and Thailand, Philippine cities are short of professional and technical staff, especially in key units such as the city planning office and the health department. Although the population-to-staff ratio for professional and technical personnel in Iloilo City is not significantly lower than in Chiang Mai, "administrative productivity" is. This is mainly due to a notorious lack of financial resources and equipment, the *"overpoliticization"* of administrative matters, and a deficient information system. In order to minimize the data processing problems of at least the RCDP, the city government acquired a computer which, however, remained unused due to the lack of trained personnel. In Davao City and Cebu City, electronic data processing facilities were available for assessment services. But here, too, lack of know-how prevented full exploitation of the the facilities. The computers were only used to store the assessed property values, but not to compute tax, prepare tax bills, and process receipts (Regional Cities Development Project 1979:24). Severe problems in record keeping, data collection, and analysis thus persisted in all Philippine regional cities. Lack of analytic capacity strongly restricted their scope of local autonomy.

While city planning in the Philippines leaves greater room for local action than in Thailand, the case of Iloilo nevertheless demonstrates that central government influence on physical and socioeconomic planning at the local level has been considerable in the Philippines as well.

The beginnings of city planning in Iloilo date back to the early 1930s. Apart from the fact that these plans concentrated exclusively on the physical aspects of urban development, city authorities did nothing to implement them. The same happened to a zoning ordinance adopted in

1958 which copied of the zoning laws of Quezon City. New efforts at instituting a planning machinery during the 1960s were shortlived and never reached the implementation stage. As a consequence, urban planning in Iloilo City was a piecemeal, ad hoc process in which applications for building permits and the respective land use were decided on a case-to-case basis by the city council (Iloilo City 1977:7-8).

In 1974, the Department of Local Government and Community Development issued a memorandum calling for the creation of a City Planning and Development Board and a City Planning and Development Staff. Three years later the city released a planning document that, for the first time, deserved its name: the Iloilo City Development Plan 1977-2000. Apart from the newly created planning bodies, several private sector committees participated in the planning process (Iloilo City 1977:9-10). Yet, although local staff did most of the work, city planners remained highly dependent on national agencies in terms of training and technical assistance. Before the planning process started, the entire City Planning and Development Staff underwent a ten-week training course in Manila conducted by the University of the Philippines' Institute of Environmental Planning. Finally, after its completion the plan had to be presented to a panel of reviewers composed of academics and representatives from national agencies at a seminar in Los Baños before it was presented to the City Council for approval (Iloilo City 1977:10). Although the City Planning and Development Staff has been in operation for more than a decade, problems in data collection and analysis still persist. During the plan revision in 1986, city planners frequently turned to the regional NEDA office or the regional offices of other national government agencies for technical assistance.

The experiences in Iloilo City and other regional cities suggest that development projects implemented by the city government did not coincide with those identified in the city development plan (Regional Cities Development Project 1980:19). This may be attributed to the highly fluid nature of project and program priorities in the Philippine policy process. Priorities laid down in planning documents can be changed at any time by the mayor, the city council, and the national government. In the past, political opportunism was one of the most decisive forces determining processes of urban development planning. The planner's role was thus limited to a powerless alibi figure, whose work was instrumentalized by politicians to disguise particularistic policies, to establish some semblance of development-orientedness for public relations purposes, and to attract funds from external sources. Not surprisingly, the City Planning and Development Boards, originally created as planning advisory bodies, became moribund soon after their inception in the mid-1970s and were frequently bypassed even in such important development projects as RCDP (Firmalino 1980:1; Regional Cities Development Project 1980:19).

Especially during the martial-law era, national ad hoc interventions frequently wrought havoc with locally defined development priorities. In Iloilo City, examples of such top-down interferences were the Ministry of Human Settlement's BLISS project[23] (1979) and the *Barangay Brigade* training programs (1980)[24] that diverted sizeable sums from capital projects (Regional Cities Development Project 1980:34). Another nationally controlled body with far-reaching influence on city planning is the Regional Development Council[25] which plays a crucial role in the selection, coordination, and implementation of development projects in the respective region. Finally, the priorities laid down in NEDA's national five- (now six-) year development plans also affect urban planning in Iloilo City to some extent. In the past, however, the impact of NEDA plans was felt to a much lesser extent than pet projects of the inner-circle of the Marcos regime. NEDA had no implemention powers and the agency's plans were frequently subjected to manipulation for the sake of short-term political moves.

National intervention in city planning was also facilitated by the fact that the planning documents stated development priorities and objectives in very broad terms. They appeared as "catch all" categories and were too general as to be translated into concrete policies and projects. They lacked a clear concept of how their objectives were to be implemented and must thus be considered more as declarations of intent than a guide for action.

An analysis of the goals and priorities outlined in the Iloilo City Development Plan 1977-2000 and the Comprehensive Development Plan of Davao City 1979-2000 revealed a bias towards infrastructural and industrial development. Although the Davao City Development Plan propagated a "holistic" development concept, very little was said about how to improve the living conditions of low-income households in the city. On the contrary, both the Iloilo and the Davao development plans contained passages that, in the long run, worsen the precarious situation of the urban poor. While the Davao City Development Plan did not mention the informal economic sector at all, which serves as a pivotal niche of survival for low-income groups, Iloilo's development plan proposed punitive action against the informal sector by calling for the "removal of sidewalk vendors from busy streets". Similarly, calls for "squatter relocation", "measures to control squatting", and the application of the antisquatting law as outlined by PD 772 were more likely to complicate the struggle for survival of the urban poor than to contribute to a "more equitable" urban development.

Although the City Development Plan 1977-2000 was an attempt in comprehensive planning, the physical dimension of planning was still predominant. Moreover, planning is not a continuous process allowing early interventions in the rapidly changing urban environment. In fact, a few years after their preparation the city development plans of Iloilo City, Cagayan de Oro, and Davao were already outdated. Thus, planning was primarily *"reactive"* instead of being *"anticipative"*. It only recorded past developments, but failed to actively steer future urban development patterns.

At first sight, this predominantly top-down pattern of planning is not fully reflected in the survey responses. When asked whether they consider themselves sufficiently consulted during the preparatory stage of long-range national government plans affecting Iloilo, only 35 percent of the respondents felt that they were not sufficiently consulted. 47 percent said that there was sufficient consultation. Lack of consultation was felt most strongly by nonincumbent politicians, whereas the majority of incumbent local politicians and city administrators claimed that they were consulted by national agencies. A closer look at the data, however, reveals that the complaints about national planning intervention in local affairs were mainly aired by long-time city officials. 62.5 percent of city officials (politicians and administrators) with more than three years' experience in local government affairs said that national agencies rarely consulted the city government when they prepared their plans. Most of Iloilo's newly appointed city officials, on the other hand, felt that central-local relations in planning were a two-way process. They based their assessment on experiences made during the brief period they were in office. Their optimistic outlook was influenced by the widespread euphoria in the Aquino camp over what was called "people's power administration" and the president's reiterated assurances of a more transparent governmental process.

When asked how they can influence plans and programs of national government agencies that have an impact on Iloilo City, almost 28 percent of the respondents mentioned "making representations with decision-makers at higher government levels" and about 21 percent "passing of resolutions by the city council" *(Sangguniang Panglungsod)*, while about 17 percent of the respondents suggested that "nothing can be done". The percentage of those who thought that nothing could be done was highest among city administrators and nonincumbent political leaders. Like Chiang Mai's leaders, decision-makers in Iloilo did not opt for militancy in their dealings with superior government levels. Only two respondents recommended the exertion of public pressure via the mass media as a suitable means to influence national government plans.

Major problems also persisted in the field of plan implementation. Coordination among city departments and between city departments and national line agencies was scarcely developed. Land-use control was an area of particular confusion as there was no clear demarcation of competencies between the City Engineer's Office, the Ministry of Public Works and Highways (MPHW), and the Human Settlements Regulatory Commission (HRSC). While the MPWH and the City Engineer's Department were responsible for enforcing the regulations of the *Building Code*, both agencies must coordinate with the HRSC in order to ensure that building permits are compatible with existing land-use ordinances. In practice, however, the MPWH and the City Engineer's Department rarely sought clarification from the HRSC. The strained relations and the noncooperation between these agencies was a major cause of widespread violations of land-use and zoning regulations, with the consequence of uncontrolled development in inner-city areas and ribbon development along the highways on the city's outskirts.

The City and the Societal Linkage Pattern

Due to unfavorable geographic and political factors, the opportunities for an expansion of Iloilo's communication and information network are limited, especially compared with Chiang Mai. Thus, Iloilo did not experience a marked increase in local autonomy due to expanded linkages with its societal environment.

The Communication Infrastructure. Because the Philippines is an archipelago, water transport is the established mode of transport between Iloilo City and other major urban centers of the country. Shipping still predominates in interisland passenger traffic. Iloilo City is linked by regular ferry service to virtually all major ports of the Philippines. Shipping, however, is a rather slow mode of transport. The journey from Iloilo to Manila, for instance, takes approximately thirty-six hours. Improvements in the transport infrastructure were mainly limited to better air transport. The frequency, travel time, and convenience of flights has noticeably improved over the past decade. In 1986, there were twenty-five flights a week from Iloilo City to Manila and eleven flights to Cebu City. Travel time to Manila is approximately one hour. However, there are no direct flights linking Iloilo City with other major urban centers of the Philippines or destinations abroad.

Recent large-scale road construction projects on Panay Island have improved Iloilo's connections with its hinterland. With the financial assistance of the International Bank for Reconstruction and Development (IBRD) and the Asian Development Bank (ADB), more than 590 km of roads have been completed during the 1980s (National Economic and Development Authority 1983:80). Travel times between Iloilo and Panay's other major urban centers such as Roxas City, Kalibo, and San José de Buenaventura have been reduced considerably.

Unlike in Chiang Mai, the upgrading of telecommunication facilities has not made much headway. The population-telephone line ratio decreased only modestly from 42:1 to 28:1 between 1977 and 1985. Although the data are not fully comparable, Iloilo City compared unfavorably with Manila and the other regional cities, except for Davao.[26]

Linkages Between the City and Other Government Units. As the government center of Region VI, Iloilo City provided numerous opportunities for interactions between the city administration and other government units. Between 1971 and 1985 the number of national government agencies with offices in Iloilo increased significantly. While in 1971 forty-seven national government agencies had offices in Iloilo, their number grew to seventy-four in 1985.

The overwhelming majority of the city government's communicative linkages were vertically structured. During the martial-law period they were primarily with cronies of the Marcoses and -- to a lesser degree -- national government line agencies. In most cases the city government was at the receiving end of these central-local communication flows, mainly reacting to initiatives from above. More often such communication was initated for political rather than developmental ends. Central-local interactions aimed primarily at maintaining the political supremacy of the regime.

Although difficult to quantify, it seems that the improved transportation and communication infrastructure strengthened vertical interactions. There were relatively frequent contacts between Manila-based political and administrative actors and the city government. Although many respondents failed to answer the respective interview questions, the data suggest that national officials travelled to Iloilo City more often than vice versa. Intergovernmental contacts were controlled by the mayor and the vice mayor. Department heads had less diversified contacts which focussed on their national line agency. Given the hierarchical structure of the central bureaucracy, these interactions occurred mainly in a top-down manner.

Central dominance in intergovernmental interactions was not effectively counterbalanced by a well-developed network of horizontal linkages. A potential pressure group of local governments, the Provincial Governors' and City Mayors' League, was unable to exert such a func-

tion and was remote-controlled by the MLG. The league had no own office and rarely met. Its day-to-day administrative work was carried out
by MLG staff. The annual conventions largely had the character of a social event and revolved around the induction rites for the newly elected
officers of the league. Even as a vehicle for the exchange of information,
the effectiveness of the league was negligible. In this respect, there were
striking similarities to the Thai case.

Horizontal bonds can also be formed through single- or multipurpose
bodies with members from neighboring cities or municipalities, for the
solution of common problems. In Iloilo City, such an example of intermunicipal cooperation was the Metro Iloilo Water District (MIWD),
which managed the water supply of Iloilo City and four adjacent municipalities. Although, as will be shown later, the efficiency of the MIWD
was low, the body's performance was further hampered by political
squabbles between the city mayor of Iloilo and the four municipal mayors over appointments to the MIWD's board.[27]

Political parties also shape the linkage pattern into which a city is integrated. While political parties had a centralizing effect even prior to
martial law, the creation of the Kilusang Bagong Lipunan-Party (KBL) in
1978 helped strengthen the vertical dimension of central-local interactions. That recruitment of the local party leadership was firmly in the
hands of national party bodies, gave them much influence on the course
of local politics. The top-heavy Philippine party structure thus further
curbed local autonomy. A new picture, however, began to appear after
the collapse of the Marcos regime. The disintegration of the KBL has
given rise to the emergence of numerous regionally or locally-based
splinter parties. Under the conditions of such a fragmented, *"floating"*
party system, political parties became a vehicle for strengthening the
position of local leaders vis-à-vis national political actors. However, as
far as Iloilo City is concerned, this trend is felt less strongly than elsewhere, as the struggle for political supremacy in the city was fought out
by nationwide-organized political groups such as the UNIDO and the
remnants of the KBL. Yet, the anticipated change towards greater
"localism" must not be mistaken for an increase of local autonomy. Its
exclusive beneficiaries are the members of entrenched local oligarchies.

Iloilo City is the headquarters of the military Regional Command, Region VI, and the Philippine Constabulary (PC) also maintains installations in the city. Although difficult to quantify, it must be assumed that
the military presence has a limiting effect on Iloilo's local autonomy.
Through the INP the PC set its own priorities in law-and-order policies,
which frequently contradicted those of the city government and for sev-

eral years in the late 1970s and early 1980s even the mayor and his clos-
est aide had a military background.

Linkages to Semi- or Nongovernmental Institutions. A well developed, locally-based network of interest groups that provides information and voluntary services to the community may be another counterbalancing force against central dominance In fact, as the major urban
center on Panay Island with a long history of educational, economic,
and political activities, there is a broad range of voluntary organizations
in Iloilo City. In 1970, a directory of civic clubs and organizations listed
thirty-seven major voluntary associations. Although the list was by no
means complete, it appears that there was a concentration of professional and civic groups. Although no data were available which could
provide an accurate picture of the more recent structure of voluntary
associations, there has been a proliferation of groups. It may serve as a
rough indicator that major civic groups such as the Lions and Rotary
Clubs now have three or four branches in Iloilo City.

Unlike in Chiang Mai, a number of linkages between the city government and the private sector, which could provide the city government with additional information and know-how, do exist in Iloilo City.
Some of them have even been institutionalized, such as the City Planning and Development Board with ten task forces composed of private
sector representatives. Unfortunately, this pool of information was
tapped only once when the city government prepared the City Development Plan 1977-2000. Thereafter, the board ceased to function until
the Aquino-appointed city government revitalized the body in April
1986.

Although hardly quantifiable, the interviews suggest that interest
groups actively sought access to the city administration and its officials.
This may to some extent be explained by the fact that in the Philippines
interactions between the city governments and the national government
are more direct than, for instance, in Thailand, where the provincial
government mediates. Nevertheless, despite these contacts it seems that
voluntary associations in Iloilo City were more involved in personality-
related than in developmental issues.

A likewise largely untapped resource of know-how that could be utilized to the advantage of urban development projects is Iloilo's educational institutions. At least two of the city's four universities, the University of the Philippines in the Visayas and the Central Philippine University, could provide badly needed expertise in the field of management, data collection, and analysis. A closer cooperation between the
city government and these universities could thus make a considerable

contribution to improved planning, monitoring, and evaluation capacities.

The pervasive influence of supralocally organized business conglomerates on local autonomy can be well illustrated in the case of Iloilo City. Before the Second World War, all major sugar exporters in the country had warehouses and offices in Iloilo from where they directed their trade operations. But technological changes since the 1930s and violent strife between labor unions over control of Iloilo's waterfront caused many trading houses to relocate their businesses from Iloilo (Leichter 1975, 1976; McCoy 1977, 1982). But even Iloilo's political elite increasingly moved the focus of their economic activities away from the city. While in 1940 most businesses of the Lopez family were located in Iloilo (McCoy 1977:165), with the acquisition of the Manila Electric Company (MERALCO) and various media enterprises their economic interests had shifted to Manila by the 1960s. In consequence, local political conditions, which created an unfavorable business climate, and the nationwide economic-cum-political interests of Iloilo's elite became more important criteria than employment generation and economic growth at home.

Political Participation

Iloilo City politics are characterized by a high level of competitiveness and "mobilized" political participation. Only during the initial phase of martial law did open political competition cease as a result of the regime's depoliticization strategies. This, however, did not mean that political competition came to a complete halt. Beneath the surface political competition continued, but was confined to squabbles between local stalwarts of the regime. Political mobilization likewise came under the complete control of the regime. Mobilization campaigns during martial law were conducted only occasionally on the eve of referenda or state ceremonies and served solely to renew the regime's legitimacy. After 1980, however, the intensity of political competition and mobilization grew rapidly and reached new heights in the two years preceding the collapse of the Marcos regime and immediately after the installation of the Aquino administration.

Competition and Political Mobilization in Iloilo City

In a political system dominated by political parties with a conspicuous lack of ideological orientation the main motivation for political action is to fill public posts (Landé 1965; Laquian 1966). It is evident that in such a *"spoils system"* elections play a pivotal role in leadership recruitment and thus constitute the climax in the political process. The next section will therefore focus on local elections and the way they influence political competition and mobilization in Iloilo City.

Political Competition, Mobilization, and Local Elections, 1955-1986. Like elsewhere in the Philippines, political competition and mobilization in Iloilo City have always revolved around elections. Local elections provided grassroots leaders with an opportunity to gain a foothold in the city government. Prior to martial law local elections were held every four years. Local elections alternated with presidential and congressional elections and took place at mid-term of the presidential tenure. At stake in Iloilo City were ten councillor posts as well as the positions of mayor and vice-mayor. After the imposition of martial law in 1972, local elections were suspended. It took until 1980, one year before the formal lifting of martial law, before new local elections were held. At the same time, the term of local officials was extended from four to six years.

The competitiveness of urban politics in Iloilo is reflected in endless factional disputes that became most evident during election time. Local elections were contested by at least two, sometimes three or even even more factions. The Nacionalista Party, Iloilo's dominant political party throughout most of the postwar period, continuously split into factions between 1955 and 1971. Factional rifts usually grew out of incompatible supralocal interests of rival party leaders, and were an expression of pronounced disagreement over the nomination of candidates for the party ticket in local elections.

Factional fluctuation within city politics was considerable. Between 1947 and 1955 the city government was completely controlled by the Lopez-Ledesma faction, which at that time was affiliated with the Liberal Party. In the 1955 local elections, Rodolfo Ganzon, a young populist wrested control of the city government from the Lopez-Ledesma faction (McCoy 1977:516). The Ganzon machine dominated urban politics in Iloilo until the 1963 elections after which -- as a result of factional realignments -- his influence on Iloilo politics began to wane. Since 1963 the factional power equation has changed at each election. In the 1967 local elections, the Ganzon candidate, Ganzon's brother Carlos, was defeated by Reinerio Ticao, a former ally, who became the standard bearer of the Lopez faction.[28] Factional dominance changed again in 1971 when, this time under the LP banner, Rodolfo Ganzon staged an impressive comeback. Ganzon was elected city mayor and his ticket made a complete sweep of all other elective positions. The newly established Ganzon supremacy was, however, shortlived, because immediately after the imposition of martial law Marcos dismantled Iloilo's factions. Yet, even Marcos' emergency rule could not eradicate the factional structure of Iloilo's politics. Factionalism began to resurface in the 1980 local elections. At the time it was widely believed in Iloilo that the NP ticket of mayoral candidate Ticao was tacitly supported by Lopez resources.

In the final years of the Marcos era factional competition in Iloilo increased tremendously. The political unrest in the aftermath of the Aquino assassination placed the Marcos administration increasingly on the defensive. Faced with defections and harsh criticism from abroad, the regime embarked on a see-saw strategy that alternated indecisively between spells of repression and cautious, yet far too late, attempts at political liberalization. At the same time the gradual disintegration of the regime encouraged oppositionist activities. Political leaders muzzled under martial law reappeared on the political scene. With a view to the local elections scheduled for 1986, Rodolfo Ganzon, for instance, began to rebuild his shattered political machine as early as 1983.

Factional competition intensified after the collapse of the Marcos regime in February 1986. In one of its first moves, the Aquino administration purged all local governments of KBL officials and replaced them with Aquino supporters. Although local elections, originally scheduled for 1986, were repeatedly postponed until January 1988, the new local officials were appointed on a temporary basis and given the status of Officers-in-Charge (OICs). On a nationwide scale, the competition over OIC appointments stepped up bitter rivalries between UNIDO and PDP-Laban, the two major coalition parties forming the Aquino government, which eventually led to a fall-out between UNIDO president Salvador Laurel and PDP-Laban chief and Minister of Local Government, Aquilino Pimentel. Laurel and, in particular, UNIDO secretary-general Rene Espina accused Pimentel of abusing his ministerial powers to expand his party's local base by favoring PDP-Laban members in the OIC-appointments. It should be noted, however, that at the time field research was conducted, the UNIDO complaints were not supported by empirical evidence. As of early July 1986, only twelve of seventy-one appointed gubernatorial OICs and twelve of fifty-four city mayoral OICs belonged to PDP-Laban.

While on the national level the OIC row erupted as a conflict between two component parties of the Aquino government, in Iloilo the ensuing competition for control over the city government was exclusively an internal UNIDO affair. No less than three factions competed for the mayoralty and city councillor positions: the Caram-faction, led by a veteran politician, former Congressman, and member of the *Batasang Pambansa*, Fermin Z. Caram, the Ticao faction, and the Ledesma faction. It was the Caram faction, a long-established political dynasty in Iloilo City, which finally prevailed over the UNIDO rival factions. Rosa "Tita" Caram, wife of the faction leader, was appointed mayoral OIC and nine supporters were appointed city councillors. Only one city councillor came from the Ticao faction, while Celso Ledesma turned down an offer of the post of vice-mayor.

With local elections expected some time in 1987, at least five major factions girded for the electoral contest: the three UNIDO factions mentioned above, the Ganzon faction, supported by the remnants of the KBL and other rightwing elements, and, finally, a heterogeneous group of politicians with roots in the so-called cause-oriented groups or *"Parliament of the Streets"*, which styled itself the progressive force on Iloilo's political scene.

Independents, however, could not capitalize on the highly competitive political climate. Although their share of candidates was sizeable in the 1971 and 1980 elections, accounting for 19.0 percent and 15.4 percent respectively, their electoral performance was dismal. While in 1971 they received 3.2 percent of the vote, by 1980 their share was as low as 1.2 percent. Only one independent (1967) has ever been elected. Independent candidates simply lack the resources available to party or faction-supported candidates.

Another feature of political competitiveness in Iloilo is the long duration of election campaigns. The campaign usually starts one year before elections, and sometimes even earlier. Prospective candidates begin gearing up their campaign machine by enlisting subleaders, mobilizing their supporters by daily house-to-house visits and establishing links to patrons at higher party echelons. This is of particular importance for securing nomination on the party ticket and to generate sufficient campaign funds.

The competitiveness of Iloilo politics is also demonstrated by the high candidate-seat-ratio which, except for the 1980 elections, is around three to one. However, as scattered data suggest, this ratio seems to be lower than the average for Philippine cities. Data of the Commission of Elections (COMELEC) for the 1959 and 1963 local elections indicate candidate-seat-ratios above four to one, and in the 1988 local election it was nearly ten to one. Cities thus displayed the highest ratio among local governments, suggesting that competition for local offices is highest in urban politics.

The high level of competitiveness is further reflected by the low percentage of reelected candidates. Since 1963 only 28 percent of the incumbents have been reelected. The highest percentage was in 1967 (41.7 percent) and the lowest in 1971 (16.7 percent).

The large majority usually won by the victorious faction both in terms of votes and seats does not contradict the view of a highly competitive political culture. The domination of the city council by the winning faction is often shortlived, ending mid-term as a consequence of factional realignments on the eve of congressional and presidential elections. Thus, although the winning faction may enjoy a clear majority at the beginning of a term, council politics again became highly competitive after realignments.

Election violence is another feature of a highly charged political atmosphere. Although no figures were available for Iloilo City, national statistics show an increasing death toll in election-related incidents. In the 1959 local elections 24 politically motivated deaths were recorded; their number rose to 29 in 1963, 128 in 1967, 200 in 1971, and 400 in 1980, and there were at least 144 in 1988 (Tutay 1969:8; Wolters 1983:167).

Voter turnout has often been taken as an indicator of political participation. But such a view overlooks that in developing countries electoral participation is based less on an "autonomous" decision of the individual citizen, but forced upon him as a result of structural dependencies on powerful patrons. Participation of this type may therefore be better termed "mobilized" participation, i.e. "activity that is designed by someone other than the actor to influence decision-making" (Hunt-ing-ton/Nelson 1976:7-10).

Electoral mobilization in Iloilo far exceeded the levels known in Chiang Mai. Turnout in local elections averaged 80.0 percent between 1947 and 1980. It was thus slightly lower than the national average (80.87), but considerably above the average for all chartered cities (1947-1971: 74.7 percent). Turnout was also higher in local than in na-tional elections. Between 1946 and 1969 the average turnout in national elections was 78.2 percent in Iloilo City. It was thus higher than the average turnout for all chartered cities (73.3 percent), but slightly lower than the national average (78.4 percent).[29]

The 1980 local elections deviated from this pattern. At 73.9 percent, turnout was markedly lower. On the one hand, such a low turnout reflected the low degree of legitimacy accorded by many voters to elections under the auspices of authoritarianism, but, on the other hand, it signaled the imminent decline of a regime increasingly unable to mobilize the population. Although election fraud was by no means unknown in premartial-law times, the 1980 election marked a new height in this respect. Opposition chances were systematically curtailed by a short campaign period, bloc voting, vote buying, and the instrumentalization of the bureaucracy.

Although President Marcos had declared earlier in 1979 that he might hold local elections within eighteen months as a further step towards "normalization", which -- according to him -- had begun in 1978 with the *Interim Batasang Pambansa* (Interim National Assembly) elections, he caught the opposition totally off-guard, when, on 15 December 1979, he announced local elections for 30 January 1980. Marcos told a stunned audience that it was the "worsening world situation" that compelled him to announce these "snap local elections". Otherwise "outside developments on later dates may not warrant the holding of any election at all". Candidates were given only two weeks to file their candidacy. With the campaign period reduced to thirty days, there was no time left for a divided opposition to organize.[30] The KBL, on the other hand, was well prepared and could get its electoral machine into high gear within a short time.

Bloc voting was another device to ensure the supremacy of the regime's candidates. It was a voting system under which a voter, by simply writing the name of a political party on the proper space in the ballot, automatically voted for all official candidates of the respective party. However, the privilege of bloc voting was limited to duly accredited political parties. A party was eligible for accreditation, if, in the preceding election, it was registered and had polled at least the third highest number of votes. On a nationwide basis this regulation would have excluded all parties except the KBL from bloc voting. That the Nacionalista Party (NP) was finally accredited as a second national political party was due only to the regime's concern for reaping maximum political legitimacy from the elections. Although it was a registered party at the time of the 1978 IBP elections, it did not field own candidates. The NP was merely one of the constituent parties of the then newly formed KBL. It was only shortly before the 1980 elections that, with the obvious consent of the regime, a NP faction headed by José Roy, who was known as a close Marcos ally, broke away from the KBL and constituted itself as a nationwide "opposition" party. The rationale behind the creation of this "fake opposition" was primarily dictated by the intention to make the 1980 local elections appear a truly democratic exercise providing a genuine choice between "alternative" political forces. At that time the regime had increasingly come under fire from abroad, especially from the US, which strongly criticized Marcos' rigid authoritarianism with its concomitant curtailment of basic civic rights and flagrant violations of human rights. A credible election would thus have relieved the regime of pressures to liberalize the political system. Apart from this, the NP accreditation was a deliberate attempt to detract votes from "genuine" opposition parties without sacrificing the democratic facade of the election. In view of the stiff competition within the KBL for slots on the party ticket, the NP provided "KBL surplus candidates" with a chance to run in the elections. It was expected that a considerable percentage of them would return to the KBL fold, if elected. On the other hand, major groups representing the moderate opposition received accredited party status only on a regional basis: Laban, which subsequently withdrew from the election, in Metro Manila, Bicol Saro in Region V, Pusyon Bisaya in Region VII, the Mindanao Alliance (MA) in Regions X and XI, and the Concerned Citizen Aggrupation (CCA) in Region IX. The National Union for Liberation (NUL) received no accreditation.[31]

Bloc voting provided good opportunities for manipulating the outcome of the elections. First, due to the relatively complicated rules for bloc voting, a high number of opposition votes would get lost in areas with lower voter sophistication. For instance, all votes for opposition parties without accredited status were to be rendered void, if only the name of the respective party appeared in the ballot instead of the names of the individual candidates of this party. Second, it is more convenient and simpler to fill in only a party's name than to list the names of individual candidates. Third, as most opposition parties were not able to field complete party slates everywhere, the space left under the heading of "individual voting" could easily be used to tamper with the election returns.[32] Finally, the bloc voting system went against the fact that local elections in the Philippines have always been determined by the personality factor. Voters usually favored candidates whom they knew personally. As a result, they rarely decided in favor of straight party slates, instead splitting the tickets of different parties (Wolters 1983:165).

The 1980 elections were overshadowed by heavy spending of the KBL candidates and widespread fraud at the canvassing stage. Candidates of the 1980 elections who were interviewed by the author claimed that in Iloilo City alone, the KBL spent more than ten million Pesos for vote-buying and other election-related activities.[33] Indeed, a content analysis of major Philippine newspapers confirmed that large amounts of money were released by the government in order to bolster the election prospects of the KBL candidates. After the election, an avalanche of protests rolled over the Commission of Elections (COMELEC). There were so many complaints against the election results that the Ministry of Justice had to create a task force for handling these cases. Until 1984 at least 209 protests were recorded.[34] In Iloilo City the defeated mayoral candidate, former city mayor Reinerio Ticao, was involved in a protracted election dispute which was finally turned down by the COMELEC. Ticao particularly denounced the statistical improbabilities in the

Table 3.7 Results of Local Elections in Iloilo City, by Factions

Party/Faction	1967ᵃ	1971	1980
LP Lopez faction	55.9	27.3	---
NP Ticao faction	---	20.5	---
NP Ganzon faction	33.5	---	---
NP	---	---	44.2
LP	10.6	49.0	---
KBL	---	---	54.6
Independents	---	3.2	1.2

ᵃFigures for vice mayor race only.

Source: Calculated from *The Visayan Tribune,* 20 November 1967, 15 November 1971, and 4 February 1980.

election results. According to him there were *barangays* where more votes were cast for the KBL than there were registered voters.

The lopsidedness of the 1980 local elections was clearly reflected in the election results. Nationwide the KBL won 81 percent of the positions at stake at the provincial, city, and municipal level. Sixty-eight of seventy-three governorships, fifty-two of fifty-nine city mayoralties and 1,187 of 1,501 municipal mayoralties went to the KBL (Ocampo and Panganiban 1985:28). Among the other twenty-two competing parties, only the NP won a noteworthy share of mandates (1,222 or 7.6 percent of the total seats).

In Iloilo province no election contest took place in seventeen out of forty-six municipalities. The NP as the major "opposition" was able to field candidates only in twenty-two municipalities and in Iloilo City itself.[35] In the end, NP candidates won the mayoralties in five towns, while in two others independents prevailed. In Iloilo City the number of candidates and turnout were the lowest since 1955. Yet, although all the odds were against it, the NP-ticket received more than 44 percent of the votes.[36] Thus, ironically, the 1980 election ended with the narrowest margin of votes between winner and loser since 1963 (See Table 3.7). This may not only be taken as another indication of the waning popularity of the martial-law regime, but also of the fact that even authoritarianism could not suppress political competition in Iloilo City. The "latent" competitiveness that could be observed in the 1980 election became more "manifest" after the regime's grip on power weakened in the aftermath of the Aquino assassination.

In the final assessment, the 1980 local election must be viewed as an internal houseclearing exercise of the ruling KBL which, in addition, helped to provide the regime with fresh legitimacy (Rüland 1982a:34). In

terms of democratic substance, however, the election was a farce. That
the election mainly served as a device to replace controversial stalwarts
of the KBL could be seen in the sizeable number of incumbents who
were dropped from the official KBL party line-up: thirteen out of seventy-three provincial governors, thirteen out of fifty-nine city mayors,
and 400 out of 1,501 municipal mayors failed to gain KBL endorsement.[1]
In Iloilo City, three KBL candidates were first timers in the political
arena, while six others were appointed councillors and subsequently
included on the KBL ticket after a major shake-up in the city council
four months before the elections.

Political Competition and Mobilization
in Everyday Politics, 1955-1986

In the pre-martial-law era political competitiveness decreased
markedly after local elections. Mobilization reached an even lower level,
with the notable exception of the presidential and congressional election
campaigns at the local officials' mid-term. National elections prompted
local party stalwarts to activate their political machines in support of
aligned national politicians, since the outcome of the elections had far-
reaching repercussions on their own position in the local arena. However, as has been shown in the previous section, the mobilization level,
if measured in terms of voter turnout, did not reach the same high level
as in local elections.

The political dynamics before and after national elections were a major reason why even large majorities of a party or a faction in the local
council were highly instable. In their struggle to win as many local allies
as possible, contenders for national offices instigated strong intraparty
or intrafactional competition that frequently led to realignments in the
local arena. In 1961 six city councillors originally elected on a NP-ticket
switched to the LP after it won the 1961 presidential elections.[2] During
the 1963-1967 term five councillors of the NP-Ganzon faction changed
sides by aligning themselves with the NP-Lopez faction.[3] Lopez influence in Iloilo got a great boost by the triumph of NP candidate Ferdinand E. Marcos and his running mate, Fernando Lopez, in the 1965
presidential contest.

Between elections, the city council formed the stage for political conflict. Although this did not change significantly after the imposition of
martial law, conflicts were less open. 47 percent of the survey respondents -- fewer than in Chiang Mai -- said that political conflicts were
usually fought behind the scenes in Iloilo.

Although local elections were suspended after 1972, local councils
continued to exist. The regime realized that an abolition of the country's

more than 1,600 local councils posed great dangers that might seriously disturb its consolidation. The turbulences created by such a measure became particularly evident after the downfall of the Marcos regime, when the newly installed Aquino administration immediately began replacing all except for a few of the country's more than 16,000 local officials. The resistance of the incumbents was so strong that it paralyzed local governments for months.

Following the declaration of martial law, the Marcos regime removed from office only those local officials whom it perceived as actual or potential opposition leaders with mass appeal. Otherwise there were no changes in the composition of the local councils till the end of 1975. In the February 1975 referendum an appointive system was adopted for the period following the term of the incumbent local officials that expired on 31 December 1975. Thereafter, four categories of local officials were gradually replaced: (1) politically unreliable officials; (2) losers of power struggles within the regime's camp; (3) local officials who fell into disgrace with the first couple and/or its cronies; and (4) officials who had become a liability for the regime.

Most of these officials were purged in early 1976 and between 1978 and 1979. But scattered data suggest that only about 25 percent of local officials were affected by these two purges. In 1976, four city mayors and nine provincial governors were among the substituted local officials. Williams reported that between 1972 and 1978 only 8 percent of the mayors in his 214 sample municipalities were replaced and an additional 18 percent between May 1978 and December 1979 (Williams 1981:264). Local officials in Iloilo City were not spared by these purges. Immediately after the proclamation of martial law, city mayor Ganzon was ousted and jailed. In April 1976, Ganzon's successor, Francisco C. Garganera, was replaced by Zafiro Ledesma, who himself was replaced three years later by Luis C. Herrera. Ledesma lost out in a protracted conflict with Fermin Z. Caram, at the time Iloilo's KBL representative in the Interim Batasan Pambansa (IBP), over the ousting of city treasurer, Romeo Manikan, a protégé of Assemblyman Caram. Finally, in September 1979, six city councillors were replaced after some of them had publicly attacked the new mayor.[40]

Except for the NCR, no marked changes in the functions of the local councils were instituted. The city councils retained their legislative functions including the powers of passing ordinances and resolutions as well as approving the annual budget. However, through PD 826, the regime was able to stifle political competition among local councillors and to exert greater control over council activities. Apart from renaming them *Sangguniang Bayans* (in municipalities) and *Sangguniang Panglung-*

sods (in cities), PD 826 built in corporatist elements into the local councils (Stauffer 1977). Council membership was expanded by ex-officio members (*barangay* captains and leaders of the *barangay* youth organization *Kabataang Barangay*) as well as hand-picked presidential appointees from the agricultural and industrial sectors. As a result of these changes, membership of local councils expanded to twice or three times the size in 1977 (Rüland 1982a:107). For the 1980 elections, however, composition of the local councils changed again as council membership was scaled down considerably. Depending on size and status, cities had between six and twelve elected councillors. In addition, the presidents of the local *Association of Barangay Captains (Katipunan ng mga Barangay)* and of the *barangay* youth organization as well as two presidential appointees from the industrial and agricultural sectors served as ex-officio members. This regulation was later incorporated into the *Local Government Code* (Sect. 173).

The creation of the *Sangguniang Bayans* (SBs) and *Sangguniang Panglungsods* (SPs) has been a major source of controversy in Philippine local government literature. A number of authors (Sultan 1976; Symons 1984; Espina 1984) uncritically accepted the regime's propaganda rhetoric, which depicted the SBs in glowing colours as a "great leap forward" in the search for an indigenous, participatory political system. Williams was somewhat more cautious, admitting that the SBs may not have contributed much in terms of participatory substance. However, he went on to state that the more important issue affecting the SBs was the question of whether they opened up new opportunities for citizen participation, which he answered in the affirmative (Williams 1981:283).

Such assessments overlook the fact that the creation of SBs was a shrewd move by the regime to outmaneuver politically unreliable incumbents elected on an opposition ticket in 1971. In Iloilo City the entire city council was affiliated with the LP opposition. Although many of these local officials had swiftly adjusted their rhetoric to the new political circumstances and formally sided with the authoritarian regime, local councils nevertheless continued to be institutional pockets of latent resistance to the martial-law administration. Through the numerical expansion of the council membership noncooperative local officials were outnumbered and, hence, politically neutralized without creating the turbulences that a wholesale purge would have caused (Rüland 1982a:107 and 1986a). At the same time, the SBs installed local officials, who did not owe their office to political skills, but entirely to the regime. Politically independent personalities were gradually replaced. Not surprisingly, four out of the six councillors, who were replaced in Iloilo City in September 1979, were seasoned politicians controlling sizeable political machines. Moreover, in other cases, like in Zamboanga City, the regime was even able to change the majority in the local council with the help of these ex-officio members. Soon after the 1980 local elections, which had established a seven-to-one majority for the oppositionist Concerned Citizens Aggrupation (CCA), two councillors of the CCA defected to the KBL. Thus, as all four ex-officio members were staunch supporters of the regime, the CCA suddenly found itself in the minority, although the party had won the local election.[41]

But despite these depoliticizing moves, local councils remained a center of political activity. Council activities became all the more lively, the more the Marcos regime lost its political cohesiveness. In Iloilo City, meetings of the council were much more frequent than in Chiang Mai. In 1984, for example, the city council held fifty regular and three special sessions, approving 235 ordinances and 378 resolutions. In the preceding year, it had been even more prolific, passing 196 ordinances and 685 resolutions (City of Iloilo 1984).

However, these facts were only partially reflected in the survey responses. When called upon to assess the city council's activities, a partisan bias dominated among the respondents. 92 percent of the newly appointed UNIDO-councillors rated "their" council's activities as either "very active" (53.85 percent) or "active" (38.5 percent), but had a low regard for the preceding KBL-controlled council. Only 23 percent of the incumbent local politicians ranked the previous council as "very active" or "active". On the other hand, nonincumbent politicians, 70 percent of whom were either KBL-members or former local officials, gave a higher ranking to the previous council. 60 percent of this group were of the opinion that in the past Iloilo's local council was "very active" or "active", while only 30 percent were convinced that the present council was "active". Not a single respondent of this group stated that the present council is "very active". However, if the responses of the city administrators are included, it would seem that a majority of Iloilo's local decision-makers thought that council activities increased after the takeover of the Aquino administration and the appointment of a new city council. Somewhat more than 70 percent of total respondents stated that the present city council is "very active" or at least "active", while only 35 percent passed the same judgement on previous councils. It must be noted, however, that a considerable percentage of respondents gave no answer -- especially local administrators and nonincumbent politicians.

During martial law and the period immediately after, political competition in Iloilo was restricted to rivalries between supporters of the regime. These conflicts usually spilled over into the city council and split its seemingly cohesive membership into factions. One of the rare conflicts that gained some publicity was the Herrera-Caram conflict in 1982 and 1983. It was a conflict that displayed typical features of the traditional Filipino value system, since it evolved from an alleged violation of the *"utang na loob"* (debt of gratitude) principle. Caram had supported Herrera's appointment as city mayor in April 1979 and backed him in the 1980 local elections.[42] Herrera, on the other hand failed to reinstate Caram's protégé, former city treasurer Romeo Manikan, who was ousted by Herrera's predecessor. Obviously in an attempt to exert political pressure on Herrera, Caram filed a case against him with the *Tanodbayan* (the Philippine anticorruption court) for alleged misuse of public funds and falsification of public documents in 1982. By the end of the year, the *Tanodbayan* had dropped the case because of "insufficiency of evidence".[43] Caram responded by filing a motion for reconsideration, but later withdrew the charges upon political pressure exerted by President Marcos himself. This, however, did not have a restraining effect on the conflict, which escalated after Herrera dismissed two other city officials linked to Caram. One of these officers and former city mayor Ticao retaliated by initiating a move for the recall[44] of Herrera.[45] It was widely speculated that the mastermind behind this move was assemblyman Caram.[46] The action, however, fizzled out, as it did not obtain the necessary minimum of 25 percent of registered voters, although the organizers claimed more than a year later that they had collected 36,000 signatures.[47]

In the meantime, the conflict between Caram and Herrera reached a new stage. After Caram fell out with KBL Region VI chairman Roberto S. Benedicto, who had vehemently opposed Caram's nomination on the KBL party slate in the 1984 *Batasang Pambansa* elections, and after Caram's victory on the UNIDO-ticket, the Caram-Herrera conflict turned into a proxy fight between the regime and the UNIDO opposition. Caram's attacks on Herrera played on local themes but aimed at the regional and national political leadership.

In the aftermath of the Aquino assassination, political competition and mobilization intensified. Moreover, as the Caram-Herrera conflict has shown, it went beyond the confines of the KBL. Mobilization reached broader segments of the population and was comparable only to the period leading up to martial law. Like other major urban areas in the Philippines, Iloilo City became a center of oppositionist activity, although to a lesser extent than Manila, Cebu, and Davao. New forms of political activity emerged. The so-called *"Parliament of the Streets"* and the *"cause-oriented groups"*, both of which grew out of the Aquinomovement, introduced militant street politics to Iloilo City. This "New Left" had a considerable following among the educated urban middle-class, the clergy, the students, the intelligentsia and, to a lesser extent, the urban poor. Between 1981 and 1986 at least seven major demonstrations were recorded in Iloilo City -- most of them sponsored by the cause-oriented groups, although in 1983 and early 1984 the UNIDO too played an important role as an organizer of rallies. The climax of street politics was the BAYAN-organized three-day *"Welgang Bayan"* (transport strike) which brought to a standstill 70 percent of transport on Panay.[48] But as the unsuccessful bid for the recall of Herrera had already shown, it was not local political themes, but national issues that mobilized the population. Foremost among these was the call to depose the Marcos regime, which grew tremendously after the Aquino assassination.

The Marcos years, with their repression, militarization, increasing impoverishment, "closed shop" politics, and the vanishing hope of substantial socioeconomic reforms, produced a fertile breeding ground for a radical counterelite that worked towards a violent overthrow of the Marcos regime and, subsequently, the oligarchical rule of the Aquino government. As the high capacity of Filipinos to sustain pain and hardship was overstrained in the Marcos years, a nationwide revolutionary movement could emerge under the leadership of the Communist Party of the Philippines (CPP) and its military arm, the New People's Army (NPA). In the mid-1980s the NPA was able to expand its military base on Panay Island considerably. While the bulk of NPA operations took place in the countryside, in recent years the CPP has attempted to penetrate the urban arena as well. To this end, links have been fostered between the revolutionary forces and urban-based, semilegal front organizations such as the National Democratic Front (NDF), cause-oriented groups, and radical labor unions. The NPA's military operations also increasingly extended into urban Iloilo, as several shooting and bombing incidents in 1986 and 1987 demonstrated. As long as the Aquino government does not address urgent socioeconomic problems such as the highly inegalitarian land distribution, and as long as the economy does not recover strongly, violent forms of political competition between the forces of the old order and a fundamentalist opposition will add another dimension of conflict to urban politics in Iloilo.

Causes of Political Competitiveness and Mobilization

One of the main reasons for the high level of political competitiveness in Iloilo were the close links between the local and the national political arena. Especially in the pre-martial-law period, politicians from Iloilo such as Thomas Confesor, Fernando Lopez, Oscar Ledesma, Rufino Hechanova, and Rodolfo Ganzon occupied high-ranking government positions and had a determining influence on the course of national politics. Yet, even such leaders of a national stature strongly depended on well-organized local party machines for the mobilization of votes in national contests. As their mobilization capacity diminished with increasing distance from their own bastion, voter mobilization on their home-turf had to be maximized and opposition eliminated to the farthest possible extent. This implied that their party or faction had to control as many local governments as possible within their perimeter of influence. National party leaders thus went a long way to ensure that they had a decisive say in the recruitment of local party stalwarts. As a result, intraparty interactions were shaped in the same top-down manner as were central-local relations in the bureaucracy.

Prior to martial law, national party juntas nominated Iloilo's mayoral candidates. Provincial leaders, depending on their access to the national party leadership, had some recommendatory influence. However, the local party conventions that eventually proclaimed the candidates, merely acclaimed decisions made elsewhere. The rank-and-file party membership thus had little say in the nomination process. Under martial law, central influence on candidate selection intensified. In the 1980 local elections, the KBL Central Committee headed by President Marcos handpicked the party's mayoral candidates for the whole country. Following the proposal of Roberto S. Benedicto, the KBL chairman of Region VI and one of the most powerful Marcos cronies, the committee nominated Luis C. Herrera as the KBL candidate for Iloilo.

While the high mobilization level of Iloilo politics is strongly influenced by national party competition, the structure of political parties in the Philippines also encourages competition. It has already been mentioned that Philippine parties are "unsteady coalitions of political factions and individuals whose primary interest is seeing their candidates win electoral contests so that they can get access to public offices and resources" (Laquian 1965:336).

There was very little ideological or programmatic commitment on the part of Philippine parties. As a result, differences between parties were purely nominal, giving rise to what Landé has called a system of "identical political parties" (Landé 1965:40). Party allegiance was correspondingly low, and changes of party affiliation frequent. Accordingly, switching of party affiliation was not negatively sanctioned, but seen rather as a pragmatic move dictated by circumstances in pursuance of the overriding objective of political activity: the access, maintenance or expansion of one's power base. An extreme example of such political opportunism was the frequent realignments of Iloilo's major factions prior to the 1953 national elections. The Zulueta faction changed party affiliation no less than four times within a seven-month period, while their opponents, the Lopez/Ledesma faction, made two realignments (McCoy 1977:516). It goes without saying that the permanently changing power configurations at higher levels of the political system left a marked imprint on the local actors. They put extreme pressure on local leaders to make the right move to strengthen -- or at least not endanger -- their position within the local arena. At the same time, supralocal leaders were faced with the necessity to win over enough local leaders in order to beat the rival faction in the next election. It is evident that in such a volatile party system, political loyalties were shortlived. Hence, politics must be viewed as an arena in which atomized political entities competed against each other. The more fragmented the political structure, the more competitive became local politics.

The importance of supralocal politics for the local arena is further reflected in the survey data. Significantly more members of Iloilo's decision-making elite were members of national political parties than their counterparts in Chiang Mai. About 41 precent of the respondents stated that they are party members. The majority of them belonged to UNIDO (42 percent), followed by the KBL (26 percent). Somewhat less than 9 percent of the respondents were affiliated with political movements (such as BANDILA and BAYAN) or locally-based political groups (such as the Timawa Party of former Senator Ganzon), while about 6 percent of the respondents classified themselves as UNIDO supporters without formal party membership. Surprisingly, however, of the incumbent local politicians, only four were UNIDO members. One city councillor claimed double membership of UNIDO and NP, while another was a BANDILA official. Even the KBL was represented in the city council through the President of the *barangay* youth organization *(Kabataang Barangay)* -- an anachronism from the Marcos days which did not survive the next election of KB officers.

The fairly heterogeneous partisan composition of the city council reflected several major trends characteristic of the early post-Marcos era:

1. the "floating" and highly fragmented nature of the Philippine party system;
2. the climate of extreme political competitiveness, in which ambitious politicians strived to build up their organizational basis in order "to keep options open" for future moves, as one councillor put it;
3. the importance of close personal relationships between leaders and subleaders, which, as the relatively high percentage of nonparty members within the city council suggests, had greater priority than party affiliation. However, as local elections approached, formal

party membership among Iloilo's decision-makers increased, because only the politicians included in an official party slate had a real chance of winning a seat.

A second reason for the high mobilization capacity of Iloilo's politicians was the city's relatively dense organizational network. Although Philippine political parties were weakly organized, most of them maintained a branch in Iloilo. Yet, in order to mobilize voters effectively, they had to rely on personal contacts to power brokers at the grassroots level *(liders)*, affiliation with voluntary associations, and, under martial law, a smooth relationship with government-sponsored neighborhood organizations *(barangays)*. In general, however, the relationship between politicians and the population was one-way, rarely enabling the citizenry to transmit demands to decision-makers. Politics at the neighborhood level very much resembled the polity at large, transforming the *barangays* into mini-arenas of factional feuds.

In premartial-law times, *"liders"* primarily acted as street level canvassers for campaigning local politicians who, once elected, rewarded them with cash, jobs, infrastructure projects and improved public services in their neighborhood, business permits, licenses, and tax exemptions, or tolerated illegal activities such as gambling, drug running, and prostitution (Benson 1970; Machado 1972a, 1972b, 1973/74; Wolters 1983).

Political control of the city governments over the grassroots became tighter and more systematical under martial law through the formation of urban *barangays* in December 1972. The regime made the *barangays* the basic administrative unit of the country. Initially they were staffed by a set of appointed, fiercely loyal officers before, in 1982, *barangay* offices became elective. In urban areas most *barangay* officials came from a "socially ambitious, status and advancement-oriented petty bourgeoisie with favorable attitudes towards authoritarianism" (Ruland 1986a:18). Their motivation for seeking a public office on the neighborhood level was dictated largely by power aspirations and the attraction of material fringe benefits.

Created as an institutional device to broaden citizen participation, to support the bureaucracy in the delivery of essential services and to act as agents of development, a closer look at *barangay* activities shows that these functions only existed in official propaganda (de Guzman 1977; Aquino 1977; Casalmo 1980; Rüland 1982a, 1984, 1986a; Rüland and Sajo 1988). In reality, they were instruments of the regime to mobilize the population for political purposes and to exert control over slums and squatter areas, which were feared as breeding grounds of political dissent and social unrest. They were major instruments in the regime's selective stop-and-go policy of mobilization and depoliticization of society. With the help of the *barangays*, the regime mobilized the population for the six referenda that took place between 1973 and 1984, five elections, and numerous state ceremonies on the occasion of the president's birthday or the anniversary of the martial-law declaration. The *barangays* were responsible for producing as many "yes"-votes as possible in the referenda and for ensuring the victory of the regime's election candidates -- by manipulation and outright fraud if necessary. During the campaign period the *barangay* officials indoctrinated the community, threatened independent-minded, abstaining or opposition voters, manipulated the voter lists and tampered with the election returns. The regime's tactics of stick-and-carrot towards the *barangay* officials through material inducements, on the one hand, and thinly veiled threats of purges, on the other, produced a remarkably high mobilization performance in the initial phase of martial law. In all referenda before 1978, turnout and affirmative votes were close to or exceeded 90 percent. The 1978 IBP and the 1980 local elections, too, ended with landslide victories for the regime.

In between such mobilization drives, the *barangays* served as the major instrument in the implementation of the regime's strategy of depoliticizing society. By carrying out intelligence functions, the *barangay* leadership had close rapport with the police and the military. The *barangay* officials became the "eyes and the ears" (Bello 1982:104) of the government at the grassroots level. They intimidated and harassed dissidents and suppressed antigovernment activities; in other words, they acted as a typical counterinsurgency instrument. At the same time, their service delivery functions were ineffective and prone to corruption, while their development performances were virtually negligible.

After 1980, the cohesiveness of the *barangay* machinery gradually decreased. The *barangays* became increasingly discredited as a haven of petty corruption, racketeers, and goons. The regime's attempt to infuse fresh legitimacy into the system by holding *barangay* elections in May 1982 proved a failure, because it came much too late and was marred by widespread election fraud. In fact, the election severely undermined the cohesion and homogeneity of the neighborhood organizations by increasing political competition at the grassroots level. In a progressively polarized national polity, *barangay* candidates became proxies of either pro-government or oppositionist local party stalwarts. Whereas previously, divisions within the *barangays* only occurred along personal lines, they now started to develop distinctly partisan overtones. Although the regime managed to have more than 70 percent of its supporters elected, the election of *barangay* officials with oppositionist leanings politicized the system and carried opposition to the regime into its own institutions. The ensuing weakening of the organization was a decisive factor in the regime's dismal performance, particularly in urban areas, in the 1984 *Batasang Pambansa* and the 1986 presidential elections.

The political role of Iloilo's *barangay* network does not differ markedly from these findings based mainly on studies of the *barangay* system in Metro Manila. In various interviews, respondents deplored the rare meetings of the *barangay* assemblies, the major forum in which citizen participation was supposed to take place, and the authoritarian style of decision-making by the *barangay* captains. In many instances, the activities of the *barangay* officials were limited to intelligence work against so-called "subversives" and collecting remunerations, hand-outs, and fringe benefits at city hall. The *barangay* elections held in Iloilo's 180 *barangays* in May 1982 were marred by anomalies such as the disenfranchisement of thousands of voters.[49] Although the elections were termed in the regime's usual euphemistic rhetoric as "elections of consensus" -- meaning that partisan involvement was banned during the campaign -- candidates loyal to the government more or less openly received the full backing of the regime.

These assessments made by individual respondents were largely confirmed by the survey results, although the latter are somewhat distorted by the fact that almost 25 percent of the interviewees evaded a clear response. In general, *barangay* activities were not held in high regard. Only 32 percent rated the *barangays* as either "very active" or "active".

Nevertheless, the basically negative assessment of Iloilo's *barangays* with regard to their participatory and developmental functions should not completely ignore some positive achievements. Some *barangays* carried out successful livelihood projects, such as running a garment factory or piggery and poultry-raising projects (Rüland and Sajo 1988:271).

However -- leaving aside their preoccupation with functions of political control -- most *barangays* were severely hampered in their developmental activities by a notorious lack of financial resources. Although *barangay* law states four major sources of revenues,[50] *barangays* received only a fraction of the revenues due to them. Bahl found that on a nationwide scale *barangays* were allocated only 11.7 percent of the total appropriated amount between 1977 and 1980 (Bahl and Miller 1983:129). As a result, *barangays* were strongly dependent on occasional hand-outs from the central government. As a newspaper analysis suggests, large amounts of funds were made available to Iloilo's *barangays* mainly before and shortly after elections.[51] With these funds, some *barangays* engaged in small-scale infrastructure projects such as the construction of *barangay* halls, foot paths, drainage systems, and wells.

Barangay activities in Iloilo were further hampered by gross inequalities in the distribution of the real property tax proceeds. As there was no scheme to equitably distribute the 10 percent share in real property tax collections among Iloilo's *barangays*, inner-city *barangays* were "wealthier" than *barangays* on the urban fringe. Due to the high land values and correspondingly relatively high real property tax collections within their jurisdiction, some *barangays* located in the central business district had annual revenues exceeding 100,000 Pesos. On the other hand, *barangays* in depressed areas or located on agricultural land had revenues of less than 1,000 Pesos. It is not surprising that developmental activities were intermittent and dependent on initiatives from above. As a result, *barangay* activities concentrated on projects which did not need financial resources or where they could rely on the resources of other institutions, as in the case of intelligence and policing. In other words, they were primarily involved in all those activities that were directed at the depoliticization of the neighborhood population.

Iloilo's voluntary associations were another intermediary institution contributing to the high level of political mobilization in the city before and after martial law. While their mobilization function was comparatively low during most of the martial-law era, they were nevertheless a major forum for intraregime competition.

Iloilo's voluntary associations were forums of the elite where opinion on local issues was formed and decisions of the city government influenced. By providing access to entire voter blocs and serving as springboards for rising local leaders, they also performed a crucial function in electoral politics. Activities in such "associational micro-arenas" (Wirsing 1973), provided opportunities to build up leadership reputation, an image of civic-mindedness, and a clientele. Occasionally, especially after the Aquino government came to power, voluntary associations were invited to participate in public hearings in order to share their expertise with local decision-makers. Unfortunately, however, the effectiveness of this practice was limited, as the local government in Iloilo and elsewhere in the country could not resist the temptation to invite only those groups with affinities to the incumbent administration. Moreover, interviews and observations suggest that only a few elitist civic clubs, such as the Rotary and Lions Clubs, had permanent influence on urban politics. Elsewhere in the Philippines, too, such an elitist interaction pattern between city government and voluntary associations seemed to be a common feature of local politics (Berner 1989). Williams, who had asked the mayors of his sample municipalities to name social and civic organizations with which they had frequent contact found that fewer than 20 percent of the organizations mentioned were those of lower-class groups (farmers, fishermen, and vendors). 30 percent of all groups mentioned were organized by the government. Williams came to the conclusion that, if there were organizations of low-income groups consulted by the mayor, they were likely to be sponsored by the national government (Williams 1981:234).

Not surprisingly, 76 percent of Iloilo's decision-makers were members of voluntary associations. Average membership of respondents was 3.24 -- somewhat higher than in Chiang Mai. Membership in voluntary associations was particularly frequent among nonincumbent politicians (90 percent), about average among incumbents (76.92 percent), and below average among city administrators (63.64 percent). On average, nonincumbent local politicians were members in 3.8, incumbents in 3.4, and city administrators only in 2.5 organizations. The lower associational affiliation level of city administrators may be attributed to the fact that, as nonelective officers, there was no need for them to build up a large clientele. This may also explain why associational membership of city administrators was clustered in professional organizations (42.86 percent). Like in Chiang Mai, the organizational affiliation of incumbents is lower than that of nonincumbents. 70 percent of nonincumbents were former office holders and thus firmly entrenched in Iloilo's organizational network, while many of the incumbent local officials were political novices and had yet to establish their political base.

The organizational membership profile of Iloilo's decision-makers differs from that of Chiang Mai's local leaders. Only civic groups played a major role in both cities. In Iloilo many local leaders were members of professional and religious groups, but in contrast to Chiang Mai, the importance of paramilitary and educational associations ranked very low (see Table 3.8). The membership pattern of Iloilo's decision-makers was far more heterogeneous, as only a few membership overlappings could be recorded. The heterogeneous structure of organizational membership is another indicator of the high level of political competitiveness in Iloilo. Iloilo's politicians were reluctant to join the same "mobilization grounds" as their rivals and tried to build up organizational networks which were free of the influence of political opponents.

A discussion of the impact of voluntary associations on local politics is incomplete without the role of the church. Despite the pervasive influence of religion on the life of the Filipinos, there is a conspicuous absence of studies dealing with the church as an actor in the local arena.

Church influence on local decision-making tends to be greater and more direct in smaller communities than in urban areas. Yet, viewed in

TABLE 3.8 Organizational Affiliation of Interviewed Local Decision-Makers, Iloilo City

Type of Organization	Total Respondents		Incumbent Mayor, Vice Mayor, SP Members		City Administrators		Other Political Leaders	
	N	%	N	%	N	%	N	%
Professional	27	24.82	11	25.00	12	42.86	4	10.53
Educational	10	9.09	9	20.45	--	--	1	2.63
Civic (= Rotary, Lions, Jaycees, etc.)	20	18.18	8	18.18	4	14.29	8	21.05
Political	7	6.36	5	11.36	--	--	2	5.26
Religious	20	18.18	4	9.09	6	21.43	10	26.32
Sports	3	2.73	3	6.81	--	--	--	--
Military	3	2.73	--	--	2	7.14	1	2.63
Social and community	7	6.36	2	4.55	1	3.57	4	10.53
Economic	8	7.27	2	4.55	1	3.57	4	10.53
Cultural	3	2.73	--	--	--	--	3	7.89
Not specified	2	1.82	--	--	--	--	2	5.26
Total	110	100.00	44	99.99	28	100.00	38	99.99
Average organizational affiliation	3.24		3.4		2.5		3.8	

Source: Survey of local decision-makers, Iloilo City, 1986.

historical perspective, in most cases, including Iloilo City, the church hindered more than promoted participatory processes. Nevertheless, it had an impact on political competition, factional feuds, and mobilization. Through its spiritual influence over the faithful, the church is the nongovernmental organization with the greatest clientele, and hence, mobilization potential. Through open or thinly veiled election recommendations from the pulpit, a frequent practice in the Philippines, the church can easily mobilize voters for a specific party or candidate. This capacity to influence voting behavior facilitates intervention by church leaders in politics.

Prior to the declaration of martial law, the church hierarchy in Iloilo fitted well the picture of an unholy alliance between the Catholic Church and the oligarchy. McCoy has amply described the great influence which the late archbishop, Monsgr. Jose Ma. Cuenco, had on Iloilo's oligarchy and how he was actively involved in factional controversies. Cuenco, who came to Iloilo in 1943 and stayed there until his death in 1972, was one of the most durable allies of the Lopez-Ledesma faction during that time (McCoy 1977:457). The scion of a powerful family from Cebu, Cuenco himself belonged to that oligarchy -- a good example of the Philippine oligarchy's sophisticated division of labor in penetrating virtually all spheres of society.

Under martial law, direct church influence on urban decision-makers began to wane as even the essentially conservative church hierarchy gradually dissociated itself from the Marcos regime. In the final years, many members of the clergy, especially those with a nationalist outlook and sympathies for the *theology of liberation,* joined forces with the cause-oriented groups and actively participated in antiregime protest. Yet, these activities were essentially national -- only in a few instances did they also have a local dimension. Socially concerned activists in the clergy, however, became increasingly involved in social action and advocacy work -- for instance, in squatter areas -- and helped to organize the urban poor which, as a result, became more vocal in articulating their demands toward the city government.

While in the final phase of the Marcos regime the more radical members of the church exercised considerable influence on local politics in Iloilo through their participation in the *"Parliament of the Streets"* and social action, the ascendance of the Aquino government seemed to reverse this trend. Although, as far as Iloilo is concerned, no definite prediction could be made at the time of the field research, it seemed that what was happening at the national level would be repeated in the local arena: a strong resurgence of the conservative forces in the church hierarchy.

An important link between local politics and the church were the numerous religious organizations, which account for almost 20 percent of the interviewed decision-makers' organizational affiliations (see Table 3.8). Parish associations and prayer groups not only provided local politicians with access to and influence on voter groups, they were also an important communication channel between them and the clergy. Dialogue with the parish priest was undoubtedly a concern of politicians as the priest's influence over the parishioners might easily undermine the politician's mobilization efforts.

A third major element in political mobilization is the mass media. Iloilo's function as a media center dates back to the period before the Second World War. At the time of field research no less than eighteen weeklies and seven radio stations competed in the city. In terms of the print media, the Western Visayas was among the three top-ranking regions in the country (Republic of the Philippines, National Economic and Development Authority, National Census and Statistics Office 1985:852). In addition, all major national newspapers were available in Iloilo -- but except for the Lopez-owned Manila Chronicle they rarely reported about Iloilo politics. The local weeklies, on the other hand, reported frequently about local politics. But since the overwhelming majority of the print media appeared in English, newspapers satisfied mainly the information needs of the educated middle- and upper-classes, while the language barrier excluded most of the poor.

To some extent this unbalanced access to news was corrected by vernacular language radio programs. With the gradual opening of the Philippine political system after 1983 and, in particular, after 1986, broadcasting increasingly gained in importance as a means of influencing public opinion and political processes. In 1986, virtually very local leader in Iloilo had his vernacular language radio program, which was used with varying skills to pursue personal or factional interests.

The watchdog function of Iloilo's media was considerably impaired by tough competition for a small market, and in some cases by questionable professional standards as well. When access to the media is traded like a commodity and commercial considerations predominate concerns for professional quality, reporting tends to become sensational, partisan, personalized, and even trivial. As a consequence, Iloilo's media contributed to the preservation of idiosyncratic divisions among politicians rather than helping to shape a greater issue-orientation in policy-making (Rüland and Sajo 1988:272).

The media were thus an integral part of the existing political culture, dominated by the same political actors competing for power in urban politics. They were not controlled by independent forces. Hence, the media were not likely to act as an institution transforming a traditional political culture into a modern one, contrary to the view of many modernization theorists. Inkeles, for instance, named three major institutions with a modernizing effect on a political system: the school, the factory, and the media (Inkeles 1969:1141). Strong media exposure -- around 52 percent of Iloilo's urban population had radios (Republic of the Philippines, National Economic and Development Authority, National Census and Statistics Office 1978:25) -- thus reinforced the elitist traits of the city's political culture.

Iloilo's Political Culture: Its Impact on Urban Development

Iloilo's political culture is not very conducive to development. It has produced a high level of mobilization which, however, must not be mistaken for people's participation in decision-making. Although lower-class interest organizations such as trade unions and vendor and squatter organizations existed, and the cause-oriented groups vocally advocated social reforms, there was hardly any political change in urban Iloilo. Contrary to the proposition of Leichter (1975), Iloilo's elitist leadership pattern did not change markedly over the years. Local politics in Iloilo was still dominated by an oligarchy consisting of a few families, which had successfully blocked the rise of new political forces.

Iloilo's decision-making bodies were firmly controlled by this oligarchy and, to a lesser extent, upper-middle-class strata. In the city council there was not even one lower-class representative. Even the activists of the cause-oriented groups had a distinct middle-class background. As students, academics, professionals, and clergymen, most of them belonged to the educated, yet less wealthy middle-class and, in the process of moving up the career ladder, many of them might well be coopted into the folds of traditional politics.

There were only short interruptions in elite domination of Iloilo politics, when upwardly mobile "new men" entered the political scene. One such example was the rise of the Ganzon faction in the mid-1950s. By the early 1960s, however, Ganzon had firmly established himself as a member of Iloilo's elite. Even under martial law, elite domination continued, though under close control and supervision of the regime. Francisco C. Garganera, mayor between 1972 and 1976, was the son of former mayor Eulogio Garganera, and his successor Zafiro Ledesma was related to the influential Ledesma clan. Only the last mayor under martial law, Luis C. Herrera, a PC officer, did not belong to one of Iloilo's elite families. Yet, even under the Herrera administration at least two members of Iloilo's traditional elite sat in the city council. Moreover, especially during the latter part of the Marcos era, Fermin Z. Caram, another scion of a prominent political family, acted behind the scene as the kingmaker in urban politics, decisively influencing the rise and fall of Iloilo's local chief executives.

The downfall of the Marcos administration led to a renaissance of traditional elite politics in Iloilo. The case of Iloilo City is thus a confirmation of similar observations made in other parts of the country: that the change of power from Marcos to Aquino was not accompanied by a change in the social status quo. It was a *"recycling"* of entrenched local oligarchies who either had been dislodged from power in the initial phase of martial law or -- after some temporary political accommodation -- broke with Marcos during the latter part of his rule for two major reasons: disappointment over losing out in internal KBL power struggles or political opportunism that made them change sides when the regime showed signs of crumbling after the Aquino murder. The Caram family, part of the hispanized mestizo elite that has controlled Iloilo since the turn of the century (McCoy 1977), emerged as the major force after the departure of Marcos. The alignment between some of the faction's core members and the Carams dates back to the 1930s. José Zaldariaga, the vice-mayor had an unmistakable elistist background, too. He is related to the Gamboa, Lopez, Ledesma, and Magallona clans, all powerful political families in the Western Visayas for many decades.[52]

Occupational background data also illustrate the upper-class background of Iloilo's decision-makers. Of the twenty-three interviewed local politicians in the sample, nine were businessmen, seven lawyers, and four other professionals. The five respondents who reported that they have no profession were housewives, pensioners or professional politicians (see Table 3.9).

There was a marked difference in the occupation pattern between incumbent and nonincumbent politicians. While a high proportion of incumbents were businessmen, lawyers were overrepresented among nonincumbents. Thus, as in Chiang Mai, Iloilo's politicians had occupations that were supportive of their political career: either professions that could be used to build up a large following through granting favors at low cost (lawyers giving free legal advice, physicians providing medical care, etc.) or occupations that could generate the wealth essential to cover spiraling campaign expenses, or a combination of both. Wealth, a large clientele, personal connections, and family prestige thus continued to be major criteria for political success.

A comparison of the occupational background data of the members of the 1986 city council and former councils showed a clear shift from lawyers to businessmen. Lawyers were the dominant profession in the city council between 1955 and 1980 -- fluctuating between 56 percent

TABLE 3.9 Occupational Background of Interviewed Local Decision-Makers, Iloilo City

Occupation	Total Interviewed Local Politicians		Incumbent Local Politicians		Nonincumbent Local Politicians	
	N	%	N	%	N	%
Lawyer	7	26.92	2	13.13	5	45.45
Businessman	9	34.62	7	46.67	2	18.18
Professor, instructor	2	7.69	1	6.67	1	9.09
Engineer	1	3.85	1	6.67	--	--
Radio broadcaster	1	3.85	1	6.67	--	--
Farmer	1	3.85	--	--	1	9.09
No profession	5	19.23	3	20.00	2	18.18
Total	26	100.01	15a	100.01	11b	99.99

[a]Three respondents named two occupations.
[b]One respondent named two occupations.

Source: Survey of local decision-makers, Iloilo City, 1986.

(1955-1971)[53] and 42 percent in 1980 (see Table 3.10). The recent dominance of businessmen in Iloilo's politics, though not as pronounced, is comparable to the occupational profile of municipal politicians in Chiang Mai. The rise of businessmen in local politics may be the result of the escalating costs associated with a successful election campaign and with the consolidation of one's political position during one's term in office.

Educational background data also clearly differentiate Iloilo's local decision-makers from the average citizen. In contrast to Chiang Mai, educational standards of Iloilo's political and administrative elite were very high. Of the thirty-four respondents, there was only one who had not at least achieved college level. All others were either college graduates or had even reached postgraduate university level. The latter group was particularly well represented among the incumbent local politicians. In addition to formal schooling, over 82 percent of the respondents had undergone professional and government training programs.

Local decision-makers were recruited from a small circle of families. 47 percent of the repondents replied that their parents had occupied political office. The percentage of politically active parents was particularly high among incumbent city officials. Almost 62 percent had parents who held public office at some stage of their life. If other relatives of the respondents had been included, the percentage of politically active family members would have been even higher. This high percentage of respondents with family members in politics suggests that kinship ties are

TABLE 3.10 Occupational Background of Iloilo City Mayors, Vice Mayors, and City Councillors, 1955-1986

Occupation	1955-1971		1980		1986[a]	
	N	%	N	%	N	%
Lawyers	25	55.56	5	41.67	2	13.33
Medical doctors	7	15.56	3	25.00	1	6.67
Other professionals	1	2.22	1	8.33	---	---
Government official	4	8.89	---	---	---	---
Businessmen	3	6.67	---	---	7	46.67
University professor	---	---	1	8.33	1	6.67
Military officer	---	---	1	8.33	---	---
Radio broadcaster	---	---	---	---	1	6.67
Others	5	11.11	---	---	---	---
No profession	---	---	---	---	3	20.00
Not identifiable	---	---	1	8.33	---	---
Total	45	100.01	12	99.99	15	100.01

[a]Three respondents stated more than one occupation, usually combining a profession with business.

Sources: Howard M. Leichter, *Political Regime and Public Policy in the Philippines: A Comparison of Bacolod and Iloilo Cities* (DeKalb: Center for Southeast Asian Studies, Northern Illinois University, Special Report No. 12, 1975), p. 70 and survey of local decision-makers in Iloilo City, 1986.

still decisive factors in the recruitment and political socialization of leaders.

Geographical mobility among Iloilo's decision-makers was relatively low. Only persons with long established roots in the city or the province had a good chance of getting into local office. Exactly 50 percent of the respondents came from Iloilo City, while another 20.6 percent were born in the province of Iloilo. An additional 12 percent of respondents came from the three other provinces of Panay Island. The rest migrated to Iloilo City from nearby Negros Occidental (8.8 percent) and Luzon (5.9 percent). The radius of mobility was thus less than 200 km around Iloilo City for nine out of ten respondents.

My thesis of a still -- or rather -- again, elite-controlled political arena in Iloilo City stands in contrast to the findings of Howard Leichter's comparative study of Iloilo and Bacolod Cities. Leichter argued that after 1955 Iloilo's political system changed from a traditional oligarchy into an emerging *polyarchy* (Leichter 1975:4). According to Leichter, the post 1955-era in Iloilo was characterized by a plurality of elites. The emergence of a middle-class that in 1955 assumed power in urban politics was possible because of an exodus of the old established elite due to political strife and economic decline (Leichter 1975:30). This reasoning, however, must be reconsidered.

1. While Iloilo's economic decline[54] undoubtedly led to an exodus of traditional elite families, the Lopezes, the most powerful among them, did not abandon their political stake in Iloilo. Leichter's assertion that the Lopezes dominated Iloilo's politics only until 1955 (Leichter 1975:53) is thus not tenable.

The Lopezes may have suffered setbacks in urban politics during the second half of the 1950s, but they never completely lost their influence. On the contrary, they regained it between 1963 and 1967, when mayor Ticao switched from the Ganzon camp to the Lopez faction.[55] Although the Lopez-supported ticket was again defeated in the 1971 elections by Ganzon, only martial law really ended Lopez dominance over Iloilo politics. With political parties dissolved, the Lopez business empire broken up, leading family members jailed or exiled, the Lopezes had lost the resource base that made them the strongest political faction in Iloilo for most of the time between 1947 and 1972. But not even martial law could totally eradicate Lopez influence in Iloilo. After Marcos was ousted, the Lopezes immediately moved to regain the hold over their former business enterprises such as the Manila Electric Company (MERALCO), or their interests in the media. In the political arena they staged a comeback with the successful candidacy of Albertito Lopez, son of former vice president Fernando Lopez, in the 1987 congressional elections. Moreover, in the local arena as well, the Lopezes attempted to expand their influence as the controversy over the governor-designate of Guimaras subprovince shows, where Abelardo Javellana, a Lopez-protégé, was involved in a dispute over the post of governor with Dr. Catalino Nava, a Caram-supporter. With the death of Fermin Z. Caram in October 1986, Lopez chances of recovering lost political ground have improved further.

2. It is misleading to gauge Lopez influence on Iloilo politics only on the basis of election results. A closer scrutiny of the periods when the Ganzon camp controlled city hall showed that Ganzon's power was seriously weakened through mid-term defections. After successfully challenging the Lopezes in the 1955 elections, Ganzon's boat was rocked when during the term two of his councillors changed sides and joined the Lopez faction. This reduced his council majority to a narrow six to four margin. The same occurred during the 1959-1963 term, although, by aligning themselves with the LP, the six defectors did not close ranks with the Lopez faction[56] -- and during the 1963-1967 term, when city mayor Ticao and five councillors left Ganzon in order to support the

Lopezes.[57] With a vice mayor who likewise favored the Lopez side, the Ganzon faction, despite a resounding electoral victory in 1963, had virtually become a minority in the city council. Thus, despite electoral defeats in 1955, 1959, and 1963 the Lopezes were nonetheless able to wield considerable influence on decision-making in Iloilo.

　　3. Leichter's assertion that the middle-class took power in Iloilo in 1955 (Leichter 1975:30) is an overstatement. Obviously Leichter became a victim of Ganzon's populist rhetoric in which he styled himself as the spearhead of the lower-class challenge to oligarchical rule. Ganzon claimed that Iloilo was controled by the Lopez-Ledesma "economic syndicate" and that the Lopezes had become rich by promoting their vested interests at the expense of public welfare (McCoy 1977:521).[58] This rhetoric blurred the fact that before Ganzon became a political force in his own right he was dependent on the support of a traditional elite politician, too. Without the material resources made available to him through his alignment with Senator Zulueta, as a young politician he would hardly have succeeded in the 1955 local elections (McCoy 1977). It further overlooks the fact that Ganzon, too, came from a politically prominent, though perhaps less wealthy, family in Iloilo City. Leopoldo Ganzon, his father, was municipal president between 1932 and 1934.[59] Moreover, the mere fact of middle-class origin does not automatically translate into a different political value pattern, although it may lead to the use of different means to attain political goals. In fact, the prime motivation for the political actions of lower-class men may be sought in their aspiration to become a recognized part of the established elite. Many Filipino politicians with lower-class backgrounds do not champion specific causes of their own social class, but acculturate to an elitist life style and value patterns with corresponding vested interests. Precisely this seemed to have been the case with Ganzon once he entrenched himself in Iloilo's power structure. Rhetorics and populist projects apart, Ganzon and other upwardly mobile "new men" shared, in large part, the same sociopolitical conservatism that is charateristic of the Filipino elite. Patronage, particularism, paternalism, and a militant anticommunism were major elements of this value pattern. There is almost no difference between the "elite by birth" and the "new elite" as far as the impact of their political actions on urban development is concerned.

　　The specious equation that a certain social background stands for a corresponding political value system is a major reason for the expectation that the appearance of "new men" in the local political arena would lead to a more pluralist, democratic, and participatory political culture in the Philippines. It was thus overly optimistic when Machado stated that 'new men' "may be expected to have a better chance of adopting less traditional conceptions of leadership than those from old families" and that they are "more likely than those from old families to be more responsive to a large segment of the population" (Machado 1972a:168).

4. The ascendancy of middle-class elements to the political arena was a natural result of institutional changes. In 1955, for the first time the city mayor and the entire council were elected. Prior to 1955, the top positions in the city government and a number of city councillor posts were filled by presidential appointment. After some bargaining, the leading families -- due to their close links to national power centers -- were able to place trusted stalwarts (often family or clan members) in these positions. The opening up of the political arena through the electoral process, and the ensuing need for mass mobilization made it necessary for the elite to recruit "mobilization specialists" (Machado 1972a:217). As the exodus of elite families had contributed to a dearth of such talents within the old elite, this vacuum had to be filled with suitable lower-class men. Given the greater number of positions at stake and the mobilizational requirements of mass politics, it is no accident that the number of politicians with middle-class backgrounds increased after 1955. But because most of them were lower-level political leaders, they were strongly dependent on elite support. This dependency in itself ensured that these middle-class politicians at least did not openly challenge the elite's political belief system, and in many cases even actively adopted it.

Urban development in Iloilo was negatively affected by the elite's extreme social and political conservatism and a development strategy that primarily served to entrench their political position.

Iloilo's decision-makers lacked a clear understanding of the city's deep-rooted social problems, preferring charity, paternalism, and occasional hand-outs over structural reforms. Like in Chiang Mai, attitudes towards development agents advocating genuine social reforms were generally negative. As shown by Table 3.11, on a list of fifteen developmental agents, social workers ranked sixth, intellectuals seventh, and trade unionists fourteenth. Businessmen/entrepreneurs received the highest ratings, followed by executives/managers and professionals -- clearly reflecting the decision-makers' own background and the shift from lawyers to businessmen as the dominant occupational group in local politics.

The interviewed politicians and administrators largely ignored the social problems confronting 30-40 percent of Iloilo's population. Squatting and the activities in the city's informal sector were frequently regarded as illegal and as criminal offenses. Remedial strategies proposed

TABLE 3.11 Opinions of Interviewed Local Decision-Makers Toward Developmental Agents in Iloilo City

Developmental Agents	Score, Total Respondents	Score, Incumbent Mayor, Vice Mayor, SP Members	Score, City Administrators	Score, Other Political Leaders
Technocrats	110	38	41	31
Government employees/civil servants	125	46	44	35
Politicians	80	33	25	22
Clergy	97	40	32	25
Intellectuals	117	44	42	31
Teachers	126	53	34	39
Businessmen/entrepreneurs	148	62	41	45
Social workers	124	50	40	34
Labor unionists	91	35	30	26
Executives/managers	137	55	45	37
Foreign experts	106	40	35	31
Officers of farmer organizations	103	39	34	30
Professionals (i.e. lawyers, architects, doctors, etc.)	129	52	46	31
Interest groups/lobbyists	97	35	34	28
Big landlords	93	36	28	29

Source: Survey of local decision-makers, Iloilo City, 1986.

by the respondents displayed a punitive and legislative bias. When, for instance, asked to name the most effective strategy to solve Iloilo's squatter problem, almost 50 percent opted for "resettlement to prepared lots in peripheral areas" (45.95 percent), and "demolition and eviction" (2.7 percent), irrespective of the highly adverse effects that relocation usually has on the living conditions of the affected households. Approaches that have proved more appropriate in dealing with the socioeconomic circumstances of low-income groups such as "slum upgrading" (21.6 percent) and "sites-and-services" (13.5 percent) ranked far behind in second and third place. The percentage of those in favor of tough antisquatting measures was particularly high among the newly appointed city councillors. Almost 84 percent of the incumbent local politicians opted for "resettlement" (76.9 percent) or "return to hometown" (7.7 percent). In view of the fact that the Aquino administration merely recycled local oligarchies in most parts of the country, and assuming that these elites display similar attitudes towards the less priviliged social strata, it was evident that the opportunities of the new government for genuine social reforms were a priori limited. In fact, shortly after the exit of Marcos, urban squatters in most cities of the country -- particularly in Manila -- faced a wave of repression that was in no way different from the Marcos era. In cooperation with the National Housing Autority (NHA), many of the newly installed local authorities launched large-scale eviction campaigns against squatters, for which they were lauded by the media.

It is striking that in a country where urban unemployment rose to nearly 20 percent,[60] urban decision-makers ranked unemployment only eighth on a list of seventeen major developmental problems confronting a city like Iloilo. The low ranking of unemployment as a developmental problem is even more bewildering as in an earlier question almost 59 percent of the respondents had stated that unemployment is a "a most serious" (23.5 percent) or a "serious" problem (32.35 percent) in Iloilo City. Inadequate housing was ranked seventh, overcrowding tenth, and social inequity thirteenth (see Table 3.12).

While Iloilo decision-makers had a fairly good grasp of their city's economic structure, attitudes towards economic development were characterized by a relatively low level of innovativeness. The majority of decision-makers tended to propose standard solutions. Over 90 percent of the respondents were in favor of industrial development through the establishment of industrial estates, and even more called for foreign investment in Iloilo City. It seems that Iloilo decision-makers were economically more outward-looking than their counterparts in

TABLE 3.12 Opinions of Local Decision-Makers on Major Urban Problems in Iloilo City

Urban Problems	Score, Total Respondents	Score, Incumbent Mayor, Vice Mayor, SP Members	Score, City Administrators	Score, Other Political Leaders
Inadequate food/malnourishment	63	24	20	19
Unemployment	126	49	38	39
Too little industrial development	137	53	43	41
Inadequate housing	129	53	37	39
Overcrowding	118	47	35	36
Social inequity	111	44	35	32
Corruption	132	57	37	38
Poor infrastructure	113	41	38	34
Poor planning	126	49	36	41
Inadequate public transport	75	30	21	24
Pollution/environmental problems	87	28	31	28
Abuse of power in office	105	41	31	33
Inadequate garbage disposal	128	55	33	40
Flooding	112	44	32	36
Poor health conditions	136	55	39	42
Inadequate financial resources	133	50	42	41
High crime rate	131	53	39	39

Source: Survey of local decision-makers, Iloilo City, 1986.

Chiang Mai. In view of Iloilo's former economic function as a colonial entrepôt, this finding may not be surprising.

Political contests in the Philippines are very costly. It was estimated by respondents that in the 1988 local elections a mayoral candidate would have to spend at least one million pesos from his own pocket to have any prospect of success. Moreover, even during the term, elective local officials are permanently approached by citizens for material favors. These requests by far exceed what a local official earns. Yet, he is under great social and political pressure to grant such favors as they create a debt of gratitude on the part of the petitioner, which in forthcoming elections can be translated into votes and other forms of political support. Likewise it establishes a reputation for generosity -- an important criterion for Filipino voters.

On the other hand, elective posts in the city government create lucrative opportunities for recovering electoral investments, accumulating funds to finance future electoral contests, expanding the political support base, and expediting self-enrichment. Wolter's finding in a Central Luzon town that politics has become business in its own right is to some extent applicable to Iloilo and most other Philippine cities as well (Wolters 1983:13). Local officials are in a favorable position to manipulate the local economy by protecting and promoting own businesses and those of their allies, while at the same time impairing the economic activities of their rivals. Land-use legislation and zoning ordinances, powers to grant or withhold permits and licenses, "kick backs" for awarding contracts, and overpricing practices provide an array of opportunities for the incumbents to reap windfall profits.[61] That corruption has been endemic in Iloilo's postwar history is implied by the fact that "corruption" was ranked fourth among the seventeen major problems confronting the city. The public pays dearly for these irregularities: the need to mobilize voters in a highly competitive poltical system favors underutilization of local tax resources, because "soft" taxation is viewed as a "discount" for voters. As a result, public services remain unequally distributed and substandard.

Patronage politics revolves mainly around personal conflicts. Their causes are factional idiosyncracies, incompatible economic interests, unrestrained political ambitions, and the craving for prestige, status, and social recognition. Disputes in Iloilo's city council were usually fueled by councillors' attempts to strengthen control over their constituencies or to ward off rival challenges. The answers of at least 50 percent of the respondents can be interpreted in this way. In such conflicts corruption charges were the most frequently used vehicle to weaken the opponent's political position. Accordingly, corruption issues were the dominant theme in Iloilo's everyday politics. This is not surprising, as in a patronage system with a limited and under the impact of the recent economic crisis, even shrinking resource base, it was almost impossible for the incumbent city administration to meet the demands of all political supporters for tangible material benefits (Landé 1973:4). Particularistic resource allocation, frustrated expectations -- which were regarded as a breach of the *utang na loob* principle -- and the exclusion of the opposition from the public resource flow created the scenario in which corruption charges were hurled at the incumbents. Policy issues, such as Iloilo's poverty problems or strategies to improve public service delivery, played a subordinate role in the factional disputes. In a political culture which derives much of its dynamics from the personality factor, mudslinging is the most promising tactic to discredit the opponent. Personal insults and assaults on a person's integrity severely reduce the chances for consensus on the rules of the political game and on approaches for tackling urban underdevelopment; more often than not they deepen existing political rifts and cause endless factional feuds (Rüland and Sajo 1988:274).

The survey results confirm the preponderance of particularism and patronage in Iloilo politics. Asked what the underlying themes of political conflicts in Iloilo City were, the items mentioned most frequently by respondents were "patronage" (29 percent), aspirations for "political control" (21 percent), and "personal interests" (12.5 percent), while the pressing economic and social problems of the city played a more than subordinate role in the responses.

The nonideological nature of and almost complete absence of issue-orientation in Iloilo's local politics can also be illustrated by an analysis of election platforms. While many factions had no explicit program at all, those which did had only rather sketchy ones. A relatively detailed platform was worked out by Rodolfo Ganzon for the 1971 elections. Yet, the platform was committed neither to clearcut and specific goals nor to existing urban issues. The introductory list of primary objectives was characterized by hazy populism. It addressed the symptoms of urban problems, but neither analyzed their roots nor offered solutions. It was a variation of themes that have become ritual in Philippine elections: pledges on public welfare, closeness to the people and promises to cut red tape, eradicate graft and corruption, refrain from increasing taxation, and promote peace and order. In the section about urban services, social services were not mentioned. Instead, the paper spoke of "charitable" services. Eleven of the twenty paragraphs devoted to urban services dealt with education, Ganzon's pet theme, but only three with health services. Moreover, there were no details of the candidate's low-cost housing policies or his proposals to upgrade the living conditions of the rapidly increasing number of slum dwellers and squatters. Nor was there anything on the problems of the informal sector -- except a paragraph on public markets. Here, the candidate proposed supermarket development of the Makati type![62]

The KBL platform in the 1980 election was even more general and did not bother to address local issues at all. The seven-point platform discussed national issues in the broadest sense -- nationalism, national unity, social justice, participatory government (meaning *barangay* "democracy"), economic development, freedom of belief, and internationalism (with a commitment to the UN ideals, ASEAN, and a pro-American foreign policy).[63]

All these arguments do not support the frequently expressed opinion that election-centered patronage politics may represent a considerable redistribution of wealth and an increase in development (Villanueva 1977:193; Schulz 1979:153). Much speaks for the observation that a high percentage of resources meant for redistribution to voters remains in the pockets of grassroots leaders (Wolters 1983:192). Patronage politics in a *"spoils system"* is not a "typical phenomenon of democratic development" as opined by the Canadian political scientist David Wurfel in one of his early writings (Wurfel 1963:773). Such reasoning, which has been reiterated by others (Scott 1969, 1972; Machado 1972a, 1972b, 1973/74), is based on an evolutionary, unilinear, and universally applicable model of political development. It rests on the historical experiences of the USA during the *Jacksonian Revolution* and nineteenth-century England. Yet, the peculiar cultural and socioeconomic conditions in the Philippines militate against the transfer of the Anglo-American model of political development to that part of the world.

Socioeconomic Development

Urban Services in Iloilo

Limited local autonomy, frequent central government interventions, financial constraints, patronage politics, and the ultraconservative political belief system of the local decision-makers produced a pattern of *"cyclical"* development in Iloilo City. Services delivery was impeded by a fragmented, poorly planned, and intermittent process of resource allocation. While performances in service delivery were satisfactory in the fields of education, public works, and transport, health services, garbage disposal, housing, and water supplies were badly neglected.

Services Provided by the City Government. The city government has done comparatively well in public works projects, a finding confirmed by the survey. Apart from the Regional Cities Development Project (41 percent), infrastructure projects (23 percent) were most prominent among the development projects cited by the respondents.

Iloilo has a better road network than most other Philippine cities. Towards the end of the 1970s the length of national, city, and *barangay* roads totaled 235 km. Three quarters of total road length was asphalted. City roads increased from 57.6 km in 1957 to 72.11 km in 1980 (National Economic and Development Authority 1978:3.19), a modest increase by all measures. Yet, unlike Chiang Mai and Penang, where more roads have been built, traffic jams are rare in Iloilo.

Although the data provided by the Land Transportation Commission are inaccurate, they support the conclusion that Iloilo did not experience the dramatic traffic growth of Chiang Mai or Penang. On the contrary, traffic volume in Iloilo declined between the mid-1970s and the early 1980s, showing a moderate upward trend only after 1982 without, however, reaching again the 1975 level.[64] This explains why the expansion of the road network has received lower priority than the maintenance and improvement of existing roads. The exception is some major radial road projects on the outskirts of the city, which were undertaken with the assistance of the national government, the International Bank for Reconstruction and Development, and the Asian Development Bank. These roads have considerably improved the city's links with the hinterland.

Nevertheless, road development in Iloilo must contend with a number of administrative constraints. Like most other public works projects, road construction is characterized by a piecemeal approach. In the Municipal Management Study it was pointed out that during the 1970s the average expenditure for road projects in Iloilo City amounted to only P 75,000 -- compared to P 82,000 in Cagayan de Oro, P 135,000 in Davao, and P 480,000 in Bacolod. The small scale of the projects is largely due to a "limited amount and type of functioning equipment available". Most heavy equipment is in poor condition and breakdowns occur quite frequently (Regional Cities Development Project 1980:36). Projects were thus often interrupted or delayed. Any delay, however, increased inflationary pressures. As a result, project targets were repeatedly scaled down.

Storm water and drainage systems worked satisfactorily in the inner-city areas. Most parts of the central business district were covered (230 ha) and so were some areas in the suburbs of Jaro, La Paz, Mandurriao, and Molo. The drainage system consisted of underground concrete pipes with some open channels and discharged into the Iloilo River

(City of Iloilo 1985:10). In general, it can be said that, except for the densely populated foreshore area, flooding was not a persistent problem in Iloilo.

The city government contributed much to make Iloilo the educational center of the Western Visayas. During the last three decades, education was the service sector given greatest attention by city authorities. The number of schools nearly trebled btween 1947 and 1985, increasing from thirty-three to ninety-six, among them fifty-six public schools. In addition, there were four universities, a teacher's training college, and a vocational school. While private educational institutions were strongly represented on the secondary and tertiary level as well as among the vocational and technical schools, the city government bore most of the cost of elementary education.

In the immediate postwar years up to 120 pupils crowded into one classroom, but educational standards improved markedly during the 1950s. During the first two terms of city mayor Ganzon (1955-1961) budgetary allocations for education increased substantially. Ganzon's free-education program was unprecedented in the country. It included an elementary program with free learning materials and free public secondary education.[65] The *Timawa* scholarship program, launched in 1961, provided 590 scholarships for poor but talented students until 1972.[66] A new attempt to restore tuition-free education in the city's secondary schools was made by Rosa Caram shortly after her appointment as city mayor in 1986. Her opponents, however, claimed that this was a political ploy to deprive Ganzon of a major campaign theme should he run against her in forthcoming local elections. Qualifications of the teachers gradually improved due to more careful recruiting, in-service training, and regular weekend seminars. School equipment likewise improved. The number of teachers increased from 390 (1946) to 1,729 (1975) and, as a result, the teacher-student-ratio declined from 1:62 to about 1:30 in the 1980s. Moreover, budgetary constraints of the city administration were eased through RA 4092 (1965), under which the state assumed responsibility for the salaries of intermediate grade teachers.[67] Due to improved educational services, the literacy rate rose from 69.3 percent in 1939 to 94 percent in 1972, a level which has not changed much since then. These achievements, however, conceal high drop-out rates: poverty and adverse economic conditions forced 34 percent of pupils in primary schools, 22 percent of students at the intermediate, and 12 percent at the secondary level to leave school prematurely (Iloilo City 1977:83).

Health services were low among the development priorities in Iloilo. Budgetary allocations for health services rarely exceeded 6 percent. Health facilities suffered from a notorious lack of inadequate premises,

qualified staff, medicaments, and medical equipment. With 52.3 per
1,000 live births, Iloilo's infant death rate was comparatively high --
lower than the national average of 58.0 (Republic of the Philippines, National Economic and Development Authority, National Census and
Statistics Office 1985:268), but considerably higher than in Cebu (34.7
per 1,000 live births) (National Economic and Development Authority
1978:3.18). Malnutrition among preschool children was also very high.
Based on *barangay* surveys, officials of the Ministry of Social Services
and Development (MSSD) estimated a figure of 65 percent, which was
slightly lower than Bacolod's and Davao's 70 percent.[68] Sanitary conditions were very poor, too. In 1979 only 22.4 percent of the city's
dwellings had satisfactory toilet facilities, and only 4.4 percent water-
sealed toilets.

Recent improvements concentrated mainly on the physical infrastructure. Between 1976 and 1980 the number of health centers increased
from twelve to twenty-eight, and the number of day-care centers from
forty-two to sixty-six. For the treatment of more serious illnesses there
were two public and six private hospitals with a total bed capacity of
1,037. This is equivalent to almost 40 percent of beds in the whole of Region VI, one of the most underserviced regions in terms of health care
(City of Iloilo 1985:33). Quantitative improvements were also recorded
for medical personnel. Between 1946 and 1985, the number of doctors in
the City Health Department increased from three to ten, the number of
nurses from seven to twenty-nine and the number of sanitary inspectors
from fifteen to twenty-two. But despite physical improvements and increases in medical personnel, health services remained inaccessible to
the majority of Iloilo's population. Most of the health centers were not
permanently staffed by doctors and other medical personnel, basic
medicines not available and public hospitals overcrowded. Yet, the
1:247 bed-to-population ratio was more favorable in Iloilo than in other
regional cities such as Davao (1:365), Bacolod (1:365), and Cagayan de
Oro (1:386).[69]

Urban Services Delivered by Non-Municipal Agencies. Water supply
was the responsibility of the Metro Iloilo Water District (MIWD). Organized as a public enterprise, the authority served the City of Iloilo and
the four adjacent municipalities of Sta. Barbara, Pavia, Maasin, and Cabatuan.

Iloilo's economic development is severely inhibited by inadequate
water supplies. Supply levels stagnated for decades at a low 4.0-4.5 million gallons per day, while minimum demand stood at 11.3 million gallons a day (Iloilo City 1977:74). Only 40-50 percent of city households
were served, and even less in the adjacent municipalities (20-25 per-

cent). Problems were further compounded by water losses of 25-40 percent due to leaking pipes.

Iloilo's waterworks system was constructed in 1928 for a target population of 30,000 with a per capita supply of 150 gallons per day. It was
designed for a period of twenty years, after which it was to be over-
hauled and expanded. However, the system has never been improved
since and is totally antiquated today.[70] In 1977, city planners estimated
that it would cost more than 200 million pesos to modernize the waterworks system, at the time an amount more than ten times the city's annual budget (Iloilo City 1977:75).

Due to the low water production and low pressure, a round-the-clock
service could not be maintained. Water was accumulated during the
day and households were served only in the afternoon and during night
time.

Water quality was poor. Bacteriological tests found all sources of
Iloilo's water supply contaminated (City of Iloilo 1980:62). The inner-city
is the most underserviced area because it is farthest away from the main
pipe. Drilling of wells is not feasible here as ground water is polluted or
salty, due to the proximity of the sea.

Alternative water supplies included the MIWD stand pipe or water
peddlers. The latter were very expensive compared with the relatively
low rates of the MIWD. One liter bought from a peddler costs about
thirty times the official MIWD rate. Commercial enterprises, hotels,
hospitals, and other large-scale consumers were supplied by barges
from Guimaras Island. In the suburbs, many households drilled their
own wells, often very shallow and hazardous to health -- or resorted to
rain water.

At the time of field research, a project was implemented with the
support of a World Bank loan of P 71.9 million to improve water supplies in the city. But even after project completion in late 1986, capacity
was not expected to be beyond 7.5 million gallons per day. This was still
almost 34 percent below the minimum requirements.[71]

The Ministry of Social Services and Development (MSSD) operated
an office at city level which -- in cooperation with the city government --
was responsible for welfare services in Iloilo City. The ministry's program aimed at socially, economically, and physically disabled persons.
The program components were summarized under the acronym
SPDEFS. "S" stands for "self-employment assistance program", "P" for
"practical skills training/job placement, "D" for "day care ser-
vices/supplemental feeding", "E" for emergency assistance", "F" for
"family planning/population awareness and sex education", and "S" for
"special social services".

The main pillar of MSSD activities was the self employment assistance program (SEYA). SEYA was a livelihood project designed to promote income-generating activities for poor families. Loans of between
300 and 1,500 pesos were provided by the MSSD without interest, and
between 3,000 and 5,000 pesos by the Development Bank of the Philippines as a support for small-scale businesses. However, the impact of
these livelihood projects is severely reduced by bureaucratic fragmentation. Apart from the MSSD, the MLG, the Population Commission
(POPCOM), the National Housing Authority (NHA), and the Ministry
of Human Settlements (MHS) implemented similar projects. In 1985, the
MSSD lent P 66,000 to 1,225 persons through SEYA. This was equivalent
to an average loan of P 54 per person. It goes without saying that such
"micro"-loans had virtually no impact on the living conditions of the
poor. The target group thus viewed them merely as hand-outs. As a result, the default rate was very high. Although no figures were given by
officials of the ministry, it seemed to be above the 50 percent margin.
One official said that a "roll back" of 25 percent of the loans can already
be considered a success.[72]

Other welfare programs of the MSSD focussed on supplemental feeding for malnourished preschool children, running day-care centers, and
training programs in simple indigenous skills for the unemployed out-
of-school youth. But most of the programs suffered from frequent inter-
ruption, due to lack of funds. Moreover, the ten field workers were
overwhelmed by the massive problems facing Iloilo's poor. As in other
cities in the Philippines, state welfare programs in Iloilo City were
hardly more than a palliative (Rüland 1982b:45; Lopez-Gonzaga
1985:19).

Like most other Philippine regional cities, Iloilo suffered from a severe housing shortage. In the 1980s, the housing backlog was estimated
at 5,652. This is equivalent to nearly 15 percent of the city's housing
stock. Construction activity was unable to keep pace with tremendous
demand, which, according to planners, exceeded 11,000 units. In the
thirteen-year period between 1973 and 1985 approximately only 6,000
new building permits (about 461 per annum) were approved by the city
government. This is also less than half of the increase in new households
over the same time.

Low construction activity led to densification of existing housing in
the 1960s. Due to slow population growth and outmigration this trend
was slightly reversed during the 1970s, but occupancy rates were still
high in 1983. Average occupancy per house stood at 6.42 in 1960, 6.81 in
1970 and 6.66 in 1983. In the mid-1980s one house was occupied by 1.15
households. However, in the severe economic crisis in the mid-1980s

construction virtually ceased, and it is expected that overcrowding will become even more serious in the latter part of the 1980s. Inflationary pressures, a skewed land ownership pattern and the lack of housing financing schemes forced an increasing number of families into squatting. Less than 15 percent of Iloilo's households can afford to buy even the cheapest subdivision lot on the open market (Government of the Philippines and International Bank for Reconstruction and Development 1982a:1). As a result, between 1970 and 1983, the percentage of squatters increased from 26 to 35 percent, most of them living in twenty-seven officially identified depressed areas. Squatters were concentrated in the foreshore area and along river banks. Apart from Davao, Iloilo has one of the largest squatter populations in the country.

Lack of funds and a generally negative attitude towards squatters on the part of local decision-makers were the main reasons why the city government did not respond adequately to Iloilo's housing problems in the past. Except for a few minor government projects, housing construction was left to the private sector.

Until very recently, housing activities of the city government were ad hoc measures in response to emergencies. Victims of the 1951 and 1966 fire disasters, for instance, were relocated to Barrio Obrero. After the 1966 fire, the city constructed 350 new houses in the barrio at a cost of P 650 each, which were handed over to the beneficiaries free of charge together with the land.[73] Other projects were undertaken by the Philippine Homesite and Housing Corporation (PHHC) in 1956 and the Ministry of Human Settlements (MHS) in 1979. None of these projects, however, alleviated the city's shortage of low-cost accommodation. The PHHC projects delivered only 276 units, and with fifty units the extravagant BLISS project of the MHS created even less (Ministry of Public Works, Republic of the Philippines, Regional Cities Development Project 1979:8). Construction costs for the BLISS project exceeded 25,400 pesos per unit, which meant that the urban poor could not afford them.

The city government was inactive in providing new shelter, but it did not destroy existing low-cost housing, although plans for large-scale evictions existed. Unlike in Manila evictions and relocations took place rarely, involved relatively small numbers of households, and were more often instigated by the private sector than by the authorities. The major evictions from publicly owned land included an unknown number of families relocated to Barrio Calumpang, Molo, in 1972, seventy-six families to make way for the Iloilo-Jaro Diversion Road, several dozen families along Rizal Street (for road widening), and forty families when the city government demolished shanties and makeshift stores in various parts of the city as part of a clean-up campaign in 1982. In the early

1970s, the city government planned the relocation of a great number of squatters to a lot in Barrio Ungka in the municipality of Pavia. However, municipal authorities in Pavia pointed out that the land bought by the city government of Iloilo was classified for industrial use. As the relocation of squatters to the plot violated the municipality's zoning laws, the controversial plan was finally abandoned (Iloilo City 1974:63).

The toleration of squatting and the relatively few evictions can to some extent be explained by the strategic importance of squatters for votes in a highly mobilized and competitive political arena. Yet, the absence of a tough antisquatting policy is not the result of organizational efforts and pressure exerted by the squatters. After the Marcos regime's strategy of depoliticizing focal points of social unrest, it took until the mid-1980s before a squatter organization named KAISOG was formed.

Large-scale housing projects have only started with RCDP. Under RCDP it is planned to upgrade 2,250 existing dwellings and to construct 2,304 sites-and-services units. As both projects are components of RCDP, their impact on the living conditions of the poor will be discussed later.

Services Provided by the Private Sector. Garbage disposal, electricity, and transport were provided by the private sector. While electricity supply and transport services could be considered satisfactory, garbage collection was a major problem in the city.

With only four to five dump trucks in operation, the city had to hire private contractors for garbage collection. Due to the usual political extra costs associated with the contract, the contractor operating the service prior to 1986 fielded only two or three dump trucks per day.[74] As a result, only 35 percent of the refuse were actually collected. The remainder was dumped openly, burnt or buried. This compared unfavorably with Cebu, where 85 to 90 percent of the garbage was regularly collected. But the situation is even worse in Davao City, where only 11.5 percent of the city area was serviced by garbage collection. The new city administration immediately discussed measures to improve the collection performances. At the time of the field research, plans existed to assign one garbage contractor to each of the city's six districts. Furthermore, as part of RCDP, a new dump site was planned in Mandurriao on the outskirts of the city.

Electricity was supplied by the Panay Electric Company (PECO). PECO had a capacity to generate a total of 65 megawatts, of which 45 megawatts were consumed on Panay Island. With 18 megawatts, Iloilo City was the greatest consumer, reflecting the low level of rural electrification.[75] However, even in Iloilo City consumption was still low as only about 60 percent of the households were connected. But unlike in

Bacolod City, there were no major fluctuations in voltage, and brownouts occurred relatively seldom.

While there was no bottleneck in energy supply in Iloilo, existing capacities were not sufficient for industrialization. An even greater deterrent to investors were the high electricity rates which, although not significantly higher than in Cebu, Bacolod or Davao, were between two and three times those of Metro Manila and other parts of Luzon. Rates were expected to decrease and supplies to increase when a project to supply Iloilo by underwater cable with geothermal power generated in Negros Island was completed in 1988.

There are no problems with transport in Iloilo City. In 1985 about 5,235 jeepneys and other public utility vehicles provided passenger transport in the city.[76] These vehicles were operated by private persons or companies with a franchise for a specific route from the Land Transportation Commission. Fares were relatively cheap. Within the boundaries of the city proper, a jeepney trip cost an across-the-board rate of 1 peso and a taxi journey 5 pesos.

Economic Development

Due to highly scattered, inaccurate and often incompatible or incomplete data it is nearly impossible to arrive at a precise empirical assessment of Iloilo City's economic development. There are wide discrepancies between data collected by the city government and those of national agencies such as NEDA or the National Census and Statistics Office. This holds particularly true for census data about business establishments and employment. For instance, the last national census of business establishments conducted by the NCSO in 1978 and the 1979 count of business enterprises undertaken by the city government revealed discrepancies of over 25 percent. A closer scrutiny of the data suggests that the NCSO census overlooked a substantial number of small-scale establishments in the service sector. On the other hand, the city government's data were plagued by major classification problems. Inconsistencies in the classification of businesses according to type of activity were the major cause for the underrepresentation of manufacturing establishments and an overrepresentation of establishments in the wholesale, retail, and service sectors. Yet, it seems that the city government data were closer to actual figures, because they covered more small-scale and backyard firms than the NCSO census. I have therefore decided to use these figures in the analysis of Iloilo's economic structure.

Iloilo's economic development has been subject to large fluctuations over the last two centuries. The successive expansion and contraction of the city's trading boundaries, its extreme dependency on the sugar trade, and its strong exposure to the world market resulted in cyclical up- and down-swings (McCoy 1982:301). The city government had only limited influence on economic development. Only after the appointment of the new city government by the Aquino administration was more systematic attention paid to attracting investors and business enterprises to Iloilo City.[77] Before, economic decentralization was a national affair, hesitantly implemented by various economic agencies, such as the Board of Investments (BOI) and NEDA, and the Ministry of Trade and Industry, while most local governments remained inactive.

Iloilo's economic development can be divided into three phases: the textile era, the sugar era, and an era of decline. Until 1850, Iloilo was a proto-industrial manufacturing center specializing in hand-woven textiles (McCoy 1982:300). The opening of Iloilo's port to direct foreign trade in 1855 and the city's subsequent integration into the colonial capitalist economy as a peripheral sugar entrepôt destroyed these embryonic forms of industrial development. Iloilo became an importer of cheap manufactured goods from England, and at the same time a transshipment center for the sugar produced in the Western Visayan Region. During the sugar era, especially the first decades of the twentieth century, Iloilo experienced its greatest economic boom. It was during this period that Iloilo acquired its reputation as the "Queen City of the South" (McCoy 1982:297). Iloilo was second only to Manila in size, economic activity, and urban amenities. In 1920, it was assumed that half of the money supply of the country circulated in Iloilo. Already at that time Iloilo had electricity, ice plants, automobiles, two cable lines, newspapers, telephone, department stores, and professionals with foreign training. But the wealth generated by the sugar trade was distributed in a very skewed manner. Periodic food shortages and grim poverty characterized the life of a large urban working class (McCoy 1982:311). Colonial capitalism was thus a major force in moulding the city's present inequitable socioeconomic structure.

The *Great Depression*, labor unrest, and technological innovation in transport and cargo handling gradually eroded Iloilo's function as the country's leading sugar entrepôt. As a result of the destruction during the war and violent factional strife in the late 1940s, many businesses were relocated to Manila, Bacolod, and Cebu. By the mid-1950s Iloilo had declined to a minor provincial center (Leichter 1975:32-35; McCoy 1982:328). The city's economic decay experienced a brief respite during the 1970s. The installation of a sugar bulk loading complex at nearby Guimaras Island and large-scale infrastructure projects strengthened Iloilo's position as a major center of the Western Visayas. Though not to the same extent as Chiang Mai, Iloilo too became the headquarters of international development organizations running projects on Panay that ultimately benefited the city as well. Propelled by the *Green Revolution*, an agricultural boom produced a strata of successful farmers in the city's fertile hinterland, creating demand for consumer goods, farm equipment, and a more diversified service sector. As a result, commerce and services expanded and economic growth rose from 3 percent in the mid-1970s to nearly 5 percent in the 1978-1982 period. Unfortunately, this temporary upswing never translated itself into a new "take-off" phase for Iloilo's economy. The effects of two oil crises and high inflation set the limits to economic recovery and prevented the manufacturing sector from acting as a catalyst for economic growth.

The gains of the 1970s were completely lost in the country's economic collapse in the mid-1980s. The debt trap, rampant cronyism during the final Marcos years, rapidly declining prices for sugar and other commodities, and the aftershock of the Aquino assassination plunged the Philippines into their worst economic crisis since the war. In Iloilo the number of business establishments declined dramatically by 21 percent from 5,701 to 4,506 within only four years. As a result, in 1985 the city had fewer businesses than in 1972 (see Table 3.13).

An in-depth analysis of Iloilo's urban economy shows that the leading sectors were retail and wholesale as well as services (financial, community, social, and personal services). Between 1967 and 1979 there was a substantial increase in establishments in the retail and wholesale sector. The sector's share in business establishments rose from 54.3 percent to 72.3 percent during that period. This growth can mainly be explained by the increased demand for agricultural and consumer goods stimulated by the province's agricultural boom during the 1970s. The lower share in 1983, on the other hand, reflects the deepening economic crisis.

While the retail and wholesale sectors dominated in quantitative terms, their contribution to employment was less significant. Although no government agency in Iloilo could provide reliable data, employment in the retail and wholesale sectors was estimated at approximately 20 percent.

Community, social, and personal services also displayed a relatively fast growth in terms of business establishments. Their share rose from 13.5 percent in 1972 to almost 25 percent in 1983 (see Table 3.13). Perhaps the most dynamic sector was finance. The number of banking institutions and investment companies more than trebled between 1968 and 1985, rising from seventeen to sixty.

The growth in commerce and services is characterized by a simultaneous decline in manufacturing, though due to classification errors this

TABLE 3.13 Number of Business Establishments, Iloilo City, 1967, 1972, 1979, 1983

Type of Industry	1967 %	1972 N	1972 %	1979 N	1979 %	1983 N	1983 %
					Number of Establishments		
Agriculture and fisheries	4.6	--	--	7	0.14	20	0.36
Mining and quarrying	0.2	12	0.26	--	--	--	--
Manufacturing	18.6	466	10.27	343	7.07	230	4.09
Electricity, water, gas	0.6	4	0.09	18	0.37	9	0.16
Wholesale, retail, restaurants, and hotels	54.3	3,159	69.61	3,506	72.26	3,626	64.46
Transport, communication, and storage	11.0	82	1.81	22	0.45	51	0.91
Finance, insurance, real estate, and business services	20.3	200	4.41	169	3.48	299	5.32
Community, social, and personal services	20.3	615	13.55	787	16.22	1,390	24.71
Total	100.1	4,538	100.00	4,852	99.99	5,625	100.01

Sources: Iloilo City, Mayor's Office, Permits and License Division; Howard M. Leichter, *Political Regime and Public Policy in the Philippines: A Comparison of Bacolod and Iloilo Cities* (DeKalb: Center for Southeast Asian Studies, Northern Illinois University, Special Report, No. 11, 1975), p. 36; City of Iloilo, *Socio-Economic Profile* (Iloilo City: City Government of Iloilo), p. 37; and City of Iloilo, *Socio-Economic and Physical Profile* (Iloilo City: City Government of Iloilo, 1985), p. 50.

is less drastic than appears from the figures in Table 3.13. Based on estimates, in the mid-1980s manufacturing had a share of 5 percent of Iloilo's establishments and provided between 10 and 13 percent of the city's employment. The decrease from almost 19 percent of establishments in 1967 to less than 5 percent is nevertheless substantial. Some observers even went so far as to speak of a deindustrialization process in Iloilo City. The continuous shut-down of manufacturing firms not only affected small-sized firms, but also large companies such as the Benedicto-owned Strachan and MacMurray metal works company. However, the failure of firms was particularly striking among small-scale enterprises -- especially those engaged in food processing, metal and machinery works, and clothing. These three branches comprised more than 77 percent of Iloilo's manufacturing firms (National Economic and Development Authority 1978:4.1).

The collapse of these firms can be explained by a whole range of factors: stiff competition from Manila-based firms, double-digit inflation, the oil crises, the bias against small-scale industries inherent in the structural adjustment policy prescribed for the Philippine government by the World Bank and International Monetary Fund, unfavorable foreign exchange regulations (after 1983), the nonavailability of cheap credit, and the sugar crisis that had severe repercussions on ancillary industries such as metal working and machine shops.

Apart from the collapse of many firms, there was a gradual relocation of companies to adjacent municipalities. Established firms such as the San Miguel Coca Cola bottling plant or Agro Industries Enterprises went to Barrio Ungka, Pavia, while a Pepsi Cola bottling plant was opened in San Miguel municipality. These nearby municipalities offer satisfactory infrastructural facilities, space for expansion, lower land prices, and lower taxes. There was virtually no fresh investment in Iloilo's manufacturing sector to replace these losses, neither from Iloilo's indigenous entrepreneurs, nor from foreign investors or companies from other parts of the country.

Agriculture and fishing remained important factors in Iloilo's economy. They still provided 10-15 percent of the city's employment. While in Thai regional cities agriculture has been declining rapidly in economic importance, under the impact of the economic crisis a different trend was likely to occur in Philippine cities. Faced with decreasing real wages and high rates of unemployment, subsistence fishing and backyard gardening were an important means of survival for a substantial segment of Iloilo's population.

Unlike in Chiang Mai, tourism did not contribute much to the city's economy. Tourist arrivals were few and have stagnated since 1980.[78]

The tourist industry of Iloilo was only weakly linked to the service, retail, and manufacturing sectors. The direct employment generated by tourism in the city's seven hotels and thirty-seven other accommodation establishments covered less than 1 percent of Iloilo's work force.

A comparison between Iloilo City's economic structure and those of other Philippine regional cities revealed many similarities. In all cities, the commercial and service sectors played the dominant role. Yet, Iloilo seems to have a more developed and diversified service sector than Bacolod and Davao, while Davao has a stronger manufacturing sector.

Iloilo's urban economy was characterized by a high level of *"tertiarization"*. Almost 95 percent of all business establishments operated in the tertiary sector. This was an even higher level than in Chiang Mai. However, it seems that in terms of employment *tertiarization* in Iloilo City was slightly lower than in Chiang Mai. The tertiary sector accounted for approximately 75-80 percent of all employment. This also included the city's large informal sector which is usually not reflected in official employment data. According to NEDA sources, there were about 10,000 hawker units in Iloilo City, with each unit employing about 1.5 workers.[79]

A second major feature of Iloilo's economy was its "small shop" structure, which was even more pronounced than in Chiang Mai. More than 97 percent of the city's registered businesses employed fewer than twenty workers, 83.6 percent fewer than five workers (Iloilo City 1977:98). Many of these establishments were notoriously short of working capital and unstable, always on the brink of collapse. While in a rapidly expanding and diversifying economy like Chiang Mai's, a "small shop" structure may contribute to the development of entrepreneurial skills and serve as a starting point for a more consolidated and balanced economy, in an environment of economic decay, small-scale and "mini"-businesses are merely a vehicle for economic survival without any real growth potential.

Social Development

Iloilo was confronted with more serious social problems than Chiang Mai and Penang were. They were the result of the city's contracting economy, the structural inequities of peripheral capitalism, elitist and, at the same time, ultraconservative value patterns of local decision-makers, and poor performance of the city government in the delivery of public services. However, from income data alone it is quite difficult to decide whether living conditions in Iloilo deteriorated over the last twenty years or not. The poverty thresholds suggested in the literature

are hardly compatible and thus not suitable for diachronic comparisons.[80] But by using nationwide socioeconomic indicators and in view
of Iloilo's past economic development, one is safe in assuming a deterioration of living conditions since the mid-1970s which affected the lower-
classes, in particular. Real wages declined by over 30 percent between
1972 and the early 1980s (Rüland 1982c:34) and most likely experienced
another sharp decline during the economic crisis following the Aquino
assassination.

By the end of 1983 there was a high poverty incidence in Iloilo City.
Based on NCSO data, 59.81 percent of the population lived below the
poverty threshold which at that time stood at P 1,163.40 per month. The
median monthly household income was P 963 in 1983 (City of Iloilo
1985:53). Iloilo's poverty incidence is thus much higher than in Chiang
Mai and Penang, albeit slightly lower than in Bacolod City. Lopez-Gonzaga computed that in Bacolod 64.5 percent of households had incomes
below the poverty threshold (Lopez-Gonzaga 1985:9).

While in Iloilo a large segment of the population must be classified as
poor, there was a relatively small middle-class -- ranging from lower-
middle-class households earning around P 1,800 a month to an upper-
middle-class with monthly incomes of more than P 15,000 (1983 income
data). This group comprised about 23 percent of the population.[81] An
additional 14 percent of households were in the income bracket of
P 1,200-1,799 per month -- which was slightly above poverty threshold
(see Table 3.14). It was obvious that these households likewise live under rather precarious circumstances. Apart from these groups there was
a very small upper-class. Less than 1 percent of Iloilo's households
earned more than P 15,000 per month in 1983.

Available data suggest a slightly lower level of social inequality in
Iloilo City than in the Philippines as a whole. While in 1980, the upper
20 percent of Filipino households earned 59.2 percent of total income,
the lowest 20 percent earned only 3.8 percent (National Census and
Statistics Office 1981). Based on 1980 data of the NCSO, the upper 20
percent of Iloilo City's households earned 56.4 percent and the lowest 20
percent slightly over 3.2 percent of total household income in the city.

Poverty was aggravated by a contracting labor market. Apart from
the closure of many business establishments between 1981 and 1985,
most employers were forced to retrench. Since vacant positions were
generally frozen, vacancies were rarely reported to the local bureau of
the Ministry of Labor and Employment (MOLE). In case of need, many
companies increasingly resorted to overtime work, which may modestly
benefit those with jobs, but aggravated the economic position of the unemployed and underemployed. Although MOLE could not provide ac-

TABLE 3.14 Monthly Family Income, by Income Class, Iloilo City, April 1983

Income	Percent	Percent, Cumulative
0-299	5.56	5.56
300-599	19.19	24.75
600-999	22.14	46.89
900-1,199	14.72	61.61
1,200-1,499	7.12	68.73
1,500-1,799	6.52	75.25
1,800-2,099	5.57	80.82
2,100-2,399	2.93	83.75
2,400-2,699	2.85	86.60
2,700-2,999	2.07	88.67
3,000 and above	11.33	100.00

Source: City of Iloilo, Socioeconomic and Physical Profile (Iloilo City: City Government of Iloilo, 1985), p. 53.

curate data on unemployment in Iloilo, the figure must be estimated at around 20 percent. Apart from that, a high percentage of workers relied on irregular and poorly paid casual work, suggesting a high rate of underemployment, too. Iloilo's labor market was thus unable to absorb the growing numbers of new entrants. Based on data of the city planners, Iloilo's labor market grew between 3.2 and 3.6 percent per year. This did not include new entrants from adjacent municipalities who sought work in Iloilo City. If new jobseekers from neighboring towns were included, Iloilo's labor market would be growing at an average annual rate of between 5.2 and 5.8 percent (City of Iloilo 1980:33).

Urban poverty and unemployment were partly cushioned by Iloilo's large informal sector and by part-time agricultural activities. Especially in Iloilo's more than thirty-two rural barangays subsistence food production and fishing complemented low monetary incomes. The city profile of 1985, for instance, recorded 24,645 fishermen, of whom, however, only 1,323 (or 5.4 percent) were engaged in commercial fishing (City of Iloilo 1985:44). The number of farms was also on the rise. Although agricultural land and open space in Iloilo City has declined continuously since the early 1970s, the number of farms within the city's boundaries rose from 1,549 in 1971 to 2,603 in 1980 (City of Iloilo 1985:42). This is equivalent to a 68 percent increase over a ten-year period. The hectarage of cultivated land also increased by 32 percent over the same period (Republic of the Philippines, National Economic and Development Authority, National Census and Statistics Office 1983a:6).

Lack of economic opportunities and the corresponding social problems made Iloilo an outmigration area with an outmigration rate of 0.7

percent in the early 1980s. Unlike other regional cities with a larger hin-terland, such as Davao, Zamboanga, and Cagayan de Oro, rural migra-tion to Iloilo was restricted to nearby municipalities and the other provinces of Panay Island. In many cases, this migration marked only the first step in the move to Manila. Due to the insurgency problems, deteriorating law and order, and declining land resources, by the mid-1980s the capital had clearly overtaken Mindanao's frontier areas in at-tractiveness for Visayan migrants. However, rural-urban migration and the related poverty problems will appreciate under the conditions of continued economic crisis. Although Panay's social and economic fabric is somewhat more resistant to destitution than that of Negros, here too displaced rural workers and impoverished peasants may move city-wards as observed by Lopez-Gonzaga in her study of Bacolod (Lopez-Gonzaga 1985:34). Moreover, in 1986 insurgency was spreading on Panay as well, constituting another reason for intensifying the *"push"* towards the cities.

The Development Potential of Iloilo City

Like Chiang Mai, Iloilo has been chosen by the central government as a development center in the Philippine Regional Cities Development Program (RCDP). The Philippine RCDP essentially pursued the same objectives as the Thai program: to transform selected cities into growth centers with the ability to stimulate economic growth in surrounding rural areas. In the following sections I will examine to what extent Iloilo City can actually perform this function.

The Regional Cities Development Program (RCDP). RCDP is part of a program package for regional development. Individual components of this package were successively initiated during the 1970s, but not pieced together into a comprehensive program as outlined in Thailand's Fifth Economic and Social Development Plan. As in the Thai case, RCDP aims at the dispersal of urban and economic growth, the diversion of migra-tory streams from the NCR, the correction of regional development im-balances, and the promotion of administrative decentralization.

RCDP has five major components: demographic, infrastructural, eco-nomic, administrative, and social (Government of the Republic of the Philippines, International Bank for Reconstruction and Development 1982b:1-10; Rüland and Sajo 1988:278). Total project costs amount to P 147.41 millon, part of which is covered by a World Bank loan. The lion's share of investments goes to infrastructure development (56.25 percent), but a substantial portion is also devoted to the social sphere (38.91 percent) (Government of the Republic of the Philippines, International Bank for Reconstruction and Development 1982b:5).

A preliminary assessment of RCDP leads to the following conclusions:

Economic Impact. The economic crisis in the Philippines severely limits the impact of the economic stimuli of RCDP. Such situations are usually characterized by a lack of investment capital and, if there is some, hesitance on the part of the private sector to found new or expand existing businesses. Moreover, prospects for relocation of firms from the National Capital Region to Iloilo are rather dim, since in times of economic crisis many entrepreneurs regard proximity to the decision-making centers in the national bureaucracy a prerequisite for survival.

While there are infrastructural foundations on which an expanding economy could build such as the international port, the fishing port complex, an airport, and a well-developed road system, there are major obstacles to a more dynamic growth of Iloilo's economy.

1. Although no studies are available, one is hardly wrong in assuming that there are only few forward and backward linkages between the city and the hinterland. Due to the structure of the manufacturing sector there are probably more backward than forward linkages. Moreover, there is much reason to believe that spread effects to the hinterland even through salaries and wages are rather limited. In order to get a foothold in the city's labor market -- which basically offers odd jobs -- one must be integrated into an informal job information network and respond quickly to opportunities. This is only possible if one resides in the city. Furthermore, many rural jobseekers are too poor to afford commuting between their hometown and the city. Many workers in fact decide to move to the city and settle in one of the numerous depressed areas.

2. The hinterland provides only a limited market for urban products and services (Rüland and Sajo 1988:280). On Panay, with a population of 2.4 million, only 10 percent of the households had enough purchasing power to buy goods and services from Iloilo's economy.[82]

Other markets in the Visayas and Northern Mindanao are controlled by economically more dynamic Cebu, while demand for less sophisticated goods and services is covered by other central places such as Bacolod, Dumaguete, and Cagayan de Oro. Taking into account the structure and state of Iloilo's economy in the mid-1980s, hopes of gaining a foothold in the country's main markets in the capital and surrounding regions were illusory.

3. Regional city development cannot be separated from development processes in the surrounding rural areas. Otherwise, investments in the city are likely to produce little more than an urban growth enclave. Re-

gional development is not a one-way process, automatically spreading from the city to the rural areas, but a mutual process. Without the demand for urban goods and services and the necessary purchasing power in the hinterland, capital investment in the regional urban center will not translate into sustained economic growth and will be a waste of scarce resources (Rüland and Sajo 1988:283).

Iloilo's prospects for economic growth would greatly improve, if RCDP were paralleled by infrastructure development outside the city, agricultural diversification, and land reform. While linkages between city and hinterland have been improved in recent years through a large-scale road construction program, efforts to diversify the agricultural production are still in the initial stages. The most important element would be an agrarian land reform that goes beyond the half-hearted approach of the Marcos administration. The highly skewed land ownership pattern on Panay is the single most important obstacle to an improvement of living conditions in the rural hinterland. Agricultural census data show that, despite minor improvements, a small number of farms still control large tracts of arable land. Furthermore, the percentage of owner-cultivators is low in all four provinces of Panay.

In addition, agrarian reform must be linked to an effective agricultural credit program. Although Iloilo City has a well-developed finance sector, there are few credit facilities for small farmers and small-scale businessmen. Commercial banks have strong objections to granting credits to farmers, because peasants with holdings of less than 5 hectares cannot provide collateral. Apart from high interest rates, deliberate delays in deciding credit applications by the banks discourages farmers from tapping existing credit facilities. Because of these difficulties many farmers simply resort to traditional forms of credit.[83]

4. RCDP does not include an attractive package of investment incentives. Existing incentives under RA 5186 *(Investment Incentives Act)* and RA 6135 *(Export Incentives Act)* had only a limited impact on industrial dispersal and regional economic growth. Of the projects promoted by the BOI under RA 5186, only 4.4 percent of the total investments and 1.99 percent of the newly generated employment benefited Region VI between 1968 and 1977. The case is similar with respect to RA 6135. Between 1970 and 1977 only 1.4 percent of the total investment, 0.7 percent of the employment, and 1.5 percent of the registered firms went to Region VI. Throughout the 1970s the NCR and Region IV remained the "core investment region". The NCR alone received between 85-90 percent of new private investment in 1979 and 1980. Furthermore, the NCR and Region IV had a share of almost 27 percent of the investments made under the *Investment Incentives Act* and 32.4 percent of the employment

generated between 1968 and 1977. Moreover, in the seven-year period from 1970 to 1977 66.4 percent of the new investments in the export sector and 82.75 percent of the employment were concentrated in the capital and its immediate surroundings. Not surprisingly, the NCR's share in industrial output increased constantly: from 42 percent of the manufacturing sector's total value added in 1948 to 50 percent in 1961 and 63 percent in the mid-1970s (Rüland 1982a:63). Region IV and the NCR also got the greatest share of public expenditure for infrastructure projects: in 1959-1961 the region's share was 49.6 percent. It decreased to 28.3 percent in 1971-1973, before rising again slightly to 32.8 percent between 1979 and 1982. In comparison, Region VI received 7.1 percent in 1959-1961, 1.8 percent in 1971-1973,[84] and 8.5 percent in 1979-1982. Nationwide, Region VI thus ranked fifth in terms of public infrastructure investment over the three periods (Bacani 1981:47-55).[85]

   5. Infrastructural problems such as inadequate water supply and high electricity rates persisted. As a result, the new fishing port complex, which depends on reliable water supplies for its refrigeration and fish processing facilities, could not operate fully after its inauguration in 1986. Water had to be hauled by truck from Pavia, 11 km away. Due to these infrastructural problems, few fish traders have so far "accepted" the new port facilities. Critics thus speak of "another white elephant" serving Japanese demand for imported marine products, but failing to benefit Iloilo's economy.

   6. The industrial estate planned in Iloilo was part of a nationwide industrial estate program drawn up in 1975 and 1976. The program envisioned the establishment of industrial estates and export processing zones (EPZs) in each region of the country. Altogether forty-two sites were planned, one of them the site in Iloilo City.

   The creation of an industrial estate will not contribute much to the economic development of Iloilo City. Due to significant changes in the world economy, the industrial estate concept based on light industries has lost its attraction in many Third-World countries. Such a concept is strongly dependent on foreign investors that -- in view of the nationwide recession and political uncertainty in the Philippines -- are unlikely to appear. In so far as such an industrial estate focusses on export-oriented firms, increasing protectionism of industrialized nations is another factor working against the estate concept. Furthermore, in the last ten to fifteen years so many industrial estates have emerged in Third-World countries that the ensuing competition for investors and the high construction costs will render economic benefits for latecomers marginal. Finally, far-reaching technological changes in the field of microelectronics cast further doubt on the estate concept. Automatized production in industrialized nations deprives developing countries and NICs of their comparative wage advantage and thus of a major incentive for foreign investors to relocate their plants to these countries. The Aquino government's decision to shelve the NEDA industrial estate program in Iloilo may thus be considered a sound decision.

7. Iloilo City does not have a comparative wage advantage over the National Capital Region. There is only a slight wage differential between Iloilo City and Metro Manila. As of November 1985, nonagricultural wages (including living allowances) were P 57.08 the National Capital Region and P 56.00 in Iloilo City.

8. Regionalization of industries is hampered by structural deficiencies of the Philippine economy. In the garments industry, which accounts for more than a quarter of Iloilo's manufacturing establishments, delivery of raw materials is controlled by Manila-based textile mills which have interests in garment manufacturing, too. Prices for raw materials are thus kept artificially high in order to prevent provincial producers from conquering substantial slices of the market in their respective region.

Apart from this, the Philippine economy is characterized by a system of interlocking directorates. The country's major banks have stakes in manufacturing enterprises, the bulk of which are located in the NCR. Credit is thus extended to provincial manufacturing firms only very hesitantly, as these companies may develop into competitors of the bank-controlled firms in the NCR. Moreover, the tendency of businessmen to favor internally integrated investments in complementary activities creates few linkages to other sectors, firms, and organizations (Rondinelli 1983a:193).

While all these factors define the limits of economic growth in Iloilo City, and neutralize many of the RCDP's infrastructural incentives, there may be growth opportunities in the agro-industrial sector. Between 1978 and 1982 agriculture was the most successful sector in terms of GDP growth in Region VI. Annual growth during these years averaged 6.4 percent. Although the sector has been adversely affected by the sugar slump in recent years, it still produced moderate growth rates on Panay Island, which is more diversified than, for instance, neighboring Negros. NEDA feasibility studies on the diversification of Iloilo's economy have identified a whole range of agricultural and aquacultural products with good prospects for processing in Iloilo City: mango and papaya drying, juice, coffee and cocoa, fish and prawns, feed milling, organic fertilizer, etc. Further opportunities exist in the production of simple agricultural machinery.

Nevertheless, it would be wrong to consider agro-industrial development a panacea for Iloilo's ailing economy. Agro-industries are propagated as a development strategy for regional cities in other Southeast Asian countries as well. Since the products are similar, possible economic gains may be neutralized by a glut of nonmarketable goods. Furthermore, as long as agro-led industrial development is controlled by a few TNCs and other monopolists, its effect on urban and rural incomes is likely to be negligible. This, at least, is the lesson of twenty years of agro-industrial development in Mindanao.

The service sector, trade, and commerce have further growth potential. Tourism, on the other hand, will not have a major impact on the city's economy in the future. Water pollution, due to the emission of the city's sewerage into the sea, and the occupation of the seashores by squatters limit the development of beach resorts in the immediate vicinity of the city. Only Guimaras Island holds some potential for tourism which will , however, hardly have a major impact on Iloilo's economy.

Social Impact. The social component of RCDP is a major portion of the project. 35.1 percent of the project costs alone are to be devoted to low-cost housing. Shelter needs of low-income groups are covered by a sites-and-services project and the upgrading of existing dwellings in various depressed areas. The sites-and-services project offers 2,304 plots ranging from 60 to 150 sqm. 1,854 units will be constructed in Mandurriao, which serves as a resettlement site for squatters from the foreshore area. Each plot includes a sanitary core, a water and sewerage connection, drainage, electricity, and access by footpath. It is also to be served with regular solid waste collection (Government of the Republic of the Philippines, International Bank for Reconstruction and Development 1982b:4; Rüland and Sajo 1988:280).

According to the 1981 household surveys, sites-and-services are affordable down to the thirteenth income percentile of the target population, which was equivalent to a monthly income of P 320. Those below the affordability margin were promised assistance under the upgrading program (Government of the Republic of the Philippines, International Bank for Reconstruction and Development 1982a:53).

The slum-upgrading projects for six depressed *barangays* in the foreshore area and in Barrio Obrero offer smaller plot sizes, ranging from 46 to 110 sqm. The project includes the construction of communal toilets, wash house blocks, solid waste collection, land filling, drainage, and improved access to the dwellings by concreted footpaths. Densities will be reduced through reblocking. The "overspill" population will be offered plots in the sites-and-services scheme in Mandurriao. Based on the same household surveys, the project planners claimed that upgrading is affordable down to the fifth income percentile of the target group. In 1981, this was equivalent to a monthly income of P 223 (Government of the Republic of the Philippines, International Bank for Reconstruction and Development 1982b:1).

While the planned 4,504 units will bring affordable housing to a greater range of low-income families, the project nevertheless has major flaws.

What was criticized in the Chiang Mai upgrading projects holds even more for Iloilo City. The housing project only provides infrastructural "hardware", but no funds are allocated for supporting social services. The relocation of around 10,000 persons to the Mandurriao site, i.e. the creation of a new community, creates enormous economic, social, and psychological strains on the relocatees. No information was available as to how, by whom, and to what extent health care, welfare services, day-care centers, nutritional programs, vocational training, etc. will be provided. In view of its constrained financial situation the city government is hardly in a position to cover these needs.

According to planning documents, the overriding objective of the project is cost recovery. One of the feasibility studies reads as follows: "it is essential . . . that every effort is made to obtain a high level of cost recovery from the benefited households" (Government of the Republic of the Philippines, International Bank for Reconstruction and Development 1982b:15). If pursued strictly, cost recovery will probably exclude the poorest families from the project.

The affordability calculations are clearly biased in favor of lower-middle-class households. The data on which the minimum monthly incomes for cost recovery were based were derived from income surveys in several depressed *barangays*. As has been pointed out earlier, costs for sites-and-services were affordable down to the thirteenth income percentile, and with upgrading down to the fifth percentile. Yet, if the income distribution for Iloilo City as a whole is used, households could afford sites-and-services only down to the twenty-eighth and with upgrading only down to the sixteenth percentile. This means that the depressed areas selected for the project were highly stratified and included a considerable proportion of lower-middle-class families -- a fact admitted by the authors of the feasibility study. It also means that there must be communities in Iloilo City which are considerably poorer, but which have been excluded were a priori from the housing program.

The affordability calculations are obsolete, due to the economic crisis and high inflation in 1984 and 1985. In times of economic crisis the poor are the group first and most severely hit by the combined effects of inflation and shrinking employment opportunities. As a result, at the time of the field research, affordability must have declined even further.

Furthermore, affordability calculations are misleading. To the rent or purchase costs additional costs must be added: property tax payments, electricity and water bills, and transport costs. The project estimated these extra costs at an additional 20 to 35 pesos. But for those relocated to Mandurriao or Barrio Obrero transport to their place of work in the inner-city would alone cost 40-60 pesos per month. Moreover, the minimum rent of 60 pesos in the sites-and-services project applies to only 11.6 percent of the plots. All other plots are considerably more expensive.

The affordability calculations are based on the assumption that beneficiaries can spend about 20 percent of their monthly income on amortization or rent (excluding extra costs for water, electricity, transport, etc.) (Government of the Republic of the Philippines, International Bank for Reconstruction and Development 1982a:20). Past experience with low-cost housing projects, however, suggests that the poor are rarely prepared to pay more than 10 percent of their monthly income for housing (Oberndörfer 1979; Bello 1982; Rüland 1982b; Oberndörfer and Rüland 1984). The affordability problem is further aggravated by the fact that there will be no employment at the relocation site in Mandurriao when the first families arrive.

All these factors lead to enormous additional financial burdens for the resettled families. But the project managers are in a dilemma, too, as their sole means of controlling exploding costs is the reduction of design and service standards. With limited scope for cross-subsidization and other equity measures the RCDP's low-cost housing component is likely to repeat the experience of such projects elsewhere: the main beneficiaries are middle-class families, who move into the project after the strong economic pressures has displaced the poorer segments of the target group. They become "urban refugees" who, after losing or giving up their rights in the project, end up moving from one squatter colony to the next.

Notes

1. Calculations based on data derived from Republic of the Philippines, National Economic and Development Authority, National Census and Statistics Office, *Philippine Yearbook* (Manila 1985), p. 137-140.

2. Ibid.

3. Legal provisions formally increasing local autonomy were, among others, Presidential Decree (PD) 144, PD 231 *(Local Tax Code)*, PD 464 *(Real Property Tax*

Code), PD 477, PD 752, PD 1256 and Proclamation No. 1759 (declaring 1979 as
the Local Government Year). These legal provisions, however, were scaled
down in their importance through other decrees which, in effect, curbed local
autonomy. Such laws included PD 824 (creation of the Metro Manila Commission), PD 826 (abolishing vice mayors and creating the *Sangguniang Bayans* and
Sangguniang Panglungsods as new local legislatures), PD 1136 (creating the Joint
Commission on Local Government Personnel Administration), PD 1396
(creating the Ministry of Human Settlements), Letter of Instruction (LOI) 265
(creating the Performance Audit Team to screen local officials) and LOI 356
(reformulating the tenure of local officials).

4. *Business Day*, Manila, 6 November 1985, p. 10.
5. *Business Day*, Manila, 13 November 1986, p. 24.
6. *Malaya*, Manila, 22 February 1987, p. 24.
7. *The Visayan Tribune*, Iloilo City, 2 October 1978, p. 1.
8. The Aquino administration abolished the MHS in 1986.
9. See Local Government Code, Book II, Title Three, Chapter Three, Article
Three, p. 71.
10. PD 1375 transferred budget supervision from the Ministry of Finance to
the Ministry of Budget.
11. If not indicated otherwise, financial data were derived from Republic of
the Philippines, Commission on Audit, *Annual Financial Report, Local Governments (Provinces, Cities, Municipalities)* (Manila: 1979-1984).
12. With a record high of 64 percent in October 1983.
13. For instance, appartments were usually classified as residential rather
than as commercial properties. The rate for residential properties (1.5 percent) is
lower than for commercial properties (2.0 percent) (Regional Cities Development Project. *Financial Study* (Manila: National Economic and Development
Authority, 1979), p.16.
14. In December 1980 textile and financial tycoon Dewee Dee fled the country
with debts amounting to P 635 million. Dee's flight caused a panic run on the
banks and a collapse of the Manila stock market. In the process, a number of
major business conglomerates, most of them controled by Marcos cronies, were
on the verge of bankruptcy.
15. *Panay News*, Iloilo City, 9-15 January 1985.
16. *The Visayan Tribune*, Iloilo City, 29 November 1982, p. 3.
17. In 1980 the city government decided to impose the maximum rates for
real properties.
18. 69.6 percent of the respondents in Sosmeña's survey were of the opinion
that local governments have inadequate taxing powers. Gaudioso C. Sosmeña,
"Policy Analysis: The Case of Local Governments," Ph.D. Thesis, Centro-Escolar
University, Manila, 1980, p. 220.
19. 45 percent for salaries and wages, an 18 percent contribution to the National Integrated Police, 8-12 percent for Infrastructure Fund Transfer, 2 percent
statutory reserve as well as expenditure for an election reserve and the
Barangay Development Fund. See Roy W. Bahl and B.D. Miller (eds.), *Local
Government Finance in the Third World. A Case Study of the Philippines* (New York:

Praeger, 1983), pp. 1-10. Under the Aquino government, these statutory obligations have been temporarily suspended, but -- as Padilla suspects -- may be reimposed at a later point of time. See Perfecto L. Padilla, *Need for a Truly Meaningful, more Substantive Decentralization and Local Autonomy* (Manila: College of Public Administration, University of the Philippines 1990), pp. 9,31

20. The Municipal Development Fund (MDF) was created through PD 1914 in May 1984 as a revolving fund. The MDF is capitalized and funded by proceeds of foreign loans, assistance or grants which are made available to the local governments for specific purposes, projects and activities set forth under international agreements between the Philippine government and foreign governments or international organizations. Funds from the MDF shall be made available to the local government as loans which shall be treated as trust fund and amortized by the local governments. The amortization (interest and principal) made by the local governments to the MDF shall form part of the MDF and be made automatically available for relending to finance similar local government projects.

21. *Manila Bulletin*, Manila, 24 February 1987, p. 12.

22. 168 employees were fired in San Fernando, Pampanga, and about 100 casuals in Danao City, Cebu. *Manila Times*, 3 April 1986, p. 2 and 3 June 1986, p. 2.

23. For similar experiences with BLISS in Angeles City, Imus and Metro Manila, see T. Firmalino, Plan Implementation: A Case Study of Angeles City, in *Philippine Planning Journal*, Vol. XI, No. 2 1980, pp. 1-7, A. Gozun-Laureta, "The Impact of Inter-Governmental Transfers on Local Government Finance" Ph.D. Thesis: University of the Philippines, Manila 1982, pp. 111, 117, and Jürgen Rüland, *Politik und Verwaltung in Metro Manila. Aspekte der Herrschaftsstabilisierung in einem autoritären politischen System* (Munich, Cologne, and London: Weltforum Verlag 1982), p. 86.

24. *The Visayan Tribune*, Iloilo City, 26 May 1980, p. 1.

25. The Regional Development Council is composed of the provincial governors of the region, the regional director of NEDA, the heads of the regional offices of other national government agencies as well as the city mayors of the region.

26. According to information provided by The Philippine Long Distance Company, the population-telephone line ratio was 12:1 in Metro Manila, 19.7:1 in Bacolod, and 51.2:1 in Davao in the first half of the 1980s.

27. *Panay News*, Iloilo City, 2-8 January 1985.

28. *The Visayan Tribune*, Iloilo City, 20 November 1967.

29. *The Visayan Tribune*, Iloilo City, 14 March 1977, p. 2; Romeo B. Ocampo and Elena Panganiban, *The Philippine Local Government System. History, Politics and Finance* (Manila: Local Government Center, College of Public Administration, University of the Philippines 1985), p. 70.

30. *Bulletin Today*, Manila, 16 December 1979, p. 1.

31. *Daily Express*, Manila, 27 December 1979, p. 1.

32. *Bulletin Today*, Manila, 19 December 1979, p. 33; Ma. Aurora Carbonell-Catilo et al., *Manipulated Elections* (Manila: College of Public Administration, University of the Philippines, 1985), p. 70.

33. According to the law, a candidate's campaign spendings were not permitted to exceed the total salary he would receive during a complete term of office.

34. *Bulletin Today*, Manila, 19 March 1984, p. 1.

35. *The Visayan Tribune*, Iloilo City, 21 January 1980, p. 1.

36. Calculated from *The Visayan Tribune*, Iloilo City, 4 February 1980, p. 1 and 11 February 1980, p. 2.

37. *Times Journal*, Manila, 13 January 1980, p. 1.

38. *The Visayan Tribune*, Iloilo City, 18 November 1963, p. 1.

39. *The Visayan Tribune*, Iloilo City, 11 September 1967, p. 1.

40. *The Visayan Tribune*, Iloilo City, 24 September 1979, p. 1.

41. Interview information.

42. *The Visayan Tribune*, Iloilo City, 19 January 1981, p. 5.

43. *The Visayan Tribune*, Iloilo City, 29 November 1982, p. 1.

44. In order to increase popular control over local officials, the Philippine Local Government Code provided opportunities to recall elected officials who lost the trust of the public. Of course, this provision could also be used by the regime to replace officials by maintaining a semblance of democratic procedure. See Local Government Code, Book I, Title Two, Chapter Three. However, according to interview sources in the MLG, local officials have so far been recalled only in a few instances.

45. *Panay News*, Iloilo City, 20-26 December 1983, p. 1.

46. *Panay News*, Iloilo City, 22-28 May 1982, 15-21 March 1983, 11-17 April 1983, 17-23 May 1983, and 20-26 December 1983.

47. *Panay News*, Iloilo City, 8-14 August 1984.

48. *Morning Sun*, Iloilo City, 28 October- 3 November 1986, p. 1.

49. *The Visayan Tribune*, Iloilo City, 31 May 1982, p. 1.

50. A 10 percent share in real property tax collections with no major restrictions on its use, a P 600 contribution of the city government to the Barangay Development Fund, a Bureau of Internal Revenue (BIR) allotment for community development, and a specific tax allotment for road, bridge and infrastructure construction, improvement and maintenance. Katipunan ng mga Barangay ng Metropolitan Manila, *Aklat-Gabay ng Barangay, Manual* (Manila: Katipunan ng mga Barangay ng Metropolitan Manila, n.d.), p. 247-258; Local Government Code, Book II, Title One, Chapter 7, pp.32-35; Roy Bahl and Barbara Miller (eds.), *Local Government Finance*, p. 128.

51. *The Visayan Tribune*, Iloilo City, 12 June 1978, p. 1, 19 February 1979; *Panay News*, 22-28 May 1985. De Guzman and Tangcanco found in their analysis of the 1984 parliamentary elections that dole outs to individual barangays amounted to between P 10,000 in Bataan and P 500,000 in Metro Manila. Raul P. de Guzman and L.G. Tangcanco, *An Assessment of the May 1984 Batasang Pambansa Elections: A Summary of Findings* (Manila: College of Public Administration, University of the Philippines 1986), p. 65.

52. *Panay News*, Iloilo City, 30 January 1985, p. 1.

53. Compiled from Republic of the Philippines, Commission on Elections, *Reports of the COMELEC to the President of the Philippines and the Congress on the Manner the Elections were Held on November 8, 1955; November 10, 1959; November*

12, *1963; November 14, 1967; November 8, 1971* (Manila: Commission on Elections).

54. For the causes of Iloilo's economic decline see Alfred W. McCoy, "Ylo-ilo: Factional Conflict in a Colonial Economy, Iloilo Province, Philippines, 1937-1955" Ph.D. Thesis, Yale University 1977; and Alfred W. McCoy, A Queen Dies Slowly: The Rise and Decline of Iloilo City, in Alfred W. McCoy and Ed. C. de Jesus (eds.), *Philippine Social History. Global Trade and Local Transformations* (Manila and Sydney: Ateneo de Manila University Press 1982).

55. *The Visayan Tribune,* Iloilo City, 20 November 1967, p. 1.

56. *The Visayan Tribune,* Iloilo City, 20 November 1963, p. 1.

57. *The Visayan Tribune,* Iloilo City, 11 September 1967, p. 1.

58. Senator Ganzon used similar words in an interview with the author by stating that he essentially represents those people "who were not born on the silver platter".

59. *The Visayan Tribune,* 25 September 1972.

60. *Malaya,* Manila, 6 January 1985, p. 1.

61. In Nueva Ecija, Wolters reported of local councillors being assigned a particular "territory" in which they could offer protection and collect money for toleating illegal activities such as gambling etc.). Willem Wolters, *Politics, Patronage and Class Conflict in Central Luzon* (The Hague: Institute of Social Studies, 1983), p. 209.

62. *The Visayan Times,* Iloilo City, 11 October 1971, p. 3.

63. *Bulletin Today,* Manila, 12 January 1980, p. 1.

64. In 1975 19,388 motor vehicles were registered in Iloilo City. This number decreased to 11,827 in 1982, before it rose again to 14,658 in 1985. Information provided by the Land Transportation Commission, Iloilo City.

65. *The Visayan Tribune,* Iloilo City, 5 September 1977, p. 2.

66. *The Visayan Tribune,* Iloilo City, 24 October 1977, p. 2.

67. *The Visayan Tribune,* Iloilo City, 19 September 1977, p. 2.

68. Interview information.

69. Data derived from the city development plans of Davao, Bacolod, and Cagayan de Oro.

70. *The Visayan Tribune,* Iloilo City, 2 October 1978, p. 1.

71. Interview information.

72. Interview information.

73. *The Visayan Tribune,* Iloilo City, 8 August 1977, p. 2.

74. Interview Information.

75. As of 1975, only 13 percent of households in Iloilo province, 10 percent in Capiz, 6 percent in Aklan, and 2 percent in Antique had access to electricity. National Economic and Development Authority, *Iloilo City Industrial Estate Project. Prefeasibility Report* (Iloilo City: National Economic and Development Authority, 1978), p. 3-11.

76. Information provided by the Land Transportation Commission, Iloilo City.

77. For instance, shortly after the appointment of the new city council, a delegation of councillors went to Cebu to study Cebu's success in becoming the Philippines' major investment center outside Manila.

78. The number of foreign tourists arriving in Iloilo declined after 1978 from 10,214 to 5,836 in 1980. See *Panay Tourism Bulletin,* Iloilo City, October 1981-January 1982, p. 9. In 1983 tourist arrivals rose again to 6,965. See Asian Institute of Tourism, *Survey on Tourism in Iloilo Province, Region VI* (Manila: Asian Institute of Tourism 1984).

79. Interview information.

80. For a further discussion see M.A.S. Abrera, Philippine Poverty Thresholds, in M. Mangahas (ed.), *Measuring Philippine Development. Report of the Social Indicators Project* (Manila: Development Academy of the Philippines, 1976), pp. 223-274.

81. This means that between 1939 and 1986 the middle-income group expanded by only 7 percent and, in fact, stagnated since 1970. See Howard M. Leichter, *Political Regime and Public Policy in the Philippines: A Comparison of Bacolod and Iloilo Cities* (De Kalb: Center for Southeast Asian Studies, Northern Illinois University, Special Report No. 11, 1975), p. 32.

82. Calculated from Republic of the Philippines, National Economic and Development Authority, National Census and Statistics Office, *Statistical Analyst, Region VI* (Iloilo City: National Economic and Development Authority, 1984), pp. 17-20.

83. This confirms what Rolf Hanisch has convincingly shown in his study *"Kleinbauernkredit in den Philippinen"* (Baden-Baden: Nomos, 1982): that the ultimate costs of the institutional agricultural credit are almost as high as in the informal credit system.

84. These figures reflect the relative strength of Iloilo's politicians in the national political arena. The figure for infrastructure investment in the region was relatively high in 1959-61, when, in a NP-led national government the influence of the Lopez/Ledesma faction was likewise high. The sharp decline in the early 1970s signified the political confrontation between Marcos and the Lopezes which ended with the defeat of the latter. Finally, the high investment ratio in the early 1980s must be attributed to the rise and immense power wielded by Roberto S. Benedicto, one of the leading Marcos cronies.

85. For a detailed analysis of regional development patterns see also Dirk Bronger, *Die Philippinen. Raumstrukturen, Entwicklungsprobleme, Regionale Entwicklungsplanung* (Hamburg: Mitteilungen des Instituts für Asienkunde, No. 159, 1987).

4

Municipal Government and Development in Penang

Introduction

Peninsular Malaysia is the most urbanized region of Southeast Asia. In 1985, 41 percent of its population lived in urban settlements of more than 10,000 inhabitants. Like in the Philippines, urbanization started very early. Already during the first decades of the twentieth century urban growth rates were remarkably high. This early urban growth was largely a result of large-scale Chinese and Indian immigration, fueled by a rapidly expanding plantation and mining economy and actively promoted by the colonial authorities to overcome labor shortages. The Chinese, in particular, frequently had an urban background before migrating to Malaysia and settled in urban centers ranging from the economically advanced Strait Settlements to the bazaar outpost at the jungle frontier (Kühne 1976; Kok 1986).

Immigration declined in the years between 1921 and 1947, following the imposition of immigration quotas by the colonial authorities. The repercussions of the Great Depression on Malaysia's colonial economy and the Japanese occupation during the Second World War further slowed down immigration and, hence, urban growth. Whereas the economic crisis in the 1930s led to a substantial remigration of aliens to their home countries, the Japanese occupation resulted in the flight of large numbers of Chinese city dwellers into rural squatterdom. Rapid urban growth resumed in the 1947-1957 intercensal period, which coincided with the *"Emergency"* (1948-1960). Widespread insecurity in the rural areas during a communist-led insurgency caused thousands of jungle farmers to move to the cities. Counterinsurgency policies further boosted urban growth, as the authorities forced more than half a million rural squatters -- mostly Chinese -- to resettle in strategic hamlets, the so-called *"New Villages"* (Kühne 1976, 1986; Kok 1986).

In the following period (1957-1970) urban growth rates slowed down, due to the massive rural development programs and land settlements schemes launched in the 1960s (Goldstein and Goldstein 1984:94). Finally, in the 1970-1980 intercensal period there was a renewal of urbanization. This new wave of urban migration was an effect of the government's *"New Economic Policy"* (NEP) which, inaugurated in 1970, was a deliberate attempt to encourage Malay urbanization through the promotion of rural industrialization and new town development in combination with numerous economic and educational privileges for Malays (Kühne 1976, 1986).

Malaysian urbanization, often considered a special case among Southeast Asia's unbalanced urban systems, resembles the settlement pattern in Thailand and the Philippines in at least one point. The major conurbation that has emerged in the Klang Valley already accounts for almost 40 percent of Peninsular Malaysia's urban population. Yet, as there are several other agglomerations such as Penang, Ipoh, and Johore Bahru (see Table 4.1), with a primacy rate of 1.3, Peninsular Malaysia has a considerably lower rate than the Philippines (4.1) and Thailand (11.0). This, however, does not mean that the Malaysian settlement system is without imbalances. The growth of a few major regional centers is clearly at the expense of the smaller urban areas. By keeping towns constant in all size classes, the two smallest categories (10,000-24,999 and 25,000-49,999) have declined continuously since 1957 (Kok 1986:63-64). Moreover, at 57 percent, the Central Region was by far the most urbanized region in 1985, followed by the Southern Region (39.4 percent), the Eastern Region (32.3 percent), and the Northern Region (32.2 percent). With a rate of 5.1 percent, the Central Region grew fastest between 1981 and 1985, closely followed by the Southern (4.5 percent) and the Eastern Region (4.2 percent) (Government of Malaysia 1986:184).

Malaysia is a *multiethnic* society. 56 percent of the population are *Bumiputras* (Malays and other indigenous peoples), 33.4 percent Chinese, 10 percent Indians, and 0.6 percent others (Shaari 1986:13). All societal issues thus have an ethnic dimension, be it politics, economics, or urbanization.

Due to the close interlinkages between immigration and urbanization, urban growth until the mid-twentieth century meant *"sinization"* (Kühne 1976:144). This process came to an end during the *"Emergency"*; the cityward migration of rural squatters and the creation of the *"New Villages"* marked the last major wave of Chinese urbanization. From then on, there has been a sharp increase in Malay urbanization. While the Chinese share of the urban population declined constantly, that of Malays increased rapidly (see Table 4.2). This was not only the result of

TABLE 4.1 Population Growth of Malaysian Regional Cities, 1957-1980

| City | Population | | |
	1957	1970	1980
Ipoh	125,776	269,316	344,627
Klang	75,649	113,607	192,080
Penang Island	338,693	432,822	489,500
(Georgetown)	234,093	269,247	250,349
Johore Bahru	74,909	155,800	247,100
Kota Bahru	38,103	55,124	167,872
Kuantan	23,034	43,358	131,547
Kuala Trengganu	29,446	53,320	180,296
Petaling Jaya	16,575	93,447	207,805

Source: Compiled from various Structure Plans such as Majlis Perbandaran Ipoh, *Report of Survey, Ipoh Structure Plan* (Ipoh: Majlis Perbandaran Ipoh, 1984), p. 29; Majlis Perbandaran Pulau Pinang, *Report of Survey. Penang Island Structure Plan* (Penang: Majlis Perbandaran Pulau Pinang, 1985), p. 33; Selangor State Government and Klang Valley Planning Authority, *Klang Draft Structure Plan 1986-2005. Statement of Policies and Proposals* (Klang: Selangor State Government and Klang Valley Planning Authority, 1986), p. 10; and L.L. Kok, "Levels, Trends, and Patterns of Urbanization in Peninsular Malaysia, 1957-1980," in Economic and Social Commission for Asia and the Pacific, ed., *Population of Malaysia, Country Monograph Series No. 13* (New York: United Nations, 1986), pp. 72-73.

TABLE 4.2 Ethnic Composition of Urban Population, Peninsular Malaysia, 1947-1980

Census	Total urban population	Malay, in percent	Chinese, in percent	Indian, in percent	Others, in percent
1947	929,928	19.0	63.1	14.7	3.2
1957	1,666,969	21.0	62.6	12.8	3.6
1970	2,530,433	27.6	58.5	12.8	1.1
1980	4,073,105	37.9	50.3	11.0	0.7

Source: Compiled from L.L. Kok, "Levels, Trends and Patterns of Urbanization in Peninsular Malaysia, 1957-1980," in Economic and Social Commission for Asia and the Pacific, ed., *Population of Malaysia, Country Monograph Series No. 13* (New York: United Nations, 1986), p. 59.

increased Malay rural-urban migration, but also of considerably higher Malay natural growth, both in rural as well as urban areas.

The *"indigenization"* of urban areas became particularly evident after the introduction of the *"New Economic Policy"* (NEP) in 1970. The NEP was formulated in the aftermath of the May 1969 racial riots which the government interpreted as an expression of widespread economic discontent among Malays. In fact, of the three major ethnic groups, the predominantly rural Malays had the lowest per capita income, the lowest share in modern sector occupations, and a minute share in the ownership of commercial and industrial enterprises in 1969 (Milne and Mauzy 1980:326). Therefore, the objective of the *New Economic Policy* was two-fold:

- to reduce and eventually eradicate poverty by raising income levels and increasing employment opportunities for all Malaysians, irrespective of race, and
- to restructure Malaysian society in order to correct economic imbalances and eliminate the identification of race with economic function and geographic location (Milne and Mauzy 1980:326; Government of Malaysia 1986:8).

Although the government claimed that the *New Economic Policy* was not to be understood as a "zero sum game", it was clear that it favors Malays at the expense of the wealthier Chinese and Indians. The NEP aims to redistribute the nation's wealth by giving Malays a minimum 30 percent share of industrial and other modern economic activities by 1990. With the NEP, the Malaysian government abandoned its former laissez-faire economic policy in favor of active government participation in the economy. By establishing public enterprises, employment quotas in all major businesses, and a quota system in higher education it aimed to create an urban Malay commercial and industrial class. As the bulk of commercial and industrial activities is concentrated in urban areas, the plan had an urban bias (Chan 1983:503). The movement of rural people to the towns thus became an essential aspect of the NEP in pursuance of its objective of narrowing down the gap between the ethnic communities.

In order to prevent the increasing cityward movement of rural Malays from concentrating primarily on the Federal Territory and the Klang Valley, the Third and Fourth Malaysia Plans outlined regionalization strategies. Major components were industrial dispersal, development of new towns, rural industrialization, and the establishment of Regional Development Authorities in Johore, Pahang, Trengganu, Kedah, Kelantan, and Penang. Yet, although the role of regional cities figured prominently in the sections on regional development of the Fifth Malaysia Plan, unlike in Thailand and the Philippines, no specific regional cities development program exists. This is despite the fact that regional cities have to absorb increasing numbers of low-skilled Malay migrants, while at the same time they are losing highly qualified labor to the Federal Territory/Klang Valley Region. As a result, the urbanization component of the NEP has been described by critics as, merely a spatial redistribution of poverty from the rural areas to the cities. If this assessment is correct, then mounting problems, aggravated by the economic recession of the mid-1980s, await Malaysia's regional cities.

Penang was selected for a case study because the regional development plans of the federal government accorded it a crucial role in the development of the Northern Region. Even in the absence of a Regional Cities Development Project like in Thailand and the Philippines, Penang was expected to be the recipient of considerable resource inputs that would strengthen its functions as a central place (Government of Malaysia 1986:196).

Data were obtained from thirty-three structured expert interviews with officials of the Ministry of Housing and Local Government, the local authorities of Penang Island, Seberang Prai, Kuala Lumpur, Klang, Seremban, and Petaling Jaya, managers of public enterprises, representatives of the private sector, and academics. Other sources of information included the published and unpublished literature,[1] official documents, newspaper reports, and statistics.

In order to avoid terminological confusion, some remarks are necessary on the nomenclature of local authorities in Penang. Until 1974, the municipal jurisdiction lay within the boundaries of Georgetown, the urban core of Penang Island, which was administered by the *City Council of Georgetown*. Suburban areas such as Ayer Itam, Gelugor, Tanjong Tokong, and Tanjong Bungah belonged to one of the two Rural District Councils, which covered all other parts of the island. In 1974 local government boundaries were redefined. The Rural District Councils were disbanded and subsumed under the *Penang Island Board of Management*, which two years later was renamed into *Penang Island Municipal Council (Majlis Perbandaran Pulau Pinang)*. This body is now the sole local authority on the island.

Local Autonomy

Central-Local Relations: Structures and Functions

The Constitutional and Institutional Framework. Malaysia is a federal state consisting of a federal government, thirteen states, and ninety-one local governments. Surprisingly, this does not imply that, at least in legal terms, local autonomy is greater in Malaysia than in unitary states such as Thailand and the Philippines. Unlike the Thai and Philippine constitutions, the Malaysian constitution of 1957 does not explicitly recognize local autonomy. There is not a single passage in the document that deals with local autonomy. Local government is only briefly mentioned in two articles: Article 76 (4) empowers the federal parliament to

enact legislation on local government "for the purpose of ensuring uniformity of law and policy", and Article 95 (A) calls for the creation of a
National Council for Local Government "to formulate from time to time,
in consultation with the federal government and the state governments,
a national policy for the promotion, development and control of local
government throughout the Federation and the administration of any
law relating thereto . . ." Finally, local government is mentioned in the
Ninth Schedule of the constitution[2] dealing with the vertical division of
powers. The *Ninth Schedule* consists of three lists of competencies: a federal list, a state list, and a concurrent list, but no local government list.
Local government outside the Federal Territory of Kuala Lumpur is regarded as a state competency. Like in India, local government is essentially a concern of the states. The state government decides whether or
not to accord municipal status to a local authority and controls the in-
corporation of new areas into local authorities or any other change of
boundaries.

At least in legal terms, the federal government was left with few
powers in respect of local government. The federal government,
through the National Council for Local Government merely acts as a
coordinator among the various states to ensure uniformity in laws and
practice (Chahl 1982:48). The powers of the Ministry of Housing and Local Government in respect of local authorities were likewise predominantly advisory and, in some cases, especially in the small municipal
and district councils, also included technical assistance. Yet, despite the
ministry's limited role, insiders speak of increasing ministerial interference in local affairs (Anthony 1971:86).

In legal terms, local authorities' scope for action has been consistently
curtailed since 1957. This erosion of local autonomy was a concomitant
of a gradual centralization process in which federal powers and functions were strengthened at the expense of the states and state competencies at the expense of local authorities (Tilman 1976; Shafruddin 1987).
Mauzy and Milne thus concluded that Malaysia is a "federation in name
only" (Mauzy and Milne 1983-84:621). Centralization in Malaysia increased markedly after the *"Emergency"* and again after the May 1969 riots, which led to the suspension of parliament and emergency rule under the National Operations Council. Tilman is right when he states that
the federal government was reluctant to give up the powers it had
usurped during these emergency periods. "Temporary centralizing
powers enunciated to meet an immediate problem thus became part of
the government corpus of laws of the Federation once the situation returned to normal" (Tilman 1976:63). In the 1970s, centralization pressures increased in the wake of the *New Economic Policy*, which led to

greater public sector involvement in the economy and, hence, a much greater central role in economic planning.

Local government powers were successively curtailed after 1957. The first federal encroachment on local government was the nationwide suspension of local elections in 1959 and 1960. Soon afterwards, in September 1960, the federal government passed the *Federal Capital Act* which, in effect, suspended elective local government in the capital. Under its provisions the powers hitherto held by the municipal council were transferred to a Federal Capital Commissioner responsible to the Minister of the Interior and Justice and, after 1964, the Minister of Housing and Local Government. The creation of the Ministry of Housing and Local Government in 1964 soon turned out to be another step towards centralization, at least as far as the adminstration of the capital city was concerned (Anthony 1971:72). One year later, in 1965, local elections were suspended throughout Malaysia, a move that was followed by the abolition of major municipal councils (Tennant 1973a, 1973b; Norris 1980). By 1972, twenty municipal councils and town boards had been abolished, in particular those of the state capitals, and their responsibilities assumed by the state governments. In 1974, the Federal Territory of Kuala Lumpur was created, governed by a lord mayor (*datuk bandar*) who is responsible to the newly established Ministry of the Federal Territory. Finally, in 1976, the *Local Government Act 171*, completely restructured local government in Malaysia. As will be shown below, the Act became the basis for a continuous strengthening of the state governments vis-à-vis local authorities.

The state government appoints the municipal councillors, the municipal secretary (the head of the municipal bureaucracy), and the municipal president. Usually, the municipal president is seconded from the federal government or he is a high-ranking state politician and, in a number of cases, the chief minister of the state (see Table 4.3). Apart from these appointive powers which also extend to the municipal staff, the state government wields far-reaching legislative, planning, and budgetary powers vis-à-vis local governments. Most council decisions need prior state confirmation which means that all major topics of the municipal council first have to be presented to the state government.[3]

Similarly, all by-laws approved by the municipal council need prior confirmation of the state government. Moreover, the state government formulates general policy guidelines which, in effect, strongly limit decision-making options of the municipal council. And, on top of this, the state government is even empowered to transfer the functions of a local authority to the chief minister (Cheema and Hussein 1978:583).

TABLE 4.3 Position of Municipal Presidents, Malaysian Regional Cities

Municipal Council	Position of Municipal President
Penang Island	Retired State Secretary
Seberang Perai	Senior Federal Civil Servant
Ipoh	Chief Minister
Seremban	Chief Minister
Johore Bahru	Chief Minister
Kangar	Chief Minister
Kota Bahru	Deputy Chief Minister
Shah Alam	State Secretary
Kuala Trengganu	Senior State Assemblymen
Kota Kinabalu	Deputy State Secretary

Sources: Compiled from *The Star*, 15 January 1980; *Malay Mail*, 5 January 1982; *The Star*, 24 February 1982; *New Straits Times*, 25 November 1982; *New Straits Times*, 11 June 1984; *National Echo*, 22 October 1984; *The Star*, 22 April 1985; *The Star*, 18 July 1986; Phang Siew Nooi, "Municipal Councils in Peninsular Malaysia After Restructuring: Issues and Problems," in *Urban Development in Asia. Readings in Subnational Development*, ed. Jürgen Rüland (Munich, Cologne, and London: Weltforum Verlag, 1988), p. 168.

Like in Thailand and the Philippines, Malaysian local officials try to overcome their legal dependence on higher government echelons by utilizing networks of informal contacts. But local councillors, especially in Penang, seem to be less successful in this respect than municipal decision-makers in Chiang Mai. The range of contacts that can be successfully tapped by Penang's municipal councillors is narrow. There are several reasons for this:

1. The ethnically segmentized nature of Malaysian politics limits contacts between municipal councillors and their ethnic peers at higher government levels.

2. In Penang the majority of state assemblymen and municipal councillors belong to Chinese-dominated parties that are part of the ruling Barisan Nasional (National Front). As the relationship between the major Chinese parties of the Barisan Nasional (BN), the Malaysian Chinese Association (MCA), and the Gerakan, is strained (Chew 1985), it is evident that Chinese municipal councillors have a reduced choice of contacts to peers even at the state level. Municipal councillors of the United Malay National Organization (UMNO) have even fewer contacts at the state level, because Penang is the only state in Malaysia where UMNO is only a junior partner in the state government.

3. The federal level, both politically as well as bureaucratically, is an UMNO domain. While this gives Penang's UMNO councillors access to higher government echelons, it severely limits MCA and Gerakan coun-

cillors (and, of course, also those of the Malaysian Indian Congress, MIC) in their access to political and bureaucratic actors at the federal level.

4. Penang has long been an opposition stronghold. In the 1986 general elections, six out of Penang's eleven parliamentary seats went to the opposition Democratic Action Party (DAP) and in the state assembly, too, the DAP won a record ten seats (out of twenty-seven) in 1986. Yet, the past experience has shown that the UMNO-dominated federal government does not hesitate to penalize states and constituencies that vote for the opposition. This was the case in Kelantan and Trengganu in the 1950s and 1960s, when the Pan-Malayan Islamic Party (PMIP), a fundamentalist Muslim party, temporarily controlled the state governments in both states. In an attempt to destabilize these state governments, Kuala Lumpur cut federal financial assistance and shelved development projects (Smith 1961:153; Tilman 1976:35; Shafruddin 1987). A similar reaction must also be anticipated for Penang, though not quite so harsh. Nevertheless, the reluctance to allocate federal resources to Penang will likewise reduce the municipal councillors' abilities to circumvent the dependencies that are dictated to them by the formal-legal framework of authority.

Municipal Functions. Since the abolition of elective local government in the 1960s, municipal councils in Malaysia have experienced a continual loss of functional autonomy. As Table 4.4 shows, there are only seven municipal functions that are exclusively local in nature. All other functions are shared with state or federal authorities or the private sector, or exercised by nonlocal agencies. Since the early 1970s, the Penang Island Municipal Council has lost the functions of low-cost housing, fire services, and water and electricity supplies. They were taken over by the national government as well as special purpose agencies at the state and federal levels. The transfer of these functions not only signified an increasing trend toward centralization and, hence, a loss of political weight on the part of local authorities, it also further diminished the chances of the local population for political participation. Service delivery became more and more bureaucratized, interaction and communication more difficult, since the headquarters of some of these special purpose agencies are located in the capital. Complaints and popular demands can thus be more easily ignored by the bureaucracy. The pressure created by discontented citizens is now absorbed by the inevitable red tape involved in long, time-consuming communication. As long as these services were the responsibility of the municipal council, the councillors, who were more accessible, could act as intermediaries, even if they were appointed and not accountable to a constituency.

TABLE 4.4 Muncipal Functions, Penang Island Municipal Council

Function	Local	State	Federal	Private
Transport	X	---	X	X
Water supply	---	X	---	---
Sewerage and drainage	X	X	---	---
Public housing	Xa	X	X	X
Parks and recreation	X	---	---	---
Health services	X	X	X	X
Fire protection	---	---	X	---
Public sanitation	X	---	---	---
Urban planning	X	X	X	---
Garbage disposal	X	---	---	X
Electricity supply	---	---	X	---
Construction and maintenance of roads	X	---	X	---
Street lighting	X	---	---	---
Conservation	X	---	---	---
Environmental protection	---	---	X	---
Abbatoir services	X	---	---	---
Police	---	---	X	---
Building control	X	---	---	---
Economic promotion	---	X	X	X
Erecting and maintaining residential houses, flats, and shops	Xb	X	X	X
Cemeteries	X	---	---	---

aUntil the early 1980s the municipal council was also involved in providing public housing.
bMinor role.

Legend: X   function performed   ---   function not performed

Source: Adapted from G. S. Cheema, "Administrative Reponses to Urbanization in Western Malaysia." *Journal of Administration Overseas* Vol.16, No. 3, p. 244. Updated and modified by the author.

The Penang Island Municipal Council spent relatively large sums on low-cost housing in the 1960s, but was eventually divested of this function by federal order. Today, low-cost housing is delivered by at least three supralocal agencies: the state government, the Penang Development Corporation (PDC), a state-level statutory body, and the Urban Development Authority (UDA), a federal, special purpose agency created to increase Malay participation in property ownership and urban businesses (Gale 1979; Wolff 1989:270-273).

For a long time water and electricity supplies were revenue-generating services of the municipality. The municipal council even built its own water reservoir, the Ayer Itam dam. Nevertheless, the water department was taken over by the State Water Board in 1973. With the *Electricity (Transfer of Electricity Installation) Act 1976*, the electricity department, became part of the National Electricity Board. In both cases, the official explanation for these measures was the deficits incurred by these departments, although -- as will be shown later -- during most of their existence they produced profits and, furthermore, were able to deliver services at lower rates than the respective state or federal agencies (Osborn 1974:220). The centralization of fire services was explained in a similar fashion. Local authorities, it was said, could no longer afford to buy the sophisticated equipment needed.

Urban planning, though still a local function, is controlled by the state government. But statutory bodies such as the Penang Development Corporation and the Urban Development Authority have also gained a lot of influence on planning (Gale 1979; Wolff 1989:270). As regards sewerage and drainage, local authorities are becoming increasingly dependent on the federal government, since maintenance and modernization are often beyond their financial capacities. Sewerage and drainage, however, have a relatively low priority in the allocation of national development funds (Norris 1980:29).

Lately, pressure on the municipal council has been growing to privatize its transport, health, and veterinary services. In a speech delivered in Penang, Deputy Local Government Minister S. Subramaniam urged that the municipal council should stop all "nonobligatory" services, as Penang was the only city to afford luxuries such as public transport.[4]

The increasing erosion of municipal functions threatens to transform Malaysian municipalities into bodies that merely deliver a few routine services -- functions that they performed already under colonial rule.

The Resource Dimension

Municipal Finance. Malaysian municipalities, too, have only limited fiscal autonomy. Hence, the frequent complaints of local officials about an inadequate revenue base that is unable to generate the financial resources needed to satisfy the growing demand for public services and to initiate dynamic urban development. This, however, should not obscure the fact that Penang and most other regional cities in Malaysia are financially better off than Chiang Mai and Iloilo City.

In absolute terms, Penang's revenues increased from M$ 31.8 million in 1977 to M$ 51.9 million in 1982, which represents an annual average growth of 10.2 percent. This is less than Chiang Mai's 15.2 percent and Iloilo's 13.8 percent. Per capita revenue, which grew by 8.8 percent per annum, was likewise below the growth rates of Chiang Mai (16.3 percent) and Iloilo (13.1 percent). On the other hand, at M$ 104, Penang's per capita revenues were slightly higher than Chiang Mai's and considerably higher than those of Iloilo in 1982.[5] But Penang's per capita revenue was exceeded by other Malaysian cities such as Ipoh and the municipal councils located in the Klang Valley like Shah Alam, Petaling Jaya, and Klang (see Table 4.5). On the other hand, east coast municipal councils (Kota Bahru and Kuala Trengganu) as well as smaller urban centers such as Seberang Prai, Taiping, and Malacca, had considerably lower per capita revenues.

Apart from higher per capita revenues, there is another major difference between Malaysian regional cities and their counterparts in Thailand and the Philippines. In Malaysian cities, a remarkably high share of municipal revenues is levied locally. In Penang, for instance, between 1959 and 1981, 96 percent of total annual municipal revenues were levied locally. After 1982, this percentage fell slightly to 94 percent. In Ipoh, locally levied revenues accounted for to 92 percent in 1983, and in thirteen other municipalities, they averaged 90 percent between 1980 and 1984.

Of the locally levied revenues, rate income is the single most important source of income. Rates are a real property tax imposed on land and buildings. Every year the municipal council fixes a certain percentage of the assessed property value -- i.e. the rates -- that the property owners must pay to the Treasury Department. Assessment is made on the basis of the estimated gross annual rent income of a holding. The rates imposed by municipal councils differ greatly throughout the Peninsula. Ipoh and Penang had the highest rates: in 1983 26 percent

TABLE 4.5 Per Capita Revenues of Thirteen Municipalities in Peninsular Malaysia, 1984

Municipality	Per Capita Revenue, in M$
Shah Alam	188.00
Ipoh	140.80
Petaling Jaya	138.95
Klang	133.76
Kuantan	83.81
Seremban	81.21
Johore Bahru	80.10
Kangar	48.03
Melaka Tengah	47.50
Seberang Perai	45.15
Taiping	41.33
Kota Bahru	25.92
Kuala Trengganu	20.58

Source: S. Pillai and H. Tan, *"Financial Management of Municipal Councils"* (Kuala Lumpur: Ministry of Housing and Local Government, 1985), p. 17.

and 25 percent respectively of the assessed property value.[6] This is considerably lower than in the 1950s and 1960s, when the Socialist Front controlled the municipal council, and rates oscillated between 30 and 35 percent. Rates imposed by municipal councils in the Klang Valley were much lower; based on land use and location, 7-8 percent in Petaling Jaya, 7-15 percent in Klang, and 3-13 percent in Kuala Lumpur.

Between 1977 and 1982 rate income in Penang averaged 52.6 percent of total revenues (see Table 4.6). This was markedly lower than in other Malaysian municipalities,[7] where rates made up 61 percent of total revenues. In Ipoh their share was even higher -- no less than 66 percent in 1983 (Pillai and Tan 1985:6).

In many Malaysian cities, the tax base of the real property tax is severely restricted by the *Rent Control Act*. The Act was introduced in 1966 to preserve the old building substance of the densely populated inner-city areas. Due to spiraling land prices, these areas were threatened with redevelopment. This would inevitably displace large numbers of low-income residents -- who found cheap, though mostly substandard and overcrowded accommodation in the cities' central areas -- and further aggravate the existing shortage of low-cost housing. According to the Act, structures built before 1948 are subjected to rent control, meaning that rents cannot be increased without the consent of the tenants. As a result, the assessed value of these houses remains at a low level. In Penang, about 25 percent of the municipality's houses are under rent control, in Malacca as much as 60 percent (Teng 1978/79:103).

Penang is the only municipal council in Malaysia that grants tax concessions for owner-occupied houses. Owner-occupiers of residential houses living in the city get a 55 percent discount on the assessed value, those living in the rural areas 50 percent and owner-occupiers of shop houses, irrespective of whether located in the city or rural areas, a 30 percent reduction.[8] The municipal government repeatedly attempted to cancel these concessions, which were introduced by the Socialist Front in the 1960s. Since 63 percent of all houses on Penang Island are owner-occupied, the municipal government argued that the concessions cost it revenues of M$ 9.8 million annually.[9] Yet, their abolition is politically not feasible. Plans to scrap the concessions met with stiff resistance from the UMNO grassroots, because the poorer Malays living on the urban fringe and in the rural areas would be particularly affected by this step, but also from the opposition Democratic Action Party (DAP) and the Socialist Democrat Party.

Critics further object to the regressive and inequitable structure of the real property tax in Malaysia. It obliges the poor to pay a larger portion of their incomes in taxes than the rich. As Chee pointed out, infrequent

TABLE 4.6 Penang Island Municipal Council, Distribution of Revenues, 1977-1982, in Percent

Revenue Category	1977	1978	1979	1980	1981	1982
Rate income	48.96	54.58	54.78	54.59	49.29	53.56
Taxes (on carts, trishaws, dogs, etc.)	0.49	0.51	0.48	0.46	0.41	0.34
Licenses	1.39	1.58	1.57	1.63	1.96	1.79
Fees, charges, rents, etc.	19.44	18.17	21.36	14.94	17.01	17.14
Contributions and expenditures recharged	5.47	5.43	2.41	8.96	12.20	8.76
Transportation department	18.61	13.90	13.81	13.98	14.30	10.84
Public housing	1.99	2.05	1.99	1.86	1.62	1.38
Grants and aids	3.64	3.79	3.61	3.59	3.22	6.19
Locally levied revenues	96.35	96.22	96.40	96.42	96.79	93.81
Total	99.99	100.01	100.01	100.01	100.01	100.00

Source: Calculated from Majlis Perbandaran Pulau Pinang, Municipal Council of Penang Island, *Epitome of Accounts and General Financial Statistics, 31st December* (Penang: Majlis Perbandaran Pulau Pinang, 1981); Majlis Perbandaran Pulau Pinang, Municipal Council of Penang Island, *Epitome of Accounts and General Financial Statistics for the Year End, 31st December* (Penang: Majlis Perbandaran Pulau Pinang, 1982), and Negri Pulau Pinang, *Report of the Auditor General 1969-1986* (Penang: Negri Pulau Pinang, n.d.).

and irregular revaluations mean that there are different rates on properties of similar design and in the same location, merely because they were built at different times and the assessment made at the time of construction has not been adjusted since. In a period of rapid inflation on the property market such rate differentials can be substantial after a few years (Chee 1978:7).

In contrast to Thai and, in particular, Philippine cities, collection efficiency in Malaysian regional cities is high. Like Kuala Lumpur (98.55 percent), Penang has a collection efficiency of almost 100 percent. Other secondary centers such as Petaling Jaya (91.4 percent in 1982 and 86.2 percent in 1983), Klang (85.3 percent in 1982), Johore Bahru (85 percent in 1985), and Kota Bahru (82 percent in 1985)[10] have achieved high collection efficiencies, too.

A major reason for the high collection efficiency is the fact that tax administration in major cities is completely computerized. Penang, which introduced computerization as early as 1978, spearheaded this development. Klang followed in 1980, and after that even small municipalities such as Kuala Muda and Kota Setar (Kedah) computerized their treasury department.[11] In 1979, the Penang Island Municipal Council could declare that it has a complete record of annual value for every single house on the island (Teng 1978/79:42). The impact of computerization on collection efficiency was demonstrated by Phang in her study of the Klang Municipal Council. Within one year of computerization, Klang's collection efficiency improved by 13.2 percent (Phang 1985:221).

In Penang, collection efficiency was further increased by mobile vans that the municipal council send out to collect taxes, especially in the rural areas. Rate payers thus do not need to travel to city hall, where they would spend considerable time waiting.

Measures to enforce tax payment do not differ markedly from those in Thai and Philippine cities. Delinquents face a 2 percent surcharge, notice and warrant fees, and, as a last resort, the auction of their property to settle the debts.[12] But as in Thailand and the Philippines, seizure of property is rarely resorted to.[13] That these sanctions have been a weak deterrent is illustrated by the fact that the municipal councils of Klang, Petaling Jaya, Kuala Lumpur, and Johore Bahru finally resorted to what was called "shame tactics" by threatening to publish the names of delinquent taxpayers in the newspapers.[14]

As indicated by the relatively high percentage of "fees, rents and charges, etc." in total revenues,[15] Malaysian cities are quite innovative in generating new revenue sources. The Penang Island Municipal Council, for instance, entered into joint ventures with the private sector for commercial development of municipal properties. This is possible, because -- unlike Chiang Mai and Iloilo City -- the municipality owns large tracts of land. How advertising was used to create additional revenues for the municipality is shown by Phang. In her study she described the Penang Island Municipal Council's efforts in persuading the private sector to donate bus shelters to the council. In return, the companies were permitted to use them to advertise their products (Phang 1985:199).

Other municipalities such as Kuala Lumpur and Petaling Jaya constructed parking complexes, shop houses or large office blocks which they rented out to the private sector. However, since such projects are risky they can also become a liability for municipal finances, as demonstrated by the Petaling Jaya office tower project. In the late 1970s the municipal council of Petaling Jaya decided to build a large office block to house the municipal council; the remaining office space would be leased to the private sector. With an initial investment of nearly M$ 50 million, the council estimated that the tower would generate an annual rental income of M$ 12 million.[16] However, when the building was finally completed in 1985, the Kuala Lumpur conurbation had already been hit by a glut of office space.[17] In 1986, the Petaling Jaya municipal council had to reduce its income estimates to less than M$ 5 million.[18] Instead of increasing municipal revenues, the office tower will severely curb the municipality's capacity for future capital investment in other service sectors because of the high interest rates for the bank loans.

Malaysian cities differ from regional cities in Thailand and the Philippines in yet another respect: they have considerably more scope for deficit spending. In a survey of thirteen municipal councils conducted by the Ministry of Housing and Local Government it was found that between 1980 and 1984 only the Klang Municipal Council had a budget surplus each year, while four municipal councils had surpluses in four out of five years. Five municipal councils, on the other hand, had deficits in all five years. All in all, the thirteen municipalities had surplus year-end accounts in twenty-six, deficits in thirty-nine cases (Pillai and Tan 1985:12). Penang, which was not included in the survey, likewise ran regular deficits. Between 1980 and 1986, a budget surplus was recorded only in 1982. Yet, in 1982, at M$ 55 per capita Penang's net debt was relatively low compared to Kuala Lumpur's M$ 518 per capita (1984).

Deficits are balanced by borrowings, grants, and own reserves. As stipulated by the *Local Government Act*, municipal councils can borrow an amount of up to five times the annual assessment value of the properties located in their jurisdiction. Given an annual value of land and buildings of M$ 118.34 million at the end of 1982, the Penang Island

Municipal Council had an authorized borrowing limit of M$ 591.7 million. This is a large amount compared to the municipality's budget.

The great borrowing capacity also had effects on capital investment. While Penang's capital investment rate of 20 percent (of total expenditure) is relatively modest, capital outlays in Ipoh averaged 50 percent between 1979 and 1982 (with a peak of 63 percent in 1982) (Majlis Perbandaran Ipoh 1984:254). In Petaling Jaya, they reached a top rate of 60.4 percent in 1983.[19]

Despite the fact that municipal incomes are greater and the proportion of locally levied revenues much higher than in Thai and Philippine cities, Malaysian municipal governments face a number of constraints that limit their fiscal autonomy. These constraints also explain the relatively low share of local government revenues in total public revenues. From 4.64 percent in 1960, the share of local government revenues declined to 3.83 in 1966, before rising again to 4.3 percent in 1979 (Teng 1978/79:95) and 4.7 percent in 1987 (Kops 1989a:149).

There are five main obstacles to greater fiscal autonomy of Malaysian municipal governments.

1. State governments must approve the annual budget estimates of municipal councils. This gives them far-reaching influence on municipal policies as they have the right to reduce or reject any item (Hussein and Cheema 1978:583; World Bank 1988:9). Due to constant rivalries between the municipality and the state government, which can be traced back to the 1950s, such interventions were a common practice in Penang. These animosities were aggravated by the fact that until the mid-1970s the municipal budget was greater than that of the state government. As a result, budget proposals of municipal councils were often severely cut by the state government (Phang 1985:67). But not only the budget estimates, borrowing also needs approval of the state government. Furthermore, the state executive councillors are empowered to inspect the accounts of the local authorities within their jurisdiction, provided they have the prior consent of the municipal president (Hussein and Cheema 1978:583; Phang 1988:177).

2. Municipal councils are dependent on the state government as far as revaluations of property assessments are concerned. Revaluation requires the approval of the state government, and, for political reasons, state governments are extremely hesitant to approve revaluations (Norris 1980:87; World Bank 1988:26; Phang, Chee, and Yahya 1989:79). Revaluations are very unpopular and usually meet vocal opposition from local ratepayer associations, economic interest groups, consumer associations, and political opposition parties. As elected politicians, the members of the state government are afraid that such a decision might

undercut their electoral base. Thus, impediments to revaluations did not disappear after the restructuring of local government -- a move that, inter alia, was legitimized with the need for greater professionalization in local administration and for putting an end to partisan politicking. In fact, the problem was only shifted to a higher government level.

Even after the *Local Government Act* was passed, only a few large municipal councils such as Penang, Petaling Jaya, Johore Bahru, and Klang adhered to the requirement of revaluating the properties within their jurisdiction every five years. After long pressuring, especially of the municipality's Treasury Department, the Penang state government finally agreed to a revaluation in 1976 which, however, did not reach its objectives. With their rigid adherence to technical criteria, the assessors ignored the social aspects of the revaluation exercise. Not even rent controlled buildings were exempted. In many cases, the new assessment levels far exceeded what people could afford to pay. In some instances, the annual value of the properties rose by as much as ten times. The result was an avalanche of protests (Norris 1980:103; Phang 1985:309). Strong objections were raised by the MCA and, in particular, the opposition DAP, but also by the House Owners and Taxpayers Association and, of course, the strong lobby of the real estate industry. It was the state government that was blamed in the first instance for not having stopped the municipal council from going ahead with the revaluation. Due to the political pressure exerted by the public, the municipal council -- and with it, the state government -- finally compromised by granting numerous concessions for social hardship (Phang 1985:309) and by reducing the assessment rate from 34 percent to 28 percent, and later to 25 percent. As a result, the revaluation increased municipal revenues by only M$ 0.8 million, instead of the anticipated M$ 5 million (Majlis Bandaraya Georgetown 1976).

The experience of the 1976 revaluation had repercussions not only on the Penang state government, but also on other state governments, which repeatedly refused for local authorities permission to revaluate properties. As a result, especially in smaller local authorities, rates were far below those justified by the actual market values (Phang 1985:66).

Whenever municipal councils implemented revaluations, the state government saw to it that assessment levels did not rise too fast and that municipal councils balanced the increase in assessment levels by lowering assessment rates. This pattern could be observed in the revaluations in Penang, Klang, Kuala Lumpur, and Petaling Jaya. Not surprisingly, despite the costs and the enormous organizational efforts involved, revenue gains in all cases were modest. An exception, it seems, was the 1981 revaluation in Penang. Although the assessment rates were lowered by 1 percent, the increase in revenues exceeded M$ 7.3 million or 36 percent.

Even the federal government undermined the tax effort of local authorities when it seemed politically opportune. In July 1986, for instance, five days before the 1986 general elections, deputy prime minister Ghafar Baba urged municipal councils to reduce rates "as a means to fight the recession". During this difficult period "efforts must be made to help the people, including the businessmen".[20]

3. State governments and the federal government are exempted from paying rates on their properties. Instead, they pay "contributions in lieu of rates". Very often, however, their payments were seriously delayed. There was very little local authorities could do to speed up these payments. In Klang the municipal council was forced to borrow from other sources in order to overcome the financial bottlenecks caused by delays in payments (Phang 1985:222).

4. Municipal councils seek to compensate their curtailed revenue-generating powers by demands for more state and federal grants. However, grants now make up only between 6 and 8 percent of total revenues in cities such as Penang and Ipoh. In the case of Penang this marked a slight increase since the 1960s, when the proportion of grants in total revenues averaged 3 percent. Grants take three main forms:

- *Launching grants* of up to M$ 3,420,000 for municipal councils and up to M$ 4,125,000 for district councils. Launching grants are one-time grants to local authorities after restructuring. They are designed as an initial assistance for development projects or other capital outlays such as the purchase of expensive equipment. Penang, as a financially relatively strong municipality received a launching grant of only M$ 1,642,293 (Chahl 1982:20).
- *Annual grants* for operating costs or balancing the budget. The maximum amount of M$ 107,500 is negligible for large municipal councils such as Penang (0.2 percent in 1982), but for district councils it may be substantial, often equal to 20 percent of their revenues.
- Government *road grants* for the maintenance of roads. The road grant for Penang was increased from M$ 9,250 to M$ 11,000 per road mile in 1982 (Majlis Perbandaran Pulau Pinang (1982:2), and to M$ 12,146 in 1987 (Kops 1989b:199).

Apart from these grants, municipal councils can apply for *federal development grants*. These are made available under the five year development plans (Malaysia Plans) upon prior application by the local authorities and submission of proposals. However, only a fraction of the grants applied for are approved. Phang, for instance, showed that under the Third Malaysia Plan (1978-1982) Penang received only 16.8 percent and under the Fourth Malaysia Plan (1982-1986) only 3 percent of the grants applied for. In Klang the share was 9 and 1.44 percent, respectively (Phang 1985:192). Under the Fifth Malaysia Plan (1986-1990) local authorities received even less. While local governments applied for M\$ 2.2 billion, the federal government approved only M\$ 20.68 million, which is less than 1 percent of the amount originally applied for (Kops 1989b:216).

Moreover, even when funds were granted, delays in the remittance were quite common. In consequence, project implementation was likewise delayed or, in the case of the Klang Municipal Council, had to be shelved. In another case reported by Phang, funds approved for a sewerage and drainage project were paid out to the state government of Selangor, which eventually implemented the project on the grounds that the Klang Municipal Council had neither the technical expertise nor the manpower (Phang 1985:172-173). In the light of such experiences, the financially stronger Penang Island Municipal Council has preferred to fund its projects as far as possible with own resources. Thanks to its great financial and land reserves, the council was able to do so in the past, but interviews with council representatives indicated that these reserves are almost exhausted by now.

State grants are another, yet quite erratic source of financial assistance. The Penang Island Municipal Council, for instance, received nothing in the 1977-1982 period. This is corroborated by Lenz, whose data on five major municipal council also suggest that state grants are lower than federal grants (Lenz 1989:103). On the other hand, in a survey covering nine municipal councils for a period of four years Phang found that state grants exceeded federal grants in 62 percent of all cases (Phang 1988:172-176).

Some municipal councils tend to overcome the federal government's unwillingness to approve grants by resorting to loans. These are either subsidized government loans at 7-8 percent interest or commercial bank loans at 11-12 percent. Yet, the demand of local authorities, supported by nongovernmental organizations such as the Consumer Association of Penang (CAP), for more grants contradicts their call for greater local autonomy, signifying the same dilemma that confronted municipal decision-makers in Chiang Mai.

5. Another factor limiting financial autonomy is the transfer of revenue generating departments to the state government, parastatal enterprises, or the private sector. In Penang, this happened with the water and electricity departments, although the latter made profits for almost

two decades. Recently, the Transport Department, which, however, recorded losses in the past, has also come under pressure to privatize. Yet, it seems that the rationale for the privatization strategy so vigorously stressed by the Malaysian government is not so much more efficient services, but pursuit of the *New Economic Policy*. Through the privatization of public services, the government obviously aims to create entrepreneurial spheres for *Bumiputra* contractors. Whether this policy will eventually contribute to greater efficiency in services delivery is open to doubt in the light of experiences with privatization elsewhere. In any case, the privatization strategy, particularly if pursued as a facet of *New Economic Policy*, increases the potential for corruption and irregularities in the bureaucracy.[21]

Managerial Resources. Like in Thailand, municipal councils in Malaysia are highly dependent for staff and recruitment on higher government levels. Autonomy in personnel affairs is thus fairly restricted. This holds particularly true for professional and managerial personnel. Although appointments are made by the municipal president, they must be approved by the state as well as the federal government through the Public Service Department (PSD) and the Treasury. New posts can only be created with the approval of the state and federal governments.[22] In the mid-1980s, due to the country's economic recession, the Public Service Department froze all vacancies, except for technical staff (World Bank 1988:10).

Compared to most other municipalities, Penang is relatively well staffed and increased its staff considerably over the last decade. The number of council employees rose from 3,770 in 1977 to 5,210 in 1986, which represents a 32.8 percent increase (see Table 4.7). At 1:102, the staff-to-population ratio is somewhat worse than in most other Malaysian and Thai regional cities, but much better than in Philippine cities. The number of professional and technical personnel is also satisfactory compared to other cities in the Southeast Asian region. However, there seems to be a serious problem in retaining qualified professional and managerial personnel. The interviews revealed that there is a considerable turnover among such personnel, due to keen competition from the private sector and higher government echelons. Both are able to provide higher salaries and better promotion prospects. At almost 89 percent, the share of council employees in manual worker and subclerical positions is extremely high. Given the fact that there is a quota for recruitment in these positions of 4:1 in favor of *Bumiputras*, it is evident that in Malaysia, too, municipal governments perform major patronage functions.[23]

TABLE 4.7 Penang Island Municipal Council, Staffing Pattern, 1977 and 1986

Personnel Category	Number of Employees	
	1977	1986
Category A	49	61
Category B	83	111
Category C	449	406
Category D	3,189	750
Workers	---	3,882
Total	3,770	5,210

Sources: Opening address by Datuk Mohamed bin Yeop Raof, President Penang Island Municipal Council, on the occasion of the first meeting of the 1977/78 session of the Council, 27 December 1977 and interview material, Penang Island Municipal Council, September 1986.

In Penang the vacancy rate in professional and managerial positions was relatively modest, usually oscillating between 10 and 20 percent. However, the situation is much more strained in smaller municipalities and district councils where vacancy rates reach up to 40 percent. Here, studies have consistently noted a desperate lack of town planners, architects, legal officers, lawyers, accountants, and assessors (Cheema 1977:247; Norris 1980:16,29; Phang 1988:178). As a result, departments are frequently headed by nonprofessional personnel. In the light of this situation, the assistance provided by the federal Ministry of Housing and Local Government in the form of a technical services unit can do little more than bridge the most urgent gaps. With seven engineers, five technical assistants, and one architect, the unit itself is severely understaffed (World Bank 1988:10). The technical services unit is thus only providing expertise for minor sewerage projects, solid waste disposal, and, to some extent, the design, repair, and maintenance of roads, buildings, and drainage (Veloo, n.d.:19-20).

There are several reasons for the limited local maneuverability when it comes to personnel recruitment.

1. State governments often refuse to approve professional positions for municipal councils.
2. Professional positions at the municipal level do not offer good career prospects. To some extent they are a dead-end. The local authority is a corporate entity with a narrow pyramid of positions, which does not allow for lateral and vertical switches as, for instance, in the Malaysian Administrative and Diplomatic Service.
3. Local authorities have increasingly become a NEP target due to the federal policy of strengthening *Bumiputra* staff at the local level. A

vacant post at the professional level cannot be filled even if there are qualified applicants, unless they are *Bumiputras*. As a result, key positions in the municipal administration are left vacant or are "frozen" for long periods (Phang 1985:68), giving rise to the allegation that ethnic policies prevail over considerations of efficiency.

Planning in Malaysian cities dates back to the 1920s (Philip 1984:13). However, under the British colonial administration, urban planning primarily meant minimizing sanitary and health hazards arising from increasing population density in the city centers. In Penang, the Engineer's Department started preparing zoning plans as early as 1939, although the local authority did not possess enforcement powers. Ten years later, in 1949, urban planning was given a stronger legal foundation through the *Enactment of the Town Board (Town Planning Provisions) (Extension) Ordinance*. However, at that time town planning was almost synonymous with land-use planning. Town plans were merely zoning and layout plans (Goh 1985a:6). Due to the lack of qualified planning personnel, such town plans were prepared only in areas under development pressure, while large areas of the city were not covered by any plan. As of 1972, only some 50 percent of Georgetown's jurisdiction was covered by zoning plans (Goh 1985a:7). Planning was thus mainly an *"ad hoc"* exercise. Like in Chiang Mai and Iloilo, it was *"reactive"*, but not *"anticipative"*. The results were gross imbalances in the city's spatial development. Relatively well-planned areas existed alongside unplanned and uncontrolled urban growth (Goh 1985a:11).

In 1974, an *Interim Zoning Plan* was enacted. Although the plan covered the whole of Georgetown, Goh termed this measure a "classic case of too little and too late" (Goh 1985a:12). There has been no major updating of existing land uses, except for the approval of specific applications for rezoning. Outside the built-up area of Georgetown -- i.e. the rural and suburban areas of Penang Island, which in 1974 were brought under the jurisdiction of the Penang Island Municipal Council -- most areas were left untouched by zoning plans. Hence, more or less the same criticism that was aired against earlier land-use planning applied to the *Interim Zoning Plan*. Moreover, zoning decisions can be changed with relative ease, as the construction and real estate industry has close ties with influential bureaucrats and politicians, both at municipal and state levels. In contrast to Bruton's positive assessment of the *Interim Zoning Plan* (Bruton 1982:322), one keen observer saw in it more a *"speculator's guide"* than an adequate instrument of town planning.[24]

Parallel to the *Local Government Act 1976 (Act 171)*, the federal government passed the *Town and Country Planning Act, 1976 (Act 172)*, which complemented the earlier *Street, Drainage, and Building Act (Act 133)*. Act 172 was a complete overhaul of the existing planning legislation. With the Act, a comprehensive system of town and country planning was introduced for the first time. Local authorities were given a mandate to prepare development plans for their jurisdiction consisting of a *structure plan* and *local plans*.

The structure plan refers to the social, economic, and physical systems of a locality, thereby interpreting national and regional policies in the context of the planning area. It is a written statement establishing broad objectives in relation to the respective local unit and formulating strategies, policies, and general proposals for achieving these goals (Majlis Perbandaran Pulau Pinang 1985:2). Goh rightly observed that as a policy plan, the structure plan constitutes an important departure from the traditional plan in the form of a map or a series of maps. With the structure plan, objectives, policies, and strategies can be expressed more precisely than before (Goh 1985a:8).

First and foremost, the structure plan aims to implement the *New Economic Policy*. Structure plans are instruments of the government to accelerate the process of economic restructuring that seeks to substantially increase the Malay share in the private sector. As a great portion of the nation's wealth is concentrated in urban areas, the cities are naturally a major target for the implementation of the NEP. Moreover, this policy also entails demographic restructuring, aimed at ending Chinese dominance in urban areas by establishing a Malay majority through accelerated rural-urban migration. Naturally, the rapid influx of poor and unskilled rural migrants puts strains on existing municipal services and employment opportunities. The structure plans are thus a device to ensure that the *"Malayanization"* of urban areas does not coincide with increasing pauperization of a large section of the population. Hence, structure plans are designed to create conditions conducive to economic growth by improving the urban infrastructure, which should, in turn, attract economic investment. Moreover, they also aim to provide an adequate reproduction sphere by upgrading and expanding social and recreational facilities as well as improving the environmental standards. This concern for environmental issues distinguishes urban planning in Malaysia from planning in Thailand and the Philippines. The emergence of a small, yet vocal and well-organized, environmental and conservationist lobby among the educated urban middle-class has increasingly forced authorities to give consideration to a more balanced relationship between development, ecology, and national heritage.

The structure plan also provides the framework for the local plans. Local plans are subarea plans and are concerned with the more detailed implementation of the policies laid down in the structure plan. Local plans are prepared on a map basis only.

Based on the stipulation that local governments "shall be the local planning authority for the area of the local authority" (Act 172, Sect. 5), the literature tended to view the *Town and Country Planning Act* as a broadening of local functions in the area of planning (Bruton 1982:323; Ibrahim and Nordin 1984:153; Asian Development Bank 1985:xv; Kassim 1986:207).[25] In reality, however, the Act left little planning autonomy to municipal councils, as the state government became the supreme body with respect to all planning in the state (Veloo, n.d.:16).

Section three of the Act, for instance, stated that the "state authority shall be responsible for the general policy in respect of the planning of the development and use of all lands and buildings within the area of every local authority in the state". The same section gives powers to the state governments to issue directions to the local planning authorities and the "local planning authority shall give effect to such directions". Furthermore, section four calls for the creation of a State Planning Committee[26] as a body of the state government to control local planning activities.

The State Planning Committee gives the final approval to the structure plan. Prior to that, the local authority must carry out surveys in virtually every urban sector in order to collect detailed and relevant planning data. These are summarized in a *Report of Survey*, consisting of the sectoral reports. Thereafter, the *Report of Survey* is submitted to the public for comments, objections, and alternative suggestions. On the basis of the representations made by the public, a *Draft Structure Plan* is prepared by the local planning authority which, together with the *Report of Survey*, must be submitted to the State Planning Committee for consideration. After the *Draft Structure Plan* has been submitted to public inspection -- and after due consideration of the objections made -- the State Planning Committee finally approves the structure plan.

Remarkably, the *Town and Country Planning Act* does not require the formal approval of the municipal council for the structure plan. In Penang, this lack of democratic legitimacy for a planning document that is likely to influence the municipality's future for the next fifteen to twenty years, was recognized by the state government. Hence, the chief minister announced that the municipal council, too, would be given the opportunity to make a decision on the structure plan. The municipal council was also represented in the Structure Plan Committee, a kind of steering committee preparing major policy decisions with regard to the structure plan. Yet, the local authority has no powers to modify or even reject decisions made by the State Planning Committee (World Bank 1988:11).

As planning is a concurrent responsibility of both the federal and state governments, functional overlappings frequently occur. In addition, state and federal statutory bodies encroach on the planning functions of local authorities, sometimes without even informing them. One report thus concluded that "most local authorities have no coherent picture of development projects planned for their areas and are often confronted with faits accomplis for new developments by other government agencies which they are then expected to service, and sometimes to maintain" (World Bank 1988:11). In Penang, the Penang Development Corporation (PDC), became the principal development agency of the state government. In this capacity, PDC is actively involved in industrial promotion and development, urbanization, urban renewal and land reclamation, tourism promotion, and agro-industrial development.

In its urbanization and urban renewal programs the PDC has taken over many planning functions of the municipal council. A case in point is the development of Bandar Bayan Baru -- a new town of 25,000 inhabitants close to the Bayan Lepas Free Trade Zone.

However, planning functions do not only overlap in the suburban areas, but also in inner-city areas. Through three major urban renewal projects, the PDC even became the leading planning agency in Central Georgetown as well.

- On behalf of the state government, PDC planned and implemented the *Kompleks Tun Abdul Razak (KOMTAR)*-project, a highly controversial urban renewal project right in the heart of Georgetown. The sixty-five-storey tower will include commercial and office space, condominiums, a five-star hotel, a car park, and civic and recreational facilities.
- The residents and shop owners displaced by KOMTAR were relocated to another PDC-managed project, the *Macallum Street Ghaut* project, which provided 4,295 housing units for approximately 20,000 people in six twenty-two-storey and two twelve-storey high-rise blocks on 33.7 ha of land, most of it reclaimed by the PDC.27
- In Kedah Road, PDC built another twenty-two-storey block with 320 residential units and forty shop lots.

Apart from these urban renewal projects, PDC is preparing the blueprints for the gigantic *Central District Development of the 21st Century Project (CDD 21)*. CDD 21 will involve the development of a new urban centre on a 244 ha site of reclaimed land stretching from the Penang

Bridge interchange at Batu Uban to Weld Quay. The M$ 1.6 billion project will include a banking and commercial center, condominiums, medium and low-cost housing, a light industrial complex, and recreational and civic facilities. It is the project's objective to transform Penang into the major trade and commerical center in northern Peninsular Malaysia, serving the entire ASEAN region (Penang Development Corporation 1986:1-6).

Federal agencies threatening the planning functions of local authorities are the Urban Development Authority (UDA) and the Regional Development Authorities (RDAs). While UDA is less active in Penang, it is involved in serious conflicts with city hall in Kuala Lumpur over planning prerogatives. UDA, established in 1971, is a federal statutory body concerned with increasing *Bumiputra* participation in urban life by implementating development projects such as shopping and commercial centers. Under the *Urban Development Authority Act*, hundreds of acres of prime land in Kuala Lumpur have been declared urban development areas by the federal government. In the process UDA has built up its own land bank for its urban renewal projects. This has pitted UDA against city hall over the question of who regulates redevelopment of vast city areas.[28] UDA projects frequently violate the local authority's planning by-laws, zoning regulations, and the building code. But UDA is politically more powerful than city hall, because it has strong connections with the federal government (Gale 1979:14).

More than by UDA, planning in Penang was affected by the creation of the *Pulau Pinang Regional Development Authority (PERDA)* in 1983. Although PERDA has not yet been very active on Penang Island, its goal of redressing the developmental imbalances between urban Penang and the rural areas of the state is likely it erode the municipal council's planning authority, especially in the rural parts of Penang Island. Not surprisingly, the DAP opposition in the Penang State Assembly rejected the creation of PERDA as a further attempt at federal intervention in local government affairs.[29]

Planning competencies have become even more confused since the creation of federal Department of Environment (DOE) (Goh 1988:227-229). The department is entrusted with the environmental aspects of planning and, hence, has to be consulted by municipal authorities.

Lack of qualified urban planners also increased municipal dependency on higher government levels. As of 1984, the overwhelming majority of urban planners was employed by the federal Department of Town and Country Planning. Of the department's 150 planners, 107 worked in the headquarters and forty-three in the states (Philip 1984:13). Local authorities had forty-six planners, thirty-nine of them employed by local governments and seven on secondment from the federal government (Philip 1984:14). With six planners, the Penang Island Municipal Council was the best staffed local authority in West Malaysia outside the capital. Finally, another fifteen urban planners were employed by UDA and an unspecified number by the various State Economic Development Corporations (SEDCs) (Philip 1984:15). Given such an asymmetrical distribution of urban planners among local authorities, states, and the federal government, it is evident that most local governments are unable to undertake complex planning such as a structure plan without staff secondment from superior government levels. For instance, the two chief planners of Penang state's mainland municipality of Seberang Prai, which is in the process of preparing the technical reports for its structure plan, were seconded from the federal government.[30]

The costs of preparing a structure plan may constitute another impediment to a greater role for local authorities in planning. The cost factor may be less decisive in larger cities such as Penang or Ipoh, which can mobilize the needed M$ 2 million for the plan with relative ease. However, a small municipal council such as Seberang Prai is forced to borrow M$ 0.8 milliom of the total cost of M$ 1.4 million from federal sources.

The Municipality and the Societal Linkage Pattern

The Communication Infrastructure. Due to its maritime location and its function as a major seaport, Penang has always been a cosmopolitan center with a well diversified communication structure. However, as an island city, Penang's linkages to other parts of the peninsula are mainly by sea and concentrated on urban centers along the peninsula's west coast. Until late 1985, the ferry between Georgetown and Butterworth was the major link with the mainland. The access to the peninsular highway system improved considerably with the inauguration of the 13.5 km Penang Bridge, another highly controversial project in view of its enormous cost. The Penang Bridge gives access to the northbound highway to Alor Setar, the East-West-Highway to Kota Bahru, and the southbound highway to the Klang Valley. Nevertheless, the highway system is still inadequate and travel time to Kuala Lumpur is eight to ten hours. The only highway that considerably improved Penang's links with the mainland was the East-West Highway, which expanded Penang's hinterland by a population of more than two million (Nathan 1970:98).

Penang Island does not have a direct railway link with the mainland, though the Bangkok-Kuala Lumpur-Singapore line passes through Butterworth, the mainland urban center opposite Penang Island. The train runs once a day in either direction, travel time to Kuala Lumpur is eight hours.

The Bayan Lepas International Airport links Penang with virtually all major urban centers in the country. There are frequent flights to Kuala Lumpur, Ipoh, and Johore Bahru. Five international airlines used Bayan Lepas, offering flights to Bangkok, Singapore, and Medan.

Penang's port, once a major international and regional transshipment center, has declined in importance. Until the early 1960s, Penang's port served a large hinterland, including southern Thailand, Burma, and Indonesia. However, due to Burma's isolationist policy after Ne Win's coup d'état in 1962 and Indonesia's *confrontasi* against Malaysia (1963-1965), Penang lost these hinterlands (Küchler 1968:128; Krüger 1989:226), although increasing export production in the free trade zones (FTZs) revitalized the city's port functions in the 1970s.

Compared with Thai and Philippine cities, Penang and other Malaysian cities have a much better telecommunications network. In Penang, there were eleven telecom exchanges with 56,500 lines (Majlis Perbandaran Pulau Pinang 1985:111), a tremendous increase on the 12,388 in 1960. With a population-to-telephone ratio of less than nine to one, Penang's ratio is more favorable than that of Chiang Mai, much better than that of Iloilo, but lower than in other Malaysian regional cities such as Klang and Ipoh.

Linkages to Governmental, Semigovernmental, and Nongovernmental Institutions. Linkages between the municipal council and higher government levels extend primarily to the state government. The greater frequency of contacts between state government and municipal council is clearly a consequence of the constitutional provision declaring local government a state responsibility. But in Penang it is also the result of the physical proximity of these two tiers of government: after the inauguration of KOMTAR in 1985, both the state government and the municipal government moved their offices to KOMTAR. It was alleged by well-informed sources that the state government put considerable pressure on the municipal council to relocate its offices to KOMTAR, hoping that this would tighten its control over the municipality (Phang 1978:145). Such moves clearly illustrate the asymmetrical relationship between the state government and the municipal council, which is essentially top-down, with the municipality on the defensive most of the time. Due to the superior powers of the state government, the physical proximity and the frequency of contacts did not help the municipal council to communicate more efficiently with the state authorities.

Compared to Chiang Mai and Iloilo, the government offices network in Penang was less dense. The federal government plan to set up regional offices in Penang in line with the Fifth Malaysia Plan's regional development strategies was thwarted because of the economic recession and the subsequent inability of the government to hire new personnel to staff the regional offices.

While there was a strong top-down communication flow from the state government to the municipal council, there were no horizontal linkages that could rectify these imbalances. Unlike in Thailand and the Philippines, there was no local government association in Malaysia that could lobby for local authorities' demands and needs.[31] More recently, however, regular meetings of the presidents of the municipal councils, the mayor of Kuala Lumpur, and the assistant state secretaries of local government have been institutionalized in order to improve horizontal and vertical coordination (Asian Development Bank 1985:94).

Political parties in Penang contributed little toward greater local autonomy. Despite some scope for grassroots dissent, the party structure favored the superior federal and state executive bodies. Moreover, contacts of party grassroots organizations and the municipal council were limited to councillors representing their own communal group. The top-down pattern of communication in the bureaucracy was thus repeated in the party system. Hence, political parties were no counterbalancing force to centralism.

There was a great variety of voluntary organizations in Penang. Many of them entertained close relationships to the municipal council. Although they lobby primarily for their members' economic interests, voluntary associations may, in the process, also offer additional information and know-how to the municipal council that broaden the existing data base and increase decision making options. Yet, the economic associations, such as the various chambers of commerce, and groups of professionals, related primarily to the real estate and building industries, monopolized contacts with the municipal council. Many of these groups are represented in SPEAD (Surveyors, Planners, Engineers, Architects, and Developers), which met monthly with representatives of the municipal government to discuss issues of mutual concern.

Other voluntary organizations such as the Consumers' Association of Penang (CAP), ALIRAN, and the environmentalist groups also had access to the municipal council, though much less frequently. Due to their sometimes vocal criticism of municipal policies, the authorities feel pressured to listen to the complaints of these groups, though they usually tend to dismiss them as unfounded. Even so, this is different from politics in Iloilo where private sector representatives or citizens groups critical of the city government were not even heard.

Unlike the local authorities in Chiang Mai and Iloilo City, the municipal council in Penang made use of the academic expertise available in the city. Not only were academics from Universiti Sains Malaysia (USM) regularly appointed as municipal councillors; the municipal council also made frequent use of the university's expertise and services through studies and consultancies. For instance, USM has prepared eight of the sixteen technical reports of the *Report of Survey* of the Penang Island Structure Plan.

This scientific approach to urban administration is a major reason for the much better data management in Penang than in Chiang Mai and Iloilo. All the data collected in the process of structure planning are computerized. A similar data bank has also been established in Seberang Prai. Through Penang's computerized planning information system, records have been completely computerized, speeding up the supply of back-up information, decision-making, and administrative action. The system enormously facilitates the processing of applications, treasury records, the payment of wages, and the keeping of personnel records. The long delays in decision-making, due to lack of storage space and unsystematic storing of data, observed in Chiang Mai and Iloilo, is a phenomenon of the past in Penang.

In the Chiang Mai and Iloilo studies I briefly discussed the influence of absentee-owned corporations on local autonomy. In Penang local autonomy is greatly reduced by economic decisions made outside the city -- and, since many of the large industrial firms in the Bayan Lepas FTZ are multinational corporations, even outside the country. Since more than 77 percent of industrial jobs available in Penang are provided by a few large foreign investors, a relocation of their plants to other places would have far-reaching effects on the island's economy. While especially the labor-intensive export-oriented firms are highly flexible in their locational decisions, the municipal council is under pressure to heed the demands of these firms in terms of service delivery, infrastructure development, environmental issues, and administration.

Political Participation

Leadership Recruitment

Until the mid-1960s most local leaders in Penang and other Malaysian cities were elected. Then, participatory elements in local gov-

ernment were curtailed. Elective local government was introduced by
the British in the immediate post-war era. Greater participatory rights
for the population were less inspired by democratic ideals than the wish
to neutralize the increasing (Malay) demands for independence and to
contain a communist-led insurgency. Elective local government was
primarily a device to give the *"New Villages"* -- a euphemism for the
strategic hamlets erected by the British in their counterinsurgency drive
-- democratic legitimacy and local identity (Norris 1980:14).

The introduction of local government did not follow a grand design
of institution-building. It was an ad hoc action dictated by political circumstances, as illustrated by the confusing proliferation of local government legislation. In the 1950s and 1960s local government was regu-
lated by no less than seven different enactments:

- the *Municipal Ordinance of the Strait Settlements* (Cap 133)
- the *Town Boards Enactment of Trengganu* (Cap 64, 3155)
- the *Town Boards Enactment of Johore* (No. 118)
- the *State of Kelantan-Municipal Enactment, No. 20/1938*
- the *Town Boards Enactment of the Federated Malay States* (Cap 137)
- the *Local Councils Ordinance, 1952*
- the *Federal Capital Act, 1960.*

Equally confusing was the variety of local authorities, their status,
powers, functions, and degree of autonomy resulting from these ordinances. Anthony listed ten different categories of local governments
(Anthony 1971:18).

Georgetown, the only city, the municipalities, the town councils, the
rural district councils,[32] and the local councils had elective legislative
bodies. Local councils were the form of local government in the *New Villages.* In line with its political propaganda functions, this form of "instant
local government" (Tennant 1973a:350) was fully elective; all other types
of local authorities included appointed members, among them usually
the president. In Georgetown, for instance, there were nine elected and
six appointed council members before the City Council eventually became fully elective in 1956. While the term "council" indicated the predominance of the electoral principle, Town Boards consisted entirely of
appointed members -- usually bureaucrats (Tennant 1973a:349). Larger
urban centers of the peninsula had city, municipality, and town councils. The others were found predominantly in rural areas. However,
more than 85 percent of the peninsula's territory was not part of any local authority (Kassim 1986:206; Phang 1988:168). Here the district officer, a federal government bureaucrat, was in charge of local affairs.

The passing of the *Local Authorities Elections Ordinance* in 1950 paved the way for local elections in Malaya. The first election took place in Georgetown, Penang, on 1 December 1951. The almost complete absence of local election studies makes it difficult to reliably assess electoral processes at the local level. Scattered data on voter turnout suggest low participation levels in the 1950s, but substantial increases in the 1960s. According to an official documentation of the 1951 local elections in Penang, not more than 20 percent of the qualified voters voted.[33] Reports of the 1956 local elections, when the city council became fully elective, indicate an even lower turnout.[34] Figures released by the Election Commission for the 1961 local authority elections showed a turnout of 76.8 percent for Peninsular Malaysia and 77.2 percent for Penang.[35] In the local council elections (*New Villages*) the turnout rose to 79.49 percent.[36] These figures are confirmed by the *Royal Commission of Enquiry into the Working of Local Authorities in West Malaysia* (1969:117), which gives a turnout of 75 percent. As far as competitiveness in the elections is concerned, the sparse data suggest a level in Georgetown more similar to that in Chiang Mai than in Iloilo. In the 1951 elections, for instance, the candidate-seat-ratio was 2.66.

The Indonesian *"confrontasi"* (1963-1965) with the newly formed Federation of Malaysia (Peninsular Malaysia, Singapore, and the East Malaysian territories of Sabah and Sarawak) marked the premature end of elective local government in Malaysia. Based on the *Emergency (Essential Powers) Act 1964*, the federal government suspended local elections throughout Malaysia on March 2, 1965 on the grounds that it was inappropriate to hold elections during a state of emergency. Although the suspension was announced as a temporary measure, and promises given to restore elective local government "the very moment peace is declared and the emergency regulations are withdrawn",[37] additional and even more restrictive measures against local authorities followed. Starting with Seremban in July 1965, by 1972 twenty councils had been abolished and taken over by state governments. The Georgetown City Council was one of them. It was abolished on 1 July 1966 and placed under the authority of the Penang State chief minister. Rabushka has shown that the abolition of both the Seremban Town Council as well as the Georgetown City Council were in fact an illegal acts. At the time of their abolition neither the Negri Sembilan nor the Penang state government had the constitutional powers to suspend or abolish local governments (Rabushka 1968:171). To avoid the accusation of unconstitutionality, the federal government subsequently passed the *Malaysia Local Government Elections (Amendments) (No. 2) Act 1966* on 29 August 1966.[38] The Act was made retroactive to 26 January 1959 and gave state legislatures the power to transfer the functions of municipal councils to the state authorities (Rabushka 1968:171; Anthony 1971:20).

The official justification for the abolition of local authorities was their alleged administrative inefficiency and corruption (Tennant 1973a, 1973b; Ibrahim and Nordin 1984). Although, as will be shown below, the circumstances raised suspicions about the legitimacy of the council abolitions, there was surprisingly little public protest. Presumably, this was a result of the confusing complexity of local government units and the fact that local government was "a late colonial intrusion" (Tennant 1973a:365) without roots in Malaysian political culture.

The abolition of local authorities sparked off an intensive debate in the local government literature. Four major explanations were offered for this drastic measure (Tennant 1973a:354):

- the racial or ethnic hypothesis;
- the political party hypothesis;
- the corruption and maladministration hypothesis; and
- perceptions and motives of state officials.

The leading proponent of the racial or ethnic hypothesis is Alvin Rabushka. Rabushka argued that the abolition was the result of increasing ethnic antagonism in Malaysia. The ruling Alliance Party perceived the major urban centers, where the bulk of the Chinese population lived, as focal points of Chinese political power, which it wanted to neutralize. In its attempt to maintain political control at all levels of Malaysian government, the Malay-dominated Alliance Party was charged with systematically discriminating against the Chinese and Indian communities (Rabushka 1968:145).

Due to the fact that voting in Malaysia largely follows communal lines, the racial or ethnic hypothesis is strongly linked to the political party hypothesis. Rabushka pointed out that elected councils were taken over by state governments especially in those cities where local government was controlled by a non-Malay opposition party. The party factor was also emphasized by Anthony, who maintained that the abolition was a "deliberate program by the Alliance to prevent municipal governments from going to the opposition in elections" (Anthony 1971:20).

With Tennant's articles (1973a, 1973b), the controversy over the causes of the abolition of elective local government came to an (premature) end (Barraclough 1986:151-159). Most scholars followed his sophisticated analysis which dismissed the racial hypothesis, played down the political dimension, and strongly emphasized the corruption factor and the negative perceptions on the part of state officials of the performance of local governments in service delivery and financial management. This in fact amounted to a confirmation of the official account of the abolitions.

Norris rightly cautions not "to strip events of their political context" (Norris 1980:25). It is surprising that the debate centered on the takeovers of the councils rather than the suspension of local elections. Abolition affected thirteen out of forty major councils,[39] whereas the suspension of local elections sounded the death knell for elective local government in Malaysia. The abolition or supersession of local authorities by state authorities is not unusual in federal states where state governments and local governments are controled by antagonistic political parties. Indian state governments, for instance, habitually resolve disputes with opposition-run municipal corporations through the supersession of the local legislature. In Malaysia, too, abolitions occurred where state government and local authorities were controled by rival political parties or factions. In Penang an Alliance-controled state government took over the Georgetown City Council, and five years later, in 1971, earlier promises to restore elective local government notwithstanding, the Gerakan state government abolished the three Rural District Councils which had Alliance majorities (Tennant 1973b:85,86). In Negri Sembilan and Malacca the state governments were also in the hands of the Alliance, whereas the Seremban and Malacca Town Councils were controled by a Socialist Front/Labor/Independent/United Democratic Party (UDP)-coalition and the Socialist Front, respectively. In Kelantan a PMIP state government assumed control of the Kota Bahru and six other town councils, all of which were run by Alliance majorities. Somewhat unique is the case of Johore, where an Alliance state government suspended the Alliance-run Johore Bahru Town Council, suggesting factional conflicts within the Alliance Party (Tennant 1973a:356).

The Penang case clearly demonstrated that the abolition was first and foremost an attempt by the state government to enforce the cooperation of an unruly Socialist Front-controled city council. Since 1963, serious policy disagreements between the two had proliferated, ranging from the increasingly militant Socialist Front opposition to the formation of the Federation of Malaysia, the refusal of the city council to heed orders of the state government to decorate the city for the Malaysia Day celebration, to divergent squatter policies and different approaches towards property assessment (Tennant 1973b:78,79). At the same time, the abolition of the city council provided a good opportunity to decisively weaken the already disintegrating and faction-ridden Socialist Front in one of its major strongholds (Vasil 1971).

Moreover, party rivalry between the state and municipal government led to a competition in development projects. When the Socialist Front-controlled municipal government started low-cost housing projects in the city, the state government countered with the Rifle Range housing project. Another large-scale project of the municipal council was the construction of the Ayer Itam dam. However, in this competition, the state government was at a disadvantage, because the city council had far greater resources at its disposal. The abolition of the city council was thus probably also guided by the motive of gaining control over the resources of the local authority.

The abolitions can only be explained on a case by case basis. What can be said with some certainty is that, with the sole exception of Kuala Lumpur, the abolitions were not masterminded by the federal government. Rather, state governments took advantage of the favorable constellation created by the suspension of local elections in order to eliminate rival political parties where the latter controlled strategic urban centers.

The debate over the abolition of some twenty local authorities blurred the real issue: that it was the earlier suspension of local elections that destroyed once and for all the basis that would allow opposition parties to systematically build up a grassroots organization from which a serious challenge to Alliance rule could be launched. Unlike the abolition of individual local authorities, the suspension of local elections was masterminded by the federal government. The growing disenchantment of the Alliance with elected local government was paralleled by the rise of opposition parties which were able to build up pockets of regional influence that eroded the Alliance's initial total control over Malaysian electoral politics. The sequence of events made the suspension of elective local government only a question of time, and the Indonesian *confrontasi* provided a convenient pretext. While local elections were considered divisive in a situation of national emergency, one year earlier, under the same circumstances, the federal government had not felt compeled to stop the much more passionate and thus divisive campaign for state and federal elections.

The first sign of weakening federal commitment to elective local government was the suspension of the 1959 local elections. This decision must be seen against the background of a serious crisis in the MCA, the Chinese party in the Alliance, the rapid increase in urban support for the Labor Party, the major party of the Socialist Front, and the equally fast expansion of the Pan-Malayan Islamic Party (PMIP) in the northern

and eastern parts of the peninsula. The results of the 1959 general
elections were a heavy blow to the Alliance Party. Its percentage of
votes dropped from 81.7 percent in 1955 to 51.8 percent (Means
1970:253). While in 1955 the party had won fifty-one out of fifty-two
parliamentary seats (Smith 1960:39; Milne and Mauzy 1980:36), in 1959
it won only seventy-four out of 104 (Smith 1960:39). The MCA, in particular, which had been assigned the task of winning the urban seats,
suffered heavy losses. At the same time, urban-based, predominantly
Chinese parties such as the Socialist Front captured 12.8 percent of the
votes and eight parliamentary seats, while the People's Progressive
Party (PPP), a left-leaning party with strongholds in Ipoh and Perak, obtained 6.9 percent and two seats (Means 1970:253).

Mainly due to these changes in the political landscape, and the fact
that -- like in other countries -- the capital increasingly developed into
an opposition stronghold (Oberndörfer 1977; Rüland 1982a), the administration of Kuala Lumpur was transferred to the federal government
through the *Local Government Elections Act, 1960*.[40] In September 1960
the federal parliament passed the *Federal Capital Act* which invested the
powers hitherto held by the Kuala Lumpur Municipal Council in a Federal Capital Commissioner directly responsible initially to the Minister
of the Interior and Justice, after 1964 to the Minister of Housing and Local Government (Anthony 1971:72), and, finally, from 1974, to the Minister of the Federal Territory. The abolition of the Kuala Lumpur Municipal Council was thus the second step in a process of gradual emasculation of Malaysian local government. It became effective on 1 April 1961,
when the Federal Capital Commission came into operation.

After 1960, demands to scrap elective local government gained momentum within UMNO, the dominant partner in the Alliance Party. In
1962 the UMNO Annual General Assembly passed a resolution calling
for the elimination of elections in all state capitals. Two years later, a
similar resolution was adopted by the Penang UMNO, urging the federal government to abolish all local elections (Anthony 1971:21). The
final suspension of local elections under the pretext of a national emergency was merely the climax of growing discontent with local government inside the ruling Alliance Party.

Another assault on the strongholds of the urban-based opposition
parties was the constitutional amendment of 1962, which gave greater
electoral weight to rural areas. It allowed for rural constituencies to
have "as little as one-half of the constituents in the more populous urban
areas" (Rachagan 1980:275). The amendment was tantamount to the introduction of a "one man, two votes" privilege for Malays, doubling

their voting power at the expense of the other communal groups (Rabushka 1968:160).

Tennant (1973a, 1973b), who paid insufficient attention to this evolution of antilocal government sentiment within the Alliance, argued that the political party factor is untenable, because the Alliance Party was not in a position of declining strength. True, the Alliance polled over 50 percent of the votes and, due to the majority system, gained 70 percent of the seats in the 1963 local elections (and made a strong recovery in the 1964 general elections). But this is not the point here. While the actual strength of the Alliance may have remained stable in the mid-1960s, Alliance perception of its political efficacy was a different matter. Opposition parties did not necessarily need to hold the majority of seats in local legislatures for the Alliance to feel threatened. The determined challenge mounted by a strong minority is sufficient to create an atmosphere of siege within the ruling party. From key urban areas such as Kuala Lumpur, Georgetown, Ipoh, and Malacca it was reported that left-leaning parties such as the Labor Party (and with it the Socialist Front) and the PPP had stepped up their efforts at voter mobilization and expanded their branch network (Means 1970:251; Anthony 1971:21). The Labor Party almost trebled the number of its party branches in Peninsular Malaysia from eighty-six to 244 between 1958 and 1960. The number of party branches rose from eighteen to thirty-two in Penang, twelve to thirty-one in Malacca, fifteen to fifty-seven in Johore, ten to twenty-one in Negri Sembilan, and eighteen to fifty-four in Selangor (Vasil 1971:126). In the 1961 local authority elections the Socialist Front polled 34.1 percent of the votes in Kedah, 48.6 percent in Penang, 36.0 percent in Selangor, 44.4 percent in Pahang, and 31.9 percent in Johore. In Penang, the Socialist Front beat the Alliance, and in Pahang and Selangor it came close to doing so. Moreover, in Perak the Alliance succumbed to the PPP. In all these states, the Socialist Front and the PPP increased their votes compared to the 1959 parliamentary election (Smith 1961:155). The Labor Party benefited considerably from the internal crisis of the MCA, which lost many disenchanted supporters to it. Moreover, even in councils where the Alliance retained a majority, Labor Party, Socialist Front, and other opposition councillors were vocal opponents. Although the organizational expansion of the Socialist Front lost momentum due to internal rifts after the 1959 general elections, it temporarily recovered when the Federation of Malaysia issue dominated the political debate in the country. But after the defeat in the 1964 general election the front finally disintegrated into its components (Vasil 1971:220-221). Although on the verge of disintegration, the leftist wing of the Labor Party became increasingly militant and radical in its opposition to the government. Though at the time of the suspension of local elections the Socialist Front had ceased to be a major threat to the Alliance, it remained a political irritant due to its militancy. It may have been the combined effects of this continuous radicalization, which was indeed perceived as a threat to national security, and the imminent disintegration of the party organization that determined the timing of the abolition of local elections.

The importance of the political factor as an explanation for the suspension of local elections was belittled by Tennant and other authors, because they overlooked the intimate relationship between local politics and control over higher government echelons. A nationwide, vertically-structured political party such as the Alliance needs strong grassroots organizations for voter mobilization. Competitive organization-building by rival parties at the grassroots level thus threatens the hegemony of the established party. In fact, in the late 1950s and early 1960s the Alliance Party faced such a situation where opposition parties had made inroads into its local network. However, the situation became worse for the Alliance when opposition parties were able to use their urban grassroots organization to seize power in major local authorities. Given the fact that cities such as Kuala Lumpur, Georgetown, Seremban, Malacca, and Ipoh are the hub of economic activities in the peninsula, losing control over these local authorities cost the alliance tremendous patronage resources. Control of patronage resources is important for maintaining or increasing the political base, for keeping the party machine going, and satisfying the supporters' expectations of symbolic and material rewards. The conquest of major local authorities by opposition parties must therefore have been viewed by the Alliance as a serious weakening of its own position and a bridgehead for the opposition, from where it could launch further assaults on Alliance power at the state and federal levels.

Tennant (1973b:355) asked whether the Alliance had gained partisan advantage over its opponents through the abolition of councils (and, one should add, the prior suspension of local elections). While he seems to answer in the negative, the opposite is argued here. The suspension of elections together with the abolition of local councils enabled the Alliance to keep control of local authorities (and their patronage resources) where it had lost influence and trust of the voters. This advantage cannot be overestimated at a time when the political arena was becoming more competitive and the popularity of the Alliance, especially its MCA component, was being eroded, a process that begun in the late 1950s, culminated in its the dismal performance in the 1969 general elections after a temporary recovery in the 1964 polls.

Soon after the suspension of elections, in July 1965, the federal government appointed a *"Royal Commission of Enquiry to Investigate into the Workings of Local Authorities in West Malaysia"*. The findings and recommendations of the Royal Commission -- also known as *Nahappan-Report* (named after the commission's chairman Senator Dato' Athi Nahappan) are amply documented and thoroughly analyzed in the writings of Malcolm Norris (1974, 1978, 1979, and 1980). Here it is sufficient to briefly summarize the major recommendations of the commission.

Contrary to what most observers expected, the commission upheld the principle of elective local government. It pleaded for autonomous local government units that would cover the entire territory of West Malaysia. Local authorities should be financially viable, exert a wide range of functions, have legislative councils that are elected on a political party basis, and have control over personnel affairs. However, the commission accepted that the management system needed urgent reform to make service delivery more efficient. The voluminous report was submitted to the government on 25 January 1969 in an atmosphere of increasing communal and political tensions. After the communal riots in Kuala Lumpur on 13 May, 1969, the report's conclusions were unacceptable to the government. Not unexpectedly, when the report was finally tabled for parliamentary debate in February 1972, Parliament did not endorse the commission's recommendations (Norris 1980: 45-65).

The federal government's negative attitudes toward strong local governments were further reflected in the deliberations of another commission. In its report the *"Royal Commission on Remuneration and Conditions of Service"*, otherwise known as the Harun Commission, proposed that local authorities should be confined to routine functions. More sophisticated, developmental services such as public housing or medical services should be handled by higher government agencies (Norris 1980:66-79).

Government plans to restructure local authorities along the line of greater administrative efficiency found initial expression in the *Local Government (Temporary Provisions) Act 124, 1973*. The Act authorized states to establish nominated boards of management, replacing the existing local legislatures. At the same time it removed from office all remaining elected councillors, although in some cases such as Ipoh or Kangar the same persons were appointed to the new boards of management (Norris 1980:24). Finally, state governments were encouraged to rearrange the jurisdiction of local authorities, thereby integrating rural areas into the newly created local units. The first response to the Act came from Penang which amalgamated its five local authorities into two large units on 1 July 1974. The Georgetown City Council and the Rural

District Councils on the island were merged into the Penang Island Board of Management while the North, Central, and South District in Wellesley Province were merged into the Seberang Prai Board of Management. The twenty-four member boards were appointed by the state government and included the former district officers of the rural districts (Norris 1980:87).

After long debates and repeated redrafting, the *Local Government Act 171, 1976* finally became law on 18 March 1976 (Norris 1980:97). The Act served as the legal basis for a complete restructuring of local government in Malaysia. In the process, the confusing plurality of local governments was reduced to two types: through mergers and boundary alterations the number of local authorities was reduced to sixteen municipal councils and seventy-five district councils (Kassim 1986:205).

However, the restructuring did not meet the recommendation of the Royal Commission to bring the entire territory of West Malaysia under the jurisdiction of local authorities. As shown by Phang, only 17.1 percent of the peninsular land area had actually come under local authorities by 1983. This is only slightly more than before restructuring. In 1971, 14.7 percent of West Malaysia's land area came under the jurisdiction of local authorities (Phang 1988:168). Explanations for this surprising fact must be sought in the resistance of the Ministry of Finance to a greater number of local authorities, because this would have considerably increased the costs of restructuring. More local authorities would have meant additional launching grants and more expenses for personnel. The Development Administration Unit, on the other hand, was against creating local authorities in all areas of the peninsula, because it would have made the district officer obsolete (Norris 1980:48). Finally, the decision also stemmed from the desire of the federal government to exempt impoverished rural Malays from assessment rates, which are obligatory for all people living within the jurisdiction of a local authority. Sabah and Sarawak were not affected by the *Local Government Act* either.

The objectives of the Act were, in this order, to boost national unity (by minimizing politicking in the local arena), to make local governments "catalysts of socioeconomic development", to improve administrative efficiency, to promote democracy (by encouraging citizen participation), and to increase local autonomy (in finance, administrative matters, and functions) (Thean, n.d.:15). However, contrary to these objectives and similar pronouncements made by high-ranking government officials, the *Local Government Act* confirmed the dominance and control of the states over local governments in all respects. As demonstrated previously, state governments were given a wide range of powers vis-à-vis local governments. Not even the revenue base of local authorities was expanded by the Act (World Bank 1988:9). Most analysts have thus expressed serious reservations as to what extent restructuring has actually eradicated the problems that the government had cited as a justification for the reform (politicking, corruption, maladministration, financial weakness) (Kassim 1986: 216; World Bank 1988:9).

Undoubtedly, the *Local Government Act* had far-reaching implications for political participation at the local level. The Act must be seen as a deliberate move to depoliticize the local arena by introducing regulations that severely curbed opportunities of political participation. People were in fact deprived of the right to control local affairs themselves. *Act 171* confirmed the suspension of local elections indefinitely. Recruitment and selection of members of the local legislatures has been placed entirely in the hands of the state government, which appoints them for a maximum term of three years, after which the appointment can be renewed.

The government used to counter such criticism, which, from time to time, was also expressed by the opposition Democratic Action Party (DAP) and nongovernmental organizations such as ALIRAN (1982), by commenting that the appointing State Executive Council is composed of freely elected persons (Abdul Karim bin Ineh 1975:22). Yet, the interpretation of Malaysian local government as a system of indirect democracy can scarcely legitimize the curtailment of participatory rights. The appointed councillors are neither accountable to a specific constituency nor to the population at large, but only to the appointing authority -- and, since most councillors are nominated for appointment by political parties, to an even greater extent to the respective party (Cheema and Hussein 1978:586; Phang 1990:32). Apart from a few prominent USM lecturers, this dependency upon the nominating and appointing bodies has created a docile breed of councillors whose main interest is to secure their reappointment. The state government, and the nominating political parties, practice a high degree of party discipline. Thus, councillors more often represent party interests than the interests of the public (Phang 1985:63). It goes without saying that only members of the ruling Barisan Nasional (National Front) have a chance of being appointed. Created in 1974, the Barisan Nasional (BN) succeeded the Alliance Party as an umbrella organization of government parties, but with a broader base than the Alliance, because it coopted former opposition parties such as the Gerakan, the PPP, and (temporarily) the PAS into the government fold. Members of the opposition parties were thus excluded from sitting on the municipal councils. Therefore, a substantial percentage of the urban population is a priori excluded from political representation.

The literature and the press are full of examples that illustrate the emasculation of the local legislature in Penang and the role of councillors as puppets of their political party or the state government. Penang was the first state in Malaysia to implement the *Local Government Act.* On 15 December 1976 the state government dissolved the Board of Management and appointed eight councillors to the Penang Island Municipal Council and fourteen councillors to the Seberang Prai Municipal Council. Yet, the decision to implement the Act did not arise from the desire to pave the way for the realization of the lofty principles laid down in it, but to defuse political controversies between the state government and the Penang Island Board of Management over the gigantic KOMTAR urban renewal project (Phang 1978:144; Norris 1980:87-88).

Interparty relationships within the Penang Barisan Nasional had never been smooth. On the one hand, fierce rivalries existed between Gerakan, Penang's leading party after its great success at the 1969 polls, and the MCA, the party which before 1969 controled Penang state politics and, like Gerakan, primarily wooed the Chinese. The Gerakan-MCA rivalry was mainly a struggle over political supremacy within the Chinese community. The other contest was between Gerakan and UMNO. UMNO criticized Gerakan for not implementing the NEP vigorously enough, making its own leadership claims for Penang state and underscoring them by repeated demands for the post of chief minister (Chew 1985:126).

In such a political environment, the KOMTAR issue sparked off sharp controversies in the Board of Management. The board subsequently split into two factions of almost equal strength: while the UMNO/MCA/MIC coucillors opposed the project, it was supported by the Gerakan and nonpolitical representatives on the board. The opponents branded the project as a "Gerakan brainchild, a pet project of Chief Minister Lim Chong Eu, planned by Lim Chong Keat (the chief minister's brother) and carried out by the PDC" (Phang 1978:144). UMNO in particular saw little advantage in the project for its Malay clientele. UMNO, MCA, and MIC further opted against moving city hall into KOMTAR. The state government finally made use of the *Local Government Act* to overcome the stalemate on the board. The implementation of the Act permitted the state government to dismiss all noncooperative board members and replace them with more compliant representatives (Phang 1978:147).

Representatives such as Gerakan councillor Yoong Guan, a university lecturer from the Universiti Sains Malaysia (USM), who openly criticized the continuous erosion of councillors's rights and of local autonomy in general, paid the price for their opposition: Yoong was not considered for reappointment. He made two council speeches in which he castigated the tokenism of local democracy. Yoong claimed that decisions had already been taken before council deliberations; that the council president took decisions without informing the council, and that the procedures and practices of the council deviated from the provisions of the *Local Government Act*. Copies of the speeches were distributed to the press, which published the highlights of the councillor's critical remarks the following day.[41]

A few years earlier, in 1978, the Penang state government had resorted to even more drastic action. It removed three MCA councillors from office five months before expiry of their term. Lim Kah Pin, Meh Cheok Tat, and Ching Teik Seng were dismissed, because earlier they had resigned from the MCA in protest over what they considered an unfair share of seats allocated to the MCA by the BN to contest in the 1978 state elections. Together with four other MCA members, they decided to contest the election as independents. Their replacement as councillors was subsequently justified by the state government, which maintained that working against BN candidates is incompatible with a council position.[42]

Instead of reducing politicking in the local arena, appointment of councillors degenerated into permanent infighting between BN component parties and within the individual parties (Milne and Mauzy 1980:287; Phang 1985:61). Although, except for the time immediately following restructuring, the party composition remained relatively stable, all parties took considerable pains to change the composition in their favor once the new council was up for appointment. Pressures to change party composition intensified in the aftermath of general elections, especially if the relative strength of BN component parties changed nationwide or locally.

Interparty rivalries within the Penang BN for a greater share of seats on the board of management led the state government to expand the board membership from twenty-four to thirty-six in 1975. UMNO demanded an increase from seven to ten seats, the MCA from two to four, and the MIC from one to two seats.[43] Conflicts increased when the chief minister drastically reduced the council membership from thirty-four to eight in line with the adoption of the *Local Government Act* in December 1976, even though it stipulated the appointment of up to twenty-four councillors. In order to diffuse the controversies over the KOMTAR project, which was in fact the rationale behind the adoption of the *Local Government Act* in Penang, the chief minister appointed four Gerakan members, one UMNO member, one independent, and the two district officers of the Northeast and Southwest Districts of Penang Island. Yet, the protest of UMNO, MCA, and MIC became so loud that, eventually, in March 1977, the chief minister was forced to appoint a new municipal council and at the same time increase its membership to twenty-four. In both the Penang Island Municipal Council as well as the Seberang Perai Municipal Council, the UMNO councillors boycotted the inauguration of the new council.[44]

Similar incidents also occurred in other municipalities. In 1980, the MCA boycotted the swearing in of new members of the Kangar Municipal Council in protest against what it claimed was unsatisfactory representation of the party. The MCA share of seats was reduced from seven to four in that year.[45] Even worse, in 1983, the three municipalities of Selangor (Klang, Shah Alam, and Petaling Jaya) were without councillors for more than three months, because the BN component parties could not reach a compromise on the distribution of seats (Phang 1985:61).

State control over municipal councils has been further strengthened by the type of councillor usually appointed. Initially, state governments tended to appoint members of the state assembly as councillors. Although this practice has ceased in Penang, in Petaling Jaya a state assemblyman still sits in the municipal council.[46] The Sultan of Selangor is also represented by a councillor (Phang 1985:84,330,332). The state government obviously expects these councillors to perform a watchdog function as regards the council activities. Similar motives must also be suspected when in 1982 the Penang state government appointed the chief minister's son, Lim Thien Aun, as a councillor.[47] In general, however, municipal councillors have been second-line politicians, particularly those of UMNO. They are branch or division chairmen, sometimes also division secretaries. The post of councillor is given to these leaders as a "political goody", as a reward for party loyalty or to assure their future loyalty. Often politicians have been appointed who failed to get nominated as candidates for state assembly or federal parliamentary elections. This appointment pattern may also explain why, unlike in the Philippines, municipal councillor posts are rarely a stepping stone to higher office. Yet, although councillor posts carry relatively little prestige among politicians (Zahari 1974:74), an appointment is usually readily accepted by these second-line leaders, because it opens up possibilities of petty influence and patronage that were hitherto inaccessible to them.

While councillors were frequently replaced in the 1970s, more recently the percentage of newly appointed council members has been

TABLE 4.8 Occupational Background of Municipal Councillors, Penang Island Municipal Council, 1952, 1979, and 1981

Occupation	1952	1979	1981
Lawyer	4	4	3
Pensioner	1	3	2
Businessman and other business-related occupations	--	10	6
Lecturer	--	1	1
Teacher	1	1	2
Medical doctor	2	1	2
Accountant	--	1	2
Military officer	--	1	--
District Officer	--	2	2
Station master	--	--	1
Meter reader	--	--	1
Technician	--	--	1
Valuer	--	--	1
Office assistant	1	--	--
Total	9	24	24

Sources: Report on the Introduction of Elections in the Municipality of Georgetown, Penang, 1951 (Kuala Lumpur: Government Printer, 1953), S. 17; W.C. Teng, "Local Government in Penang. A Study to Assess the Changes Brought about by the Local Government Act 1976," (BA Thesis, Faculty of Law, University of Malaya, Kuala Lumpur, 1978/79), p. 55; and Phang Siew Nooi, "The Aftermath of Local Government Restructuring in West Malaysia: The Experience of the Penang Island and Klang Municipalities," (Ph.D. Thesis, University of Birmingham, Birmingham, 1985), p. 329.

much lower. Moreover, in many cases newly appointed councillors were by no means "new", because they had already served on the council in previous terms. The fact that after a break of one or two terms the same persons were again appointed suggests that a group of local politicians had emerged that were favored in council appointments. Several of Penang's municipal councillors have served on the council for ten and even more terms.

Most councillors in Penang have an upper-middle-class background (Chahl 1982:54, Phang 1985:329). Like in Chiang Mai and Iloilo, the overwhelming majority of councillors are businessmen, professionals or both (see Table 4.8). Hence, there has been no social change in the council composition over time.

The same social strata had dominated local politics long before restructuring. Occasionally, the lower-classes are represented by low-ranking government employees. This, again, is a move to make sure that social discontent does not spill over into local political bodies. It does not need much imagination to realize that government employees can be easily "guided" in their political behavior by higher government levels. Scattered data from other municipal councils seem to confirm the Penang data. In Seberang Prai, for instance, ten councillors came from the commercial and business sector, while eight were professionals and the remainder civil servants (among them three district officers) (Teng 1978/79:54). A similar profile was found in Petaling Jaya[48], and in Kota Setar where the municipal president was the local president of the Chinese Chamber of Commerce.[49]

Among the businessmen-professional group, housing developers, architects, and engineers are particularly strongly represented. This group wields great influence on municipal decision-making in cities such as Penang and Petaling Jaya. Inherent in this constellation is the danger that municipal development decisions will coincide with the business interests of a small societal group.

Participation in Everyday Politics

The previous section revealed how little influence the public has on the recruitment of its municipal representatives. In the following section I turn to the municipal decision-making pattern: i.e. how and where decisions are made, to what extent societal groups and interests are able to influence them, which groups are involved, what are the issues at stake, and what are the channels through which interests are articulated.

Based on the frequency of meetings, the Penang Island Municipal Council appears to be quite active. Throughout the 1970s there was an average of twenty-six ordinary and special council meetings a year, although frequency of meetings declined towards the end of the decade. In addition, there were numerous committee meetings. In 1979, for instance, apart from nineteen full council sessions, there were 113 committee meetings (Majlis Bandaraya Georgetown 1975, 1979).

Decision-making, however, rarely takes place in full council sessions. Debates are usually very short, and -- like in other municipalities (University of Birmingham, Institute of Local Government Studies 1973:8) -- often last less than 30 minutes. What followed was an acclamation of decisions already taken earlier behind closed doors in pre-council meetings or in the General Purposes Committee. Thus, while full council meetings in Penang are open to the public and the press, the actual debate and decision-making is a "closed shop" affair (Phang 1988:180). However, in many other municipal councils meetings not even open to the public "pro-forma". Despite public protests, in Kuantan, Ipoh, Kota Setar, Seberang Perai, and Klang the public and the press are completely excluded from all council deliberations.[50]

How tightly information on council meetings and municipal decision-making was supervised by the authorities was evident from the repeated admonitions to municipal councillors in Penang, Seberang Prai, and Kuala Lumpur by the state government, the municipal president or the Lord Mayor (*datuk bandar*) of Kuala Lumpur to avoid statements outside the council that did not agree with decisions taken at its meetings.[51] In Seberang Prai and Kuala Lumpur councillors and city hall staff were even exhorted to secure approval before making public statements.

In order to counteract the frequently raised criticism that the Malaysian local government system lacks democratic substance and that councillors do not have effective links to the citizenry (Cheema and Hussein 1978:583; Phang 1988:179), the Penang Island Municipal Council instituted so-called *"meet-the-people-sessions"*. Starting in 1978, these sessions took place at city hall every Wednesday. Four councillors were present, one from each component party of the BN on a rotational basis. The public was invited to attend these sessions and air demands, complaints, and suggestions. In an attempt to make the sessions more effective and more representative, the municipal council decided in 1981 to go to the people once a month. These "outdoor sessions" were held in specific residential areas of the municipality with the intention of giving the rural people in particular better access to municipal decision-makers through this "service at the doorstep".[52]

Yet, appraisals of these sessions produced mixed results. While the municipal council maintains that, in principle, the sessions provide effective feed-back from the public to councillors and administrators, it is admitted that very often the sessions suffer from poor attendance. However, given the fact that sessions were scheduled in the afternoon between 2.30 and 4.15 p.m., when most people were at work, it is not at all surprising that attendance was poor.[53]

Another reason for the public's indifference is the fact that the political efficacy of such sessions was considered low. Frequently, complaints were made that the administration did not respond to demands and suggestions or reacted slowly. Furthermore, councillors assigned to attend the meetings repeatedly did not turn up.[54] While councillors justified this with what they regarded as a low level of public responsiveness towards the sessions and the trivial nature of issues brought up, the public tended to interpret the councillors' behavior as a lack of commitment to political participation.

Political parties played a major role in raising popular demands in Malaysian cities. In Penang, all major political parties set up a tight network of party branches. Due to the communalist structure of political parties, demands are made along ethnic lines. The interviews and issue analysis, however, suggest that all parties have a clearly recognizable middle- and upper-middle-class bias in their interest representation. But this should hardly come as a surprise, given the socioeconomic background of most local party leaders.

The Gerakan, for instance, can be described as a "developmentalist" party. On the basis of western modernization theories, its leaders pursue the rapid transformation of Penang into a modern urban center. Singapore may be the tacit underlying model. It is obvious that the beneficiaries of such development are primarily the groups best equipped to make use of the new opportunities: the educated middle-class, professionals, and businessmen.

The other Chinese component party of the BN, the Malaysian Chinese Association (MCA), appears as a "property owners' party" in Penang. The MCA rejects rent control for pre-1948 buildings and has frequently organized protest campaigns against rate increases.

As a Malay political organization, the United Malay National Organization (UMNO) follows the prime objective of implementing the *New Economic Policy*. This automatically implies a strong bias towards developmentalism, since Malays can only increase their share of the economic pie through participation in large-scale, capital-intensive modern-sector projects. Again, this means that it is primarily a well-to-do conglomerate of Malay businessmen, professionals, politicians, and bureaucrats that have benefited from this policy. It is not surprising, therefore, that, contrary to the avowed targets, numerous appraisals of the NEP suggest increasing disparities of wealth within the Malay population.

Yet, UMNO is in a delicate position, because the overwhelming majority of party followers come from the poorer sections of the Malay population who regard UMNO as their protector and patron. From UMNO they expect service improvements, jobs, and better income opportunities -- in short, an upgrading of their living conditions. These expectations, however, often clash with the interests of the "NEP-elite": for instance, when Malay bona fide settlers or squatters are threatened with eviction to make way for urban renewal projects or subdivision development. A particularly illustrative case was the squatter colony half-way between Georgetown and Bandar Bayan Baru. In 1984 a tract of land was invaded by predominantly Malay squatters who subsequently built houses, investing up to M$ 7,000.[55] When the municipal council made several moves to evict the squatters and demolish the houses, UMNO was caught in a dilemma. The party establishment could hardly tolerate the invasion, because implicitly it militated against its developmentalist attitudes. Publicly, therefore, the Penang-

UMNO establishment gave reserved support to the squatters, at the same time however describing them as victims of a few ruthless "squatter entrepreneurs" who had sold the lots to them. Thus they gave the invasion the stamp of an illegal act without blaming their own constituency. Nothwithstanding these tactics, the UMNO state leadership came under heavy fire from grassroots party leaders in the area. The UMNO Bandar Bayan Baru youth division threatened to stage a mass resignation of 600 UMNO members, unless the party leadership heeded the squatters' demands to legalize the settlement and provide it with basic public services. UMNO grassroots pressure became strong enough to cause that a stalemate: in November 1986 the squatter colony was still there.[56]

Finally, the Democratic Action Party (DAP), a predominantly Chinese-based opposition party with a strong base on Penang Island, cultivates an image that portrays the party as advocate of the less advantaged. It frequently represents (Chinese and Indian) squatters threatened by eviction or relocation and hawker groups facing economic hardships resulting from regulatory measures of the municipal council. Moreover, the DAP is the only party that from time to time articulates demands for more political participation and the restoration of elective local government (Norris 1980:81).[57] The party's strategy is to find or create issues on which to expand its grassroots base. Yet, due to the exclusion of DAP stalwarts from municipal and state decision-making bodies, the party can do little more than try to raise public awareness of the failings of the authorities. It is not in a position to directly effect changes in the municipal council's policies.

As has already been pointed out, a great spectrum of voluntary associations flourishes in Penang. This seems to contradict the widely held belief that interest groups do not play a prominent role in Malaysian politics. However, as will be seen in the following paragraphs, this channel of political participation was almost exclusively utilized by the middle- and upper-classes.

At least three types of voluntary groups can be distinguished in Penang; economic groups, traditional associations such as clan and trade associations, and organizations working for societal objectives (Doh 1980:44).

Economic groups are particularly active in municipal politics. Among them are the various chambers of commerce, organizations of professionals such as the Board of Engineers or the Architects Association, interest groups of the housing and real estate industry such as the Housing Developers Association, landlord organizations such as the Penang Ratepayers, Taxpayers, and Landowners Association, as well as numerous hawkers' associations. The issues at stake are zoning decisions, land development for residential and commercial purposes, assessment levels and assessment rates, hawkers' sites, fees, and permits for stalls.

However, with the exception of hawker associations, most of these organizations represent interests of the propertied classes and big business. The latter were the groups that made use of the participatory channels offered by the *Town and Country Planning Act, 1976.* When the *Report of Survey* of the Penang Structure Plan was laid out for public response, it mainly drew comments and suggestions from property owners and the real estate and construction industries.[58]

The most prominent organizations working for societal objectives are the Consumers' Association of Penang (CAP), a group protecting, educating, and organizing consumers, ALIRAN, an organization for developing ideas and social awareness, environmentalist groups such as the Environmental Protection Society or Sahabat Alam Malaysia (SAM), and squatter organizations. The latter, however, were frequently linked to political parties which took up their issues -- especially in the case of Malay squatters, whose interests were usually represented by UMNO branches. Most of these societal groups were strongly involved in lower-class representation -- supporting the poor when they were threatened by eviction or hawkers facing relocation of their stalls. Moreover, they mobilize public opinion to combat pollution or to conserve the city's architectural heritage. Yet, despite their advocacy work for less vocal and impoverished segments of the population, the activists of these organizations come predominantly from the educated urban middle-class. Even today there are few horizontally-structured, intercommunal organizations of the poor. They are divided by ethnicity and thus most are linked to patrons of the same communal group (Chan 1983).

Malaysian authorities have always viewed the activities of organizations working for societal objectives with suspicion. It is this type of political participation that is kept under strict control through the *Societies Act, 1961.* This Act, originally intended to register and control secret societies, was amended in 1972 and 1981 to facilitate state supervision of the activities of what were believed to be anti-governmental organizations (Mauzy and Milne 1983-84:622). Under the *Societies Act*, any voluntary association of seven or more persons, whatever its nature or objective, must be registered. After registration, tight control over these organizations is exercised by the regular submission of reports or any other information required (Doh 1980:46; Barraclough 1984:151).

Due to their high degree of organization, housing and subdivision developers and the construction industry were able to maintain permanent contacts with municipal decision-makers. Interaction between this group and the municipal council was institutionalized with the creation of SPEAD in 1979. SPEAD and representatives from the municipal council meet at least once a month to discuss issues of mutual concern. While these economic interest groups had ready access to municipal decision-makers, organizations with a reputation for criticizing the government had much greater difficulty in making themselves heard. Moreover, many of the smaller voluntary associations were not permanently active; they voiced their demands only on issues important to them.

Patterns of interaction with the authorities vary greatly. This is primarily a tactical question, but it depends also on the stage of conflict. Frequently, the leadership of voluntary organizations utilized personal contacts to politicians or prominent administrators. Other means of making demands were petitions or signature campaigns. In the majority of cases, however, most groups preferred to operate behind the scenes, since in Malaysian political culture going public is not generally accepted. Pressure politics via media exposure, demonstrations or strikes were adopted only rarely -- and, if so, usually by opposition organizations.

The Malayanization of Urban Politics

The restructuring of local government consolidated BN influence in urban areas. Opposition parties were left with little chance of building up sizeable grassroots machines in their former strongholds. Among BN component parties, UMNO undoubtedly was the winner of the restructuring exercise. The redrawing of local government boundaries brought urban and adjacent rural areas under one jurisdiction. This was officially explained as a move to avoid ethnic polarization, but had the advantage of substantially increasing the share of the Malay (i.e. UMNO-supporting) population in urban local authorities. The merger of rural and urban areas significantly changed the ethnic composition of municipal jurisdictions, since the urban fringe and the immediate rural hinterland are inhabited by Malay majorities. This, in turn, enabled UMNO to demand a larger share of council seats. In Penang, for instance, with nine councillors, UMNO got more seats than any other party, although even after the formation of Penang Island Municipal Council Malays were still an ethnic minority on the island. UMNO can now exert much greater control in urban areas than under the old Alliance Party, when it had to rely strongly on its MCA partner.

The growing influence of UMNO was only one aspect of the *Malayanization* of urban politics. Yet, it was a necessary condition for the other aspect: the implementation of the *New Economic Policy*. Strong UMNO representation in municipal councils was essential, because the *New Economic Policy* is necessarily an urban-biased policy.

Urban areas are the hub of commerce and industry. It is here that the greatest economic assets are located. Hence, the goal of a 30 percent share for Malays in commercial and industrial enterprises can only be achieved if Malays get access to the urban economy. This also explains why the government encourages Malay migration to urban centers.

Local government restructuring thus not only facilitated UMNO control over the implementation of the *New Economic Policy* in key areas, at the same time it gave UMNO access to vast patronage resources that can be utilized to consolidate or expand its political grassroots machine in urban centers. The provision that municipal councillors do not represent specific constituencies must also be seen in this context. If bound to individual constituencies, UMNO urban and periurban representation would be confined to the economically much less attractive areas where Malays predominated.

Although surrounded by an air of secrecy, politically-supported Malay penetration of the urban economy is increasingly gaining momentum. Especially the federal government's privatization policy has opened up opportunities for *Bumiputra* entrepreneurs and in public biddings *Bumiputra* firms have now an edge over their competitors. Of the 407 contractors registered with the Penang Island Municipal Council, 237 (or 58.2 percent) were *Bumiputra* entrepreneurs. *Bumiputra* contractors were awarded contracts worth M$ 7.7 million or 49 percent of the total value of all contracts.[59] This is striking in an economic environment such as Penang, where businesses and services are controlled almost exclusively by Chinese entrepreneurs.

Bumiputra participation in business can be further promoted by licensing policies. Already in 1975, a policy paper prepared by the Ministry of Housing and Local Government urged that "efforts must be heightened to increase the number of *Bumiputra* businessmen and this would be done through the provision of licenses and quota reservations for them" (Ahmad Idris Mohd. Noor 1975:16). This policy is currently being implemented in virtually every Malaysian city.[60] Municipal approval for housing developers, shophouses, and commercial complexes is given on condition that 30 percent of these units must be sold or rented to *Bumiputras*.[61] Hawker licenses are given out on a *"Bumiputra first"* basis. Municipal approval for setting up factory buildings in Petaling Jaya requires a declaration of intent to restructure the business in accordance with the objectives of the *New Economic Policy*.

TABLE 4.9 Land Ownership in Malaysian Regional Cities, by Ethnic Group, in Percent

| City | Percent of Land Owned by | | | |
	Malays	Chinese	Indians	Othersa
Ipohb	2.86	51.86	0.84	44.61
Penang Island	16.8	52.5	2.6	28.1
Central Georgetownc	1	85	13	1
Butterworth	9	76	15	--
Kota Bahru	82.9	9.6	0.3	7.3

aIncludes foreigners, associations, and state owned land
bCentral Business District only
cBased on 1973 data

Sources: H.D. Evers and Goh Ban Lee, "*Urban Landownership in Kota Bahru and Jeli, Kelantan,*" (Penang: Centre for Policy Research, Universiti Sains Malaysia, Project Paper No. 5, 1976), p. 20; Goh Ban Lee and H.D. Evers, "Urban Development and Local Landownership in Butterworth, Malaysia," in *Journal of Southeast Asian Studies*, Vol. 9, No. 1, p. 42; Goh Ban Lee, "Urban Landownership by Capital in Penang," (Ph.D. Thesis, University of California, Los Angeles, 1981); Majlis Perbandaran Ipoh, *Report of Survey, Ipoh Structure Plan* (Ipoh: Majlis Perbandaran Ipoh, 1984), p. 124 and Majlis Perbandaran Pulau Pinang, *Report of Survey. Penang Island Structure Plan* (Penang: Majlis Perbandaran Pulau Pinang, 1985), p. 176.

Companies without 30 percent *Bumiputra* participation risk not obtaining approval for their plans.[62]

The sector of greatest opportunity opened up to Malay businessmen with the help of political influence is the property market. Until the mid-1970s, Malays were strongly underrepresented in urban property ownership (see Table 4.9). The increasing control over municipal councils, further supported by the leading role that UMNO plays at the state level, has helped to create a group of Malay housing and real estate developers (in some cases as junior partners in established Chinese companies) that gained a foothold in the booming market of the late 1970s and early 1980s. In the Petaling Jaya Municipal Council, at least three UMNO councillors were reputed to be large-scale *Bumiputra* entrepreneurs in the housing and construction industry. Not surprisingly, they utilized their political leverage to get approval for their development projects, even though they were highly controversial and opposed by a sizeable number of residents in the respective areas.[63] And the Petaling Jaya Municipal Council president was repeatedly accused in the press of having close ties with the firms constructing the MPPJ-office tower.[64]

According to the Far Eastern Economic Review, the approval required for building plans or rezoning of land uses created sources of "instant wealth" for UMNO politicians through generous kick backs from the applicants.[65] These politicians and administrators were able to influence the approval of applications in such a way that *Bumiputra* entrepreneurs, often closely linked to them, gained a substantial edge over their non-*Bumiputra* competitors.

The increased political influence of UMNO in the municipal areas thus created access to tremendous patronage resources that could be used to cement the party's grassroots organization. However, it benefited mainly a *Bumiputra*-class of businessmen-politicians and the UMNO coffers, while only some of these resources trickled down to the average Malay in the form of licenses, flats, service improvements, or protection from eviction and relocation. This clearly supports previous critical appraisals of the *New Economic Policy* which indicate increasing social and economic disparities among Malays (Wolff 1989:145). If this trend continues, in the long run it will erode the political gains UMNO has made through the *New Economic Policy* and the restructuring of local government.

While Penang's socioeconomic development was undoubtedly boosted by the modernization-theory inspired developmentalism of its state and municipal politicians, the large-scale, capital-intensive nature of many projects increasingly impaired the livelihood base of those groups which were not yet integrated into the modern economic sector: hawkers, fishermen, mini- and small-scale backyard firms, etc. The discontent of groups excluded from rapid development was muzzled by a political system that allowed for only controlled political participation. Only those societal groups with key roles in the development game had relatively free access to decision-making channels, whereas those economically disadvantaged considered a threat were deprived of free access to decision-making. This is one of the major reasons why 10-20 percent of the urban population still live below the poverty line. There are only few channels that these groups can utilize to articulate their demands -- either on a communalist basis through the respective BN component party, or through an opposition party or intercommunal advocacy groups such as CAP. Yet, in the latter cases the chances of demands being accepted by municipal authorities are limited, as this would resemble an admission of political failure. In the case of BN component parties much depends on the political weight of the party in question, the extent to which the interests of the clientele of these parties are affected and whether the demands clash with the interests of the party establishment. In most cases, therefore, demands of the lower-classes articulated via party channels are filtered through many layers of compromises -- which means that they usually only constitute a slight improvement for the groups affected.

Socioeconomic Development

Compared to Chiang Mai and Iloilo, and also to other Malaysian cities, services in Penang are of a high standard in virtually all sectors (see Table 4.10). The last two decades saw not only tremendous infrastructure improvements, but also a steady improvement in social services. Today, the basic material needs such as food, health, education, clothing, employment, water, and electricty supply of about 80 percent of Penang's population can be satisfied. Service standards are less satisfactory in the fields of housing and transport. Yet, despite huge investments, poverty is far from eradicated. Due to the harsh recession that hit Malaysia's formerly booming economy in the mid-1980s, the strict controls on political participation, and the relentless, officially encouraged Malay migration to urban centers, poverty will remain a challenge for municipal decision-makers for a long time. While "developmentalism" was able to improve the living conditions of about 80 percent of Penang's population to varying degrees, the benefits of economic growth scarcely trickled down to the poorest 20 percent. Especially in the rural areas of Penang Island, service standards have improved very slowly.

Municipal Services

The provision of health services is shared by the municipal council, the Ministry of Health, and the private sector. Through its Health Department the municipal council is involved in a wide range of activities such as primary health care, maternal-and-child care, control of infectious diseases, and immunization. The municipal council runs clinics and health centers, mobile health clinics, and X-ray facilities. Apart from these activities directly related to health care, the Health Department provides street cleaning and conservancy as well as mosquito, rodent, and pest control services. In addition, it is responsible for market administration and health inspection of eateries and restaurants. As a result, the health department always received the lion's share of municipal expenditures. Between 1977 and 1982 an average of 39.4 percent per annum was spent on health services -- although, as in the case of Chiang Mai, the bulk went to the sanitation section.

There are nine major hospitals in Penang Island, two run by the Ministry of Health, the others privately owned. Altogether they provide 1,975 beds. The bed-to-population ratio of 1:248 is favorable; it is the same as that of Kuala Lumpur. At the lower levels of the health-care system, there are thirty-one government-run clinics, 111 private medical clinics and thirty-one dental clinics on Penang Island. The ratio of one

TABLE 4.10 Services Matrix of Regional Cities in Peninsular Malaysia

Service Sector	Penang	Ipoh	Klang	Kuala Lumpur
Total water production (in million gallons per day)	32.3	31	10.9	n.d.
Percentage of households supplied with piped water	97	92.1	93	88.1
Installed electricity (in MVA)	245.8	35	120	n.d.
Percentage of households supplied with electricity	94.3	n.d.	82 (1974)	95.7
Number of hospitals	9	5	3	22
Government	2	1	2	4
Private	1	4	1	18
Number of hospital beds	1,975	1,537	n.d.	n.d.
Public	1,378	1,000	809	4,177
Private	596	537		
Bed-to-population ratio	1:248	1:224	1:386	1:248
Percentage of households with flush toilet	69	n.d.	55.7	n.d.
Number of schools	148	87	87	256
Primary	107	64	63	171
Secondary	41	23	24	85
Student-teacher ratio				
Primary	n.d.	30.6	24.2	n.d.
Secondary		22.5	22.1	n.d.
Fire engines	20	n.d.	6	n.d.
Length of roads	182 (1972)	n.d.	n.d.	n.d.

Sources: Compiled from Structure Plans such as Dewan Bandaraya Kuala Lumpur, *Kuala Lumpur Draft Structure Plan* (Kuala Lumpur: Dewan Bandaraya Kuala Lumpur, 1982); Majlis Perbandaran Ipoh, *Report of Survey, Ipoh Structure Plan* (Ipoh: Majlis Perbandaran Ipoh, 1984); Majlis Perbandaran Pulau Pinang, *Report of Survey. Penang Island Structure Plan* (Penang: Majlis Perbandaran Pulau Pinang, 1985) and Selangor State Government and Klang Valley Planning Authority, *Klang Draft Structure Plan 1986-2005. Statement of Policies and Proposals* (Klang: Selangor State Government and Klang Valley Planning Authority, 1986).

medical doctor for every 1,600 inhabitants is one of the most favorable in the country (Majlis Perbandaran Pulau Pinang 1985:91-92).

Sanitary conditions are much better than, for instance, in Iloilo City. 69 percent of housing units have a flush toilet system. Only 3 percent are without any toilet facilities. Yet, 19 percent of houses, mostly located in the densely populated inner-city areas, still use the bucket system, while seven percent, particularly households in the rural areas, use pit latrines (Majlis Perbandaran Pulau Pinang 1985:82).

Compared with other cities in Southeast Asia, Penang's health system is relatively well developed. The infant mortality rate declined from 38 per 1,000 live births (1972) to 14.0 in 1983. Medical services are less costly in Malaysian cities than in other countries of the region and even the needs of the poor are met to a considerable extent by the public sector (Meerman 1979:623). Yet, it should not be overlooked that 78 percent of Penang's health facilities are concentrated in Georgetown (Majlis Perbandaran Pulau Pinang 1985:92) -- a clear indication that, despite local government restructuring, the urban-rural service disparities are still substantial.

Penang's road network was consistently expanded over the last two decades through construction of new roads and bridges and the widening of existing major thoroughfares. A system of six radial and three ring roads has helped considerably to deal with the rapid increase in traffic. While the northern and eastern parts of the island were well-served with new roads, the predominantly rural western part benefited to a much lesser extent. Since restructuring of local government only one new road linking Balik Pulau with Bayan Lepas, has been built (Phang 1985:54). Although the municipal government was frequently blamed for this inequitable distribution of services, in the case of road construction it could hardly do more, because only the roads within the Georgetown area are under the management of the municipal council. All other roads are the reponsibility of the state government's Public Works Department.

Despite considerable investments in road and bridge construction, maintenance work and traffic lighting, traffic flow improved only slightly. This is due to the limited space for road expansion and the explosion in the number of motor vehicles. The number of cars increased by 8.5 percent between 1961 and 1979 and by 9.8 percent between 1980 and 1983. The increase in motorcycles was even greater: 11.3 percent between 1965 and 1979 and 13.8 percent between 1980 and 1983 (Majlis Perbandaran Pulau Pinang 1985:165). Traffic volume is more than double that of Chiang Mai and almost ten times that of Iloilo City.

Apart from Kuala Lumpur, Kota Kinabalu, and Shah Alam, Penang is one of the few cities with a water-borne central sewerage system. However, the system serves only about 45 percent of Penang Island (Majlis Perbandaran Pulau Pinang 1985:113). The new town of Bandar Bayan Baru has its own sewerage system. About 25 percent of the Penang Island population, especially in the old parts of Central Georgetown, still depend on the night-soil system. Another 20 percent rely on septic tanks, while 10 percent of the population are without any proper sewerage system (Majlis Perbandaran Pulau Pinang 1985:113). A considerable portion of the sewage, sullage from pig farms, and industrial effluents are discharged into rivers and the open sea. This has led to high and possibly even dangerous levels of marine and water pollution (Nathan 1970:112; Barrow 1981; Majlis Perbandaran Pulau Pinang 1985:130).

The Penang Island Municipal Council is the only local government in Peninsular Malaysia that provides transport services. The municipal council has ninety-one buses of which sixty to sixty-five are run daily on thirteen routes.[66] Private companies own an additional 180 buses. Yet, public and private bus services only account for 20 percent of total passenger trips, the remainder being made by private car, motorcycle, or the 330 factory buses ferrying workers to and from work. In addition, there are approximately 390 school buses and 500 taxis. The latter also offer shuttle services along major thoroughfares. In the inner-city areas, around 3,300 registered and unregistered trishaws offered their services. However, as in Chiang Mai, trishaws became a victim of rapid modernization and the municipal council decided to phase out this mode of transport by refusing to issue new licenses (Majlis Perbandaran Pulau Pinang 1985:166).

Garbage disposal is shared by the municipal council and private contractors. Refuse is collected daily in most parts of the city, although in some squatter areas only every second day (Chahl 1982:34). As the council was unable to collect more than 60 percent of the island's 400 tons of daily refuse, part of the collection service was contracted out to the private sector (Khoo 1987:4). However, the Penang example clearly shows that the privatization concept espoused by the Malaysian government does not automatically lead to improved services and lower costs. While initially the experiment worked satisfactorily, complementing municipal efforts and reducing costs, considerable problems arose later. Garbage trucks frequently broke down, areas were not served daily, and the municipal council had to field its own workers (Khoo 1987:7). Collections only improved when a more competitive system, involving several contractors, was introduced in 1984 (Khoo 1987:10).

Non-Municipal Services

In Penang and other Malaysian cities, housing was a municipal function until the mid-1970s, although it was shared with state and federal agencies. In contrast to Thai and Philippine cities, Malaysian municipalities had launched their own low-cost housing programs. In Penang, the Socialist Front-controlled city council started low-cost housing schemes as early as the late 1950s. Until the early 1970s, the municipal government constructed 1,377 low-cost housing units. With rents between M$ 20 and M$ 75, these apartments were quite attractive for low-income groups.[67] The envisioned expansion of the program was eventually blocked by the federal government in the mid-1970s, when it rejected the municipal council's application for federal grants to finance further low-cost housing projects. Municipal councils were downgraded to support agencies of the state government which, together with state and federal statutory bodies, were then entrusted with the provision of housing (Phang 1985:197-198).

The housing situation in Malaysian regional cities is not as bad as in Kuala Lumpur. The percentage of squatters in Penang, Ipoh, Klang, and Johore Bahru is considerably lower than in the capital, or in Thai and, in particular, Philippine regional cities. Only 3.0 percent of Penang Island's population lived in squatter areas (see Table 4.11). Equally low percentages of squatters are found in Ipoh and Klang. However, the number of squatters can be expected to rise in the future, mainly as a result of the government policy of encouraging Malay migration to the cities. Malay migrants are usually at the bottom of the urban income distribution and thus hardly able to meet the escalating rents on the free market. Many of them cannot even afford the rents of public low-cost housing projects. Moreover, given the previous pace of housing construction, the discrepancy between supply and demand will widen, so that new arrivals will have no alternative but to squat. Already by the early 1980s, there was an estimated backlog of approximately 30,000 housing units (Chahl 1982:9). Finally, government housing projects provide mainly high or medium-rise tenement blocks, but Malays are very much averse to living in apartments.

The percentage of dilapidated or deteriorating housing stock is also relatively low in Malaysian cities. In Penang, the percentage of substandard dwelling units declined from 10.9 in 1970 to 6.0 in 1980. Yet, at 31 percent of the total housing stock, the percentage of nonpermanent or semipermanent structures in Penang is relatively high. Most of this so-called "indigenous" housing consists of timbered or half-wooden structures. In general, these houses have piped water and electricity. While Penang's planners recognize that these dwellings are an "important part of the housing stock" (Majlis Perbandaran Pulau Pinang 1985:80), time and again the municipal council has discredited this type of housing as "squatting" -- especially when justification was sought for removing these structures, because they stood in the way of large-scale subdivision or commercial development. Goh rightly speaks of "a disturbing trend" characterized by the progressive destruction of cheap indigenous housing for high-priced condominiums and subdivision units (Goh 1986:13).

TABLE 4.11 Housing Conditions in Malaysian Cities

City	Percent of Squatter Population	Percent of Substandard Housing[a]	Number of Households per Occupied Unit	Number of Persons per Occupied Unit	Housing Backlog	Units to be Constructed 1980-2000
Penang Island	3.0	6.0	1.23	6.3	30,000	65,416
Georgetown	--	--	1.31	7.47	--	--
Central Georgetown	--	--	1.53	8.72	--	--
Ipoh	3.1	11.2	1.14	6.89	--	56,800
Klang	3.8	11.2	1.11	5.9	--	112,800[b]
Kuala Lumpur	25-30	40.3[c]	1.2	5.9	89,100	326,300
Johore Bahru	13.0	--	--	--	--	--
Seremban	--	--	--	--	--	47,200

[a]Defined as dilapidated or deteriorating units.

[b]Until 2005.

[c]Defined as temporary or semitemporary units.

Sources: Compiled from various Structure Plans. Dewan Bandaraya Kuala Lumpur, *Kuala Lumpur Draft Structure Plan* (Kuala Lumpur: Dewan Bandaraya Kuala Lumpur, 1982), p. 38-41; *Johore Bahru/Pasir Gudang Structure Plan Study* (Johore Bahru: Mimeographed Report, n.d.); Majlis Perbandaran Ipoh, *Report of Survey, Ipoh Structure Plan* (Ipoh: Majlis Perbandaran Ipoh, 1984), pp. 63-80; Majlis Perbandaran Pulau Pinang, *Report of Survey, Penang Island Structure Plan* (Penang: Majlis Perbandaran Pulau Pinang, 1985), pp. 79-88; Seremban Municipal Council, *Draft Seremban Structure Plan* (Seremban: Seremban Municipal Council, 1986); and Selangor State Government and Klang Valley Planning Authority, *Klang Draft Structure Plan 1986-2005. Statement of Policies and Proposals* (Klang: Selangor State Government and Klang Valley Planning Authority, 1986), pp. 62-69.

The loss of indigenous low-cost housing, the increased influx of poor Malay migrants into the cities and the nonachievement of construction targets are major reasons why overcrowding is still a major problem in Malaysian cities. Density is particularly high in the old city centers, where most buildings are rent controlled. In Central Georgetown, for instance, 1.53 households or 8.72 persons live in one dwelling, while for the whole of Georgetown and Penang Island the figures are 1.31 (= 7.47 persons) and 1.23 (= 7.01 persons), respectively (Majlis Perbandaran Pulau Pinang 1985:80; Asian Development Bank 1985:57). But not only in the inner-city areas do problems of overcrowding persist -- the same holds true for the new town of Bandar Bayan Baru. Due to its proximity to the Bayan Lepas Free Trade Zone, many low-skilled workers live in Bandar Bayan Baru flats. In order to be able to pay their rent from their meagre incomes, there are cases of up to eighteen persons sharing a three-room flat.

Despite many shortcomings, it seems that Malaysian housing policies have been more dynamic than those of Thailand (until 1987) and the Philippines. At least quantitatively, output of newly constructed units was greater in Malaysian than in Philippine and Thai cities, although the targets were only partially met: in the Third Malaysia Plan (1976-1980) 55 percent of the planned public sector units were actually completed, and in the Fourth Plan (1981-1985) only 51 percent (Khor 1989:14). Already in the 1960s, Penang had a remarkably high average construction rate of more than 1,230 units per year. In the 1970s, a rate of 1,200 new houses a year was maintained until 1978, when the average rate rose to 1,705 units (Majlis Perbandaran Pulau Pinang 1985:86). In Ipoh, an average of 1,583 new housing units a year were built between 1970 and 1982 -- which meant that the population increase could be accommodated (Majlis Perbandaran Ipoh 1984:72). Nevertheless, housing policies in Malaysia faced the same problems as in Thai and Philippine cities. Prime Minister Mahatir's vision of a "home-owning democracy" is strongly biased in favor of the middle- and upper-income brackets as well as public servants. The latter are eligible for heavily subsidized government credits at an interest rate of four percent. In Penang, 80 percent of the population cannot afford to buy a house for more than M$ 70,000. The high prices are due to the tremendous increase in the cost of land in densely populated urban areas. In Penang, land prices soared by 500-600 percent between 1973 and 1979 (Goh 1981:5). In the early 1980s, a single-storey terrace house cost at least M$ 100,000, two-storey terrace houses over M$ 200,000 (Goh 1981:5). But an average household could afford at most M$ 40,000. Nevertheless, there is a large oversupply of high-cost houses, because the private sector avoided participating in the construction of low-cost housing on the grounds that profits were too marginal. Low-cost housing projects often did not benefit the urban poor. In Penang's Rifle Range project, only 27 percent of the beneficiaries were in the low-income bracket, while the majority belonged to the lower-middle-class (Abraham n.d.:241). This is, in part, also a consequence of affordability calculations that assume that low-income households can spend at least 30 percent of their monthly income on housing (Majlis Perbandaran Pulau Pinang 1985:85). The figure is also 30 percent in Kuala Lumpur, 33 percent in Ipoh and Klang. This is even higher than World Bank affordability calculations which proved far too high for the majority of the urban poor in the bank's Philippine projects. Rents and amortization in Malaysian low-cost housing are further inflated due to the emphasis on high or medium-rise building. In Penang, the government did not embark on the cheaper slum upgrading and sites-and-services options, the latter apparently for lack of space. But also in cities with greater land reserves suitable for residential use than Penang, only a few sites-and-services or upgrading projects have been undertaken (Johnstone 1983:266).

Housing projects are also ethnically biased. Low-cost housing serves, above all, to absorb Malay rural-urban migration. In Penang, the state government stipulated a ratio of 45:45:10 for the allocation of low-cost flats to *Bumiputras*, Chinese, and Indians respectively (Majlis Perbandaran Pulau Pinang 1985:84). Not surprisingly, *Bumiputras* constituted only a relatively small percentage of Penang's waiting list for government low-cost apartments. Of 46,240 applicants, many who had been waiting for five to six years, some even ten years, 60 percent were Chinese, 23.6 percent *Bumiputras*, and 16.4 percent Indians.[68] Private housing developers are obliged to reserve at least 30 percent of houses in their schemes for *Bumiputras* and must give them a 5 percent discount (Majlis Perbandaran Pulau Pinang 1985:85).

Penang's housing policy has a latent bias against indigenous housing. As in the Philippines, antisquatting drives were particularly harsh when the government saw dangers to the national security. In most cities, frequent antisquatting drives took place during the *"Emergency"*, because (Chinese) squatter areas were suspected as sanctuaries for communist insurgents, and in the years following the May riots of 1969 (Johnstone 1983:257).

In recent times, antisquatting drives have become more selective -- squatters were usually only evicted when a relocation site already existed. Especially where Malay squatters were concerned, a strategy of appeasement was pursued by municipal governments: squatters were either relocated, paid compensation or given an apartment in low-cost housing schemes. Nevertheless, the Penang Island Municipal Council with its 65-man enforcement squad embarked periodically on anti-squatting drives. However, all these evictions involved relatively small numbers of squatters. Much more serious is the continuing encroachment of land developers on existing cheap indigenous housing. In view of the increasing discrepancy between cheap accommodation and demand, it is hardly foreseeable how the large numbers of migrants expected in Malaysian cities until the turn of the century can be housed.

Penang is the educational center of the northern part of Peninsular Malaysia. It is the seat of the prestigious Universiti Sains Malaysia (USM) and has a teacher's training college and forty-one secondary schools (four of them private). Average class size is 35.4 in secondary and 37.0 in primary schools, while the student-teacher ratio is 20.9:1. However, school facilities are concentrated in Georgetown, where almost 81 percent of secondary schools are located (Majlis Perbandaran Pulau Pinang 1985:90).

Water and electricity supplies are considerably better in Penang than in most other Malaysian or in Thai and Philippine regional cities. With 32.3 million gallons a day, total water production in Penang was seven times higher than in Iloilo and ten times higher than in Chiang Mai. More than 97 percent of Penang Island's population had access to piped water. This is a higher percentage than for all urban areas in Malaysia (93 percent), Ipoh (92.1 percent), and Kuala Lumpur (88.1 percent) (Asian Development Bank 1985:66; Government of Malaysia 1986:183). Water rates are subsidized for small consumers and residential rates are lower than those for industrial users (Majlis Perbandaran Pulau Pinang 1985:108).

With a capacity of 245.8 MW, electricity supplies far exceed those of Chiang Mai and Iloilo. 94.3 percent of Penang Island's households have electricity -- only slightly less than in Kuala Lumpur (95.7 percent), but more than in urban areas of Malaysia as a whole (92 percent). Water and electricity supplies are thus no obstacle to economic development, unlike in Chiang Mai and Iloilo City (Majlis Perbandaran Pulau Pinang 1985:109; Government of Malaysia 1986:183).

With the rapid industrialization and development of Penang, pollution has become an increasingly serious problem. Rivers were generally treated as natural sewers, so that pollution of drinking water now exceeds the legally permitted levels. The ecological balance of streams and coastal waters is increasingly endangered. Hillside development has led to soil erosion, while motorized traffic has aggravated air pollution. Existing environmental legislation is still inadequate to deal with pollution. There are still too many loopholes in the *Environmental*

Quality Act, 1974. The regional office of the federal Department of Environment is acutely short of staff to be effective in enforcing pollution control (Majlis Perbandaran Pulau Pinang 1985:139; Selangor State Government/Klang Local Planning Authority 1986:99; Goh 1988:227).

Greater environmental awareness has encouraged policy-makers to show greater concern for the city's architectural heritage. Old premises and architectural monuments are under increasing threat from redevelopment and urban renewal projects. The *Antiquities Act*, passed by the Penang state government in 1976, was intended to formulate an effective conservation policy. However, so far only Fort Cornwallis, St. George's Church, City Hall, and Town Hall have benefited from the Act (Majlis Perbandaran Pulau Pinang 1985:159). Unfortunately, the Act does not apply to private buildings. Hence, the city planners concluded in the *Report of Survey* of the Structure Plan that "at the moment there is no comprehensive and effective policy to protect the historic cultural and architectural heritage from disrepair and destruction" (Majlis Perbandaran Pulau Pinang 1985:161).

Economic Development

Penang has experienced tremendous economic growth since the late 1960s. It not only benefited from a favorable national economic environment with an impressive average annual growth of 7.9 percent in the gross domestic product (GDP) between 1970 and 1980, but, in particular, from Penang State's manufacturing boom initiated by the Gerakan state government after its electoral triumph in 1969.

Although GDP data are not broken down by municipality, available data for Penang State is nevertheless a crude indicator of the island's economic development, as it constitutes 30 percent of the state's land area and 51 percent of its population. However, as the island was more developed than the mainland part of the state prior to 1970, state growth rates slightly overestimate the island's actual economic growth.

In 1965, Penang State ranked fifth in terms of GDP and sixth in terms of per capita income among the eleven states of West Malaysia (Nathan 1970:28). Its per capita GDP at the time was almost 8 percent below the national average. In 1980 it was second only to the Federal Territory/Selangor -- almost 28 percent above national per capita GDP. With an average annual increase of 11.6 percent and 9.6 percent respectively, Penang State recorded both the fastest GDP growth rate and the most rapid per capita increase of all states of Peninsular Malaysia during the 1970s (Majlis Perbandaran Pulau Pinang 1985:40, 42).

However, after 1980 economic growth slowed considerably. While the national GDP grew at 5.8 percent per annum between 1981 and 1985 (Government of Malaysia 1986:40), Penang State's GDP only grew at an annual average of 4.9 percent between 1981 and 1983. And at the time of field research the island was in a recession.

Manufacturing was the engine of Penang's economic growth. While in Peninsular Malaysia the manufacturing sector grew at an average of 11.4 percent per annum between 1970 and 1980, in Penang State it recorded a phenomenal annual increase of 16.8 percent. In 1985, Penang State contributed no less than 15.5 percent of Malaysia's manufacturing output (Yeoh 1985:1), second only to the Federal Territory/Selangor, which accounted for 26.6 percent. The sector's contribution to Penang's GDP rose from 21.0 percent in 1970 to 34.1 percent in 1983, with a peak of 37.7 percent in 1977. Manufacturing thus grew much faster than commerce, which expanded at a rate of 8.5 percent (Majlis Perbandaran Pulau Pinang 1985:54).

After coming to power in Penang State, the Gerakan government completely restructured Penang's manufacturing sector. It immediately embarked on a strategy of rapid industrialization in order to reduce widespread urban unemployment that was estimated at 16-17 percent in 1969 (Georgulas 1972:263; Krüger 1989:227). Emphasis subsequently shifted from the previous *import substitution industrialization (ISI)* strategy to an outward-looking *export-oriented industrialization (EOI)*. Central to this strategy were eight industrial estates and three *Free Trade Zones (FTZ)*, which were created during the 1970s. Mainly because of company investment in these industrial estates, the product structure of manufacturing changed markedly. In 1968 the leading products were basic metals, paper, printing, and publishing and chemical products; ten years later electronics and electrical goods, food, beverages and tobacco, textiles, and clothing accounted for almost 70 percent of the sector's value added.

As shown by Table 4.12, the restructuring of Penang's economy has altered sectoral employment. Manufacturing has become the single most important source of employment, accounting for 52.3 percent of the net increase in employment, far exceeding the increase in the commercial (18.6 percent) and service sectors (12.8 percent). Based on an average annual employment growth of 9.7 percent, manufacturing almost doubled its sectoral share in employment from 15 percent in 1970 to 27 percent in 1980. Commerce, government/community services, and public utilities were relegated to second and third place, providing 23 percent and 21 percent of jobs, respectively. Ten years earlier, in 1970, manufacturing had still lagged far behind these two sectors; govern-

TABLE 4.12 Sectoral Employment Trend in Penang Island, 1970-1980

Sector	1970	1980	1970 Percent of Total Employment	1980 Percent of Total Employment	Average Annual Growth Rate 1970-1980, in Percent
Agriculture and mining	13,500	12,800	12	7	-0.5
Manufacturing	18,300	46,200	15	27	9.7
Construction	3,700	10,300	3	6	10.8
Transport/communication	11,400	7,500	10	4	-4.1
Wholesale, retail, hotel, and catering	28,100	38,800	24	23	3.3
Finance, insurance, real estate, and business services	---	5,900	---	4	---
Government/community services, and public utilities	42,200	36,000	36	21	2.7
Personal and other services	---	13,000	---	8	---
Total	117,200	170,500	100	100	3.8

Source: Majlis Perbandaran Pulau Pinang, *Report of Survey. Penang Island Structure Plan* (Penang: Majlis Perbandaran Pulau Pinang, 1985), p. 45.

ment/community services and public utilities was the leading employer (36 percent), followed by commerce with 24 percent.

Manufacturing in Malaysian cities provides more employment than in Thai and Philippine regional cities. Except for Kuala Lumpur, in all Malaysian regional cities manufacturing accounts for more than 20 percent of total employment. This finding contradicts Rondinelli's assumption that secondary centers are usually characterized by a considerably smaller manufacturing sector than the capital city (Rondinelli 1983a:146). Penang Island's manufacturing sector, however, is exceeded in size by that of Klang, which has grown rapidly over the previous decade and had a slightly greater share in total urban employment. Moreover, the average firm in Penang and other Malaysian cities is almost three times as large as in Chiang Mai and Iloilo.

Despite its rapid growth, Penang Island's manufacturing sector is not free from distortions. It seems that EOI even reinforced the dualistic nature of the sector. The expansion of the manufacturing sector relied almost exclusively upon a few large-scale, foreign-owned firms and a few products. Of 1,285 manufacturing firms, only fifty-one (or 4 percent) had more than 100 employees. Forty-five of them were located in the Bayan Lepas FTZ. These large-scale companies account for 77 percent of total employment and 90 percent of the gross value added in manufacturing (Majlis Perbandaran Pulau Pinang 1985:58). On the other hand, very small firms (with less than five workers) were 58 percent of all manufacturers, but provided only 5 percent of the sector's employment. Small firms (5-49 workers) accounted for 37 percent of manufacturing establishments and provided 15.5 percent of all jobs. Noticeable is the almost complete absence of medium-sized firms (50-99 workers). They constitute only 1.1 percent of firms and provide less than 2.5 percent of manufacturing employment (Majlis Perbandaran Pulau Pinang 1985:58). Thus, excluding the large-scale establishments, the average firm in Penang's manufacturing sector employs only 8.61 workers. In other words, 96 percent of Penang's manufacturing sector differed little in its employment structure from that of Chiang Mai and Iloilo.

The large-scale companies in the Bayan Lepas FTZ did not contribute much to the growth of local industries. Technology transfer has been disappointingly low. Moreover, there were only few linkages between EOI-companies in the FTZs and other Penang-based firms. Forward linkages accounted for only 7.3 percent of total sales (Yeoh 1985:3). Local content (including services and utilities) in the products of the semiconductor industry, for instance, was below 20 percent. Efforts of the Penang Development Corporation (PDC) to foster linkages between

MNCs and local companies have so far met with only modest success. The PDC attempts to establish linkages through promoting subcontracting work of local firms for MNCs. A list of engineering firms registering the kind of work that could be done locally was offered to MNCs, but the response was disappointing.[69] Furthermore, in order to strengthen interindustry linkages an Industrial Research and Consultancy Services (IRCS) link was created by the Universiti Sains Malaysia with the aim of making the university's expertise, personnel, and facilities available to the government and industry (Sadasivan 1985:9).

The manufacturing sector not only relies upon a few large-scale companies and foreign investment capital, it also depends on two major products. The overwhelming majority of EOI companies is engaged in the electrical/electronic and garment/textile subsectors. Electronics and textiles and clothing alone provide almost 70 percent of employment in manufacturing. This narrow industrial base makes Penang's economy vulnerable to adverse external influences such as world market fluctuations. The sluggish demand in the semiconductor industry, for instance, caused massive lay-offs in the mid-1980s. According to trade-union estimates, more than 6,000 workers were retrenched in 1985.[70] Moreover, wages rise, several major American companies in the labor-intensive, low-wage semiconductor industry reportedly plan to relocate their plants to the Bangkok area, where wages are more competitive than in Penang.[71]

The developmental potential of indigenous family-based micro- and small-scale industries is also limited. Many firms suffered from under-capitalization, low productivity, higher than normal wastage, obsolete technology, inferior or inconsistent product quality, and poor export skills (Yeoh 1985:5). These deficiencies were, in large part, the consequence of an outmoded patriarchical management system that places great emphasis on family tradition, seniority, and Confucian values. These traditional business and managerial attitudes forestall technological and managerial innovation that could serve as a starting point for more dynamic growth by these firms. Economic growth was further impeded by public sector inertia. Due to the delay in granting licenses and permits, between nine and twelve months elapsed from company formation to full-scale operation. In other NICs just half of that time is needed (Yeoh 1985:11-12).

The growth of employment in the manufacturing sector was exceeded by the construction sector. Employment in construction increased by an average of 10.8 percent per annum between 1970 and 1980. The construction sector thus doubled its share of employment from 3 percent in 1970 to 6 percent in 1980. This rapid growth was mainly the result of the large-scale infrastructure projects such as KOMTAR, land reclamation, the Penang Bridge, road construction, and the boom in the housing and subdivision industries.

Due to the rapid expansion of the secondary sector, Penang Island's economy was less *tertiarized* than Iloilo's or Chiang Mai's or, except for Klang, that of other Malaysian regional cities. In 1980, only 56 percent of the workforce was employed in the tertiary sector, which marks a slight decrease on 1970 (60 percent). However, *tertiarization* in Malaysian cities is similar to that of Chiang Mai and somewhat lower than in Iloilo in terms of sectoral distribution of firms. Between 83 and 86 percent of all registered business establishments in Penang Island, Ipoh, Johore Bahru, and Klang are in the tertiary sector (see Table 4.13).

After manufacturing, commerce is the most important contributor to Penang's GDP. In 1983, commerce accounted for 21.1 percent of the state's GDP, a decline of 5 percent compared to 1970. Also in terms of employment, commerce ranked second. Yet, with 7.7 workers, the average size of commercial establishments is much smaller than in the manufacturing sector and even smaller than its counterpart in Chiang Mai (8.1 workers).

The relative decline of commerce is primarily a result of the expansion of the manufacturing sector, but it is also due to the loss of the city's entrepôt functions. On the other hand, the losses in the entrepôt trade were compensated in the 1970s by the growth of the tourism industry. The number of foreign tourists increased 13.2 percent per annum between 1970 and 1981, whereas there was a much more modest 1 percent increase in local tourist arrivals. With daily spendings of M\$ 491, expenditures of foreign tourists were higher than in Chiang Mai (Majlis Perbandaran Pulau Pinang 1985:142). In 1983, tourism contributed no less than 15 percent to the state's GDP, but only 2.2 percent of jobs (Hamzah Abdul Majid 1985:4).

However, after peaking in 1981 tourist arrivals declined drastically. Hotel occupancy fell to 60 percent. There were a number of reasons: the prolonged world recession seriously affected ASEAN countries (from where the bulk of foreign tourists come), the stability of the Malaysian Dollar (making Malaysia expensive), stiff competition from other destinations in the region such as Pulau Langkawi, Phuket, Bali, and the Maledives and, finally, the deterioration of the island's environment through water pollution and pollution of the beaches (Muhammed Ikhbal bin Mhd. Hamzah 1985:2). This trend gave rise to doubts about whether the ambitious growth projections can be met in the light of the leading role that the state government has assigned to tourism in the future development of Penang. If the anticipated annual average increase

TABLE 4.13 Sectoral Distribution of Business Establishments in Malaysian Cities

Sector	Penang Island N	%	Ipoh N	%	Johore Bahru N	%	Klang N	%
Agriculture	--	--	--	--	--	--	--	--
Mining and quarrying	--	--	--	--	--	--	--	--
Manufacturing	1,285	13.61	871	11.66	571	14.06	623	14.28
Construction	n.d.	n.d.	76	2.03	n.d.	n.d.	n.d.	n.d.
Transport	n.d.	n.d.	152	1.02	130	3.20	n.d.	n.d.
Wholesale and retail	4,065	43.07	4,320	56.62	1,402	34.52	1,989	45.61
Hotels and restaurants	996	10.55	n.d.	n.d.	n.d.	n.d.	n.d.	n.d.
Finance, insurance, real estate, and business services	994	10.53	253	3.39	170	4.19	n.d.	n.d.
Other services	2,099	22.24	1,898	25.28	1,788	44.03	1,749	40.11
Total	9,439	100.00	7,471	100.00	4,061	100.00	4,361	100.00

Sources: Compiled from *Johore Bahru/Pasir Gudang Structure Plan Study* (Johore Bahru: Mimeographed Report, n.d.); Majlis Perbandaran Ipoh, *Report of Survey, Ipoh Structure Plan* (Ipoh: Majlis Perbandaran Ipoh, 1984); Majlis Perbandaran Pulau Pinang, *Report of Survey, Penang Island Structure Plan* (Penang: Majlis Perbandaran Pulau Pinang, 1985); Selangor State Government and Klang Valley Planning Authority, *Klang Draft Structure Plan 1986-2005. Statement of Policies and Proposals* (Klang: Selangor State Government and Klang Valley Planning Authority, 1986).

of 6.5 percent in foreign tourist arrivals is not attained, another major sector of Penang's economy will stagnate.

Like in Thai and Philippine regional cities, a major source of employment in Malaysian cities is the informal sector. Among regional cities in Malaysia, Penang seems to have the largest informal sector, although figures for other cities may be understated. On Penang Island, there were some 13,000 hawker units. With 1.5 workers per unit the sector employs nearly 20,000 people, many of them new entrants into the labor market or secondary earners (Majlis Perbandaran Pulau Pinang 1985:64). The informal sector thus accounts for almost 20 percent of the labor force and, hence, is a major source of income.

Despite a large area of agricultural land -- about 40.7 percent of Penang Island's total land area is classified as agricultural land -- the economic importance of agriculture for the city has declined over the last fifteen years. Only 5 percent of the island's GDP came from agriculture and the agricultural workforce dropped from 12 percent in 1970 to 7 percent in 1980. Most agricultural workers earned meagre incomes slightly above or even below the poverty line of M$ 300 per month (Majlis Perbandaran Pulau Pinang 1985:70-71). Due to the boom in housing and industrial development large tracts of agricultural land were converted for nonagricultural use (Mohd. Yusof bin Hashim 1985:8). The farms, many less than 1 hectare in size, were uneconomic and left idle by the farmers. Particularly the young migrated to the urbanized parts of the island, seeking industrial jobs. As a consequence, the agricultural workforce is aging: the average age of agricultural workers in Penang State was fifty-two years (Mohd. Yusof bin Hashim 1985:13). Faced with this dilemma, the state government is attempting to replace traditional farming methods by capital-intensive agriculture: agro-horticultural industries, fruits, floriculture, and vegetables.

Economic development in Penang Island seems to have benefited mainly the built-up, urbanized areas. Spread effects to rural areas were modest. In 1983, 90 percent of all commercial establishments and 97.7 percent of manufacturing establishments were concentrated along the highly urbanized east coast in Georgetown, Ayer Itam, and Bayan Lepas (Majlis Perbandaran Pulau Pinang 1985:63). Only 10 percent of the commercial and 2.3 percent of manufacturing establishments were located in rural areas. Employment is also concentrated on the east coast: 51 percent of jobs were in Georgetown, 21 percent in Bayan Lepas, and 15 percent in other suburbs; rural areas provide 14 percent (Majlis Perbandaran Pulau Pinang 1985:45). As probably half of the latter are agricultural, nonagricultural jobs in the rural areas constitute only 7 percent of the island's total employment. Nevertheless, it should not be overlooked that the Bayan Lepas FTZ has made industrial employment more accessible to the rural population living in the western part of the island. Thus, at least indirectly, some decentralization of employment has been achieved within the jurisdiction of Penang Island Municipal Council.

Social Development

Improvements in municipal service delivery, a substantial increase in employment opportunities, and dynamic growth have resulted in better living conditions for a large part of Penang's population. Like in Chiang Mai, in Penang too a broad middle-income stratum has emerged that includes nearly 50 percent of all households. This is a slightly smaller percentage than in Ipoh and Kuala Lumpur, and considerably below Klang's share of middle-income households (see Table 4.14).

Household incomes on Penang Island increased from M$ 774 per month in 1976 to M$ 1,335 in 1983. This is equivalent to an annual average increase of 8.11 percent. However, with an average inflation rate of 5.6 percent between 1976 and 1983, growth in real incomes was much lower. Nevertheless, at 2.4 percent, Penang's household incomes grew faster in real terms than in Johore Bahru (1.6 percent) between 1976 and 1982 (see Table 4.14).

Among Malaysian regional cities, Penang exhibits one of the highest average household income. It is, however, considerably lower than the adjusted Kuala Lumpur average household income and also lower than the average for total urban Malaysia. The latter figure reflects the high income levels in Kuala Lumpur and other Klang Valley municipalities, especially Petaling Jaya. In terms of median household income Penang still lags behind Johore Bahru and urban Malaysia as a whole, but ranks higher than Kuala Lumpur, Ipoh, and Klang. Although data did not allow to compute the Gini coefficient for Penang, it can be concluded from the existing data that social inequities in Penang are lower than in Klang and Kuala Lumpur, but higher than in Johore Bahru, Ipoh and total urban Malaysia (see Table 4.14).

Poverty incidence in Malaysian cities is lower than in Thai secondary centers and much lower than in Philippine regional cities. According to government statistics, urban poverty in Peninsular Malaysia declined from 21.3 percent in 1970 to 17.9 percent in 1976 and 8.2 percent in 1984 (Government of Malaysia 1986:86).

Statistics on poverty in Penang vary. The municipal council operated with a poverty incidence of 18 percent, while structure plan estimates were as low as 10 percent. Given the harsh economic recession in Malaysia's EOI-companies in the mid-1980s, the real figure for Penang

TABLE 4.14 Household Incomes and Income Distribution in Malaysian Cities

Income	Penang Island 1983	Ipoh 1980	Johore Bahru 1982	Klang 1984	Seremban 1980	Kuala Lumpur 1979	Total Urban Malaysia 1984
Average household income	1,335	692	1,053	1,078	722	1,447	1,541
Annual average increase since 1976, in percent	8.11	--	5.47	--	--	--	--
Real increase	2.4	--	1.6	--	--	--	--
Median household income	705	533	800	480	--	570	1,027
Average household income (1984 prices)	1,387	865	1,135	1,078	903	1,931	1,541
Median household income (1984 prices)	732	667	862	480	--	760	1,027
Gini coefficient	--	0.3686	0.3215[a]	--	--	0.5626	0.4216[a]
Percentage of households below poverty line:							
< 300 M$ per month	10	17.45	7.5	4.9	--	12.7	8.2
< 500 M$ per month	30	44.67	27.5	44.1	--	36.9	--
Percentage of households between M$500 and M$1,999 per month	49	52	46	82	--	52	--
Income of Malay households as percentage of Chinese household incomes	67.6[a]	79.9[b]	74	63.4	--	--	56.7

[a]Based on 1976 data

[b]Bumiputra as percentage of non-Bumiputra

Source: Calculated from various Structure Plans. Dewan Bandaraya Kuala Lumpur, *Kuala Lumpur Draft Structure Plan* (Kuala Lumpur: Dewan Bandaraya Kuala Lumpur, 1982); *Johore Bahru/Pasir Gudang Structure Plan Study* (Johore Bahru: Mimeographed Report, n.d.); Majlis Perbandaran Ipoh, *Report of Survey, Ipoh Structure Plan* (Ipoh: Majlis Perbandaran Ipoh, 1984); Majlis Perbandaran Pulau Pinang, *Report of Survey. Penang Island Structure Plan* (Penang: Majlis Perbandaran Pulau Pinang, 1985); Selangor State Government and Klang Valley Planning Authority, *Klang Draft Structure Plan 1986-2005. Statement of Policies and Proposals* (Klang: Selangor State Government and Klang Valley Planning Authority, 1986); and Seremban Municipal Council, *Draft Seremban Structure Plan* (Seremban: Seremban Municipal Council, 1986).

was most probably higher than 10 percent. Penang's poverty incidence seems to be higher than the national urban average, but lower than that of Ipoh and Kuala Lumpur (see Table 4.14).

The most poverty-stricken group in Penang Island are undoubtedly agricultural workers. A fisherman's income was as low as M$ 150 per month, paddy smallholders had a monthly income of around M$ 250. Incomes of unskilled workers in the commercial and manufacturing sectors were also low, averaging M$ 266 in the commercial sector and M$ 308 in manufacturing. However, household incomes were usually higher because there was more than one breadwinner per household.

Bumiputra households had lower average incomes than non-*Bumiputras*. Based on 1976 statistics, Penang Island's *Bumiputras* earned only 67.6 percent of the average employment income of Chinese households. Yet, this differential is an understatement of real ethnic disparities, because household employment income excludes nonemployment income such as rents, profits, interest, transfer income, capital gains, etc. In view of the overwhelming dominance of the Chinese in business and property ownership (see Table 4.15), the *Bumiputra-non-Bumiputra* gap is certainly wider than 32 percent. The Malay-Chinese income differential is even wider in Klang and for total urban Malaysia, but considerably lower in Ipoh and Johore Bahru (see Table 4.14).

These ethnic disparities can easily be explained. Malays were underrepresented in the better paying managerial, professional, commercial, and clerical jobs in the private sector, but overrepresented in low-skill manufacturing jobs as well as in the government service and utility sectors. Moreover, there was a high concentration of Malays in the agricultural sector.

Viewed against the background of Penang's development model, improvements in living conditions came mainly as trickle-down effects of the island's rapid economic growth. Yet, this trickle-down benefited the city's social strata disproportionately. The top income groups received most, while the bottom 10-20 percent derived little or no benefit. As has already been seen, the municipal council contributed little to the island's economic upswing. Economic development policies were the prerogative of the state government, supported by the parastatal Penang Development Corporation. Moreover, when the state's large EOI program was initiated, conditions in the world economy were favorable. Penang, and Malaysia as a whole, started this program when there was little competition from other developing countries -- only the "four tigers" Singapore, Hong Kong, Taiwan, and South Korea had embarked on the same development strategy somewhat earlier. Furthermore, the industrialization program was not hit by the two oil crises, as, for instance,

TABLE 4.15 Ownership of Industrial Enterprises in Malaysian Cities, by Industrial Group

| City | Shares Owned by | | | |
	Malays	Chinese	Indians	Others[a]
Penang Island	2.0	90.0	3.0	3.0
Johore Bahru	4.9	81.3	2.1	11.7
Klang	22.6	44.0	1.2	32.2
Kuala Lumpur[b]	9.15	83.56	1.18	6.11
	6.33	35.11	1.83	56.76

[a]Includes foreigners
[b]Column one refers to small industries, column two includes only large industries

Sources: Dewan Bandaraya Kuala Lumpur, *Kuala Lumpur Draft Structure Plan* (Kuala Lumpur: Dewan Bandaraya Kuala Lumpur, 1982), p. 105; *Johore Bahru/Pasir Gudang Structure Plan Study* (Johore Bahru: n.d., Mimeographed Report), p. 4.32; Majlis Perbandaran Pulau Pinang, *Report of Survey. Penang Island Structure Plan* (Penang: Majlis Perbandaran Pulau Pinang, 1985), p. 56; and Selangor State Government and Klang Valley Planning Authority, *Klang Draft Structure Plan 1986-2005. Statement of Policies and Proposals* (Klang: Selangor State Government and Klang Valley Planning Authority, 1986), p. 51.

the Philippines, because Malaysia is an oil-producing country. Nor were industrialized countries yet threatening the infant industries in developing nations with protectionism. The then low wage levels and a comparatively well-developed infrastructure added to Penang's attractiveness as a center for industrial investment.

Nevertheless, the municipal council has also made contributions to the improvement of living conditions in the city. The infrastructure was consistently improved, and generally well-maintained. Social services were improved, as were recreational facilities. Contributions of the local authority to a better quality of life in the city thus mainly concentrated on services in the reproduction sphere.

On the other hand, the land development and urban renewal policies of the council have made it increasingly difficult for the urban poor to find decent accommodation. Long-time residents are faced with relocation to distant sites which very often do not coincide with their economic needs and their cultural predispositions. The property and subdivision boom, facilitated by the council's zoning and rezoning decisions, exerts increasing pressure on families living in low-priced, low-density housing stock on the urban fringe or in cheap, but old town houses in central Georgetown.

Ambivalent too is the council's informal sector policy. While, in contrast to many other city governments in the region, the informal sector is recognized as a vital part of the island's economy, a tendency towards overregulation reduces the sector's economic potential. Hawkers must go through time-consuming application procedures for a license and are subject to regulations severely limiting their mobility and flexibility, as the municipal government tends to concentrate hawkers in so-called "hawker centers". Ethnic considerations also play an important role in deciding whether an application for a license is approved or not, because in line with the NEP, *Bumiputras* must be given priority.

The municipal council was not very successful in narrowing the gap between urban and rural incomes and quality of life. Household incomes in Penang Island's rural areas were still more than 20 percent below those in urban areas. Major goals of the local government restructuring have thus not been attained: neither did local governments become catalysts of socioeconomic development, nor were rural-urban disparities in wealth diminished.

Notes

1. Very informative are the writings of Goh Ban Lee, Malcolm W. Norris, and Phang Siew Nooi. The dissertation of Phang Siew Nooi is perhaps the most enligthening analysis of municipal government in Malaysia. See Phang Siew Nooi, "The Aftermath of Local Government Restructuring in West Malaysia: The Experience of the Penang Island and Klang Municipalities" (Ph.D. Thesis, University of Birmingham, 1985).
2. A kind of annex to the Constitution.
3. *The Star*, Kuala Lumpur, 21 July 1985, p. 9.
4. *The Star*, Kuala Lumpur, 12 February 1984.
5. By 1986, Penang's per capita revenues had risen to M$ 144.
6. Rates for houses and shop houses outside the city area or located in Malay reservation areas are considerably lower. In Penang property owners in rural areas were charged a rate of 20 percent.
7. Calculation includes revenues of Transport Department. Without these additional revenues Penang's rate income would likewise be around 63 percent.
8. *New Straits Times*, Kuala Lumpur, 23 December 1982.
9. Interview information.
10. *The Star*, Kuala Lumpur, 28 February 1986, p. 10.
11. *The Star*, Kuala Lumpur, 15 September 1984.
12. *Local Government Act, 1976 (Act 171)*, Section 148.
13. *Malay Mail*, Kuala Lumpur, 9 January 1985.
14. *The Star*, Kuala Lumpur, 15 September 1984.
15. In Penang they averaged 18 percent between 1977 and 1982.
16. *New Straits Times*, Kuala Lumpur, 7 January 1984.
17. *Far Eastern Economic Review*, Hong Kong, 8 March 1984, p. 62.
18. *The Star*, Kuala Lumpur, 24 March 1986.
19. *Malay Mail*, Kuala Lumpur, 17 January 1983.
20. *The Star*, Kuala Lumpur, 29 July 1986, p. 1.

21. Mixed experiences with privatization are reported in Khoo Thean Chin, "Private Participation in Public Services/Functions -- Solid Waste Disposal," in National Institute of Development Administration, *Course on Urban Finance and Management in East Asia* (Kuala Lumpur: National Institute of Development Administration, September 7-October 2, 1987) and World Bank, Malaysia. *Municipal Services Review Mission. Finale Aide Memoire* (Washington, D.C.: World Bank 1988), pp. 37, 47.

22. Interview information.

23. Interview information.

24. Similar asssessments were made by planners in Seberang Prai municipality. Interview information.

25. For a deviating assessment see G. Shabbir Cheema, "Administrative Responses to Urbanization in Western Malaysia," in *Journal of Administration Overseas*, Vol. 16, No. 3, p. 242.

26. The *State Planning Committee* is composed of seven senior representatives of the state government, four non-official members, all appointed by the state government, and headed by the chief minister (*Act 172*, Section 4 (1). Remarkably, no representative of the municipal government sits on the body.

27. *The Star*, Kuala Lumpur, 22 August 1985, p. 2.

28. *Malay Mail*, Kuala Lumpur, 13 May 1981.

29. *New Straits Times*, Kuala Lumpur, 2 August 1983.

30. Interview information.

31. The *Consultative Committee of Municipalities* created in 1955 with Penang, Malacca, Kuala Lumpur and (since 1962) Ipoh as members was not very efficient in representing the interests of the member cities. See Malcolm W. Norris, *Local Government*, p. 27.

32. Existing only in the states of Penang and Malacca.

33. Calculated from the *"Report on the Introduction of Elections in the Municipality of Georgetown, Penang 1951"*, (Kuala Lumpur: Government Printer 1953), p. 9.

34. According to the figures of Lim, less than 40 percent of the registered voters actually voted in the 1956 local elections in Penang. See Lily Lim, *The Municipal Government of Georgetown, Penang, 1946-1957* (Singapore: 1960).

35. See Malaya. Election Commission, Local Authority Elections 1961. *Results and Statistics of Voting* (Kuala Lumpur: Government Printer 1961).

36. Malaya, Election Commission, Local Council Elections 1962. *Results and Statistics of Voting* (Kuala Lumpur: The Commission, 1963).

37. Quoted by Malcolm W. Norris, *Local Government in Peninsular Malaysia* (Aldershot: Gower 1980), p. 23.

38. The abolition of the Georgetown City Council was legitimized by the state government through the *Municipal (Amendment) (Penang) Enactment, 1966*, passed by the state assembly on 23 March 1966, and the *City of Georgetown (Transfer of Functions) Order, 1966*, passed on 30 June 1966. Both enactments were ultra vires. See Paul Tennant, The Decline of Elective Local Government in Malaysia, in *Asian Survey*, Vol. XIV, No. 4, 1973, pp. 347-365.

39. As well as seven minor councils and rural district councils.

40. The Act also paved the way for the temporary restoration of local elections in 1961.

41. *The Star*, Kuala Lumpur, 24 March 1984.

42. *The Star*, Kuala Lumpur, 25 July 1978.

43. *New Straits Times*, Kuala Lumpur, 1 July 1975.

44. *New Straits Times*, Kuala Lumpur, 12 December 1976; *The National Echo*, Penang, 15 January 1977.

45. *The Star*, Kuala Lumpur, 15 Jaunary 1980.

46. *Malay Mail*, Kuala Lumpur, 29 February 1984.

47. *The National Echo*, Penang, 5 January 1982.

48. *The Star*, Kuala Lumpur, 21 July 1985, p. 9.

49. *The Star*, Kuala Lumpur, 24 February 1982.

50. *The Star*, Kuala Lumpur, 28 May 1982; *New Straits Times*, Kuala Lumpur, 27 April 1982, 18 August 1982, 3 February 1986, 4 April 1986.

51. *The Malay Mail*, Kuala Lumpur, 2 March 1982; *New Straits Times*, Kuala Lumpur, 15 December 1983.

52. *The National Echo*, Penang, 12 March 1981; *The Star*, Kuala Lumpur, 11 September 1981, 27 April 1982, 28 May 1984.

53. *The National Echo*, Penang, 12 March 1981.

54. *The Star*, Kuala Lumpur, 10 September 1981, 1 November 1982.

55. *New Straits Times*, Kuala Lumpur, 13 September 1984.

56. *The Star*, Kuala Lumpur, 1 October 1984, 20 October 1984; *The National Echo*, Penang, 30 September 1984.

57. *New Straits Times*, Kuala Lumpur, 17 August 1976.

58. *The Star*, Kuala Lumpur, 1 October 1985.

59. *The Star*, Kuala Lumpur, 7 January 1984.

60. The Klang Structure Plan, for instance, states that "operating license for large retail stores shall be granted only to those that allocate a minimum share of 30 percent investment to *Bumiputras*". See Selangor State Government/Klang Local Planning Authority, *Klang Draft Structure Plan 1986-2005. Statement of Policies and Proposals* (Klang: Selangor State Government/Klang Local Planning Authority 1986), p. 75.

61. *Malay Mail*, Kuala Lumpur, 27 February 1985.

62. Ibid.

63. *The Star*, Kuala Lumpur, 21 July 1985, p. 9.

64. *New Straits Times*, Kuala Lumpur, 7 January 1984.

65. *Far Eastern Economic Review*, Hong Kong, 2 April 1987, p. 18.

66. *The Star*, Kuala Lumpur, 22 August 1983.

67. *The Star*, Kuala Lumpur, 10 March 1984.

68. *The Straits Times*, Kuala Lumpur, 10 May 1984.

69. Interview information.

70. Government figures, however, were lower, placing lay-offs caused by the recession in Penang at 2,000 in 1985. *Far Eastern Economic Review*, Hong Kong, 19 September 1985, p. 79.

71. *Far Eastern Economic Review*, Hong Kong, 19 September 1985, p. 82.

5

Local Autonomy, Urban Government, and Development in Southeast Asian Regional Cities: Conclusions

Local and Supralocal Determinants of Socioeconomic Development in Southeast Asian Regional Cities

The concluding chapter focusses on comparative aspects. Returning to the questions raised in chapter one, an attempt is made at some general assessments of local government in the Southeast Asian region. In a first step, I try to identify the factors fostering or inhibiting urban development in Southeast Asian regional cities -- especially those responsible for the different levels of development in the cities investigated. Based on the model outlined in chapter one, the effect of extra-local social, economic, and political factors as well as endogenous factors on the developmental performance of the three regional cities will be examined. In a second step, the direction of analysis is reversed. I turn to the "feedback" dimension in the model by asking in how far urban and -- more generally -- local government affects the national political system. What are the functions of local government for the respective polity? And third, with the empirical evidence of the case studies in mind, an attempt is made to reappraise the interlinkages between local autonomy, political participation, and socioeconomic development.

The Pattern of Socioeconomic Development

Based on data and findings of the previous chapters, Table 5.1 provides an overview on the developmental performance of the three cities examined. It shows that, in terms of socioeconomic development, Penang is most advanced, followed by Chiang Mai, and then Iloilo City. Penang leads in twelve out of sixteen selected indicators, Chiang Mai in

TABLE 5.1 Socioeconomic Development in Southeast Asian Regional Cities

Indicator	Penang	Chiang Mai	Iloilo City
Average annual growth of Gross City Product (1970-1980), in percent	10	8-10	3-5
Average household employment income, in US $	301	183	84
Poverty incidence, in percent	10	18	65
Unemployment rate, in percent	5.2	7-8	17-20
Water supply, in gallon/day/person	65.99	18.60	17.53
Percentage of households supplied with piped water	94	55	64.22
Percentage of households supplied with electricity	95	88	n.d.
Electricity supply, installed capacity, in MW	245.8	18	n.d.
Sanitary conditions, percentage of households with flush toilets	69	n.d.	47.68
Housing, squatter incidence, in percent	3	10-15	35
Housing construction activity, houses constructed per capita	0.00357	0.00403	0.00259
Health facilities, hospital beds per capita	0.00403	0.01298	0.00404
Educational facilities, persons per school (primary, secondary, vocational)	3,307 (148 schools)	1,234 (122 schools)	2,852 (90 schools)
Number of business establishments per capita	0.01926	0.017452	0.01754
Percentage of employment provided by manufacturing	27	15.9	10-13
Average firm size, manufacturing, workers per firm	25.96	12.7	n.d.

Sources: Compiled from Tables 2.11, 2.13, 2.14, 3.14, 4.10, 4.11, 4.12, 4.13, 4.15.

three; in the case of one indicator Penang and Chiang Mai share the lead. Iloilo City ranks last in terms of nine indicators.

Penang has experienced dynamic economic growth over the last one and a half decades, has higher household incomes than the other cities, a lower incidence of poverty, and a superior infrastructure. Only in social services, such as health and education, does its performance appear to be inferior to that of Chiang Mai and Iloilo. It must, however, be borne in mind that these data reflect the extension of Penang's municipal jurisdiction in 1974, which almost doubled its population. The apparently less favorable indicators for these service sectors thus suggest low service levels in the rural areas of the municipality, compared with the much denser, better service network in the city center. With these development differentials in mind, I now turn to the question of which factors have been responsible for the different patterns of development in these cities.

External Factors Determining Urban Development. The examination of development processes in the three Southeast Asian regional cities showed that factors relating to the local government system influenced socioeconomic development to a lesser extent than theory suggests. In Penang, Chiang Mai, and Iloilo City the influence of supralocal factors on urban development patterns was found to be strong. These supra or extralocal factors can be classified as follows: (1) world market fluctuations; (2) regional economic peculiarities; (3) changes in the national economy; and (4) changing power constellations in national politics.

1.World Market Fluctuations. World market forces affected development in all three cities. Penang's industrialization, for instance, strongly benefited from the new international division of labor that emerged in the 1970s. Rising wage levels, shorter working hours, reformist labor legislation, intense trade-union activism, and stricter antipollution legislation in industrialized countries prompted manufacturing firms to divide production into stages and relocate labor-intensive (assembly) work to low-wage countries in the Third World, retaining the technology-intensive components in industrialized countries (Fröbel, Heinrichs, and Kreye 1977). Due to its comparatively well-developed infrastructure, favorable investment incentives, an English-speaking, well-trained labor force, Penang was a particularly attractive location for foreign investors. The opportunities arising from the new international division of labor were apprehended by Penang's state government and skilfully employed as a basis for its dynamic *export-oriented industrialization* (EOI) policy. Industrialization created mass employment, which raised income levels especially among the lower-income groups on the island. At the same time, unemployment rates declined significantly from 16 percent at the end of the 1960s (Georgulas 1972:263) to 5.2 percent in 1983 (Majlis Perbandaran Pulau Pinang 1985:44). However, today, nearly twenty years after Penang started its EOI-policy, what had initially appeared as a platform for economic take-off could prove a liability. This is less a problem of a -- probably temporary -- set-back in the semiconductor industry, which provides the largest percentage of jobs in Penang's manufacturing sector, than of structural problems. EOI has brought about only modest technology transfer and created few linkages with the local industry.[1] While Penang's industrial estates attracted large numbers of low-skilled (Malay) female migrants from the northern parts of the peninsula, the sluggish growth of the island's local industry caused the migration of skilled workers and professionals to the Klang Valley region (Majlis Perbandaran Pulau Pinang 1985:19). Moreover, technological innovations in microelectronics increasingly erode the comparative wage advantage of developing and newly industrializing countries by facilitating automatization of production in industrialized nations. While this in itself severely dims future prospects for foreign investments, the footloose nature of EOI-industries also takes advantage of the increasing competition among low-wage countries for foreign investment. The adoption of an EOI-strategy by an increasing number of developing nations in Asia has led to keen competition in offering attractive incentives to foreign investors. This leaves the first generation EOI-countries in an unfavorable position, if they have not shifted to more technology-intensive manufacturing in the meantime. Meanwhile, Malaysia, including Penang, with its comparatively high wage level has lost its competitive edge in the race for foreign investments. Those foreign companies which, despite progress in automatization still relocate plants to Third-World countries, seem to prefer EOI-latecomers with their extremely low wage level, as do several of Penang's large-scale semiconductor firms which are considering relocating their plants to the Bangkok area.[2] The difficulties in attracting export manufacturing firms to industrial estates is underscored by the Chiang Mai experience. Two years after its inauguration, the Northern Industrial Estate, located between Chiang Mai and Lamphun, had attracted only seven investors.

World market forces also aided Chiang Mai in its long-term economic upswing, although the initial stimuli were home-made. While the city successfully exploited the economic opportunities offered by the international tourism boom that started in the mid-1960s, two-thirds of the visitors were Thais. By promoting Chiang Mai's scenic location and environment as well as its ancient history and rich cultural heritage, tourism has become the leading sector in the city's economy, indirectly benefiting other sectors such as commerce, services, handicrafts, and even manufacturing.

While world market forces had -- at least in macroeconomic terms -- a predominantly positive impact on socioeconomic development in Penang and Chiang Mai, Iloilo City's economy was badly hit by the fluctuations of the international economy. Although tremendous wealth was accumulated in Iloilo during the heyday of the sugar industry in the early twentieth century, the same forces had a destructive impact on the city's economy when technological innovations made Iloilo's function as the leading Philippine sugar entrepôt increasingly obsolete

(McCoy 1977, 1982) and when, in the 1980's, commodity prices fell to an all-time low. Sugar prices fell from 14 cents per pound in 1976 to an unprecendented low of 2.5 cents per pound in 1985. As a consequence, Iloilo's ancillary industries serving the sugar centrals of the region collapsed as did the sugar marketing and shipping companies. The depression in the manufacturing and utility sectors affected on the commercial sector, as lay-offs and wage cuts severely reduced purchasing power in the city. The effects of this crisis were reinforced when the Philippine economy nearly collapsed in the two years prior to Marcos' overthrow.

2. Regional Economic Peculiarities. Penang's economic stagnation in the 1960s prior to its industrial boom was mainly caused by the decline of its function as an entrepôt serving Indonesia, the southern parts of Burma, and Thailand. It was affected by the Indonesian *confrontasi* policy against the young Federation of Malaysia (1963-65), the isolationist policies of Burma after Ne Win's seizure of power (1962), and increasing competition from Singapore. As a result, Penang's economic growth fell behind the national average in the second half of the 1960s, and its per capita GDP growth was overtaken by several other states in the peninsula. The port, shipping and commerce -- all labor-intensive subsectors -- bore the brunt of the economic contraction, resulting in the high unemployment rate that marked Penang's economy at the end of the 1960s. Yet, unlike Iloilo after the war, Penang was able to recover rapidly by making use of the economic opportunities provided by the emerging new international division of labor.

Apart from tourism, Chiang Mai benefited greatly from its strategic location as the "gateway to the Golden Triangle". Chiang Mai is the center of an illegal but extremely lucrative cross-border trade with Burma, and to a lesser extent, with Laos (Vatikiotis 1984a:19). The city benefits from the fact that this smuggling trade is the major source of revenue for Burmese minorities, such as the Karen, the Wa, the Shan, and others who control the rugged terrain along the border. They are involved in a protracted insurgency against the central government in Rangoon. To maintain their armies, they need the revenues from the trade as well as taxes imposed on the smugglers trespassing on their territory. Shipments of all kinds of western consumer goods into Burma are organized from Chiang Mai. This trade includes consumer electronics and electrical appliances such as TVs, VCRs, radios and refrigerators, as well as cosmetics, pharmaceutical products, and liquor. The bulk of these goods reappear on Burma's flourishing black market. In return, opium, teak, gems, bamboo, rattan, handicrafts, antiques, and cattle find their way into Thailand, where they are either used as raw materials by the local industry (teak, bamboo, rattan), channeled into the tourist trade (handicrafts and antiques), or transshipped to other destinations (gems, antiques, opium) such as Hong Kong, Europe, and the United States. This smuggling trade produces enormous wealth in Chiang Mai that never appears in official statistics. Yet, Chiang Mai is not a unique case among Thai regional cities. There are several other urban centers that benefit from such cross-border trade: Udon Thani and Ubon Ratchathani in the Northeast, Trat and Aranyaprathet in the East, and Hat Yai in the South. It is estimated that as much as 40 percent of Thailand's foreign trade is illegal cross-border trade with Burma, Laos, Malaysia and -- to a lesser extent -- Cambodia (Vatikiotis 1984b:150).

Chiang Mai's position as a strategic regional center has also made the city a headquarters for international and foreign development agencies. From their Chiang Mai offices these agencies manage development projects in northern Thailand. The steady influx of development aid and expatriates has had an impact on the city's economy by increasing the demand for more sophisticated goods and services.

3. The National Economy. Urban areas are not self-contained entities but an integral part of the national political and economic system. Consequently, the national economy sets parameters for urban development.

While Chiang Mai and Penang have benefited from a generally favorable national economic environment, Iloilo City suffered severely from the crisis that hit the Philippines after 1983. National economic growth was reflected in Penang and Chiang Mai in the foundation of new and the expansion of existing businesses and a growing informal sector. The Thai economy grew steadily by 5.8 percent between 1977 and 1986, and reached record-breaking double-digit growth rates in the late 1980s, while Malaysia displayed an average annual growth rate of 7.15 percent (1972-1985), until its economy was affected by declining commodity and oil prices in 1985 and 1986. Both cities further benefited from new regional development strategies of the central government that declared them regional growth centers and subsequently allocated extra resources for infrastructure development (Government of Malaysia 1986:182,196). Iloilo's economy, on the other hand, was severely rocked by the country's economic crisis; this was reinforced by the city's dependence on the declining sugar industry. The Philippine economy, after sluggish growth in 1982 and 1983 (2.5 percent and 1.3 percent, respectively), contracted by almost 10 percent in 1984 and 1985 (Asia Yearbook 1986:6-7); in 1986 growth was a negligible 0.13 percent. Under these circumstances, economic growth incentives such as the Regional Cities Development Project (RCDP), could make little noteworthy impact on Iloilo's economy.

4. Power Constellations in National Politics. Power constellations also influence urban development if a city is a power base of supporters or opponents of the regime. In the former case, this is likely to result in sizeable resource allocations from the central government, in the latter it will almost certainly result in central government funds being cut off.

The Iloilo case study has shown how the changing political fortunes of the local oligarchy, especially the Lopez family, have influenced the flow of central government resources for public infrastructure projects to the city and the entire Western Visayan Region. The stronger the political links between the local arena and higher government levels, the greater is the impact of power constellations at the center on urban development (Landé 1965; Benson 1970; Machado 1972a, 1972b, 1973/74). The changing fortunes of politicians at both levels and the frequent factional realignments work against continuity in urban development. The latter is subjected to stop-and-go policies and intermittent and unpredictable resource flows from the center to the locality. Similar processes can also be observed in Malaysia, where the federal government punished constituencies or states supporting opposition parties by cutting off federal assistance for development projects (Smith 1961; Tilman 1976; Shafruddin 1987). Whether this pattern will be repeated in Penang after the opposition won six of eleven parliamentary seats and ten out of twenty-seven mandates in the state assembly in 1986 remains to be seen.

The reverse is demonstrated by Chiang Mai. Local political leaders in Thai regional cities are less closely identified with a specific group at the power center. Links are usually more informal than in the Philippines. Hence, changing political fortunes at the center have affected urban development to a lesser extent. On the other hand, Chiang Mai interests have always been well-represented in any national government through informal links to politicians and top bureaucrats -- often persons originating from Chiang Mai itself or other parts of northern Thailand (Noranitipadungkarn and Hagensick 1973). Moreover, many top ranking military officers, politicians, and administrators have chosen Chiang Mai as a second residence, which has made it even easier for the municipality's local elites to ensure a steady flow of government resources to the city.

Factors Relating to Local Government Performance

Political Participation. Of the factors affecting local government, the lack of accountability and limited political participation seem to have the most profound impact on the patterns of urban development. Table 5.2 compares political participation in the three case studies on the basis of various indicators commonly used in the general literature on politi

TABLE 5.2 Political Participation in Southeast Asian Regional Cities

Indicator	Penang	Chiang Mai	Iloilo City
Local elections			
Take place regularly		X (since 1974)	
Take place intermittently			X (1971, 1980, 1988)
Do not take place at all	X (since 1963)		
Average voter turnout	no electoral contest since 1963	28.56 (1967-1985)	80.77 (1947-1980)
Competitiveness of local elections			
Candidate-seat ratio	no electoral contest since 1963	3	2.9
Frequency of changes of political party or group in power during last 20 years	no electoral contest since 1963	2	3
Social profile of local decision-makers			
Elitist			X
Upper-middle-class	X	X	
Middle-class			
Lower-class			
Lower-class representation in local decision-making bodies			
Strongly represented			
Adequately represented			
Weakly represented	X	X	
Not represented at all			X
Frequency of local council meetings			
> 50 per year	X		X
12-49 per year		X	
< 12 per year			
Intensity of council debates			
Very intensive			
Intensive			X
Not intensive	X	X	
No debate at all			
Involvement of voluntary organizations in local politics			
Strongly involved			
Involved, but only specific groups	X		X

continued

TABLE 5.2 *(continued)*

Indicator	Penang	Chiang Mai	Iloilo City
Weakly involved		X	
Government control over political participation through government-sponsored grassroots organizations			
Strong control			X (1972-1986)
Some control		X	
Little control			
No control	X		
People's control over local administration			
Very strong			
Strong			
Moderate	X		
Weak		X	X
Intensity of media reporting on local politics			
Very frequently			
Frequently			X
Occasionally	X	X	
Rarely			
Very rarely			

Sources: Table summarizes major findings of previous chapters.

cal participation in the Third World. Such a comparison reveals that in a formal sense, participation is strongest in Iloilo City. At the same time, however, these indicators show how misleading an analysis based purely on statistical evidence can be. Data on Iloilo's political culture before and after martial law seem to reflect basic premises of a participatory political culture: regular elections (until 1972), high voter turnout, high competitiveness, the existence of representative political bodies, regular changes in the party or factional composition of these bodies, an active local council, a broad spectrum of voluntary associations, and intense media reporting on local politics. The uncritical interpretation of such data is one of the major reasons why the pre-1972 Philippines have frequently been termed the "showcase of democracy in Asia" (Day 1974) and why it has become fashionable to speak of redemocratization in the post-Marcos Philippines. However, these indicators do not convey the highly elitist nature of local politics in Iloilo (and elsewhere in the Philippines). This reserves the benefits of participatory politics to a tiny oligarchy, which makes use of the masses in its inter- and intrafactional power struggles. The analysis of quantitative as well as qualitative data and, in particular, the author's observation of Philippine local politics for almost a decade suggest that the participatory performance of the country's local governments is quite low. What appears to the casual observer as participation is merely mobilization, although participatory elements increased after the forced opening of the political system in the final years of Marcos rule.

In order to assess the participatory contributions of local government in Southeast Asia, it may be useful to introduce Cohen and Uphoff's (1980) distinction between participation in decision-making, participation in implementation, participation in benefits, and participation in evaluation as well as Huntington and Nelson's distinction between autonomous and mobilized political participation (Huntington and Nelson 1976:7). In all three cities examined, participation in implementation predominates over the other forms of participation; furthermore, participation is much more mobilized than autonomous. While in periods of nonauthoritarian rule some participation in evaluation also took place in the Philippines and Thailand in the form of local elections, there has been virtually none in Malaysia since the suspension of elective local government in the mid-1960s.

Urban development is greater where local decision-makers have a broader social base, as in Penang and in Chiang Mai, whereas the elitism characteristic of Iloilo City and other Philippine cities appears to have a retarding influence on the city's development. The Chiang Mai and Penang cases further demonstrate that local decision-makers with middle-class backgrounds tend to be more oriented towards "developmentalism" or "housekeeping", although this does not ensure a sufficiently equitable distribution of growth benefits. Especially the Penang type of "developmentalism" is strongly biased toward the modern sector and usually coincides with the decision-makers' own economic interests.

Local politics in Iloilo City, on the other hand, is dominated by a few old, well-entrenched, extremely conservative family clans. This elitist structure was also preserved throughout the martial-law era. While at the national level a "new oligarchy" of cronies emerged (Canoy 1980:101-120; Hanisch 1989:68-69), the Marcos regime recruited its local stalwarts in Iloilo from among those groups of the "old elite" that agreed to cooperate with the new government. That prominent local leaders and their factions were ousted by the regime,[3] reflected little more than the cyclical ups and downs in factional politics that have always been part of political competition in Iloilo (McCoy 1977).

This elitist pattern of politics was a major block to development. Despite the fact that, with the exception of much of the martial-law era, participatory channels formally existed, political participation other than voting was blocked by rigid socioeconomic barriers. Participatory politics was reduced to money politics, which left little room for the organized articulation of lower-class demands. Cleavages in Iloilo politics were of a primarily idiosyncratic nature, with elites sharing the belief that any lower-class challenge to their privileges had to be opposed. Iloilo elites were, as shown in chapter three, extremely conservative in their social and political outlook. In addition, local politics was massively influenced by national political interests, personalism, particularism, and excessive patronage. The result has been *"cyclical"* development, in contrast to *"linear"* development in Chiang Mai and Penang. While "linear" development signifies steady socioeconomic growth, "cyclical" development denotes an intermittent process of resource allocation that is mainly based on short-term political goals, and thus creates an erratic rhythm of development and premature decay. The major focus of resource allocation are political exercises such as elections (or referenda under martial-law), while patronage serves as the lubrication. The cycle of events is basically the following:

Long before the election, candidates can be found on the campaign trail, scrambling for funds and projects that can be channelled into their constituencies for "developmental purposes". However, many of these election-related projects are ill-conceived and uncoordinated with long-term development schemes. They are seldom need-oriented, and are carried out ad hoc without proper planning and feasibility studies. Their only justification is the availability of funds and the candidate's intention to display some semblance of political efficacy, generosity, and development-orientedness. The ostensible political objective of these projects is to improve the living conditions in the constituency. They are usually labor-intensive, and by promising employment for low-income groups they have a high public relations value for the sponsoring politician. Yet, most of these projects are too small in scale and rather shortlived. Scarce resources are spread too thinly to have any lasting developmental impact. Many remain unfinished, as money runs out before project completion.

After the elections there are no funds left to continue or maintain the projects, let alone for new projects. Especially in the fiscal year immediately following the elections, governments can hardly do other than impose austerity. Consequently, many projects disintegrate. Moreover, after the elections the sparse funds available are spent in those constituencies which have supported the incumbents, while constituencies that voted for the opposition are punished by poor services and exclusion from whatever development projects can be undertaken in the face of empty public coffers. Excessive patronage politics thus also has an inbuilt tendency to increase spatial imbalances in service delivery and development. The case of the asphalted road that all of a sudden turns into a dirt road as it passes an "opposition" neighborhood can be found throughout the Philippines (Rüland and Sajo 1988:273).

Penang and Chiang Mai differ markedly from Iloilo. Although in both cases, too, patronage plays an important role in stabilizing local power bases, fewer scarce resources are wasted on elitist electoral contests than in the Philippines. Based on rough calculations, a local election in the Philippines nowadays costs more than three billion pesos -- funds which are allocated for doubtful "development" projects and vote buying, but which subsequently are desperately lacking for public and private investments.[4] Election-related patronage regularly causes serious government budgetary deficits, bouts of inflation, and a disruption of economic growth.

Like in the Philippines, in Malaysia too there are vertically structured parties reaching down to the local level. However, there are no local elections. The incentive to periodically waste scarce resources in order to maintain or build up a party base at the local level in an electoral contest is thus reduced to the general elections every four years.

In Thailand the electoral contest takes place largely among locally confined groups of citizens with no or only loose connections with national political parties. Moreover, except for the Democrat Party and, to a lesser extent, the Social Action Party (SAP), political parties do not have a nationwide network of branches (Tongdhamachart 1982; Samudavanija 1987). As parties have only regional bases and are mainly Bangkok-centered, the local level is much less significant for the success or failure of political parties in national elections. Furthermore, voter turnout and mobilization levels are much lower in Chiang Mai than in Iloilo. Hence, in the past there was less need to spend large amounts of money and other patronage resources in local elections.[5] Consequently, there were more funds left for projects between elections and fewer pressures on the elected local officials to recover their "political investments" by corrupt practices while in office.

The lower level of patronage and political competitiveness and the stronger role of the bureaucracy in Chiang Mai and Penang have helped local development by creating a more favorable business climate and greater economic security than, for instance, in Philippine cities, where harassment of the businesses of political opponents by the incumbent faction is common practice. It is evident that such a situation inhibits long-term investment strategies on the part of local entrepreneurs and -- given the uncertain nature of factional fortunes -- encourages business-men to reap windfall profits via political manipulations.

Moreover, the developmental draw backs of patronage politics are less pronounced in societies with an expanding resource base than in societies with stagnating or shrinking resources. In other words, while in Malaysia and Thailand cities can "afford" a certain degree of patron-age politics, Philippine cities cannot.

Participation levels are low in all three cities. At present channels for political participation formally exist in all cities, but they were almost nonexistent during the first eight years of martial law in the Philippines and the Sarit (1958-63) and Thanom/Praphat (1963-1973) dictatorships in Thailand. Yet, participation is tolerated only to the extent that it does not militantly espouse radical social change. Lower-class opposition, be it from leftist unions or squatter organizations, is often stigmatized as subversion and accordingly suppressed, if necessary with physical force. Not surprisingly, there is little participation of the lower-classes in all three cities. Lower-class political participation is usually limited to *"defensive participation"* to prevent the destruction of their source of livelihood or eviction from their residential quarters. Viewed in com-parative perspective, data and observations suggest that, despite Malaysia's semiauthoritarian political culture, lower-class interests are better and more effectively represented in Penang than in Chiang Mai and Iloilo. Low-income Malays have a powerful patron in the UMNO, which has set up a branch in virtually every Malay *kampung*, although relationships between grassroots officials and supralocal party leaders are often strained. Chinese and Indian low-income groups, however, are less well represented by political parties (Chan 1983:498). The party that often champions their cause, the DAP, is an opposition party with lim-ited influence on decision-making. The same holds true for nongov-ernmental groups representing the urban poor such as ALIRAN and CAP. Yet, the demands of the DAP, ALIRAN, or CAP cannot be taken lightly by the government, because, especially in urban areas, all three groups are well able to mobilize public opinion.

In most Philippine cities, squatter organizations (re-)emerged during the final years of the Marcos era. Some of them were closely aligned with the leftist National Democratic Front (NDF) or "cause-oriented" groups such as BAYAN. While in Iloilo the formation of squatter organizations was still in its initial stages during field research, in other cities squatter groups reflected the cleavages of the political system at large. The somewhat artificial, largely idiosyncratic division of groups into nationalist and social-democratic organizations, weakens their bargaining power, because for the state it is relatively easy to contain these movements through a policy of divide and rule. In Thailand, except for Bangkok, there were no organized groups championing the cause of the urban poor. Nor have the political parties made any noticeable inroads into Chiang Mai's slums and squatter colonies.

Some of the barriers against lower-class political involvement have already been named: the dominance of narrow elites or of upper- and upper-middle-class groups which usually share conservative attitudes towards social change and the redistribution of societal wealth and, hence -- although to a varying degree -- view social movements and organized lower-class interest representation as a threat to the state and government authority. Another barrier against lower-class political participation is the "constant pie" thinking of the poor themselves (Scott 1968:91), i.e. the widespread belief among poverty groups that they are competing for the same scarce resources: jobs, housing, and other basic services. Moreover, slums and squatter settlements rarely live up to the romantic ideal of some adherents of the "development-from-below" approach: as pointed out by Oberndörfer, it is a myth to believe that they are "egalitarian communities of the poor" (Oberndörfer 1979:37). Usually their social structure is highly heterogeneous, so that common political actions are difficult to organize. The exception is situations in which the existence of the settlement as a whole is threatened (as in the case of demolition or eviction). After goal achievement the political organization normally disintegrates. Moreover, broad coalitions of the urban poor under a common umbrella organization are inhibited by the structure of slums and squatter settlements. Except for some Philippine cities, communities of the poor are usually scattered all over the city in small poverty pockets surrounded by better-off neighborhoods.

Organized political action by the poor is further inhibited by the fact that the permanent day-to-day struggle for economic survival completely absorbs their energies. Thus political organization is a last resort in cases of emergency. Due to the preoccupation of household heads with securing the family's livelihood, very often the politically most active strata among the poor are women. Much also depends on whether poverty groups consider their stay in the city as temporary or permanent. In case of a temporary stay, there is less readiness to get involved in political activities.

The fact that participatory channels are open to -- or utilized -- by only a numerically small group strongly affects the distribution of socioeconomic growth benefits. It is a major reason for the uneven distri-

bution of socioeconomic development in Penang and Chiang Mai and
for low-income groups in Iloilo suffering much more than middle- and
upper-classes during the present economic depression. Apart from the
middle and upper-class-biased development strategy, strict government
control over political participation is largely responsible for the fact that
in Chiang Mai and Penang about 20 percent of the population remain
excluded from developmental gains.

Local government in Iloilo is characterized by *overpoliticization*,[6] in
Chiang Mai by *overbureaucratization*, and in Penang it is somewhere
between these two extremes. From the case studies it appears that overpoliticization is a greater obstacle to urban development. In Iloilo overpoliticization has often paralyzed local decision-making and the implementation of development projects.

Overpoliticization is caused by high political competitiveness in an
environment of limited or shrinking patronage resources. It usually occurs when intraparty or intrafactional cohesion is low, political alignments are fluid, conflicts frequent, the abilities of political actors to
compromise low, conflict-solving capacities of representative bodies
and interest-aggregating organizations underdeveloped, political issues
emotionalized, and political cleavages much more idiosyncratic than
issue-oriented. In addition, the better personal and particularistic interests can be protected and the more resource allocation can be manipulated through local offices, the greater overpoliticization tends to be.
Hence, overpoliticization in Iloilo reached particularly high levels between 1955 and 1972 and again after the demise of the Marcos regime
and the formal restoration of basic political liberties by the Aquino government. It was less prevalent in the initial years of martial law, when
the local power bases of regime opponents in Iloilo were systematically
dismantled, but started increasing again after 1979, when the regime
announced local elections for the first time since 1971. Overpoliticization
intensifies political conflicts and sharply increases political costs. Expenditure for winning a local mandate rises fast.

The consequences are counterproductive to urban development in at
least two ways:

1. Political investments such as campaign expenses must be recouped
   or amortized during the term of office.
2. To this end, a political machine lubricated by patronage must be established, expanded or diversified. The maintenance and strengthening of the politcal machine is indispensible for the consolidation
   of the power base of political actors. Yet, it withdraws additional
   resources from development programs. Moreover, political ma-

chines, due to their vertical structure, impede the development of horizontal ties among societal groups -- in other words, they hamper incipient processes of sociopolitical differentiation.

Through patronage elected local politicians try to fill major posts in the local bureaucracy with loyal, yet very frequently administratively incompetent supporters. This is done to minimize potential intraadministrative opposition and to allocate public resources according to the political and personal needs of the incumbent power elite (Landé 1965; Benson 1970; Machado 1972a; Wolters 1983).

Yet, the system is not so much monolithic as unstable. In a political situation, such as after the departure of Marcos, which is characterized by a high level of fragmentation and deinstitutionalization (a legacy of the Marcos years) and, hence, competitiveness (Rüland 1985c, 1986b), the local bureaucracy becomes highly vulnerable to the frequently changing local power constellations.

Political machines in Iloilo (and the Philippines in general) are not very cohesive. Political opportunism is the driving force behind frequent defections and factional realignments. In the case of defections, the respective subleaders *(liders)* take their own political machine with them to the new faction. Thus, a local leader like the mayor will not only lose support in the city council, he will suddenly also face resistance to his policies from inside the bureaucracy, since former bureaucrat allies, following their political patron, have all of a sudden turned into adherents of a rival faction. Moreover, the national government and also the Civil Service Commission (CSC) have a decisive say in the filling of positions within the local bureaucracy. Thus, nonincumbent local leaders may utilize personal connections to national politicians and the CSC to influence staffing and bureaucratic leadership patterns within the local bureaucracy by installing their own supporters.

Occasionally, attempts by rival factions to move supporters into strategic administrative positions lead to double appointments; this happens when the incumbent official and his faction leaders refuse to recognize a transfer order and the appointment of a new official handed down to them by the center. Until the ensuing protracted legal struggles over who is the legitimate office holder are resolved, the respective administrative function is virtually paralyzed.

Incumbent leaders attempt to protect themselves against such inroads into their administrative support base by imposing an informal administrative superstructure on the formal bureaucratic hierarchy. To this end posts for advisors and consultants are created and staffed with relatives or trusted friends. The son of the mayor as an influential actor

behind the scenes is ubiquitous in Philippine local politics.7 As a consequence, decision-making often takes place in the shadowy sphere of informal channels, bypassing the formal structures. It is, for instance,
quite common in the Philippines that a mayor deliberately ignores the
Local Government Code, which stipulates that during a leave of absence
the vice mayor "shall exercise the powers, duties and functions of the
mayor" (*Local Government Code*, Sect. 52). Instead of the vice mayor, who
is frequently a political rival of the mayor, the mayor prefers to name
his son or another close aide as acting mayor.

As a result, the political fragmentation is reflected within the local
administration. Even matters of administrative routine turn into emotionalized proxy fights of political actors. Issue- and public welfare-ori-
ented decision-making are thus relegated to a back seat.

Intense political competition, a high degree of fragmentation, and
frequent factional realignments also lead to a high personnel turnover in
the local bureaucracy. Like the political arena, the bureaucracy becomes
a *"floating system"*. There is little personnel and programmatic continuity, and since -- usually inept -- political appointees in the bureaucracy
hardly have time to improve their poor administrative know-how, poor
service delivery is perpetuated in a process of messy and scandal-rid-
den muddling through.

Overbureaucratization as found in Chiang Mai is characterized by excessive red tape, overregulation, and the involvement of a great number
of screening committees, ad hoc working groups, and other bureaucratic bodies in the preparation and implementation of decisions. This is
a reflection of Thai bureaucratic culture which places great emphasis on
consensual decisions, harmonizing of contradictory positions, and the
avoidance of open conflict. Issues are preferably resolved before they
reach the public arena and the formal decision-making bodies. As a result -- especially if serious objections are raised against a project or a
certain public policy -- decisions are often deferred and projects
shelved. This notoriously slows down decision-making (World Bank
1986:169). Ironically, however, slow decision-making has saved Thai
governmental units from developmental fashions and "white elephants"
that characterized urban development policies in other developing
countries.

Despite factionalism inside the bureaucracy, this "consultative system" of decision-making provides more checks and balances against
corruption than in Iloilo and against unsound prestige projects than in
Penang. The local administration in Thai municipalities is much more
independent of political decision-makers than its Iloilo counterparts.
First, local administrators are part of a national municipal career service

that is tightly administered by the Ministry of the Interior (MOI) and characterized by regular transfers of officers. Second, the Thai bureaucracy has developed its own esprit de corps and a general dislike of politics, which also serves as a protection against becoming too involved in political maneuverings. Civil service rules thus have a stronger impact on administrative behavior than external political influences. This esprit de corps has grown out of the traditionally strong position of the bureaucracy that can be traced back to the times of the absolute monarchy and the divine sanction it received. Third, due to the lower level of political competition and mobilization in Chiang Mai, there is less need to recover large amounts of electoral expenses, although in Thai municipal elections vote-buying is also very common. Yet, due to its structural independence of elected politicians, the local administration cannot be so readily instrumentalized by political actors for particularistic objectives.

In Penang and other Malaysian cities, political influence on the local administration is greater than in Chiang Mai. This is largely a result of the *New Economic Policy* (NEP) and the strategic importance of urban areas as a political base for general elections in a vertically-structured party system. Nor are there any local elections which might induce local officials to recover campaign investment. Moreover, like in Thailand a strong esprit de corps among local bureaucrats -- a legacy of British civil service tradition -- serves as a counterbalance to excessive, politically motivated corruption at the local level.

Local Autonomy

Indicators operationalizing the scope of local autonomy in the three cities suggest that legal-constitutional autonomy is greatest in the Philippines, and that central control of the legal framework of Malaysian and Thai cities is very tight. Except for the Philippines, especially after the ratification of the 1987 Constitution, a trend of increasing central control can be observed in Southeast Asian countries. The powers and functions of municipal government have been progressively curbed, despite the lip service paid to decentralization (Tilman 1976; Shafruddin 1987; Demaine and Malong 1987).

The case studies do, however, show that the restriction of the legal-constitutional scope of local self-government can be counterbalanced to a certain extent by informal communication processes that have in the past frequently been overlooked in local government research (Krannich 1982). In all three cities, local politicians and local administrators have established personal links to key decision-makers at higher government levels that can be tapped to varying degrees to modify or change central government directives, if these are incompatible with locally perceived interests.

The case studies also show that legal-constitutional factors determine the scope of local autonomy to a much lesser extent than usually assumed in the literature. Thus, at first sight it may be surprising that Penang, the city with the narrowest scope of legal-constitutional autonomy, has nevertheless achieved the fastest socioeconomic development. An important reason is Penang's greater resource endowment and the superior efficiency in resource utilization. In addition, both Penang and Chiang Mai are better integrated into the societal network of linkages than Iloilo City.

However, what can be observed from a comparison of the resource dimension of Southeast Asian cities, is an overall relative decline of the city's locally levied financial resources. This decline was most pronounced in Chiang Mai and other Thai regional cities, somewhat less dramatic in Iloilo, and only marginal in Penang. At the same time, there was a general increase in dependency on central grants, which was more strongly felt in Iloilo than in Chiang Mai and Penang. Although all cities displayed impressive revenue increases, growth in real terms was slow and could not keep pace with the rapid increase in service demands. Major problems also persisted in the field of staffing, especially as far as professional and technical personnel is concerned. Nongovernmental management resources, too, were rarely tapped and horizontal linkages to other governmental units only very weakly developed.

In general, it was found that there was little local autonomy in all three cities (see Table 5.3). Yet, based on a broadened concept of local autonomy, it was nevertheless greater in regional cities than in other types of city. This stands in contrast to the literature on local government, which usually makes sweeping assessments about the extent of local autonomy. Statements about local autonomy must thus be differentiated according to city size. It is relatively low in the metropolitan areas, higher in regional cities, and very low in small municipalities and hinterland towns.

Due to the political sensitivity of the metropolitan area as the seat of the national government, legal-constitutional, administrative, procedural, and physical controls affect their autonomy more than that of smaller cities. In the capital these aspects of supervision predominate over all other elements of the autonomy concept -- especially the linkage dimension, which admittedly is stronger in the metropolitan area than in hinterland cities.

TABLE 5.3 Matrix of Local Autonomy

Indicator	Penang	Chiang Mai	Iloilo City
Legal-Constitutional Dimension			
Constitution			
Constitutionally guaranteed local autonomy			
Guaranteed local autonomy with minor limitations			Philippines
Guaranteed local autonomy with major limitations		Thailand	
No constitutionally guaranteed local autonomy	Malaysia		
Central control and supervision over local government			
Very strong		X	
Strong	X		
Moderate			X
Weak			
Very weak			
Functions of local government			
No. of functions exclusively local	8	7	7
No. of functions shared with superior government levels/public enterprises/private sector	5	11	16
No. of functions exclusively executed by superior government levels/public enterprises/private sector	8	2	3
Resource Dimension			
Per capita revenues, in US $	44.1	43.9	8.9
Real increase of revenues, in percent	3.84	3.62	5.23 (1977-1982) -5.86 1980-1984)
Percentage of locally levied revenues	93.81	29.98	59.99
Decline of locally levied revenues, in percent, 1977-1982	2.54	5.99	2.83 (1980-1984)
Percentage of central government grants	6.18	21.0	40.01
Tax collection efficiency	100	67	54
Capital investment ratio, in percent of total expenditure	20	23.3	5.7

(continued)

TABLE 5.3 *(continued)*

Indicator	Penang	Chiang Mai	Iloilo City
Staff-population ratio	1:94	1:118	1:212
Urban planning			
Planning by national government		X	
Planning by national government with local participation			
Planning by local government with assistance by national/state government	X		X
Planning by local government			
Linkage Dimension			
Communication			
Telephone-population ratio	1:9	1:22 (1985) 1:7 (1989)	1:30.31
Transport linkages			
City well connected			
City sufficiently connected	X	X	
City weakly connected			X
Information management capacities			
Well developed	X		
Adequate			
Little developed		X	
Undeveloped			X
Linkages to nongovernmental sources of know-how			
Strong	X		
Moderate			
Weak		X	X

Source: Table summarizes major findings of previous chapters.

All capital cities of the countries investigated are more or less run like a national government ministry. In all countries the elected metropolitan governments were dissolved and the administration of the capital either placed under direct supervision of the national government or transferred to centrally appointed agents. Only the Thai government, after passing the *Bangkok Metropolitan Administration Act, 1985,* made the governor and the city council elective. In November 1985 a strong charismatic governor was elected in the person of Chamlong Srimuang, and the Democrat Party won two-thirds of the seats in the Bangkok Metropolitan Assembly.[8] In the Philippines, local legislatures in the Metropolitan Manila Area (MMA) have been revitalized, but no metro-wide legislature had been introduced by 1988.

Regional cities are less tightly controlled in legal, administrative, political and physical terms than the metropolitan center. Moreover, lack of legal autonomy can partly be compensated by close informal ties with national decision-makers. With the exception of Malaysia, regional cities are not much weaker in financial terms (based on per capita revenues) than the capital cities, while they are considerably better-off than small municipalities. Also in terms of staffing, regional cities fare well, though they may be less well-off as regards professional and technical personnel -- at least, if compared with Bangkok and Kuala Lumpur. In addition, Chiang Mai, Penang, and even Iloilo have comparatively large potentials of nongovernmental sources of information and know-how within their cities that could be tapped for development projects. All regional cities are -- to a varying degree -- incorporated into a fairly good communicative network that facilitates all kinds of external inputs which can be utilized for developmental purposes.

Small cities, on the other hand, are extremely weak in financial terms and highly dependent on the central government for grants, staff, and technical assistance. Moreover, decision-makers and administrators in small municipalities are usually more junior than their national counterparts (unlike in regional cities), which further strengthens the latter's supervisory authority. Finally, small cities are less integrated into the societal linkage network and have fewer sources from which to obtain additional information that could broaden decision-making.

One of the major differences in services output and rate of development between Penang and the other cities is Penang's superior information management and organizational capacities. Planning, tax administration, licensing, personnel affairs, and population are completely computerized. In terms of information management, Malaysian regional cities are five to six years ahead of Thai regional cities, which only recently started to utilize electronic data processing devices, and about ten years ahead of Philippine regional cities. Malaysian secondary centers are thus less dependent on superior government levels as far as data collection and analysis is concerned. Moreover, Penang has made frequent use of nongovernmental sources of know-how such as the university and private sector consultancies, while Thai and Philippine cities have more or less ignored such sources of expertise. The superior capabilities of Malaysian regional cities in information management have, notwithstanding persisting shortcomings, also led to greater revenue collection efficiency than in Thai and, in particular, Philippine secondary centers. Not surprisingly, therefore, capital investment rates were higher in Malaysian cities than in Thailand and the Philippines, although in some cases at the expense of considerable indebtedness. Borrowing capacities of local authorities are much more substantial in Malaysia than in Thailand and the Philippines, though in Malaysia, too, they are subject to close scrutiny and approval by superior government levels.

While the Iloilo city government only recently adopted measures to promote investment, Chiang Mai has pursued a deliberate strategy aimed at improving the business climate by providing services that increase the city's attractiveness for tourists. While this policy in some instances collided with lower-class interests by pushing up land prices, violating zoning regulations, or overregulating the informal sector (Wahnschafft 1984:218), the net effect has been to expand economic opportunities. Despite rapid modernization, traditional life styles such as the *muban*-type of settlement still exist, even in close proximity to the central business district.

Urban-Level Socioeconomic Factors

The informal sector can be considered as a kind of traditional subsistence mechanism. The case studies have shown that all cities have a large informal sector. While in all three cases city governments tend to treat the sector with overregulation and at times even with punitive action, its existence is more or less tacitly accepted. Nevertheless, the general economic development level of the respective city also determines the income-generating capacity of the informal sector. Whereas in Penang and Chiang Mai -- rapidly growing and diversifying urban economies -- the sector offers a wide range of economic opportunities, in Iloilo, due to the low level of economic development and lack of growth incentives, it is no more than a niche for survival.

Beyond the local government sphere it appears that Thai society has preserved relatively intact subsistence mechanisms such as voluntary (welfare) organizations and religious institutions. The Buddhist monasteries, for instance, not only provide poor Thais with a channel for upward mobility through education via the institution of novicehood (Suksamram 1982; Keyes 1989), they also provide land for housing, primary education, and other services that are normally offered by the state but cannot be afforded by low-income families living in the vicinity of the temple grounds (Vatikiotis 1984b:393). In Iloilo and also in Penang welfare services provided by nongovernmental organizations are less developed. Iloilo's civic clubs such as the Jaycees, the Rotary and Lions Clubs or church institutions usually only offer charity that may mitigate the most acute needs in cases of emergency, thus often obscuring the necessity for structural reforms. In Penang the Chinese clans or religious foundations, too, are primarily charity-oriented.

That Chiang Mai exhibits social disparities to a lesser degree than Iloilo and probably even Penang is also due to the fact that so far there is no push of impoverished rural migrants into the city. A flexible urban labor market that permits the utilization of urban and rural employment opportunities to a maximum (Singhanetra 1982a), and thus encourages commuting, a well-developed road system, and cheap mass transport between the city and most parts of the hinterland has so far forestalled an exodus from the villages. Chiang Mai has thus been spared large slum or squatter colonies. Iloilo, on the other hand, has a large impoverished hinterland. Commuting between Antique or Aklan provinces and Iloilo is impossible. Penang is the destination of low-income rural Malays from the entire northern region of Peninsular Malaysia. However, due to the long distances involved and the city's island location, commuting is not an alternative.

Thai municipal governments enjoy yet another great advantage that facilitates their efforts to deliver better service and developmental performances. They are considerably smaller than their counterparts in Malaysia and the Philippines. Solutions, especially for infrastructure development, are financially as well as politically less costly: in a context of low urbanization there is less need to remove already established social and physical structures before a project can be started. Hence, development may commence without directly affecting the interests of sizeable groups of the urban population.

The Regional Cities Development Projects (RCDP) are so far the most systematic approach to counteract urban primacy and to reshape the imbalances in the urban hierarchy. Especially in Thailand, the project is based on a very carefully designed strategy laid down in the Fourth National Economic and Social Development Plan (1977-1981). Since in Thailand as well as in the Philippines, RCDP entered its implementation stage only a few years ago, it is premature to draw conclusions about its impact. The Chiang Mai and Iloilo case studies have, however, shown that the impact of these projects on urban development is limited. It benefits mainly the urban areas; so far there have been few spread effects to the surrounding rural areas (Ladavalya et al. 1987). The project's impact is much greater in Chiang Mai than in Iloilo -- largely due to the fact that in Chiang Mai and other Thai cities economic and political factors both at the national and regional level are much more conducive to translating RCDP resource inputs into economic growth.

Local Government and the
National Political System

Having analyzed the factors explaining the different levels of socioe-conomic development in the three regional cities, the next step is to ex-amine the role of local governments in the context of the respective na-tional polity. In the model outlined in chapter one, this is the feed-back relationship between local government and the national political system.

Most scholars and practitioners have so far treated local government as "wholly dependent on national government, its laws, resources and institutions defining the capabilities and influence of local level units" (Ashford 1975:92). Undoubtedly, this assumption is a legacy of the le-gal-institutional approach and its legal formalism, which looks at local government solely in its dependency on the national system. However, the relationship between national and local government is interdepen-dent, though unequal. In the case studies, the conventional research perspective was pursued by focussing on the impact of national politics on the local arena; in this section an attempt is made to analyze the in-fluences of local government on the national political system.

Local government in Southeast Asia is less an independent than a dependent variable in political and socioeconomic development. In other words, local governments are much more influenced by national political events and actors than vice versa. The more authoritarian the regime, the weaker are local governments as an independent variable and the more are they instrumentalized for the regime's political goals. On the other hand, however, the impact of local government on national politics grows in periods of political decay and disintegration of au-thoritarian regimes, and may become a factor accelerating the collapse of the regime.

As the previous sections have demonstrated, local governments play a relatively limited role as catalysts of urban and regional and, cumula-tively, of national socioeconomic development. Higher government lev-els and here, in particular, central government agencies are far more important as planning, decision-making, and implementing bodies. In the Philippines, Thailand, and Malaysia local governments have only supportive functions in national development. Most municipal gov-ernments cannot do more than exert maintenance functions ("*house-keeping*"), offering services that facilitate the reproduction of the labor force or else simply muddle through to satisfy the most basic needs of the population. Especially in the Philippines, many local governments cannot even perform these minimum functions -- here they are often merely a mechanism to sustain themselves, i.e. the local bureaucracy, the single largest employer in many cities. Local government, notably in urban areas, is little more than an institution cushioning the unemployment rate that approached 20 percent in most Philippine cities in the crisis years between 1984 and 1986.

Local governments also play a very limited role in strengthening democracy, pluralism, and political participation in the respective societies. For they themselves are *"penetrated systems"* (Jones 1975) under more or less tight control of the national government, they are instrumentalized by the national ruling cliques, factions, dominant party or ethnic group to exert grassroots control. In other words, local governments and, due to the concentration of patronage resources in urban areas, city governments in particular, are utilized as a device to depoliticize and demobilize the political system. It is a truism that these functions are diametrically opposed to the principles of classical democratic theory.

Yet, if Chiang Mai is a representative case for Thailand, it must appear surprising that despite their strong dependence on the national government, the larger Thai municipalities have contributed more to national socioeconomic development than comparable local units in Malaysia and the Philippines during much of the last decade.

Moreover, in terms of democratization and vertical division of powers, Thai municipalities also made greater contributions than Philippine and Malaysian urban governments, because local political actors and groups are less closely linked to superior levels of the national polity. In Thai municipalities, for instance, the nomination of candidates for local elections is much less controlled from above than in the Philippines. While electoral and party politics leave some room for local autonomy and localism, the centralizing element in Thai local government is the bureaucracy. However, due to its traditionally strong position in the Thai polity, the bureaucracy clearly dominates elected politicians in decision-making. In the complex web of Thai bureaucratic rules, by-laws, and procedures, civil servants are superior in administrative competence and in the application of these regulations. Unlike in Thailand, centralization of government in the Philippines and Malaysia was more pronounced in the political sphere as a result of vertically structured political parties. At present, centralization via political institutions seems to be stronger in Malaysia than in the Philippines, mainly because political parties in Malaysia are more cohesively organized and less regionally fragmented.

The functions of local government within the national political context vary according to regime type. In the period covered by this study three regime types can be distinguished: (1) *authoritarian* or *semiauthoritarian* regimes; (2) *patronage oligarchies;* and (3) *liberalizing regimes.*

Local Government in Authoritarian and Semiauthoritarian Regimes

Authoritarianism was practiced in the Philippines between 1972 and 1986, in Thailand until 1973, and again from 1976 to 1978, whereas government in Malaysia, after a short, fully-fledged authoritarian period under the National Operations Council (1969-1971), may presently be best categorized as semiauthoritarian.

A salient strategy of the authoritarian regimes was to make sure that local governments did not influence the political system in a way that was beyond regime control. Under authoritarian regimes, local governments exerted little influence on the national polity other than contributing to the depoliticization and demobilization of society and organizing the necessary grassroots support in legitimization exercises such as (manipulated) elections, referenda, or state ceremonies (Carbonell-Catilo et al. 1985). The function of local governments was thus primarily to stabilize rule by eliminating or preventing the emergence of grassroots bases of opposition forces. Through tight grassroots control, exerted by loyal local officials and their political machines, counterelites were left with few chances to build up their own organizational network (Thai University Research Association 1976; Aquino 1977; Canoy 1980; Casalmo 1980; Noranitipadungkarn 1981; Bello et al. 1982; Rüland 1982a; Wurfel 1988).

All the authoritarian and semiauthoritarian regimes engineered sophisticated systems of direct political and administrative control over their capital cities. In Thailand, the Bangkok Metropolitan Administration (BMA) and its predecessors stood under close supervision of the Ministry of the Interior (Thai University Research Association 1976; Patom 1978; Kongridhisusakorn 1984) Elected representative bodies were dissolved and replaced by an appointed advisory body. In Kuala Lumpur the (partly) elected municipal council was abolished in face of increasing opposition and embarassing government losses in the capital's constituencies in the 1959 general elections. The capital was subsequently placed under direct supervision of the central government: first the Ministry of the Interior and Justice (1961), then the Ministry of Housing and Local Government (1964) and, finally, in 1974, the newly created Ministry of the Federal Territory (Anthony 1971). In the Philippines, three years after the imposition of martial law, the National Capital Region (NCR) was placed under the jurisdiction of the Metropolitan Manila Commission (MMC) with Imelda R. Marcos, the president's wife, as governor (Caoili 1988:158). In 1978, the MMC became an attached agency of the country's superministry, the Ministry of Human Settlements (MHS), which was also chaired by Imelda R. Marcos. The creation of a supralocal metropolitan government had the effect of emasculating the seventeen formerly elected, traditionally pro-opposition local governments located within the boundaries of the metropolitan agglomeration (Rüland 1982a, 1985a).

Another feature of authoritarian and semiauthoritarian regimes is the abolition or suspension of local elections and the appointment of local officials. Local elections were abolished after almost every coup in Thailand (Thai University Research Association 1976; Patom 1978), suspended in the Philippines after the declaration of martial law in 1972, suspended (1965) and later completely abolished (1976) in Malaysia (Tennant 1973a, 1973b; Norris 1980; Phang 1978, 1988; Kassim 1986).

Apart from exercising functions of political grassroots control during phases of authoritarian rule, municipal government in Thailand was used by the ruling clique to consolidate or preserve its power. As the classical Thai "bureaucratic polity" (Riggs 1966) was essentially based on a delicate balance between rival military and bureaucratic factions, maintenance of power to a great extent hinged on the ruling group's ability to enlarge its support base by rewarding its clientele with promotions and other material and symbolic benefits. While the dismissal of elected municipal assemblies and the suspension of municipal elections was legitimized as a device to reduce the divisiveness of politics, to create unity and to maintain national security, the subsequent appointment of military officers and civil servants as municipal councillors were steps to consolidate factional support at the lower echelons of the governmental system.

In the Philippines, despite the suspension of local elections, local officials elected in the 1971 local polls were allowed to stay in office until their term expired in 1975. Only the most vocal adversaries of the regime were ousted right at the start of the martial-law period. Many local councillors were even retained after the introduction of new local legislatures, but completely outnumbered and, hence, politically neutralized by appointed regime-loyal ex-officio members. These new legislatures -- the *Sangguniang Bayans* in municipalities and the *Sangguniang Panglungsods* in cities -- appealed to nationalist and nativist values, blurring the fact that they left little scope for local self-determination and political participation. Later, in 1979/1980, under increasing pressure from abroad as well as from within the Philippines, the regime repeated what it had done two years earlier at the national level, and what in many countries appears to be an almost inevitable sequence of events some time after the imposition of authoritarian rule: it created a "multi-party" system with one dominant party, allowed a limited degree of political competition, and held token elections. The 1980 local elections served primarily to provide the Marcos regime with fresh "democratic" legitimacy and enable a spring-cleaning exercise within the dominant party (Rüland 1982a).

An additional measure adopted by authoritarian regimes to utilize local government for the depoliticization and demobilization of society is the creation of regime-sponsored neighborhood organizations. As has been shown in chapter three, the Philippine *barangays* served as ex-tended arms of the security agencies, suppressing political dissent at its roots. While a politico-administrative organization extending down to the barrio level already existed in the rural Philippines long before the declaration of martial law (Laquian 1965, 1968), due to their reputation as opposition strongholds, the Marcos regime took great pains to build up *barangays* especially in the urban areas. Moreover, since urban areas in the Philippines usually harbor large concentrations of poverty groups, social unrest was anticipated in the cities. Hence, the strategy of the regime to tighten the *barangay* network particularly in the residential quarters of the urban poor (Aquino 1977; Rüland 1986a).

Though they did not pretend to work for participatory and develop-mental ends (as the Philippine *barangays*), the Thai village scouts also served mainly to suppress or eliminate political opponents striving for a radical redistribution of public and private assets (Muecke 1980). The indoctrination sessions and emotional initiation rites of both the *barangays* and the village scouts clearly espouse antidemocratic and authoritarian values.

Attempts to build up grassroots organizations in Malaysia, the *Rukun Tetenggas*, have met with much less success. The *Rukuns* initially orga-nized night patrols in their respective neighborhoods, but in Penang and most other cities they are moribund today.[9]

While authoritarian regimes attempted to build up strong govern-ment-controled neighborhood organizations, nonconformist social movements, regime-critical NGDOs, and self-help organizations are stigmatized and prosecuted as subversive communist-infiltrated orga-nizations (Simon 1987; Wan G'aeo 1989) . This happened to squatter or-ganizations in the Philippines and antinuclear, environmentalist, and consumer organizations in Malaysia (Husin Ali 1989). The strategy of muzzling demands critical of government policy, especially if they bear

social overtones, has legislative, organizational, and physical components. First of all, the organization of antigovernment groups is impeded by legislative means. The Marcos regime did this by restricting
the right of assembly, press freedom, and the free expression of opinion
(Wurfel 1988:123), whereas in Thailand and Malaysia laws were enacted
that made registration of all kinds of interest groups, societies, and voluntary organizations compulsory (Chenvidyakarn 1977; Jumbhala 1987).
The *Malaysian Societies Act* obliges registered groups to report periodically to the government about their activities and to provide any information that is required (Doh 1980; Barraclough 1984). The second step
was to organize grassroots associations loyal to the government as described above. If these precautions still did not discourage opposition
groups from organizing themselves, the military was employed to suppress them by physical force.

Not surprisingly, the local arena could not contribute to the democratization of decision-making or to building up a more pluralistic structure of nongovernmental organizations and interest groups. Local decision-making remained a closed-shop affair, as did national politics. In
authoritarian regimes local governments thus have quite the opposite
function than stipulated in democratic theory: they do not foster, but
rather prevent the emergence of a democratic polity.

Beyond their functions of regime stabilization -- depoliticization and
demobilization at the grassroots level -- local governments have exerted
little influence on the national political system in authoritarian states.
However, autocratic processes of leadership recruitment, decision-
making, and policy execution permit little *"elasticity of control"* (Werlin
1974:20). Elasticity of control denotes a cooperative relationship
between rulers and ruled, in which political power takes a persuasive
rather than a coercive form. The more a political system is considered
legitimate by the people, the less the need for control, because subordinates are more trusted by the rulers, and the greater is the elasticity of
control. On the other hand, constant enforcement of obedience by
means of structural coercion, intimidation, and outright repression, as is
the case in authoritarian regimes, is politically the most costly way to
gain compliance (Werlin 1974:26). Such political costs cannot be sustained over a long period. Hence, the attempt of regimes to win greater
democratic legitimacy by introducing limited party competition and
forms of *"guided democracy"*. Yet, during the autocratic phase so much
political frustration and opposition has accumulated that moves to liberalize the political system -- or, in other words, to establish greater
elasticity of control -- lead to a rapid erosion of the regime's power.

Accordingly, in the Philippines, the 1980 elections and the *barangay* elections of 1982 contributed more to the disintegration of the regime than to the absorption of political discontent. These elections were events in a sequence of moves (parliamentary elections in 1978, formal lifting of martial law in 1981, presidential elections in 1981, and parliamentary elections in 1984) that were advertised by the regime as stages of a "normalization" process that would eventually return the country to democracy (Wurfel 1988).

Towards the end of the 1970s the Marcos regime was facing mounting opposition on two fronts: from parts of the traditional oligarchy (the so-called moderate opposition) and an armed leftist insurgency. Although they were attempts to provide the regime with fresh legitimacy, the above-mentioned political exercises were also limited concessions to the moderate opposition. Hence, these moves were designed to appear as a liberalization of the political system that would give opposition forces a chance to gain access to political decision-making bodies. The ultimate goal of this maneuvering, however, was to isolate the radicals, who categorically denied the possibility of reformist changes within the parameters set by the Marcos regime, from the moderate opposition. Despite crushing electoral defeats, the moderate opposition gained a foothold in local governments and, to an even greater extent, in the *barangays*. The existence of only a single opposition councillor in a city or municipal council broke the once more or less monolithic control of the regime and led to an increasing politicization in the local arena. Whereas political competition and conflicts had hitherto been relegated to personal controversies within the confines of the dominant KBL-party and received little publicity, the local arena now developed into a battle field between proxies of the Marcos regime and the oligarchical elite opposition. This confrontation became much more intense after the Aquino assassination in 1983, especially in the urban areas. The battle cry under which the show-down was fought -- "dictatorship or democracy" -- guaranteed a high level of public attention and the more the regime appeared to be on the defensive, the easier it was for the opposition to mobilize support. Defections of KBL-stalwarts increased dramatically at the local level, eroding the machine that the regime had systematically built up after 1972.[10] The defections of KBL politicians to the UNIDO and the noncommitment of many other "near defectors" were one of the major reasons why the regime, despite the total mobilization of the government machinery, its superior material resources, and rampant election fraud, failed to win the 1986 presidential elections (Rüland 1986b) that preceeded its collapse in February 1986.

Besides depoliticization and demobilization, urban-based local governments in Malaysia have two other functions important for the political system as a whole. They serve as *"shock absorbers"* for the state governments. State officials and politicians frequently hold municipal governments responsible for poor service even if they are beyond local governments' financial means or not their legal responsibilty. While it is of little political consequence if state-appointed local offcials are blamed for such deficiencies, the deflection of criticism that should actually be addressed to the state government saves elected state officials from serious repercussions at forthcoming polls. If the state government appeared as the main culprit, this would inevitably result in a sizeable loss of votes in urban areas and lead to shifts in favor of the opposition at the national level.

The second major function of urban governments in Malaysia has already been amply discussed in chapter four. Control over municipal governments is a major precondition for implementing the federal government's pro-Malay *New Economic Policy*, as the most lucrative assets are concentrated in the urban centers. Here, municipal government also has an ethnic dimension.

Local Government in Patronage Oligarchies

The post-independence Philippine political system until 1972 and the order emerging after the fall of Marcos are classical cases of a patronage oligarchy. Unlike in authoritarian regimes, in a Philippine-type patronage oligarchy there is greater scope for local governments to influence the national political system in a way that cannot be controlled by the central government. This is due mainly to the democratic formalism of patronage oligarchies, which guarantees a considerable level of political competitiveness. Greater competitiveness, on the other hand, increases the political instability of power relationships in a political system that is built on loosely-structured, personalized horizontal and vertical alliances. These alliances are highly fluid and -- as shown in chapter three -- characterized by frequent factional realignments based on pragmatic and opportunistic considerations as well as conflicting economic interests within the oligarchy. Local governments are the foundations of these power pyramids engineered by rivaling factions of the national oligarchy (Landé 1965). The extent to which these factions control local authorities determines their influence in national politics and their numerical strength in national representative bodies. Urban areas are particularly sensitive spots in these alliance systems -- especially for the incumbent national leadership -- because in cities competition is much stronger than in the countryside, the cost of political mobilization much higher, and, due to the existence of an educated, though numerically small, politically vocal, and independent-minded middle-class, there are usually strong pro-opposition sentiments. In a country with an urbanization rate of 40 percent, the urban political arena is an important factor in determining the path of national politics.

Like in authoritarian regimes, the national elite attempts to exert political control over the local level to the greatest possible extent. This is done by influencing the nomination of candidates in local elections, a complex system of rewards and sanctions in order to ensure political loyalty, appointments in the bureaucracy, and even intimidation and physical force through private armies, the police or the military. But the formal existence of democratic and constitutional institutions such as courts, press freedom, and the ability of rival factions to employ exactly the same legal and illegal mechanisms has a restraining effect on control over local governments by the incumbent central government. As a result, changing alliances, although in many instances instigated by supralocal political forces, may have a decisive influence on national power distribution. For instance, if a local faction aligned with the faction running the national government defects to the opposition, then the center loses its ability to implement projects and political plans in the respective locality. This -- and the cut in central resources to the local unit that usually follows -- undermines the credibility of the national government to work for national development, and eventually leads to a loss of legitimacy. This loss of legitimacy reinforces the "natural" erosion of government legitimacy that is built into patronage oligarchies with limited patronage potential. The incumbent administration is rarely able to meet the expectations of rewards held by powerful local individuals and groups supporting it. The apparent inability -- or perceived unwillingness -- of the government to repay political debts is interpreted as a breach of the traditionally respected norm of reciprocity. Those not or insufficiently participating in the allocation of government resources start to criticize and attack the incumbent administration as corrupt and incompetent -- thus further undermining its legitimacy. Since local leaders organize the election campaign of national politicians within their locality and are thus instrumental in delivering sizeable vote packages, power constellations at the local level are decisive for the outcome of national political contests. Massive shifts in local factional alignments have always been the rule in Philippine politics, and one of the main reasons why before 1969 no president was able to win a second term.

Another function of the local political arena for the polity as a whole is its decisive role in leadership recruitment for national offices. In this respect the Philippines differs markedly from Thailand and Malaysia. Ocampo and Panganiban found that 61 percent of the members of the national assembly had been local officials at some point in their political careers (Ocampo and Panganiban 1985:15). Local offices thus constitute a field for political apprenticeship and provide a fall-back position for established leaders who have lost national office. In Thailand's House of Representatives, on the other hand, only 25 percent of the MPs in 1975/76 had previous political experiences in municipal or provincial assemblies (Morell and Samudavanija 1981:116).

Yet, Philippine local governments should not be mistaken for a *"school of democracy"* that supports an incipient process of national democratization. It is argued here that neither in the pre-1972 nor in the post-Marcos Philippines were local governments "democracies in the making" or "polyarchies" as argued by Leichter (1975), Scott (1969 and 1972), and Machado (1972a, 1972b, and 1973/74).

The analysis in chapter three has shown that the three major preconditions for a polyarchy do not exist in the Philippines -- neither at the national nor at the local level. These preconditions are:

1. nonleaders exert a high measure of control over policy-makers, thereby introducing a reciprocity relationship between the governors and the governed;
2. different social groups participate in the political process; and
3. there is a pluralist social order. A pluralist social order is characterized by a decentralized and diversified economy, a high degree of egalitarianism in the distribution of resources, and a separation or neutralization of the societal means of coercion (Zipfel 1982).

None of these preconditions is fulfilled in the Philippines. Nonleaders exert a minimal degree of control over leaders, the political process rests on a narrow social base, and there is no pluralist social order -- at best a plurality of interests. Despite the existence of a formal division of powers, its impact on the political process is limited at best. Members of the executive, legislative, and the judiciary are, in large part, recruited from the family clans of the oligarchy. Spreading out from its landed base, the Philippine oligarchy developed a sophisticated division of labor that enabled it to diversify into virtually every economic sector. Upward mobility by other groups without the consent -- or, rather, cooptation -- of this oligarchy is severely restricted. Because of this narrow social base, economic growth may fuel contradictions and conflicts among factions of the oligarchy, but hardly translate into a broadening of political actors. The elements of control and accountability, key principles in a democracy, are thus severely underdeveloped at all levels of the Philippine governmental system.

It is therefore questionable to interpret the existence of democratic formalism as an incipient form of democracy (Wurfel 1963; Scott 1969; Machado 1972a). Patronage oligarchies are not part of an unilinear evolutionary process from traditional forms of government to a western-type democratic polity, as suggested by the experience of the Anglo-American political systems. Only a long period of uninterrupted and dynamic economic growth could differentiate and diversify Philippine society to such an extent that the oligarchy would lose their monopoly of political power and economic resources. New functional groups must emerge, develop, articulate their interests, and, finally, become actors in the political game. Only when rapid, long-term economic growth, and group differentiation coincide, do patronage oligarchies stand a chance of developing into a political system with some democratic substance. These conditions, however, did not exist in the years preceding martial law and do not exist now after the collapse of authoritarian regimes in many parts of the Third World has given rise to another round of discussion on the prospects of democracy in developing countries (Huntington 1984; Berg-Schlosser 1985; Vanhanen 1990; Rüland and Werz 1991).

Local Government in Liberalizing Political Systems

Liberalization in Thailand began with the fall of the Thanom/Praphat dictatorship in 1973. Yet, the experiment with parliamentary democracy was short-lived. It was torn apart between an increasingly radical left and rightest reaction (Morell and Samudavanija 1981; Girling 1981; Prizzia 1985). But the coup that brought to power the ultraconservative Thanin administration in 1976 could not restore the old order. Another coup ended Thanin's premiership one year later. Under his successors, retired army generals Kriangsak Chomanand and Prem Tinsulanonda, a gradual and careful liberalization was initiated -- despite two abortive coups by opposition factions within the military in 1981 and 1985. Parliamentary and local elections were restored in 1979 and 1980 respectively, and the powers of the military-dominated Senate vis-à-vis the House of Representatives were curbed in 1983 (Suriyamongkol 1988).

Although the social base of political decision-makers is broader, and there are formal participatory channels, liberalizing systems have many obstacles to participation in common with patronage oligarchies. The liberalizing political regime in Thailand is characterized by distortions in the political process at all levels of the government system. Elections, both national and local, are marked by vote-buying and electoral manipulation, although not to the same extent as in the Philippines, neither in terms of the amount of money spent nor of the gravity of electoral fraud. Moreover, in Thailand the political value system of local decision-makers remains essentially conservative. Restriction of political participation to the upper-middle- and middle-classes is one of the main reasons why the bottom 20 percent of the urban population are more or less excluded from resource allocation. Yet, the major difference compared with a Philippine-type patronage oligarchy is that the situation is not static. Social group formation continues and, once resourceful enough, the new groups find access to the political arena. Given the diversification of interests represented in political bodies, services output and the allocation of public resources will become more complex and cover more societal groups than before -- assuming that economic growth continues and the resource base expands.

In the context of this liberalizing political system, municipal government has become an important participatory platform for a socially ambitious, upwardly mobile urban middle-class with business backgrounds. Since the country's rapid economic growth was paralleled by a rapid expansion of the educational system and specialization of the economy, new political interest groups able to articulate their demands emerged. In this process, a fledgeling urban-based middle-class, which had been hitherto more or less excluded from the political arena by the traditional military and bureaucratic elites, sought to protect its economic interests through access to political decision-making bodies. Since considerable individual and collective economic interests are at stake for these groups, to exclude them from access to political decision-making would in the long run create dangerous frustrations. The opening of the municipal arena for new groups is helping to broaden the social base of Thai politics. It may serve as an outlet for political pressures that would otherwise be directed against the central government. In this sense, the opening of the local level to competitive politics is an important contribution to the stability of the political system as a whole, and in keeping with the present policy of gradual democratization.

Concluding Remarks on the Interrelations Between Local Autonomy, Political Participation, and Socioeconomic Development

After discussing at length the extent of local autonomy, the patterns of political participation, and the trends in socioeconomic development in three Southeast Asian regional cities, I now turn to the model outlined in chapter one in order to draw more definite conclusions about the interrelations between these three variables. These concluding remarks may be understood as an ideological critique of the mainstream local government literature and its excessive normative bias. In all events it is a reminder of Ylvisaker's plea to avoid "emotional, dispassionate or mythical attachment" to the theme (Ylvisaker 1959:29-30).

As pointed out in chapter one, the entire decentralization debate, of which local government is a central subtheme, is characterized by anachronistic conceptual premises. Derived from nineteenth-century liberalism, concepts such as decentralization, local autonomy, local government, and participation were advocated as ends in themselves (Faltas 1981:1). This frequently tempted western or western-educated scholars as well as international aid organizations to make a puristic view of these concepts the basis for judging Third-World political systems. The functions of these concepts in the specific historical situation of the West were overlooked and it was widely assumed that a mechanical transfer of these organizational principles to developing societies would greatly accelerate national development. Although scholars such as Riggs (1959, 1964), Fesler (1968), Leemans (1970), and Faltas (1981, 1982) repeatedly warned that the "romantic idealization of decentralization is a fallacy" (Leemans 1970:20), these voices were a small minority and went largely unheard. This should not come as a surprise, since the appeal for a more differentiated view of the decentralization strategy and its related concepts is incompatible with the programmatic declarations of international and foreign donors of development assistance. As shown in Rondinelli's (1983b) evaluation of decentralization programs in Asia, in four out of eight cases the decentralization ideology was in fact introduced by the foreign donor. Both the foreign donor as well as the recipient are under *"decentralization pressure"*: the recipient because he wants to secure development aid and hence must fulfill certain requirements set by the donor, the donor because he must legitimize his aid programs vis-à-vis a critical public at home. In consequence, he is forced to sell development assistance as a device that facilitates decentralization, democratization, and participation, even in essentially nondemocratic societies. This fact also explains the frequently observed discrepancy between the decentralization rhetoric of many Asian governments and actual implementation. While central governments eagerly pay lip service to strengthening their subnational government units, in reality decentralization is not taklen seriously. Rarely is power devolved upon local authorities. The most that is done is deconcentration of powers -- i.e. the limited transfer of authority to central government field agencies. Yet, deconcentration must -- contrary to general opinion -- be clearly distinguished from decentralization because its effects in fact tend to strengthen central authority (Mawhood 1974:7; Rowat 1983:64-67; Rüland 1991:288). Thus, paradoxically, what is advertised as decentralization in reality leads to increased centralization.

A normative dimension is introduced into local government research from yet another side. A number of Third-World scholars critical of development strategies imitating western experience speak of a continuous loss of local autonomy since the colonial era. The yardstick for this assessment was ancient traditions of "autonomous village republics", which were equated with equality and democracy (Subramaniam 1980:582). This idea was a major element in Gandhian philosophy which later resurfaced in Schumacher's slogan that *"small is beautiful"* (Schumacher 1977). Such village republics with an "extremely vigorous system of self-government were said to have existed in large parts of Southeast Asia, South Asia, and Africa prior to the arrival of the European colonial powers" (Subramaniam 1980:582).

Yet, the glorification of a *"Great Tradition"* of democratic and egalitarian local self-government in precolonial times is a myth similar to that of the autonomy concept derived from liberal doctrine in the Western hemisphere. Already in 1955 Virginia Thompson had warned that "the democratic nature of the area's (i.e. Southeast, J.R.) local government institutions, before their contact with the West, should not be exaggerated" (Thompson 1955:122). As argued by Wittfogel, the *"Asian Despoty"* left little room for village autonomy, let alone local self-government. If there was anything resembling local autonomy, it could only develop on the periphery of the *"hydraulic society"*, in remote areas protected by geographical barriers which the imperial power could only weakly penetrate (Wittfogel 1977:160-164). This type of "local autonomy" is better circumscribed as isolation or "local autonomy by default" (Lockard 1968:458). It should be compared neither with the liberal autonomy concept nor with modern central-local relations, because precolonial village republics had no legal-constitutional dimension -- i.e. were not corporate entities -- and because the participatory element was tightly circumscribed, if it existed at all. Local entities in India, for instance, were characterized by highly stratified, rigid caste structures, while village structures in Thailand and the Philippines were far from egalitarian, too (Phelan 1973).

Moreover, this nativist version of a *"paradise lost"* syndrome was frequently abused by authoritarian regimes to legitimate new local government bodies which served the sole purpose of consolidating the regime's grip on power. Examples par excellence of such a strategy were the creation of the *Sangguniang Bayans*, the *Sangguniang Panglungsods* and the *barangays* by the Marcos regime in the Philippines.

Also in the tradition of this precolonial autonomy concept is Stöhr and Taylor's (1981) strategy of *"selective regional closure"* -- a spatial decentralization strategy complementary to political and administrative decentralization. Stöhr and Taylor's concept is based on "little-developed, small-scale cellular societies" which, in order to avoid major external dependencies, pursue endogenously motivated development strategies (Stöhr and Taylor 1981:473). Regional or local isolation and a strong subsistence economy are the major pillars of their model, that also borrows from Senghaas' *dissociation theory* (Senghaas 1977). However, the idealization of *"subsistence affluence"* found among adherents of the *"Great Tradition"* myth as well, collides in most Asian societies with demographic realities and shrinking land resources. Selective regional closure -- as a spatial autonomy concept -- may temporarily have some equalizing effect. In the long run, however, it does not lead to "affluence", but to impoverishment of the respective region.

Ylvisaker's plea for sobriety in dealing with concepts related to decentralization and local government is underscored by the result of this comparative study on local government in Southeast Asia. While in Chiang Mai and Penang there was very little local autonomy and a rather low level of political participation, there had been considerable socioeconomic progress. This finding runs counter to conventional assumptions of democratic theory and local government research which see local autonomy and political participation as necessary and sufficient conditions for development.

This leads me to some further, though possibly provocative conclusions. Contrary to Michael Calavan, who holds that "building local autonomy is essential for socioeconomic development" (Calavan 1984:247), it is be argued here that in the initial stage of development, local autonomy is not a necessary condition for urban development. The low degree of autonomy granted by centralist political systems may at this point not seriously hamper urban development, if external conditions are conducive to development. What I mean by favorable external conditions is this: few fluctuations and predictability of the world market forces in localities with strong links to the international economy, long-term national economic growth, and a less inegalitarian local distribution of societal resources.

However, under unfavorable environmental conditions such as existed in the Philippine city of Iloilo, lack of autonomy, together with the combined negative effects of elitism, authoritarianism, and an economic crisis, tends to reinforce the negative effects on urban development and may, moreover, become a factor seriously undermining the legitimacy of the central government. What is needed in a situation of crisis is flexibility that enables improvisation to overcome resource constraints. Overly rigid rules and regulations would be counterproductive for this purpose. Greater local autonomy may provide the potential for flexible administrative maneuvering. Yet, this type of local autonomy is little more than a device for crisis-management. It hardly offers opportunities for developing a consolidated local government system and institutions.

In a situation of crisis, the central state -- or rather the political forces dominating it -- tend to withdraw scarce resources from the local authorities that the national ruling clique urgently needs to secure its own political survival. The distribution of societal resources thus becomes increasingly top heavy. The lopsidedness of the distributional pattern corresponds with the extent of local autonomy. In an austerity situation, local authorities have the least priority in the process of national resource allocation. In the Philippines the Marcos regime, under severe economic and political pressure, did not hesitate to deny the local authorities legitimate national resources. Illegal appropriations of resources by the central state included the nonallocation of the internal revenue allotments as well as the specific tax allotments (Bahl and Miller 1983:102; Cordero and Santiago 1990:26-27). While the central state is able to overcome resource constraints through borrowing, restrictive legislation deprives Philippine and Thai cities of this option. In as much as local governments are only extended arms of the state in a centralized, authoritarian political system, the crisis and its concomitant political culture of decay make a strong impact on the local level as well. Corruption and mismanagement -- reflecting the intensifying struggle over scarce resources -- then characterize the local governmental process to a much greater extent than under normal conditions. But as a result of the proximity of the rulers and the ruled, the local arena is more transparent than the national level. Scandals, mismanagement, abuse of power, and excessive corruption in local government more easily become common knowledge and thus increase popular discontent with the regime. As a consequence, the erosion of legitimacy accelerates at the bottom of the political system and -- as the rapid expansion of the New People's Army in large parts of the Philippines shows -- may even translate into violent fundamentalist opposition.

More local autonomy will also be needed once an urban center has reached a certain development threshold. Penang, for instance, has clearly reached this stage, Chiang Mai is on the verge of it. As society becomes more complex, the need for accelerated, local-based decision-making increases. The more complex an urban system, the more difficult it is for distant central authorities to make competent decisions. The present arrangement of central-local decision-making in Chiang Mai, and, to a lesser extent, in Penang is too time-consuming, not elastic enough, and may thus become a political liability.

Much more important for urban development than autonomy is political participation. Participation is not merely an intervening variable as stipulated during the first decentralization debate in the 1950s and 1960s. Rather, is it an independent variable for development.

This finding contradicts the results of Uphoff and Esman's comparative study on local organization. Uphoff and Esman conclude that participation "does not appear to be a necessary or sufficient condition for development" (Uphoff and Esman 1983:200). In contrast to Uphoff and Esman, it is argued here that participation is indeed a major prerequisite for ensuring that socioeconomic development is not distributed in too skewed a manner. It may be recalled that lack of participation was one of the key reasons why, despite rapid economic growth in Penang and Chiang Mai, about one-fifth of the population was virtually excluded from developmental gains. Thus, not surprisingly, Iloilo, the city with the most elitist local political culture, had by far the highest urban poverty incidence. A strategy of "participatory centralization" may thus be as effective in stimulating development as autonomy and participation, the twin engines of development in the conventional decentralization approaches.

Greater participation also safeguards against increasing local autonomy, which is often the autonomy of local elites or the local bureaucracy instead of the community as a whole. Political participation -- preferably, but not necessarily, within institutionalized, legitimate channels -- is thus a decisive element of leadership control.

With increasing socioeconomic development, a diversification of the socioeconomic structure and a broader distribution of growth benefits, pressure for more participation in local politics arises, because municipal politics essentially affects economic opportunities in the city, and more people will thus have a greater stake in decision-making. Such a process could be observed in Chiang Mai, where socioeconomic development went hand in hand with a modest expansion of the social base of local leadership, including more leaders with a middle-class background. In Penang, on the other hand, such a process did not take place, first, because in the given situation of ethnic tensions most participatory channels at the local level are tightly controlled by the ruling Barisan Nasional and, second, because electoral politics at the state level provides at least some outlets for upwardly mobile social groups.

Socioeconomic development has some impact on the degree of local autonomy. Though development does not directly affect the legal-constitutional dimension of central-local relations, the increase of local government resources, both in terms of finances as well as staff and know-how, will broaden local decision-making options. If development is not based on just one economic sector, institutional, organizational, and communicative linkages will also expand -- further strengthening the information base for decision-making at the local level (Williams 1981; Uphoff 1986). Such a trend will be reinforced, if socioeconomic growth also increases spatial interdependencies -- i.e. changes the radial structure of communication and financial and trade flows away from the national capital towards denser horizontal networking. Then, again, the dependency on the capital would diminish. For instance, absentee-owned corporations with their headquarters in the capital or abroad would lose some of their influence on local politics in the hinterland cities. Thailand with its good transport and improving telecommunications infrastructure stands a good chance of effecting such a change towards greater horizontal networking.

Yet another aspect must be kept in mind. The stronger a municipality in economic terms, the more important is its role within the national economy. As the case of Chiang Mai shows, this strengthens its bargaining power vis-à-vis national political decision-making bodies and the bureaucracy. In fact, economically advanced regional cities tend to be comparatively well represented in national politics, and are thus able to circumvent rigid centralism by means of informal contacts.

Whether more participation leads to greater local autonomy remains to be seen. In Thailand there are indications that such a trend may occur.[11] A new municipal law that professes to grant more autonomy to municipal government was introduced in parliament during the Prem V administration (1986-1988).[12] Various symposia attended by academics and government representatives pleaded for greater local autonomy, a plea eventually echoed by the Municipal League as well. Even the Ministry of the Interior is now showing greater flexibility towards such demands. From Penang and Iloilo no conclusions could be drawn, because in Penang has been no increase in political participation and in Iloilo basic civic rights were formally restored only a few months before the second field research phase started.

Notes

1. *Far Eastern Economic Review*, Hong Kong, 19 September 1985, pp. 79-85.
2. Ibid., p. 82.

3. Such as the Lopez/Ledesma faction and the Ganzon machine in Iloilo.

4. For the escalation of Philippine campaign costs see David Wurfel, "Comparative Studies in Political Finance, The Philippines," in *The Journal of Politics*, Vol. 25, No. 4, 1963, pp. 757-773. The campaign costs of the 1986 presidential election were estimated at P 10 billion (= US $ 250 million) which is equivalent to 12.3 percent of the national budget. In contrast, with an estimated spending of B 3 billion (= US $ 115 million), the Thai parliamentary elections of July 1986 were comparatively cheap (about 1.5 percent of the national budget).

5. This situation may however be changing, due to increasing competitiveness in Thai politics and the rising stakes in municipal government.

6. The problem of *"overpoliticization"* has been discussed extensively by Huntington. See Samuel P. Huntington, *Political Order in Changing Societies* (New Haven: Yale University Press, 1968). However, the concept as it is used here, has a different meaning. While for Huntington the institutional bottlenecks are the main causes that political systems cannot cope with increasing participation, here the emphasis is placed on resource constraints causing overly high mobilization levels.

7. Political "apprenticeship" is also an important step for political dynasties in generating new leaders. See Aprodicio A. Laquian and R.M. Pangilinan, *The 1963 Elections in Manila: A Study of the Recruitment of Political Leaders and its Relation to Administration* (Manila: College of Public Administration, University of the Philippines, 1968).

8. In January 1990, Chamlong was reelected in a landslide victory.

9. Interview information.

10. See Jürgen Rüland, *Die Philippinen. Anatomie einer Krise* (Bonn: Friedrich-Ebert-Stiftung, 1985), p. 20; For Panay, see *Panay News*, Iloilo City 1-7 May 1985, p. 1, 5-11 June 1985, p. 1, and 22-28 January 1986, p. 3.

11. Already in 1980 Friedman stated that "Thailand may be the situation where events are moving to more autonomy and more participation, but less bureaucratization". See H.J. Friedman, "Other Asia," in *International Handbook on Local Government Reorganization*, ed. Donald C. Rowat (London: Aldwych Press, 1980), p. 464.

12. After the take over of the Chatichai government (1988-1991), the bill has not been revitalized. Interview information.

Acronyms

ADB	Asian Development Bank
ASEAN	Association of Southeast Asian Nations
BA	Bachelor of Arts
BAYAN	Bagong Alyansang Makabayang
BLISS	Bagong Lipunan Sites and Services
BMA	Bangkok Metropolitan Administration
BN	Barisan Nasional
BOI	Board of Investment
CAP	Consumer Association Penang
CCA	Concerned Citizen Aggrupation
CDD	Central District Development
COMELEC	Commission on Elections
CPP	Communist Party of the Philippines
CSC	Civil Service Commission
DAP	Democratic Action Party
DLGCD	Department of Local Government and Community Development
DOE	Department of Environment
DOLA	Department of Local Administration
EOI	Export-Oriented Industrialization
EPZ	Export Processing Zone
ESCAP	Economic and Social Commission for Asia and the Pacific
FTZ	Free Trade Zone
GDP	Gross Domestic Product
GSIS	Government Services Insurance System
HSRC	Human Settlements Regulatory Commission
HY	Hat Yai
IBP	Interim Batasang Pambansa
IBRD	International Bank for Reconstruction and Development
IEAT	Industrial Estate Authority of Thailand
IRCS	International Research and Consultancy Services
ISI	Import-Substituting Industrialization
IULA	International Union of Local Authorities
KB	Kabataang Barangay
KBL	Kilusang Bagong Lipunan

KK	Khon Kaen
KOMTAR	Kompleks Tun Abdul Razak
LOI	Letter of Instruction
LP	Liberal Party
MA	Master of Arts
MA	Mindanao Alliance
MCA	Malaysian Chinese Association
MDF	Municipal Development Fund
MERALCO	Manila Electric Company
MHS	Ministry of Human Settlements
MIC	Malaysian Indian Congress
MIWD	Metro Iloilo Water District
MLG	Ministry of Local Government
MMA	Metropolitan Manila Area
MMC	Metropolitan Manila Commission
MNC	Multinational Corporation
MOH	Ministry of Health
MOI	Ministry of the Interior
MOLE	Ministry of Labor and Employment
MP	Member of Parliament
MPHW	Ministry of Public Works and Highways
MSSD	Ministry of Social Services and Development
NACIDA	National Cottage Industries Development Authority
NAWASA	National Water and Sewerage Authority
NCR	National Capital Region
NCSO	National Census and Statistics Office
NDF	National Democratic Front
NEDA	National Economic and Development Authority
NEP	New Economic Policy
NESDB	National Economic and Social Development Board
NGDO	Nongovernmental Development Organization
NHA	National Housing Authority
NIC	Newly Industrializing Country
NIDA	National Institute of Development Administration
NP	Nacionalista Party
NPA	New People's Army
NR	Nakhon Ratchasima
NSO	National Statistics Office
NUL	National Union for Liberation
OIC	Officer-in-Charge
PAS	Parti Islam
PC/INP	Philippine Constabulary/National Integrated Police
PD	Presidential Decree

PDC	Penang Development Corporation
PDP	Phalang Dharma Party
PDP	Philippine Democratic Party
PEA	Provincial Electricity Authority
PECO	Panay Electric Company
PERDA	Pulau Pinang Regional Development Authority
PHHC	Philippine Homesite and Housing Corporation
PMIP	Pan Malaysian Islamic Party
POPCOM	Population Commission
PPP	People's Progressive Party
PSD	Public Service Department
PWA	Provincial Water Authority
RA	Republic Act
RCDP	Regional Cities Development Project
RDA	Regional Development Authority
SAM	Sahabat Alam Malaysia
SAP	Social Action Party
SB	Sangguniang Bayan
SEDC	State Economic Development Corporation
SEYA	Self-Employment Assistance Program
SP	Sangguniang Panglungsod
SPEAD	Surveyors, Planners, Engineers, Architects, and Developers
SSS	Social Security System
TDRI	Thailand Development Research Institute
TNC	Transnational Corporation
TV	Television
UDA	Urban Development Authority
UDP	United Democratic Party
UMNO	United Malay National Organization
UN	United Nations
UNDP	United Nations Development Program
UNESCO	United Nations Educational, Scientific and Cultural Organization
UNIDO	United Nationalist Democratic Party
US	United States
USAID	United States Agency for International Development
USM	Universiti Sains Malaysia
VCR	Video Casette Recorder

Bibliography

I. General Literature

Alderfer, Harold F. 1964. *Local Government in Developing Countries*. New York: McGraw-Hill.

Ali, Husin S. 1989. "Comparative Experience of Nongovernmental Organizations in ASEAN." *Asian Exchange*, Vol. 6, No. 1, pp. 45-57.

Allen, Hubert B.J. 1987. "Decentralization for Development: A Point of View." *Planning and Administration* 14: 23-30.

_____ . 1990. *Cultivating the Grass Roots. Why Local Government Matters*. Bombay: International Union of Local Authorities.

Almond, Gabriel A. and Sidney Verba. 1963. *The Civic Culture. Political Attitudes and Democracy in Five Nations*. Princeton: Princeton University Press.

Ashford, Douglas. 1975. "Theories of Local Government. Some Comparative Considerations". *Comparative Political Studies* 8: 90-107.

Asia Yearbook. 1986. Hong Kong: Far Eastern Economic Review, 1986.

Asian Development Bank. 1980. *Key Indicators of Developing Member Countries of ADB*. Manila: Asian Development Bank.

Bahl, Roy W., D. Holland, and Johannes F. Linn. 1983. *Urban Growth and Local Taxes in Less Developed Countries*. Honolulu: Papers of the East-West Population Institute No. 89.

Bahl, Roy W., Jerry Miner, and Larry Schroeder. 1984. "Mobilizing Local Resources in Developing Countries". *Public Administration and Development* 4: 215-233.

Bahl, Roy W., D. de Ferranti, and W. Dillinger. 1987. *"Financing Urban Local Governments in Developing Countries."* Paper Presented at the Second Congress of Local Authorities for Development of Human Settlements in Asia and the Pacific, June 29, Nagoya.

Behrendt, Richard F. 1965. *Soziale Strategie für Entwicklungsländer*. Frankfurt: Verlag Fischer.

Berg-Schlosser, Dirk. 1985. "Zu den Bedingungen von Demokratie in der Dritten Welt," in Franz Nuscheler, ed., *Dritte-Welt-Forschung. Entwicklungstheorie und Entwicklungspolitik*. Pp. 233-266. Opladen: Westdeutscher Verlag, Politische Vierteljahresschrift Sonderheft 16.

Byrne, Tony. 1981. *Local Government in Britain*. Harmondsworth: Penguin Books.

Calavan, Michael. 1984. "Appropriate Administration: Creating a Space where Local Initiative and Voluntarism Can Grow," in Robert F. Gorman, ed., *Private Voluntary Organizations as Agents of Development*. Pp. 215-247. London and Boulder: Westview Press.

Cheema, G. Shabbir. 1983. "The Role of Voluntary Organizations," in: G. Shabbir Cheema and Dennis A. Rondinelli, eds., *Decentralization and Development. Policy Implementation in Developing Countries*. Pp. 203-230. Beverly Hills, London, and New Delhi: Sage Publications.

Cheema, G. Shabbir and Mitsuhiko Hosaka, eds. 1983. *Administration of Regional and Local Government*. Nagoya: United Nations Centre for Regional Development.

Cheema, G. Shabbir and Dennis A. Rondinelli, eds. 1983. *Decentralization and Development. Policy Implementation in Developing Countries*. Beverly Hills, New Delhi, and London: Sage Publications.

Clark, Terry N. 1973. "Inputs and National Societal Characteristics: The Issue of Local Autonomy," in: Terry N. Clark, ed., *Community Power and Policy Outputs. A Review of Urban Research*. Pp. 5-11. Beverly Hills and London: Sage Publications.

Cochrane, Glynne. 1983. *Policies for Strengthening Local Government in Developing Countries*. Washington, D.C.: World Bank Staff Working Papers, No. 582.

Cohen, John M. and Norman Uphoff. 1980. "Participation's Place in Rural Development: Seeking Clarity through Specificity." *World Development* 8: 213-236.

Conyers, Diane. 1983. "Decentralization: the Latest Fashion in Development Administration." *Public Administration and Development* 3: 97-109.

_____ . 1984. "Decentralization and Development: a Review of the Literature." *Public Administration and Development* 4: 187-197.

_____ . 1986. "Decentralization and Development: A Framework for Analysis." *Community Development Journal* 21: 88-100.

Corfmat, F. 1985. "Computerisierung von Finanzverwaltungen in Entwicklungsländern." *Finanzierung und Entwicklung* 22: 45-47.

Dahl, Robert A. 1971. *Polyarchy. Participation and Opposition*. New Haven and London: Yale University Press.

Dahl, Robert A. and Charles E. Lindblohm. 1953. *Politics, Economics and Welfare. Planning and Politico-Economic Systems Resolved into Basic Social Processes*. New York, Evanston, and London: Harper & Row Publishers.

Davey, Kenneth. 1983. *Financing Regional Government: International Practices and their Relevance to the Third World*. Chichester: John Wiley.

Demaine, Harvey and Romana E. Malong, eds. 1987. *Decentralization: Area Development in Practice in Asia*. The Hague and Bangkok: Institute of Social Studies and Asian Institute of Technology.

Dillinger, William. 1988. *Urban Property Taxation in Developing Countries*. Washington, D.C.: The World Bank, Office of the Vice President, Development Economics, Background Paper.

Drewski, Lutz, Klaus Kunzmann, and Holger Platz. 1989. *Förderung von Mittel-städten. Ein Ansatz der Entwicklungszusammenarbeit.* Eschborn: Deutsche Ge-sellschaft für Technische Zusammenarbeit.

Dürr, Heiner and Rolf Hanisch. eds. 1986. *Südostasien. Tradition und Gegenwart.* Braunschweig: Westermann.

Dwyer, Denis J.. ed. 1972, *The City as a Centre of Change in Asia.* Hong Kong: University Press.

Easton, David. 1965. *A Systems Analysis of Political Life.* New York, London, and Sydney: John Wiley & Sons.

Esman, Milton E. and Norman Uphoff. 1984. *Local Organizations. Intermediaries in Rural Development.* Ithaca: Cornell University Press.

Evers, Hans-Dieter, ed. 1980. *Sociology of Southeast Asia. Readings on Social Change and Development.* Kuala Lumpur, Oxford, New York, Melbourne: Ox-ford University Press.

Faltas, Michael. 1981. *"The Changing Role of the State. Decentralization, Adminis-trative Reform and Technical Assistance: Trends and Prospects."* Paper Presented at the Development Policy Seminar for UNDP Executives, October 26-No-vember 6, The Hague.

_____. 1982. *"Decentralization and the Design of Planning Systems."* Paper Pre-sented to the Meeting of the D.S.A. Study Group on Regional Development and Planning at Nottingham University, March 5-6.

Fesler, J.W. 1968. "Centralization and Decentralization," in David L. Sills, ed., *In-ternational Encyclopedia of Social Sciences,* Vol. 2. Pp. 370-379. New York: MacMillan and The Free Press.

Friedman, Harry J. 1973. *Local Government in Third World Asia.* Morristown: Ge-neral Learning Press.

_____. 1980. "Other Asia," in Donald C. Rowat, ed., *International Handbook on Local Government Reorganization.* Pp. 458-469. London: Aldwych Press.

_____. 1983. "Decentralized Development in Asia," in Dennis A. Rondinelli and G. Shabbir Cheema, eds., *Decentralization and Development, Policy Imple-mentation in Developing Countries.* Pp. 35-57. Beverly Hills, New Delhi, and London: Sage Publications.

Fröbel, Folker, Jürgen Heinrichs, and Otto Kreye. 1977. *Die neue internationale Arbeitsteilung.* Reinbek: Rowohlt.

Girling, John L.S. 1981. *The Bureaucratic Polity in Modernizing Societies.* Singa-pore: Institute of Southeast Asian Studies Occasional Paper No. 64.

Goldblum, Charles. 1987. *Metropoles de L'Asie du Sud-Est, Strategies Urbaines et Politiques du Logement.* Paris: Éditions L'Harmattan.

Hackenberg, Robert A. 1980. "New Patterns of Urbanization in Southeast Asia: An Assessment." *Population and Development Review* 6: 391-419.

Hamer, Andrew M., Andrew D. Steer, David G. Willimas. 1986. *Indonesia. The Challenge of Urbanization.* Washington, D.C.: The World Bank.

Hampel, Rainer and Jürgen Rüland 1987. "Urbanization in the Third World: Growth without Development?" in Salim Nasr and Theodor Hanf, eds., *Ur-ban Crisis and Social Movements. Arab and European Perspectives.* Pp. 25-43. Beirut: The Euro-Arab Social Research Group.

Hanisch, Rolf, ed., 1983. *Soziale Bewegungen in Entwicklungsländern*. Baden-Baden: Nomos.

Hardoy, Jorge E. and D. Satterthwaite, eds. 1986. *Small and Intermediate Urban Centers. Their Role in National and Regional Development in the Third World*. London: Hodder & Stoughton.

Hauck Walsh, A. 1969. *The Urban Challenge to Government. An International Comparison of Thirteen Cities*. New York: Praeger.

Hennings, Gerd, Bernd Jenssen, and Klaus R. Kunzmann. 1978. *Dezentralisierung von Metropolen in Entwicklungsländern. Elemente einer Strategie zur Förderung von Entlastungsorten*. Dortmund: Institut für Raumplanung, Universität Dortmund.

Hicks, Ursula K. 1961. *Development from Below. Local Government and Finance in Developing Countries of the Commonwealth*. Oxford: Clarendon.

Hsueh, S.S. 1969. "Local Government and National Development in Southeast Asia." *International Social Science Journal* 21: 45-56.

Humes, Samuel and Eileen Martin. 1969. *The Structure of Local Government*. The Hague: Martinus Nijhoff.

Huntington, Samuel P. 1968. *Political Order in Changing Societies*. New Haven: Yale University Press.

_____. 1984. "Will more Countries Become Democratic?" *Political Science Quarterly*, Vol. 99, No. 2, pp. 190-214.

Huntington, Samuel P. and Joan M. Nelson. 1976. *No Easy Choice. Political Participation in Developing Countries*. Cambridge, Massachusetts, and London: Harvard University Press.

Illy, Hans F. 1982. "Some Basic Considerations with Respect to Local Government Reforms," in Korel Göymen, Hans F. Illy, and Winfried Veit, eds., *Local Administration: Democracy Versus Effciency?* Pp. 9-15. Bonn: Friedrich-Ebert-Stiftung.

_____. 1986c. "Dezentralisierung und Entwicklung. Anmerkungen zu einigen neueren Ansätzen," in Hans F. Illy and Klaus Schimitzek, eds., *Entwicklung durch Dezentralisierung?* Pp. 9-23. München: Minerva Publikation.

Illy, Hans F., Rüdiger Sielaff, and Nikolaus Werz. 1980. *Diktatur -- Staatsmodell für die Dritte Welt?* Freiburg and Würzburg: Ploetz, 1980.

Illy, Hans F. and Jürgen Rüland. 1984. "Kommunalpolitik in der Dritten Welt," in: Rüdiger Voigt, ed., *Handwörterbuch zur Kommunalpolitik*. Pp. 248-251. Opladen: Westdeutscher Verlag.

Illy, Hans F., Eugen Kaiser, and Jürgen Rüland. 1987. "Verwaltung," in Dieter Nohlen and Peter Waldmann, eds., *Pipers Wörterbuch zur Politik, Bd. 6, Dritte Welt*. Pp. 532-648. München: Piper.

Inkeles, Alex. 1969. "Participant Citizenship in Six Developing Countries." *American Political Science Review* 63: 1120-1141.

International Union of Local Authorities. 1979. *Die kommunalen Finanzen*. The Hague: International Union of Local Authorities.

_____. 1983. *The Local Council. A Collection of 32 National Reports and a Covering Commentary*. The Hague: International Union of Local Authorities.

Jones, Rodney W. 1975. *Urban Politics in India. Area, Power and Policy in a Penetrated System*. Delhi: Vikas.

Kammeier, H. Detlef and Peter J. Swan, eds. 1984. *Equity with Growth. Planning Perspectives for Small Towns in Developing Countries*. Bangkok: Asian Institute of Technology.

Kasfir, Nelson. 1983. "Designs and Dilemmas: An Overview" in Philip Mawhood, ed., *Local Government in the Third World. The Experience of Tropical Africa*. Pp. 25-48. Chichester: John Wiley.

Kornhauser, W. 1959. *The Politics of Mass Society*. Glencoe: The Free Press.

Korten, David C., ed. 1986. *Comunity Manangement. Asian Experience and Perspectives*. West Hartford: Kumarian Press.

Koyano, Shogo. ed. 1985. *Sociological Study of Urbanization in Southeast Asia*. Kyoto: International Joint Team for Overseas Scientific Surveys.

Leemans, Arne. 1970. *Changing Patterns of Local Government*. The Hague: International Union of Local Authorities.

Lehner, Franz. 1984. "Dezentralisierung," in Rüdiger Voigt, ed., *Handwörterbuch zur Kommunalpolitik*. p. 112-114. Opladen: Westdeutscher Verlag.

Linz, Juan J. 1970. "An Authoritarian Regime: Spain," in E. Allardt and Stein Rokkan, eds., *Mass Politics*. Pp. 251-283. New York and New Haven: The Free Press and Collier-MacMillan.

_____. 1975. "Totalitarian and Authoritarian Regimes," in Fred I. Greenstein and Nelson W. Polsby, eds., *Handbook of Political Science*. Pp. 175-411. Reading, Mass.: Addison-Wesley Publication.

Lockard, D. 1968. "Local Government," in David L. Sills, ed., *International Encyclopedia of Social Sciences, Vol. 2*. Pp. 451-459. New York: MacMillan and The Free Press.

Maass, Arthur R., ed. 1959. *Area and Power. A Theory of Local Government*. Glencoe: The Free Press.

Maddick, Henry. 1963. *Democracy, Decentralization and Development*. Bombay: Asia Publishing House.

Mahar, Dennis J. and William R. Dillinger. 1983. *Financing State and Local Government in Brazil. Recent Trends and Issues*. Washington, D.C.: World Bank Staff Working Papers No. 612.

Malo, Manasse and P.J.M. Nas. 1991. "Local Autonomy: Urban Management In Indonesia." *Social Issues in Southeast Asia* 6: 175-202.

Mathur, Kuldeep. 1983. "Administrative Decentralization in Asia," in G. Shabbir Cheema and Dennis A. Rondinelli, eds., *Decentralization and Development. Policy Implementation in Developing Countries*. Pp. 59-76. Beverly Hills, New Delhi, and London: Sage Publications.

Mathur, Om Prakash, ed. 1982. *Small Cities and National Development*. Nagoya: United Nations Centre for Regional Development.

Mawhood, Philip. 1974. "Negotiating from Weakness: the Search for a Model of Local Government in Countries of the Third World." *Planning and Administration* 1:17-32.

_____, ed. 1983. *Local Government in the Third World. The Experience of Tropical Africa*. Chichester: John Wiley.

_____. 1987. "Decentralization and the Third World in the 1980s." *Planning and Administration* 14: 10-22.

Muttalib, M.A. and M. Akbar Ali Khan. 1982. *Theory of Local Government.* New Delhi: Sterling.

Nassmacher, Hiltrud and Karl-Heinz Nassmacher. 1979. *Kommunalpolitik in der BRD.* Opladen: Leske Verlag & Budrich GmbH.

Nie, Norman H. and Sidney Verba. 1975. "Political Participation," in Fred I. Greenstein and Nelson W. Polsby, eds., *Handbook of Political Science, Vol. 4, Nongovernmental Politics.* Pp. 1-74. Reading, Mass: Addison Wesley Publication.

Nohlen, Dieter and Franz Nuscheler. 1982. "Was heißt Entwicklung?," in Dieter Nohlen and Franz Nuscheler, ed., *Handbuch der Dritten Welt. Unterentwicklung und Entwicklung: Theorien, Strategien, Indikatoren.* Pp. 48-72. Hamburg: Hoffmann und Campe.

Oberndörfer, Dieter. ed. 1977. *Kommunalverwaltung in Mittelamerika. Eine Studie über die Hauptstädte Guatemalas und El Salvadors.* Mainz: von Hase & Köhler GmbH.

Oberndörfer, Dieter and Wolfgang Jäger, eds. 1971. *Klassiker der Staatsphilosophie.* Stuttgart: K.F. Köhler Verlag.

Oberndörfer, Dieter and Jürgen Rüland. 1984. "Slum- und Squattersanierung in der Dritten Welt," in Michael von Hauff and Brigitte Pfister-Gaspary, eds., *Entwicklungspolitik. Probleme, Projektanalysen und Konzeptionen.* Pp. 219-243. Saarbrücken and Fort Lauderdale: Breitenbach Publishers.

O'Donnell, G.A. 1973. *Modernization and Bureaucratic Authoritarianism. Studies in South American Politics.* Berkeley: University of California Press.

Offe, Claus. 1975. "Zur Frage der Identität der kommunalen Ebene," in Rolf-Richard Grauhan, ed., *Lokale Politikforschung 2.* Pp. 303-309. Frankfurt and New York: Campus Verlag.

Pendakur, Setty V. 1984. *Urban Transport in ASEAN.* Singapore: Institute of Southeast Asian Studies.

Prakash, Ved. 1986. "Role and Structure of User Charges in Financing Urban Services in Developing Countries." *Regional Development Dialogue* 7: 1-31.

Prantilla, E.B., ed. 1988. *Financing Local and Regional Development in Developing Countries. Selected Country Experiences.* Nagoya: United Nations Centre for Regional Development.

Putnam, R.D. 1976. *The Comparative Study of Political Elites.* Englewood Cliffs: Prentice Hall.

Renaud, Bertrand. 1981. *National Urbanization Policy in Developing Countries.* New York: Oxford University Press.

Riggs, Fred W. 1959. "Economic Development and Local Administration: A Case Study in Circular Causation." *Philippine Journal of Public Administration* 3: 86-145, Special Issue on Local Government.

_____. 1964. *Administration in Developing Countries. The Theory of Prismatic Society.* Boston: Houghton Mifflin Company.

Rodenstein, Marianne. 1974. "Thesen zum Wandel der kommunalen Selbstver-
waltung in Deutschland," in Rainer Emenlauer, Herbert Grymer, Thomas
Krämer-Badoni, and Marianne Rodenstein, eds., *Die Kommune in der Staats-
organisation*. Pp. 35-71. Frankfurt: Suhrkamp Verlag.

Rondinelli, Dennis A. 1983a. *Secondary Cities in Developing Countries. Policies for
Diffusing Urbanization*. Beverly Hills, New Delhi, and London: Sage Publications.

_____ . 1990. "Decentralization. Territorial Power and the State: A Critical Response." *Development and Change* 21: 491-500.

Rondinelli, Dennis A. and G. Shabbir Cheema. 1983. "Implementing Decentralization Policies: An Introduction," in: Dennis A. Rondinelli and G. Shabbir
Cheema, eds., *Decentralization and Development. Policy Implementation in Developing Countries*. Pp. 9-34. Beverly Hills, New Delhi, and London: Sage
Publications.

Rostow, Walt W. 1960. *The Stages of Economic Growth*. Cambridge: Cambridge
University Press.

Rowat, Donald C., ed. 1980. *International Handbook on Local Government Reorganization*. London: Aldwych Press.

_____ . 1983. "The Centralizing Effect of Recent Local Government Reorgani-
zations." *Planning and Administration* 10: 64-67.

Rüland, Jürgen. 1985b. "Small Cities, Decentralization and Regionalization." *Internationales Asienforum* 16: 165-174.

_____ , ed. 1988a. *Urban Government and Development in Asia. Readings in Subnational Development*. Munich, Cologne, and London: Weltforum Verlag.

_____ . 1988b. "Urban Government in Southeast Asian Regional Cities: Issues
and Problems in Dispersing Urban Growth," in Jürgen Rüland, ed., *Urban
Government and Development in Asia. Readings in Subnational Development*. Pp.
54-121. Munich, Cologne, and London: Weltforum Verlag.

_____ . 1990. "Continuity and Change in Southeast Asia. Political Participation
in Three Intermediate Cities." *Asian Survey* 30: 461-480.

_____ . 1991. "Demokratisierung in Asien." *Aussenpolitik* 42: 281-289.

Rüland, Jürgen and Nikolaus Werz. 1991. "Mehr Chancen für Demokratie in der
Dritten Welt?" in Peter J. Opitz, ed., *Grundprobleme der Entwicklungsländer*.
Pp. 245-266. München: Verlag C.H. Beck.

Savelsberg, Joachim J. 1980. *Kommunale Autonomie. Gemeindeautonomie, Macht
und Entscheidungen in Gemeinden*. Frankfurt: Haag & Herchen.

_____ . 1982. "Macht in Gemeinden oder Macht über Gemeinden. Zur Relevanz
lokaler Autonomie für kommunale Machtstrukturen und Entscheidungs-
prozesse," in Klaus M. Schmals and Hans-Jörg Siewert, eds., *Kommunale
Macht- und Entscheidungsstrukturen*. Pp. 153-184. München: Minerva Publikation.

Schmidt, Einhard, ed. 1989. *Squatters' Struggles and Housing Policies in Asia. Experiences from Five Countries in Southeast and South Asia*. Dortmund: Institut
für Raumplanung, Universität Dortmund.

Schmitter, Philippe G. 1973. "The Portugalization of Brazil?," in Alfred Stephan, ed., *Authoritarian Brazil. Origins, Policies, and Future*. Pp. 179-232. New Haven and London: Yale University Press.

Schulz, Ann. 1979. *Local Politics and Nation State. Case Studies in Politics and Policy*. Santa Barbara: Clio Books.

Schumacher, Ernst F. 1977. *Die Rückkehr zum menschlichen Maß*. London: Rowohlt.

Scott, James C. 1969. "Corruption, Machine Politics and Political Change." *American Political Science Review* 63: 1142-1158.

———. 1972. "Patron-Client Politics and Political Change in Southeast Asia." *American Political Science Review* 66: 91-113.

Senghaas, Dieter. 1977. *Weltwirtschaftsordnung und Entwicklungspolitik. Plädoyer für Dissoziation*. Frankfurt: Suhrkamp Verlag.

———. 1982. *Von Europa lernen. Entwicklungsgeschichtliche Betrachtungen*. Frankfurt: Suhrkamp Verlag.

Sivaramakrishnan, K.C. and Lesley Green. 1986. *Metropolitan Management. The Asian Experience*. New York: Oxford University Press.

Smith, Brian C. 1985. *Decentralization. The Territorial Dimension of the State*. London: George Allen & Unwin.

Statistisches Bundesamt. 1985. *Datenreport. Zahlen und Fakten über die Bundesrepublik Deutschland*. Bonn: Bundeszentrale für politische Bildung.

Stöhr, Walter B. and Fraser D.R. Taylor, eds. 1981. *Development from Above or Below?*, Chichester: John Wiley.

Subramaniam, V. 1980. "Developing Countries," in Donald C. Rowat, ed., *International Handbook on Local Government Reorganization*. Pp. 583-593. London: Aldwych Press.

Symons, C., eds. 1984. *Comparative Local Government, Country Papers*. Mosman.

Tocqueville de, Alexis. 1976. *Über die Demokratie in Amerika*. München: Deutscher Taschenbuch Verlag.

Tolley, George S. and Vinod Thomas, eds. 1987. *The Economics of Urbanization and Urban Policies in Developing Countries*. Washington, D.C.: World Bank.

United Nations. 1970. *Administrative Aspects of Urbanization*. New York: United Nations.

United Nations Economic and Social Commission for Asia and the Pacific and National Institute of Development Administration. 1987. *Managing Intermediate Cities*. Bangkok: United Nations Economic and Social Commission for Asia and the Pacific and National Institute of Development Administration.

United Nations/Economic and Social Commission for Asia and the Pacific. 1982. *Regional Congress of Local Authorities for Development of Human Settlements in Asia and the Pacific*. Yokohama: United Nations/Economic and Social Commission for Asia and the Pacific.

Uphoff, Norman. 1986. *Local Institutional Development: An Analytical Sourcebook with Cases*. West Hartford: Kumarian Press.

Uphoff, Norman and Milton J. Esman. 1974. *Local Organization for Rural Development. Analysis of Asian Experiences*. Ithaca: Rural Development Committee, Cornell University, Special Series on Rural Local Government.

_____ . 1983. "Comparative Analysis of Asian Experience with Local Organization and Rural Development," in Norman Uphoff, ed., *Rural Development and Local Organization in Asia, Vol. II: East Asia.* Pp. 263-337. Delhi: MacMillan.

Vanhanen, Tatu. 1990. *The Process of Democratization: A Comparative Study of 147 States, 1980-1988.* New York: Crane Russak.

Walton, John. 1979. "Urban Political Movements and Revolutionary Change in the Third World." *Urban Affairs Quarterly* 15:3-22.

Walton, John and Louis H. Masotti, eds. *1976. The City in Comparative Perspective. Cross-National Research and New Directions in Theory.* New York: John Wiley.

Werlin, Herbert H. 1974. *Governing an African City. A Study of Nairobi.* New York and London: Africana Publishing Co.

Wirsing, Robert G. 1973. "Associational 'Micro-Arenas' in Indian Urban Politics." *Asian Survey* 13:408-420.

Wittfogel, Karl August. 1977. *Die Orientalische Despotie. Eine vergleichende Untersuchung totaler Macht.* Frankfurt: Ullstein.

World Bank. 1979. *Policies for Efficient and Equitable Growth of Cities in Developing Countries.* Washington, D.C.: The World Bank: Staff Working Paper No. 342.

Ylvisaker, Paul N. 1959. "Some Criteria for a 'Proper' Areal Division of Governmental Powers," in Arthur R. Maass, ed., *Area and Power. A Theory of Local Government.* Pp. 27-49. Glencoe: The Free Press.

You, Nicholas and Tomasz Sudra. 1988. "Innovative Experiences in Local Finance in South Asia." *Planning and Administration* 15: 34-43.

Zipfel, Horst C. 1982. "Demokratietheorie zwischen Norm und Wirklichkeit: Das Polyarchie-Konzept Robert A. Dahls." *Zeitschrift für Politik* 29: 376-398.

II. Malaysia

Abdul Karim bin Ineh. 1975. *"Restructuring of Local Authorities."* Paper Presented at the National Seminar on Local Government. Local Government Towards National Objectives, Kuala Lumpur, 30th June-4th July.

Abraham, Collin E.R. n.d. *"Impact of Low-Cost Housing on the Employment and Social Structure of Urban Communities: A Case Study of Penang."* Penang: Universiti Sains Malaysia, Mimeographed Article.

Ahmad Idris Mohd. Noor. 1975. *"Local Government and the Restructuring of Society."* Paper Presented at the National Seminar on Local Government. Local Government Towards National Objectives, Kuala Lumpur, 30th June-4th July.

Ahmad Mahdzan Ayob. 1985. *"An Agricultural Policy for Penang."* Paper Presented at the Convention on the Future of Penang, May 6-8, Penang.

Aliran Speaks. 1982. Penang: Aliran.

Anthony, James M. 1971." Urban Politics in Malaysia. A Study of Kuala Lumpur." Ph.D. Thesis, Australian National University, Canberra.

Asian Development Bank. 1985. *Malaysia Urban Sector Profile.* Manila: Asian Development Bank.

Barraclough, Simon. 1984. "Political Participation and its Regulation in Malaysia: Opposition to the Societies (Amendment) Act 1981." *Pacific Affairs* 57: 450-461.

_____. 1986. "A Re-Assessment of Political and Communal Factors in the Abolition of Elected Local Government in Malaysia." *Contemporary Southeast Asia* 8: 151-159.

Barrow, C.J. 1981. "Urbanization and Growth: Growth and Environmental Degradation in Penang (Georgetown)." *Third World Planning Review* 3: 407-418.

Bass, J. 1984. "Malaysia in 1983: A Time of Troubles." *Asian Survey* 24: 167-177.

Brookfield, Harold, Abdul Samad Hadi, and Zaharah Mahmud. 1991. *The City in the Village. The In-Situ Urbanization of Villages, Villagers and their Land around Kuala Lumpur, Malaysia.* Singapore, Oxford, New York: Oxford University Press.

Bruton, M.J. 1982. "The Malaysian Planning System." *Third World Planning Review* 4: 315-335.

_____. 1985. "Peninsular Malaysia. Conflict between Economic and Social Goals." *Cities* 2: 124-139.

Chahl, Lakhbir Singh. 1982. *"The Institutional Structure and Capabilities of Local Authorities in Metropolitan Areas of the ESCAP Region."* Paper Presented at the Regional Congress of Local Authorities for Development of Human Settlements in Asia and the Pacific, Yokohama, Japan.

_____. 1984. *"Urban Management in Penang."* Paper Presented at the Fourth IULA Large Cities Forum '84, October 30-November, Osaka.

_____. 1989. "Revitalizing the Harbour Front Area of Central George Town, Penang: A Collection and Analysis of the Socioeconomic and Physical Inventory Assets. *Regional Development Dialogue* 10: 59-84.

Chan, Paul. 1983. "The Political Economy of Urban Squatting in Metropolitan Kuala Lumpur." *Contemporary Southeast Asia* 4: 486-508.

Chee, K.L. 1978. *An Experiment in Local Property Taxation Reform.* Penang: Universiti Sains Malaysia, Centre for Policy Research.

Cheema, G. Shabbir. 1977. "Administrative Responses to Urbanization in Western Malaysia." *Journal of Administration in Overseas* 16: 240-247.

Cheema, G. Shabbir and Hussein, S.A. 1978. "Local Government Reform in Malaysia." *Asian Survey* 23: 577-591.

Chew, H.H. 1985. "Some Observations on Coalition Politics in Penang." *Modern Asian Studies* 19: 125-146.

Choo, E.G. 1970. "A Study of the Administrative Process of the City Council of Georgetown, Penang." BA Thesis, University of Malaya, Kuala Lumpur.

Commission of Enquiry to Enquire into the Affairs of the City Council of Georgetown, Penang, 31st December 1958 up to 30th June 1966. 1967. Alor Star: Government Printer.

Davies, Chris J. and Malcolm W. Norris. n.d. *"Kelang Town Council. A Functional and Financial Profile."* Klang: Mimeographed Paper.

Dewan Bandaraya Kuala Lumpur. 1982. *Kuala Lumpur Draft Structure Plan.* Kuala Lumpur: Dewan Bandaraya Kuala Lumpur.

Diaz, Ralph. 1982. "Restructuring Services to Reach the Urban Poor in Kuala Lumpur." *Assignment Children* 57/58: 135-156.

Doh Joh Chien. 1980. "Voluntary Organizations with Special Reference to Malaysia." *Prisma* 16: 44-50.

Economic and Social Commission of Asia and the Pacific. 1987. *City Monograph Kuala Lumpur*. Bangkok: Economic and Social Commission of Asia and the Pacific.

Evers, Hans-Dieter and Goh Ban Lee. 1976. *"Urban Landownership in Kota Bahru and Jeli, Kelantan."* Penang: Centre for Policy Research, Universiti Sains Malaysia, Project Paper No. 5.

Gale, Bruce. 1979. "'Restructuring' Malaysian Cities: The Politics of the Urban Development Authority." *Review of Indonesian and Malaysian Affairs* 13: 1-24.

_____, ed. 1986. *Readings in Malaysian Politics*. Petaling Jaya: Pelanduk Publications.

Georgulas, N. 1972. "Penang State: A Spatial Analysis. A Study of Existing and Potential Settlement Patterns." *Town Planning Review* 43: 361-378.

Goh Ban Lee. 1979. "Patterns of Landownership: Case Studies in Urban Inequalities," in K.C. Cheong, S.M. Khoo, and R. Thillainathan, eds., *Malaysia. Some Contemporary Issues in Socio-Economic Development*. Pp. 64-74. Kuala Lumpur.

_____. 1981. "Urban Landownership by Capital in Penang." Ph.D. Thesis, University of California, Los Angeles.

_____. 1985a. *"Evolution of Town Planning Praxis - Case Study of Penang."* Penang: Centre of Policy Research, Universiti Sains Malaysia, Mimeographed Paper.

_____. 1985b. *"Muddling Toward Better Urban Environment in Penang."* Paper Presented at the Convention on the Future of Penang, May 6-8, Penang.

_____. 1986a. *"The Role of Town Planners in a Peripheral Capitalist Society."* Paper Presented at the National Planning Conference, Penang, 9-10 September.

_____. 1986b. *"The Role of Conservation in Planning -- with Reference to Malaysian Cities."* Paper Presented at the International Conference on Urban Conservation and Planning, June 23-24, Penang.

_____. 1987. "Import of Urban Planning into Malaysia." *Planning History* 10: 7-12.

_____. 1988a. *"Urban Environmental Problems: A New Challenge to Local Governments in Malaysia. The Case of Penang Island,"* in Jürgen Rüland, ed., Urban Government and Development in Asia. Readings in Subnational Development. Pp. 209-236. Munich, Cologne, and London: Weltforum Verlag, pp. 209-236

_____. 1988b. "The Foundation of Urban Planning in George Town and Adelaide." *Kajian Malaysia* 6: 44-67.

Goh Ban Lee and Hans-Dieter Evers. 1978. "Urban Development and Local Landownership in Butterworth, Malaysia." *Journal of Southeast Asian Studies* 9: 28-49.

Goldstein, Sidney and Alice Goldstein. 1984. "Interrelations between Migration and Fertility: Their Significance for Urbanization in Malaysia." *Habitat* 8: 93-103.

Government of Malaysia. 1970. *Report of the Royal Commission of Enquiry to Investigate into the Workings of Local Authorities in West Malaysia.* Kuala Lumpur: Government Printer.

_____. 1986. *The Fifth Malaysia Plan 1986-1990.* Kuala Lumpur: National Printing Department.

Hamzah Abdul Majid. 1985. *"Towards a State Tourism Policy."* Keynote Adress Delivered at the Convention on the Future of Penang, May 6-8.

Ibrahim, Nik Hashim and Mohd. Yahya Nordin. 1984. "Local Government System in Malaysia," in K. Hanaoka, ed., *Comparative Study of the Local Public Administration in Asian and Pacific Countries.* Pp.146-168. Tokyo: Eastern Regional Organization of Public Administration, Local Government Center.

Johnstone, Michael. 1983. "Housing Policy and the Urban Poor in Peninsular Malaysia." *Third World Planning Review* 5: 249-271.

Johor Bahru/Pasir Gudang Structure Plan Study. n.d. Mimeographed Report.

Karim, Gulrose, ed. 1986. *Information Malaysia. 1986 Yearbook.* Kuala Lumpur: Berita Publishing Sdn. Bhd.

Kassim, Shamsuddin. 1986. "Toward Effective Delivery of Public Services at the Local Level: Restructuring of Local Government in Peninsular Malaysia," in Suchitra Punyaratabandhu-Bhakdi et al., eds., *Delivery of Public Services in Asian Countries. Cases in Development Administration.* Pp. 202-218. Bangkok: National Institute of Development Administration.

Khoo, T. C. 1987. "Private Participation in Public Services/Functions - Solid Waste Disposal," in National Institute of Public Administration et al., eds., *Course on Urban Finance and Management in East Asia, September 7 - October 2, 1987.* Kuala Lumpur: National Institute of Public Administration et al.

Khor Kok Peng. 1989. *Why Malaysia Has so far Failed to Meet Housing Needs of the Poor.* Penang: Consumers' Association of Penang and Southeast Asian Forum on Development Alternatives.

Kok, L.L. 1986. "Levels, Trends and Patterns of Urbanization in Peninsular Malaysia, 1957-1980," in Economic and Social Commission for Asia and the Pacific, ed., *Population of Malaysia, Country Monograph Series No. 13.* Pp. 53-72. New York: United Nations.

Kops, Manfred. 1989a. "Imbalances in the Vertical and Horizontal Distribution of the Local Revenues in Malaysia," in Ministry of Housing and Local Government, Malaysia, and Deutsche Gesellschaft für Technische Zusammenarbeit (GTZ) GmbH, eds., *Local Financial Equalization System, Proceedings of the Higher Level Seminar on Local Financial Equalization System, 5-6 September 1988, Cameron Highlands.* Kuala Lumpur: Ministry of Housing and Local Government.

_____. 1989b. "A Critical Look at the Present Intergovernmental Transfers in Malaysia," in Ministry of Housing and Local Government, Malaysia, and Deutsche Gesellschaft für Technische Zusammenarbeit (GTZ) GmbH, eds., *Local Financial Equalization System, Proceedings of the Higher Level Seminar on Local Financial Equalization System, 5-6 September, 1988, Cameron Highlands.* Kuala Lumpur: Ministry of Housing and Local Government.

Koschatzky, Knut. 1988. "Development of Industrial Systems in West Malaysia," in Ludwig H. Schätzl, ed., *Growth and Spatial Equity in West Malaysia*. Pp.98-168. Singapore: Institute of Southeast Asian Studies.

Krüger, Klaus. 1989. *Regionale Entwicklung in Malaysia*. Bern, New York, and Paris: Verlag Peter Lang.

Küchler, Johannes. 1968. *Penang: Kulturlandschaftswandel und ethnisch-soziale Struktur einer Insel Malaysias*. Gießen: Gießener Geographische Schriften.

Kühne, Dietrich. 1976. *Urbanisation in Malaysia. Analyse eines Prozesses*. Wiesbaden: Harrassowitz.

_____. 1986. *Vielvölkergesellschaft zwischen Dorf und Metropole. Fortentwicklung und neue Wege der Urbanisation in Malaysia (1970-1980)*. Wiesbaden: Harrassowitz.

Lau Lee Ching. 1978. "Urban Management in Malaysia. A Study of the Federal Territory." MA Thesis, University of Malaya, Kuala Lumpur.

Lee, B.T. 1983. "Planning and the Kuala Lumpur Metropolis." *The Asian Journal of Public Administration* 5: 76-86.

Lenz, Dieter. 1989. "Local Government Statistical System: Methodological Proceedings and Empirical Results," in Ministry of Housing and Local Government, Malaysia, and Deutsche Gesellschaft für Technische Zusammenarbeit (GTZ) GmbH, eds., *Local Financial Equalization System, Proceedings of the Higher Level Seminar on Local Financial Equalization System, 5-6 September 1988, Cameron Highlands*. Kuala Lumpur: Ministry of Housing and Local Government.

Lim, L. 1960. *The Municipal Government of Georgetown, Penang, 1946-1957*. Singapore.

Loh, T.L. 1982. "The Images of Malaysian Cities. A Case Study of Georgetown." Student Thesis, School of Housing, Building and Planning, Universiti Sains Malaysia, Penang.

Majlis Bandaraya Georgetown, Pulau Pinang. 1972-1979. *Annual Reports*. Penang: Majlis Bandaraya Georgetown.

Majlis Perbandaran Ipoh. 1984. *Report of Survey, Ipoh Structure Plan*. Ipoh: Majlis Perbandaran Ipoh.

Majlis Perbandaran Pulau Pinang, Municipal Council of Penang Island. 1981. *Epitome of Accounts and General Financial Statistics, 31st December*. Penang: Majlis Perbandaran Pulau Pinang.

Majlis Perbandaran Pulau Pinang. 1982. *Municipal Council of Penang Island, Epitome of Accounts and General Financial Statistics for the Year End, 31st December*. Penang: Majlis Perbandaran Pulau Pinang.

_____. 1985. *Report of Survey. Penang Island Structure Plan*. Penang: Majlis Perbandaran Pulau Pinang.

Mauzy, Diane K. 1984. "Malaysia," in: Diane K. Mauzy, ed., *Politics in the ASEAN States*. Pp. 138-185. Kuala Lumpur: Maricans.

Mauzy, Diane K. and R.S. Milne. 1983-1984. "The Mahatir Administration in Malaysia: Discipline through Islam." *Pacific Affairs* 56:617-648.

Means, Gordon P. 1970. *Malaysian Politics*. London: University of London Press.

_____. 1991. *Malaysian Politics. The Second Generation.* Singapore, Oxford, New York: Oxford University Press.

Meerman, J. 1979. "Public Services for Basic Needs in Malaysia." *World Development* 7: 615-634.

Milne, Robert S. and Diane K. Mauzy. 1980. *Politics and Government in Malaysia.* Singapore: Times Book International.

Mohamed Talha bin Haji Alithamby. 1985. *"An Urbanization and Environmental Policy for Penang."* Paper Presented at the Convention on the Future of Penang, May, 6-8, Penang.

Mohd. Yusof bin Hashim. 1985. *"An Overview of Current and Future Potential of Agricultural Development in Penang."* Paper Presented at the Convention on the Future of Penang, May 6-8, Penang.

Muhammed Ikhbal bin Md. Hamzah. 1985. *"A State Tourism Policy."* Paper Presented at the Convention on the Future of Penang, May 6-8.

Nathan, Robert R. and Associates. 1970. *Penang Master Plan. The Resource Base and the Socio-Economic Programme.* Penang: Mimeographed Report.

Negri Pulau Pinang. n.d.. *Report of the Auditor General 1969-1986.* Penang: Negri Pulau Pinang.

Noh bin Haji Abdullah. 1975. *"Local Government Finance with Special Reference to Lembaga Pengurus Kerajaan Tempatan Seberang Perai."* Paper Presented at the National Seminar on Local Government Towards National Objectives, 30th June-4h July, Kuala Lumpur.

Norris, Malcolm W. 1974. "Local Government in West Malaysia - The Royal Commission Report and After." *Studies of Comparative Local Government* 8: 5-21.

_____. 1978. *Recent Malaysian Reform.* London: University of London. A Revival of Local Government and Administration. Collected Seminar Papers No. 13.

_____. 1979. "Local Government Reform in Malaysia." *IDS Bulletin* 10: 47-51.

_____. 1980. *Local Government in Malaysia.* Aldershot: Gower.

Oestereich, Jürgen. 1978. "Städtische Entwicklungssteuerung als Illusion." *Internationales Asienforum* 9:131-154.

Osborn, J. 1974. *Area, Development Policy and the Middle City in Malaysia.* Chicago: University of Chicago, Dept. of Geography, Research Paper No. 153.

Penang Development Corporation. 1986. "Penang Looks to 21st Century." *Penang Development News* 2: 1-6.

Penang Island Structure Plan: An Aliran Analysis 1986. *Aliran Monthly* 6: 14-15.

Phang Siew Nooi. 1978. "Administration of Urban Redevelopment in Penang: The Case of the Penang Urban Centre." MA Thesis, University of Malaya, Kuala Lumpur.

_____. 1982. "The Relationship between the State and Local Government in West Malaysia. The Case of Penang Island Municipal Council." *Planning and Administration* 9: 66-73.

_____. 1985. "The Aftermath of Local Government Restructuring in West Malaysia: The Experience of the Penang Island and Klang Municipalities." Ph.D. Thesis, University of Birmingham, Birmingham.

_____ . 1987. "Local Government Reform - A Comparative Study of Selected Countries in Africa and Southeast Asia." *Planning and Administration* 14: 31-38.

_____ . 1988. "Municipal Councils in Peninsular Malaysia after Restructuring. Issues and Problems," in Jürgen Rüland ed., *Urban Government and Development in Asia. Readings in Subnational Development.* Pp. 167-186. Munich, Cologne, and London: Weltforum Verlag.

_____ . 1989. *Sistem Kerajaan Tempatan di Malaysia.* Kuala Lumpur: Dewan Bahasa dan Pustaka Kementerian Pendidikan Malaysia.

_____ . 1990." Issues and Problems in Local Government Management -- Improving Local Government Performance." *Jurnal Produktiviti* 9: 30-41.

Phang Siew Nooi, Stephen Chee, and Siti Rohani Yahya. 1989. "Local Authority Functions and Service Performance," in Ministry of Housing and Local Government, Malaysia, and Deutsche Gesellschaft für Technische Zusammenarbeit (GTZ) GmbH, eds., *Local Finance Equalization System, Proceedings of the Higher Level Seminar on Local Financial Equalization System, 5-6 September, Cameron Highlands.* Kuala Lumpur: Ministry of Housing and Local Government.

Philip, P. 1984. "Planning in the Public Service." *Journal JPBD Lembaga Penyunting* 1: 13-19.

Pillai, S. and H. Tan. 1985. *"Financial Management of Municipal Councils."* Kuala Lumpur: Ministry of Housing and Local Government.

Quah, H.C. 1970. "The City Council of Georgetown and its Finance." BA Thesis, University of Malaya, Kuala Lumpur.

Rabushka, Alvin. 1968. "Ethnic Components of Political Integration in Two Malaysia Cities." Ph.D. Thesis, Washington University, Seattle.

_____ . 1970. "A Note on Overseas Chinese Political Participation in Urban Malaya." *American Political Science Review* 64: 177-178.

Rachagan, S. 1980. "The Development of the Electoral System," in: Harold Crouch, H., K.H. Lee, and M. Ong, eds., *Malaysian Politics and the 1978 Election.* Pp. 235-292. Kuala Lumpur: Oxford University Press.

Report on the Introduction of Elections in the Municipality of Georgetown, Penang 1951. 1953. Kuala Lumpur: Government Printer.

Sadasivan, N. 1986. "Towards a State Industrial and Trade Policy." Paper Presented at the Convention on the Future of Penang, May 6-8, Penang.

Schätzl, Ludwig H. ed. 1988. *Growth and Spatial Equity in West Malaysia.* Singapore: Institute of Southeast Asian Studies.

Schmidt, Einhard. 1979. *Raumplanung in Malaysia. Imperialistische und nationale Einflüsse auf räumliche Planung in einem Land der Dritten Welt.* Bochum: Studienverlag Brockmeyer.

Scott, James C. 1968. *Political Ideology in Malaysia: Reality and Beliefs of an Elite.* Kuala Lumpur: University of Malaya Press.

Selangor State Government and Klang Valley Planning Authority. 1986. *Klang Draft Structure Plan 1986-2005. Statement of Policies and Proposals.* Klang: Selangor State Government and Klang Valley Planning Authority.

Seremban Municipal Council. 1986. *Draft Seremban Structure Plan.* Seremban: Seremban Municipal Council.

Saari bin Abdul Rahman, "Basic Composition of Population," in United Nations Economic and Social Commission for Asia and the Pacific, eds., *Population of Malaysia. Country Monograph Series No. 13.* Pp. 7-20. New York: United Nations.

Shafruddin, B.H. 1987. *The Federal Factor in the Government and Politics of Peninsular Malaysia.* Singapore: Oxford University Press.

Singh, C. 1974. *"Urbanization -- Penang's Strategy."* Paper Presented at the Seminar on Urbanization and Urban Renewal, 25th and 26th October.

Singh, C. and P.H. Cheah. 1974. *"The Penang Urban Center Project. A Strategy of Urban Development."* Paper Presented at the Joint ECAFE/IULA Regional Seminar on Local Government Finance, August 12-17, Penang.

Singh, Gurmit K.S. 1984. *Malaysian Societies. Friendly or Political?* Petaling Jaya: Environmental Protection Society Malaysia, Selangor Graduates Society.

Smith, T.E. 1960. "The Malayan Elections of 1959." *Pacific Affairs* 33: 38-47.

_____ . 1961. "The Local Authority Elections 1961 in the Federation of Malaya." *Journal of Commonwealth Political Studies* 1: 153-155.

Snider, Nancy L. 1968. "What Happened in Penang?" *Asian Survey* 8: 960-975.

Tan, S.H. 1976. "Financing of Penang State, 1960-1972. An Enquiry into Malaysian Federal-State Fiscal Relationship." MA Thesis, Universiti Sains Malaysia, Penang.

Tan, Simon. 1990. "The Rise of State Authoritarianism in Malaysia." *Bulletin of Concerned Asian Scholars* 22:32-42.

Teng, W.C. 1978/79. "Local Government in Penang. A Study to Assess the Changes Brought About by the Local Government Act 1976." BA Thesis, Faculty of Law, University of Malaya, Kuala Lumpur.

Tennant, Paul. 1973a. "The Abolition of Elective Local Government in Penang." *Journal of Southeast Asian Studies* 4: 72-87.

_____ . 1973b. "The Decline of Elective Local Government in Malaysia." *Asian Survey* 13: 347-365.

Thean Lip Shien. n.d.. *"Local Government in Peninsular Malaysia."* Kuala Lumpur: National Institute of Public Administration, Mimeographed Paper.

Thillainathan, R. 1985. *"State Governments Consolidated Finance. Trends and Implications."* Paper Presented at the Convention on the Future of Penang, May 6-8, Penang.

Tilman, Robert O. 1976. *The Centralization Theme in Malaysian Federal State Relations 1957-1975.* Singapore: Institute of Southeast Asian Studies, Occasional Paper No. 39.

University of Birmingham, Institute of Local Government Studies. 1973. *"Case Study of the Committee System of Management in Ipoh Municipal Council: Malaysia."* Birmingham: Institute of Local Government Studies, University of Birmingham Mimeographed Research Paper.

Vasil, R.K. 1971. *Politics in a Plural Society. A Study od Non-Communal Political Parties in West Malaysia.* Kuala Lumpur and London: Oxford University Press.

_____ . 1980. *Ethnic Politics in Malaysia.* New Delhi: Radiant Publication.

Veloo, S. n.d. *"Some Aspects of Local Government Reforms in Malaysia."* Kuala Lumpur: Ministry of Housing and Local Government, Mimeographed Paper.

Wolff, Jürgen H. 1989. *Stadtplanung in Kuala Lumpur: Politik und Verwaltung in einer pluralen Gesellschaft.* Frankfurt, Bern, New York, Paris: Verlag Peter Lang.

World Bank. 1988. *Malaysia. Municipal Services Review Mission. Final Aide Memoire.* Washington, D.C.: World Bank.

Yeoh, P.S. 1985. *"A Look at Penang's Industrialization from a Business Perspective."* Paper Presented at the Convention on the Future of Penang, May 6-8, Penang.

Zahari, A.R. 1974. "The Path of Local Government in West Malaysia." MA Thesis, University of Birmingham, Birmingham.

Zainol bin Mahmood 1975. *"Local Government and the Eradication of Poverty."* Paper Presented at the National Seminar on Local Government, Local Government Towards National Objectives, 30th June-4th July, Kuala Lumpur.

III. Philippines

Abiado-Gicole, T. 1981. *Socio-Demographic Characteristics and Fertility Behavior of Slum Dwellers in Iloilo City.* Cagayan de Oro City: SEAPRAP Research Report No. 75.

Abrera, Ma. Alcestis. 1976. "Philippine Poverty Thresholds," in Mahar Mangahas, ed., *Measuring Philippine Development. Report of the Social Indicators Project.* Pp. 223-274. Manila: Development Academy of the Philippines.

Aklat-Gabay ng Barangay. 1978. *Katipunan ng mga Barangay ng Metropolitan Manila Manual.* Manila: Katipunan ng mga Barangay ng Metropolitan Manila.

Aldon, C. et al. 1982. "Some Changes and Developments in the Local Governments in the Transitional Period." *Philippine Law Journal* 54: 121-135.

Aquino, Belinda A. 1977. *"Politics in the 'New Society': Barangay 'Democracy'."* Paper Presented at the Annual Meeting of the Association of Asian Studies, New York City.

_____ . 1977/78. "Dimensions of Decentralization: The Philippine Case." *Journal of Asian Pacific and World Perspective* 1: 47-62.

Asian Institute of Tourism. 1984. *Survey on Tourism in Iloilo Province, Region VI.* Manila: Asian Institute of Tourism.

Bacani, R.C. 1981. Framework of Regional Development Policies, in: *Philippine Budget Management,* 3: 41-59.

Bacolod City. 1985. *Socio-Economic Profile.* Bacolod City: City Government of Bacolod.

Bagatsing, Ramon D. 1978. "A Critical Study of the Metropolitan Manila Government." Ph.D. Thesis , Santo Tomas University, Manila.

Bahl, Roy W. and Barbara D. Miller, eds. 1983. *Local Government Finance in the Third World. A Case Study of the Philippines*. New York: Praeger.

Bello, Walden, D. Kinley, and E. Ellison. 1982. *Development Debacle: The World Bank in the Philippines*. San Francisco: Institute for Food and Development Policy.

Benitez, Teresa V. 1969. *The Politics of Marawi*. Manila: University of the Philippines.

Benson, L.P. 1970. "Political Leadership through Political Liders: A New Approach for the Analysis of Philippine Provincial Leadership Positions." Ph.D. Thesis, University of Hawaii, Honolulu.

Bernabe, Daisy G. 1969. "National Government Controls Affecting Cities: Some Issues and Problems." M.A. Thesis, University of the Philippines, Manila.

_____. 1969. *Philippine City Charters: A Formal Comparison*. Quezon City: University of the Philippines.

Berner, Erhard. 1989. *"Clubs and Associations in a Philippine Small Town -- Social Funtions and Political Significance."* Paper Presented at the IXth Bielefeld Colloquium on Southeast Asia, "Lowland Christian Filipino Civilization."

Brillantes, Alex. 1987. "Decentralization in the Philippines: An Overview." *Philippine Journal of Public Administration* 31:131-148

Bronger, Dirk. 1979. *Die Industrie der Philippinen. Geschichte, Struktur, Entwicklungsprobleme*. Hamburg: Mitteilungen des Instituts für Asienkunde No. 108.

_____. 1987. *Die Philippinen. Raumstrukturen, Entwicklungsprobleme, Regionale Entwicklungsplanung*. Hamburg: Mitteilungen des Instituts für Asienkunde No. 159.

Calaguio, H. 1982. "Financial Administration in the Metropolitan Manila Commission: Options for Development." M.A. Thesis, University of the Philippines, Manila.

Canoy, Reuben R. 1980. *The Counterfeit Revolution. Martial Law in the Philippines*. Manila: Philippine Editions Publishing.

Caoili, Manuel A. 1972. *Central Government Grants to Local Governments: A Comparative Study of England and Wales, the Netherlands and the Philippines*. Manila: College of Public Administration.

_____. 1985. "Reflections on Metropolitan Manila Reorganization and Social Change." *Philippine Journal of Public Administration* 29: 1-26.

_____. 1988. *The Origins of Metropolitan Manila. A Political and Social Analysis*. Quezon City: New Day Publishers.

Carbonell-Catilo, Ma. Aurora et al. 1985. *Manipulated Elections*. Manila: College of Public Administration, University of the Philippines.

Carino, Ledivina V. and Wilfredo B. Carada. 1990. *Philippinen. Verwaltungsprofile*. Eschborn: Deutsche Gesellschaft für Technische Zusammenarbeit.

Casalmo, Felix. 1980. *The Vision of a New Society*. Manila.

City Government of Davao. 1979. *Comprehensive Development Plan of Davao City*. Davao City: City Government of Davao.

City of Cagayan de Oro. 1986. *Socio-Economic Profile, 1983-'84-'85*. Cagayan de Oro City: City Government of Cagayan de Oro.

City of Iloilo. 1980. *Socio-Economic Profile*. Iloilo City: City Government of Iloilo.

_____ . 1984. *Annual Report*. Iloilo City: City Government of Iloilo.

_____ . 1985. *Socio-Economic and Physical Profile*. Iloilo City: City Government of Iloilo.

City Planning and Development Board and City Planning and Development Office. 1979. *A Profile of Davao City*. Davao City: City Planning and Development Staff.

Clemente II, Wilfedo A. 1974. "Philippine Bureaucracy and Local Development: The Case of Two Municipalities." Ph.D. Thesis, University of Connecticut.

Clemente II, Wilfredo A. and C. Fernandez 1972. "Philippine Corruption at the Local Level." *Solidarity* 7: 75-81.

College of Public Administration. 1973. *Handbook on City Government and Administration*. Manila: College of Public Administration, University of the Philippines.

Cordero, Rosa R. and Jocelyn R. Santiago. 1990. "Local Government Finance." *Local Government Bulletin* 25: 23-28.

Cullinane, Michael. n.d. "Implementing the 'New Order'. The Structure and Supervision of Local Government During the Taft Era," in Norman G. Owen, ed., *Compadre Colonialism: Studies on the Philippines under American Rule*. Pp. 9-34. Manila: Solidaridad.

David, Randolph S. 1984. "Crisis and Transformation: The Philippines in 1984." *New Asian Visions* 1: 3-22.

Day, Beth. 1974. *The Philippines. Shattered Showcase of Democracy in Asia*. New York: M. Evans & Company, Inc.

Dillinger, William. 1988. "*Urban Property Tax Reform. The Case of the Philippines' Real Property Tax Administration Project*." Washington, D.C.: The World Bank, Policy Planning and Research Staff, Discussion Paper.

Doronila, A. 1985. "The Transformation of Patron-Client Relations and its Political Consequences in Postwar Philippines." *Journal of Southeast Asian Studies* 16: 99-117.

Espina, G.S. 1984. *Philippine Constitution and Government*. Quezon City: Panamao Publications.

Firmalino, T. 1980. "Plan Implementation: A Case Study of Angeles City." *Philippine Planning Journal* 11: 1-7.

Gabot, Alfedo G. 1975. *Manila Directory and Barangay Guidebook*. Manila.

Government of the Republic of the Philippines. 1979. *Regional Cities Development Project. Metropolitan Cebu*. London: Government of the Republic of the Philippines.

Government of the Republic of the Philippines and International Bank for Reconstruction and Development. 1982a. *Regional Cities Development Project. Project Preparation Stage. Draft Final Executive Summary*. Iloilo City: Government of the Republic of the Philippines and International Bank for Reconstruction and Development.

_____ . 1982b. *Regional Cities Development Project. Project Preparation Stage. Draft Final Report on Shelter, Iloilo City, Vol. 1*. Iloilo City: Government of the Republic of the Philippines and International Bank for Reconstruction and Development.

Gozun-Laureta, A. 1982. "The Impact of Inter-Governmental Transfers on Local Government Finance." Ph.D. Thesis. College of Public Administration, University of the Philippines, Manila.

Guzman, Raul P. de. 1966. "Local Government: Issues, Problems and Trends." *Philippine Journal of Public Administration* 10: 231-241. Special Issue on Local Government and Development.

Guzman, Raul P. de and Proserpina D. Tapales. 1973. *Philippine Local Government: Issues, Problems and Prospects*. Quezon City: Local Government Center, University of the Philippines.

Guzman, Raul P. de and Associates. 1977. "Citizen Participation and Decision-Making under Martial Law Administration: A Search for a Viable Political System." *Philippine Journal of Public Administration* 21: 1-19.

Guzman, Raul P. de and Ma. Aurora Carbonell. 1978. "Toward Meaningful Partnership in Government: Citizen Participation Mechanism at the Local Levels." *Local Government Bulletin* 13: 3-8. Special Issue.

Guzman, Raul P. de and Ric Tan Legarda. 1984. "Local Governments in the Philippines," in: Keiso Hanaoka, ed., *Comparative Study on the Local Public Administration in Asia and Pacific Countries*. Pp. 180-205. Tokyo: Eastern Regional Organization of Public Administration, Local Government Center.

Guzman, Raul P. de and Luz G. Tancangco. 1986. *An Assessment of the May 1984 Batasang Pambansa Elections: A Summary of Findings*. Manila: College of Public Administration. University of the Philippines.

Guzman, Raul P. de, Mila R. Reforma, and Elena M. Panganiban. 1988. "Local Government," in Raul P. de Guzman and Mila R. Reforma, eds., *Government and Politics of the Philippines*. Pp. 207-240. Singapore, Oxford, and New York: Oxford University Press.

Hanisch, Rolf. 1982. *Probleme und Perspektiven des Kleinbauernkredites im Reissektor der Philippinen*. Frankfurt: Alfred Metzner Verlag.

⎯⎯⎯⎯. 1989. *Philippinen*. München: Beck.

Hollnsteiner, Mary Racelis. 1963. *The Dynamics of Power in a Philippine Municipality*. Quezon City: Community Development Research Council.

Illy, Hans F., Eugen Kaiser, and Klaus Schimitzek. 1988. *Lokale Verwaltungsinstitutionen und Selbsthilfemaßnahmen in Entwicklungsländern. Problemaufriß, Fallstudien, Ansatzpunkte für die entwicklungspolitische Förderung*. Munich, Cologne, and London: Weltforum Verlag.

Iloilo City. 1974. *Socio-Economic Profile*. Iloilo City: City Government of Iloilo.

⎯⎯⎯⎯. 1977. *City Profile*. Iloilo City: City Government of Iloilo.

Integrated Research Center, De La Salle University. 1983. *The Delivery of Basic Services in Three Selected Urban Centers: Implications for a Participatory Management Model*. Manila: De La Salle University.

Javier, E.P. 1976. "Economic, Demographic and Political Determinants of the Regional Allocation of Government Infrastructure Expenditure in the Philippines." *Journal of Philippine Development* 3: 281-312.

Landé, Carl H. 1965. *Leaders, Factions and Parties. The Structure of the Philippines*. New Haven: Yale University, Southeast Asia Studies Monograph Series No. 6, Southeast Asia Studies.

_____ . 1971. "Party Politics in the Philippines," in: George M. Guthrie, ed., *Six Perspectives on the Philippines*. Pp. 85-132. Manila, Makati, Cebu: Bookmark.

_____ . 1973. *Southern Tagalog Voting, 1946-1973. Political Behavior in a Philippine Region*. Chicago: Northern Illinois University, Sepcial Report No. 7

Laquian, Aprodicio A. 1965. "Politics in Metropolitan Manila." *Philippine Journal of Public Administration* 9: 331-342.

_____ . 1966. *The City in Nation Building. Politics and Administration in Metropolitan Manila*. Manila: School of Public Administration, University of the Philippines.

_____ . 1971. *Slums are for the People: The Barrio Magsaysay Pilot Project in the Philippine Urban Community Development*. Honolulu: East-West-Center Press.

Laquian, Aprodicio A. and R.M. Pangilinan. 1968. *The 1963 Elections in Manila: A Study of the Recruitment of Political Leaders and its Relation to Administration*. Manila: College of Public Administration, University of the Philippines.

Leichter, Howard M. 1975. *Political Regime and Public Policy in the Philippines: A Comparison of Bacolod and Iloilo Cities*. DeKalb: Center for Southeast Asian Studies, Northern Illinois University, Special Report, No. 11.

_____ . 1976. "Politics and Policy in Two Philippine Cities." *Comparative Political Studies* 8: 379-412.

Liem Ngo-Huy. 1982. *Ausländische Privatinvestitionen auf den Philippinen. Voraussetzungen und Auswirkungen auf die sozialökonomische Entwicklung. Eine Fallstudie*. München and Mainz: Kaiser und Grünewald.

Local Government Center. 1986. *National Seminar on the Administration of the Metropolis and Highly Urbanized Cities. November 4-6*. Manila: College of Public Administration, University of the Philippines.

Lopez-Gonzaga, Violeta B. 1985. *Crisis in Sugarlandia: The Case of Bacolod*. Bacolod: La Salle Social Research Center.

Lopez-Nerney, S., M.E. Chiong-Javier, and C. Montiel. 1976. *Socio-Economic Profiles of Six Selected Towns*. Quezon City: Ateneo de Manila University, Institute of Philippine Culture.

Machado, Kit G. 1972a. "Leadership and Organization in Philippine Local Politics." Ph.D. Thesis, University of Washington, Seattle.

_____ . 1972b. "Changing Patterns of Leadership Recruitment and the Emergence of the Professional Politician in Philippine Local Politics." *Philippine Journal of Public Administration* 16: 147-169.

_____ . 1973/74. "From Traditional Faction to Machine: Changing Patterns of Political Leadership and Organization in the Rural Philippines." *Journal of Asian Studies* 33: 523-547.

Mariano, L.C. 1958a. "Congress and Local Autonomy." *Philippine Journal of Public Administration* 2: 363-378.

_____ . 1958b. "The Supreme Court and Local Autonomy." *Philippine Journal of Public Administration* 2: 38-53.

Martir, Rolando L. 1990. "League of Governors Elect New Officers." *Local Government Bulletin* 25: 11.

McCoy, Alfred W. 1977. "Ylo-ilo: Factional Conflict in a Colonial Economy, Iloilo Province, Philippines, 1937-1955." Ph.D. Thesis, Yale University, New Haven.

_____ . 1982. "A Queen Dies Slowly: The Rise and Decline of Iloilo City," in Alfred W. McCoy and Edilberto C. de Jesus, eds., *Philippine Social History. Global Trade and Local Transformations*. Pp. 297-356. Manila and Sydney: Ateneo de Manila University Press.

Ministry of Finance and National Tax Resource Center. 1982. *A Study on Local Government, 7 Vols.* Manila: Ministry of Finance and National Tax Resource Center.

Ministry of Human Settlements. 1978. *Settlement Profiles*. Manila: Ministry of Human Settlements.

Ministry of Public Works, Republic of the Philippines, COWI Consult. 1979. *Regional Cities Development Project, Davao*. Manila: Ministry of Public Works.

Ministry of Public Works, Republic of the Philippines, Regional Cities Development Project. 1979. *Iloilo and Bacolod, Project Identification, Draft Research, Volume 2*. Manila: Ministry of Public Works.

National Census and Statistics Office. 1974. *1970 Census of Population and Housing, Final Report, Vol. 1*. Manila: National Census and Statistics Office.

_____ . 1981. *"Office of the Executive Director, Special Release,"* Manila, June 12.

National Economic and Development Authority. 1978. *Iloilo City Industrial Estate Project, Prefeasibility Report*. Iloilo City: National Economic and Development Authority.

_____ . 1983. *Regional Profile, Region VI*. Manila: National Economic and Development Authority.

Nimsdorf, Udo, ed. 1988. *Anatomie einer Revolution. Herrschaft, Krise und Umbruch in den Philippinen*. Saarbrücken and Fort Lauderdale: Breitenbach Publishers.

Oberndörfer, Dieter. 1979. *Strukturdaten zum Squattergebiet Tondo/Manila. Beschreibung und Analyse der amtlichen Förderungsmaßnahmen in dieser Region*. Freiburg: Arnold-Bergstraesser-Institut.

Ocampo, Romeo B. 1963. "The Reorganization Program of Quezon City: Mayor-City Council Relations in the Formulation and Implementation of Reform Policy." *Philippine Journal of Public Administration* 7: 184-219.

_____ . 1982. *Low-Cost Transport in Asia. A Comparative Report on Five Cities*. Ottawa: International Development Research Centre.

Ocampo, Romeo B. and Elena M. Panganiban. 1985. *The Philippine Local Government System. History, Politics and Finance*. Manila: Local Government Center, College of Public Adminitration, University of the Philippines.

Paderanga, C.W. Jr. 1984. *Real Property Taxation in the Philippines: Issues and Research Directions*. Manila: Philippine Institute for Development Studies, Staff Paper Series No. 84-01.

Padilla, Perfecto L. 1990. *Need for a Truly Meaningful, more Substantive Decentralization and Local Autonomy*. Manila: College of Public Administration, University of the Philippines.

Pernia, Ernesto M., C.W. Paderanga Jr., V.P. Hermoso, and Ass. 1980. *The Spatial and Urban Dimensions of Development in the Philippines*. Manila: Philippine Institute for Development Studies.

Pertierra, Raul. 1987. "An Anthropological Perspective on Philippine Politics," in Peter Krinks, ed., *The Philippines under Aquino*. Pp. 115-133. Canberra: Australian Development Studies Network.

Phelan, John Leddy. 1973. *The Hispanization of the Philippines*. Mandaluyong: Cacho Hermanos, Inc., Filipiana Reprint Series.

Philippines, Office of the President. 1984. *Accomplishment Report for the Period 1978-1983/84. Province of Iloilo*. Manila: Office of the President.

Prantilla, E.B., R.C. Bacani, and Y.A. Choong. 1986. "Problems and Strategies of Financing Sub-National Development: The Case of the Philippines and the Republic of Korea." *Regional Development Dialogue* 7: 157-184.

Provincial Planning and Development Office, Province of Iloilo. 1983. *Socio-Economic Profile*. Iloilo City: Provincial Planning and Development Office, Province of Iloilo.

Ramos-Jimenez, Pilar, Ma. Elena Chiong, and Judy Carol C. Sevilla. 1988. "The Poor in Philippine Cities. A Situation Analysis." *Social Issues in Southeast Asia* 3: 79-89.

Regional Cities Development Project. 1979. *Financial Study*. Manila: Government of the Republic of the Philippines and International Bank for Reconstruction and Development.

Regional Cities Development Project. 1980. *Municipal Management Study*. Manila: Government of the Republic of the Philippines and International Bank for Reconstruction and Development.

Republic of the Philippines, City of Iloilo. 1977. *Comprehensive Urban Development Plan 1977-2000*. Iloilo City: City Government of Iloilo.

Republic of the Philippines, Commission on Audit. 1985. *1984 Annual Financial Report, Local Governments (Provinces, Cities and Municipalities)*. Manila: Commission on Audit.

Republic of the Philippines, Commission on Elections. 1956. *Report of the Commission on Elections to the President of the Philippines and the Congress on the Manner the Elections were held on November 8, 1955*. Manila: Commission on Elections.

_____ . 1960. *Report of the COMELEC to the President of the Philippines and the Congress on the Manner the Election was held on November 10, 1959*. Manila: Commission on Elections.

_____ . 1965. *Report of the COMELEC to the President of the Philippines and the Congress on the Manner the Elections were held on November 12, 1963*. Manila: Commission on Elections.

_____ . 1968. *Report of the COMELEC to the President of the Philippines and the Congress on the Manner the Elections were held on November 14, 1967*. Manila: Commission on Elections.

_____ . 1973. *Report of the COMELEC to the President of the Philippines and the Congress on the Manner the Elections were held on November 8, 1971*. Manila: Commission on Elections.

_____. 1979. *Report of the COMELEC to the President/Prime Minister of the Philippines and the Batasang Pambansa on the Manner the Elections of Representatives to the Batasang Pambansa were held on April 7 and 27, 1978*. Manila: Commission on Elections.

Republic of the Philippines, National Economic and Development Authority, National Census and Statistics Office. 1971. *Census of Agriculture, Vol. 1, Final Report*. Manila: National Economic and Development Authority, National Census and Statistics Office.

_____. 1978. *Statistical Analyst*. Iloilo City: National Economic and Development Authority, National Census and Statistics Office.

_____. 1983. *Statistical Analyst, Region VI*. Iloilo City: National Economic and Development Authority, National Census and Statistics Office.

_____. 1983. *1980 Census of Population and Housing, Vol. 1, Final Report*. Manila: National Economic and Development Authority, National Census and Statistics Office.

_____. 1984. *Statistical Analyst, Region VI*. Iloilo City: National Economic and Development Authority, National Census and Statistics Office.

_____. 1985. *1980 Census of Agriculture, Vol. 1, Final Report*. Manila: National Economic and Development Authority, National Census and Statistics Office.

_____. 1986. *Philippine Yearbook 1985*. Manila: National Economic and Development Authority, National Census and Statistics Office.

Romani, John H. and Ladd M. Thomas. 1954. *A Survey of Local Government in the Philippines*. Manila: Institute of Public Administration, University of the Philippines.

Rondinelli, Dennis A. 1980. "Regional Disparities and Investment Allocation Policies in the Philippines: Spatial Dimensions of Poverty in a Developing Country." *Canadian Journal of Development Studies* 1: 262-287.

Rüland, Jürgen. 1982a. *Politik und Verwaltung in Metro Manila. Aspekte der Herrschaftsstabilisierung in einem autoritären politischen System*. Munich, Cologne, and London: Weltforum Verlag.

_____. 1982b. *Squatter Relocation in the Philippines. The Case of Metro Manila*. Bayreuth: University of Bayreuth, Research Papers No. 5, Fachgruppe Geowissenschaften.

_____. 1982d. *Die Philippinen: Zwischen Repression und Widerstand. Ein Überblick über neueste Entwicklungen*. Freiburg: Arnold-Bergstraesser-Institut.

_____. 1984. "Political Change, Urban Services and Social Movements: Political Participation and Grass-Roots Politics in Metro Manila." *Public Administration and Development* 4: 325-334.

_____. 1985a. "Metropolitan Government under Martial Law: The MMC Experiment." *Philippine Journal of Public Administration* 29: 27-41.

_____. 1985c. *Die Philippinen. Anatomie einer Krise*. Bonn: Friedrich-Ebert-Stiftung.

_____. 1986a. "Authoritarianism at the Grass Roots: Urban Neighborhood Organizations in Metro Manila." *The Asian Journal of Public Administration* 8: 2-42.

_____ . 1986b. *Die Philippinen. Das Marcos Erbe.* Bonn: Friedrich-Ebert-Stiftung.

Rüland, Jürgen and Tomas A. Sajo. 1988. "Local Government and Development in a Regional City: The Case of Iloilo City, Philippines." *Public Administration and Development* 8: 261-287.

Soberano, José D. and H. Odell Waldby. 1965. *Philippine Public Fiscal Administration.* Manila: College of Public Administration.

Solano, M.S. 1974. "The Local Political Elite: A Study of its Composition." *Saint Louis University Research Journal* 5: 1-44.

Soriano, L.V. 1966. *Local Officials' Understanding, Willingness and Attitudes Towards Local Autonomy.* Manila: College of Public Administration, University of the Philippines.

Sosmeña, Gaudioso C. 1980. "Policy Analysis: The Case of Local Governments." Ph.D. Thesis, Centro-Escolar University, Manila.

_____ . 1988. " Philippine Cities: Limits and Opportunities for Local Autonomy," in Jürgen Rüland, ed., *Urban Government and Development in Asia. Readings in Subnational Development.* Pp. 187-208. Munich, Cologne, and London.

Stauffer, Robert B. 1977. "Philippine Corporatism: A Note on the "New Society." *Asian Survey* 17: 393-407.

Stinner, W.F. and M. Bacol-Montilla. 1981. "Population Deconcentration in Metropolitan Manila in the 20th Century." *The Journal of Developing Areas* 16: 3-16.

Sultan, K.M.T. 1976. "Citizen Participation and Political Development in Asian Perspectives: A Comparative Study of Bangladesh and the Philippines." M.A. Thesis, College of Public Administration University of the Philippines, Manila.

Tapales, Proserpina D. 1970. "Philippine Cities: Government Partners or Parasites?" *Philippine Journal of Public Administration* 14: 67-77.

Tutay, Filemon V. 1969. "Violence and Terrorism in Elections," in José Veloso Abuenva and Raul P. de Guzman, eds., *Foundations and Dynamics of Filipino Government and Politics.* Pp. 81-84. Manila, Quezon City, Makati, and Cebu: Bookmark.

United Nations/Economic and Social Commission for Asia and the Pacific. 1982. *Local Authorities and Human Settlements Development in Manila.* Yokohama: United Nations/Economic and Social Commission for Asia and the Pacific.

University of the Philippines Law Center. 1985. *MMC: Issues, Problems and Proposals.* Manila: Law Center, University of the Philippines.

Villanueva, A.B. 1976. "Congressional Legitimization of Municipal Reform in the Philippines, 1954-1960." *Modern Asian Studies* 10: 285-301.

_____ . 1977. "Central-Local Relations in Philippine Municipal Reform 1954-60." *Journal of Administration Overseas* 16: 186-194.

Williams, Arthur R. 1981. "Center, Bureaucracy, and Locality: Central-Local Relations in the Philippines." Ph.D. Thesis, Cornell University, Ithaca.

Wolff, Jürgen H. 1983. *Planung in Manila.* Bayreuth: University of Bayreuth, Fachgruppe Geowissenschaften, Research Papers No. 7.

Wolters, Willem G. 1983. *Politics, Patronage and Class Conflict in Central Luzon.* The Hague: Institute of Social Studies.

_____. 1989. "Rise and Fall of Provincial Elites in the Philippines." *Social Issues in Southeast Asia* 4: 54-74.

World Bank. 1988. *The Philippine Poor: What Is to Be Done?.* Washington, D.C.: The World Bank.

Wurfel, David. 1963. "Comparative Studies in Political Finance, The Philippines". *The Journal of Politics* Vol. 25:757-773.

_____. 1988. *Filipino Politics. Development and Decay.* Ithaca and London: Cornell University Press.

Yeh, G.A. 1980. "Urban System Structures and Development in the Philippines." Ph.D. Dissertation, Syracuse University, Syracuse.

Yoingco, Angel Q. 1976. *Land Tax Policy in Developing Countries. With Particular Reference to the Philippines.* Manila: National Tax Resource Center.

_____. 1986. "Credit-Financing for Local Governments in the Philippines." *Regional Development Dialogue* 7: 65-93.

IV. Thailand

Angel, Shlomo. 1985. *"Where Have all the People Gone? Urbanization and Counter-Urbanization in Thailand."* Paper Presented at the International Seminar on Planning for Settlements in Rural Regions: The Case of Spontaneous Settlements, United Nations Centre for Human Settlements (Habitat), Nairobi, Kenya, 11-20 November 1985.

Angel, Shlomo and Sopon Pornchokchai. 1988. *Bangkok, Slum Lands: The Policy Implications of Recent Findings, Technical Report.* Bangkok: Planning and Development Collaborative International.

Bänziger, Hans. 1987. "How Wildlife is Helping to Save Doi Suthep: Buddhist Sanctuary and National Park of Thailand" in I. Hedberg, ed., *Proceedings of the Symposium "Systematic Botany. A Key Science for Tropical Research and Documentation,"* Sweden, 14-17 September 1987. Pp. 255-267. Stockholm.

Boesch, Ernst E. 1970. *Zwiespältige Eliten. Eine sozialpsychologische Untersuchung über administrative Eliten in Thailand.* Bern, Stuttgart, Wien: Huber.

Boonchorntarakul, Daranee. 1976. "The Impact of the Growth Center on Rural Areas: A Case Study in the North of Thailand." MA Thesis, Asian Institute of Technology, Bangkok.

Boonyabancha, Somsook. 1983. "The Causes and Effects of Slum Eviction in Bangkok," in Shlomo Angel, Ray Archer, Sidhijai Tanphiphat, and Emiel Wegelin, eds., *Land for Housing the Poor.* Pp. 254-280. Singapore: Select Books.

Chananan, P. 1987. *Investors and Merchants. The Origin and Growth of Commercial Enterprises in Northern Thailand, 2464-2523.* Bangkok: Chulalongkorn University Social Research Institute (CUSRI) Publications (in Thai).

Chenvidyakarn, Montri. 1977. "Economic Interest Groups in Thailand: Some Observations on the Legal Aspects, Public Policy and Political Process." *Social Science Review,* pp. 224-277.

Chiang Mai Chamber of Commerce. 1985. *Chiang Mai Directory 1985-1986*. Chiang Mai: Chiang Mai Chamber of Commerce.

_____. 1990. *Chiang Mai Directory 1990-1992*. Chiang Mai: Chiang Mai Chamber of Commerce.

Chiang Mai Municipality. 1985a. *Municipal Long-Range Plan (15 Years) 1985-2000*. Chiang Mai: Chiang Mai Municipality (in Thai).

_____. 1985b. *Report on Overcrowded Communities Development in a Regional Center*. Chiang Mai: Chiang Mai Municipality (in Thai).

_____. 1990. *Municipal Development Plan 1990*. Chiang Mai: Chiang Mai Municipality (in Thai).

Chiang Mai University. 1985. *Profile of Northern Thailand*. Chiang Mai: Chiang Mai University.

Department of Local Administration. 1988. "Policy to Develop Municipal Revenues." *Tesaphiban Krom Gan Bokkrong* 83: 19-31 (in Thai).

Dhiratayaninant, K. 1986. "Taxing Powers of Local Government in Thailand: Present Performance and Potential." *Regional Development Dialogue* 7: 96-123.

Dhiravegin, Likhit. 1978. *The Bureaucratic Elite of Thailand. A Study of Their Sociological Attributes, Educational Backgrounds and Career Advancement Pattern*. Bangkok: Thai Khadi Institute, Thammasat University.

_____. 1983. "Centralization and Decentralization: The Dilemma of Thailand" in: Ernst E. Boesch, ed., *Thai Culture. Report on the Second Thai-European Research Seminar 1982*. Pp. 47-64. Saarbrücken: University of the Saar, Socio-Psychological Research Centre on Development Planning.

_____. 1984. *Social Change and Contemporary Thai Politics. An Analysis of the Interrelationship between the Society and the Polity*. Bangkok: Research Center, Faculty of Political Science, Thammasat University.

Dias, Hiran D. 1981. *"The Legal Framework for Public Participation in the Management of Human Settlements in Thailand."* Bangkok Asian Institute of Technology, Human Settlements Division, Working Paper 7.

Donner, Wolf. 1989. *Thailand. Räumliche Strukturen und Entwicklung*. Darmstadt: Wissenschaftliche Buchgesellschaft.

Douglass, Michael. 1981. "Thailand: Territorial Dissolution and Alternative Regional Development for the Central Plains," in Walter B. Stöhr and Fraser D. R. Taylor, eds., *Development from Above or Below? The Dialectics of Regional Planning in Developing Countries*. Pp. 183-208. Chichester: John Wiley.

Evers, Hans-Dieter, ed. 1969. *Loosely Structured Social Systems. Thailand in Comparative Perspective*. New Haven: Yale University Southeast Asia Studies.

_____. 1978. "The Formation of a Social Class Structure: Organization, Bureaucratization, and Social Mobility in Thailand," in Clark D. Neher, ed., *Modern Thai Politics*. Pp. 170-185. Cambridge, Mass.: Schenkman.

Girling, John L.S. 1981. *Thailand. Society and Politics*. Ithaca and London: Cornell University Press.

Government of Thailand. 1981. *The Fifth National Economic and Social Development Plan (1982-1986)*. Bangkok: National Economic and Social Development Board, Office of the Prime Minister.

Hennings, Gerd and H. Detlef Kammeier. 1978. *Zur Entwicklung von Sekundar- zentren in Thailand. Bericht der Projektfindungskommission im Bereich Stadt- und Regionalplanung in Thailand.* Bangkok and Dortmund: Mimeographed Report.

Horrigan, Frederick. 1959. "Local Government and Administration in Thailand: A Study of Institutions and Their Cultural Setting." Ph.D. Thesis, Indiana University, Bloomington.

Horrigan, Wilkinson & Associates. 1982. *Regional Cities Development Programme. Technical Assistance in Valuation and Taxation of Real Property, Final Report, 2 Vols.* Canberra: Horrigan, Wilkinson & Associates.

Hutaserani, Suganya and Somchai Jitsuchon. 1988. *"Thailand's Income Distribution and Poverty Profile and their Current Situations."* Paper Presented at the 1988 TDRI Year-End Conference on "Income Distribution and Long-Term Development." Bangkok: Thailand Development Research Institute.

Ikemoto, Y. and K. Limskul. 1987. "Income Inequality and Regional Disparity in Thailand, 1962-1982." *The Developing Economies* 25: 249-269.

Industrial Estate Authority of Thailand. 1985. *The Northern Industrial Estate Chiang Mai-Lamphun. Golden Town for Industries.* Bangkok: Industrial Estate Authority of Thailand.

Ingavata, Chaichana. 1990. "Community Development and Local-Level Democracy in Thailand: The Role of Tambol Councils." *Social Issues in Southeast Asia* 5: 113-143.

Ingle, M. 1974. *Local Governance and Rural Development in Thailand.* Ithaca: Rural Development Committee, Center for International Studies, Cornell University.

Janssen, P. 1982. "Chiang Mai on the Brink of Industrialization." *Bangkok Post,* October 31, p. 5.

Jumbhala, P. 1987. "Interest and Pressure Groups" in Somsakdi Xuto, ed., *Government and Politics of Thailand.* Singapore, Oxford, New York: Oxford University Press, pp. 110-167.

Kammeier, H. Detlef. 1986. "Thailand's Small Towns: Exploring Facts and Figures Beyond the Population Statistics," in Karl Husa, Christian Vielhaber, and Helmut Wohlschlägl, eds., *Beiträge zur Bevölkerungsforschung. Festschrift Ernest Troger zum 60. Geburtstag.* Pp. 299-320. Vienna: Ferdinand Hirt Publications.

Karnjanaprakorn, Choop. 1962. *Municipal Government in Thailand as an Institution and Process of Self Government.* Bangkok: Institute of Public Administration, Thammasat University.

Kemp, Jeremy H. 1988. *"Community and State in Modern Thailand."* Bielefeld: University of Bielefeld, Sociology of Development Research Centre, Southeast Asia Programme, Working Paper No. 100.

Keyes, Charles F. 1989. *Thailand. Buddhist Kingdom as Modern Nation-State.* Bangkok: Editions Duang Kamol.

Kingdom of Thailand, Ministry of Interior, Australian International Development Assistance Bureau. 1988a. *Regional Cities Development Project II. Pre-Feasibility Study, Vol. 3, Nakhon Sawan.* Bangkok: Sinclair Knight & Partners PTY Ltd., Pal Consultants Co. Ltd.

_____. 1988b. *Regional Cities Development Project II. Pre-Feasibility Study, Vol. 10, Institutional Issues Report.* Bangkok: Sinclair Knight & Partner PTY Ltd., Pal Consultants Co., Ltd.

Kingdom of Thailand, Ministry of Interior, United Nations Development Programme. 1983. *Feasibility Studies for Regional Cities Development. Final Report, Vols 1-7.* Bangkok: Ministry of Interior, United Nations Development Programme.

Kongridhisuksakorn, P. 1984. "Local Government in Thailand," in: K. Hanaoka, ed., *Comparative Study on the Local Public Administration in Asian and Pacific Countries.* Pp. 206-231. Tokyo: Eastern Regional Organization for Public Administration, Local Government Center.

Korff, Rüdiger. 1986. *Bangkok: Urban System and Everyday Life.* Saarbrücken and Fort Lauderdale: Breitenbach Publishers.

_____. 1989. *"Political Change and Local Power in Thailand."* Bielefeld: University of Bielefeld, Sociology of Development Research Centre, Southeast Asia Programme, Working Paper No. 119.

Krannich, Ronald L. 1975. "Dimensions of Urban Political and Administrative Behavior: The Role of the Municipal Clerk in Thailand." Ph.D. Thesis, Northern Illinois University, DeKalb.

_____. 1978a. *Mayors and Managers in Thailand. The Struggle for Political Life in Administrative Settings.* Athens, Ohio: Ohio University Center for International Studies, Southeast Asia Program.

_____. 1978b. "The Politics of Street-Level Bureaucracy in Thailand." *Philippine Journal of Public Administration* 22: 113-130.

_____. 1979. "The Politics of Intergovernmental Relations in Thailand." *Asian Survey* 19: 506-522.

_____. 1980. "Administrative Leadership of Mayors: The Politics of Mayor-Manager Relationships in Thailand." *Public Administration Review* 40: 330-341.

_____. 1982. "Governing Urban Thailand: Coping with Policies and Administrative Politics." *Urban Affairs Quarterly* 17: 319-342.

Ladavalya, Bhansoon M.L. et al. 1987. *The Development of Chiang Mai as a Regional City: Its Impact on the Modernization of Upper Northern Thailand.* Chiang Mai: Social Research Institute, Chiang Mai University (in Thai).

Laothamatas, Anek. 1988. "Business and Politics in Thailand. New Patterns of Influence." *Asian Survey* 28: 451-469.

London, Bruce. 1979. "Internal Colonialism in Thailand. Primate City Parasitism Reconsidered." *Urban Affairs Quarterly* 14: 485-514.

Mabry, Bevars. 1977. "The Thai Labor Movement." *Asian Survey* 17: 931-951.

Mawhood, Philip. 1981. *"Local Government Reform in Thailand. Case Studies."* Birmingham: Development Administration Group Occasional Paper No. 12.

Meyer, Walter. 1988. "Beyond the Mask. Toward a Transdisciplinary Approach of Selected Social Problems Related to the Evolution and Context of International Tourism in Thailand." Ph.D. Thesis, University of Geneva, Geneva.

Morell, David and Chai-anan Samudavanija. 1981. *Political Conflict in Thailand. Reform, Reaction, Revolution.* Cambridge, Mass: Oelgeschlager, Gunn & Hain Publishers, Inc.

Muecke, Majorie A. 1980, "The Village Scouts of Thailand." *Asian Survey* 20: 407-427.

Mulder, Niels. 1985. *Everyday Life in Thailand. An Interpretation.* Bangkok: Edition Duang Kamol.

Multiman. 1982. *Municipal Management and Finance Study, Concept Report, 3 Vols.* Bangkok: Multiman, Royal Government of Thailand, Ministry of Interior, and United Nations Development Programme..

Murashima, Eiji. 1987. "Local Elections and Leadership in Thailand: A Case Study of Nakhon Sawan Province." *The Developing Economies* 25: 363-385.

National Institute of Development Administration. 1983. *Regional Cities Development Programme: Municipal Finance and Management. Final Report.* Bangkok: National Institute of Development Administration.

_____ . 1984. *Regional Cities Development Programme: Municipal Finance and Management. Final Report. Planning and Budgeting.* Bangkok: National Institute of Development Administration.

National Statistical Office, Office of the Prime Minister. 1980. *1978 Agricultural Census Report. Thailand.* Bangkok: National Statistical Office.

National Statistical Office, Office of the Prime Minister. 1984. *Statistical Reports of Changwat.* Bangkok: National Statistical Office.

_____ . 1984. *1983 Intercensal Survey of Agriculture.* Bangkok: National Statistical Office.

_____ . 1988. *Statistical Yearbook Thailand 1987-1988.* Bangkok: National Statistical Office.

Neher, Clark D. 1977. "Political Corruption in a Thai Province." *The Journal of Developing Areas* 11: 479-492.

_____ , ed. 1979. *Modern Thai Politics: From Village to Nation.* Cambridge, Mass.: Schenkman.

_____ . 1984. "Thailand," in Diane K. Mauzy, ed., *Politics in the ASEAN States.* Pp. 13-55. Kuala Lumpur: Maricans.

_____ . 1990. Change in Thailand. *Current History* 89: 101-130.

Neher, Clark D. and Budsayamat Bunjaipet. 1989. Political Interaction in Northern Thailand. *Southeast Asian Journal of Social Science* 17: 53-69.

Noranitipadungkarn, Chakrit. 1981. *Elites, Power Structure and Politics in Thai Communities.* Bangkok: The National Institute of Development Administration.

Noranitipadungkarn, Chakrit and Clarke Hagensick. 1973. *Modernizing Chiang Mai.* Bangkok: Research Center, National Institute of Development Administration.

Norconsult, A.S. 1977. *Chiang Mai Urban Pre-Investment Study, Thailand THA/75/024.* Final Report: Bangkok: Norconsult.

Office of the National Economic and Social Development Board. 1986. *Bangkok Metropolitan Regional Development Proposals: Recommended Strategies and Investment Programmes for the Sixth Plan (1987-1991)*. Bangkok: Office of the National Economic and Social Development Board.

Pakkasem, Phisit. 1977. "The Role of Local Government in Regional Development. Thailand Case Study." *Social Science Review* 46-70.

_____ . 1981. "Thailand: Urbanization and Government Policy," in M. Honjo, ed., *Urbanization and Regional Development*. Pp. 179-199. Nagoya: United Nations Centre for Regional Development.

_____ . 1984. "Urban Energy Development Issues and Infrastructure Requirements in the 1980s and the 1990s," in Thailand Development Research Institute, ed., *Seminar on Development Research and National Development, December 1-2, Pattaya*. Bangkok: Thailand Development Research Institute.

_____ . 1987. "Decentralization is not the Answer." *The Nation Review*, 5 July, p. 10.

_____ . 1988. *Leading Issues in Thailand's Development Transformation 1960-1990*. Bangkok: D.K. Book House.

Parananond, Usadank. 1985. "The Chiang Mai City Plan." *Political Science Review* 6: 73-83 (in Thai).

Patom, Manirojana. 1978. "Governing a Metropolitan Area in Thailand: A Study of Public Policies in Bangkok Metropolis." Ph.D. Thesis, Syracuse University, Syracuse.

Pongquan, Shanvit. 1980. "Municipal Boundaries of the Towns in Thailand: Implications for Development Planning." MA Thesis, Asian Institute of Technology, Bangkok.

Prabudhanitisarn, Nitaya. 1982. *Problems of People Participation in Chiang Mai City Urban Land Use Planning*. Chiang Mai: Chiang Mai University (in Thai).

_____ . 1985. "A Study of Transportation Planning in Chiang Mai City." MA Thesis, San Jose State University, San Jose.

Prachid na Bangchang. 1981. *Migration to Chiang Mai and Kampaeng Petch*. Bangkok: Chulalongkorn University Social Research Institute.

Prasith-rathsint, Suchart. 1987. *Thailand's National Development: Policy Issues and Challenges*. Bangkok: Thai University Research Association and Canadian International Development Agency.

Prizzia, Ross. 1985. *Thailand in Transition. The Role of the Oppositionist Forces*. Honolulu: University of Hawaii Press.

Raksasataya, Amorn. 1990. *Thailand. Verwaltungsprofile*. Eschborn. Deutsche Gesellschaft für Technische Zusammenarbeit.

Research Division, Department of Local Administration, Ministry of the Interior. 1977. *Report on Chiang Mai City Research*. Bangkok: Ministry of the Interior (in Thai).

Riggs, Fred W. 1966. *Thailand. The Modernization of a Bureaucratic Polity*. Honolulu: East-West Center Press.

Rüland, Jürgen. 1989. *Another Asian Miracle Economy in the Making? Thailand's Prospects for Becoming a NIC in the Nineties*. Freiburg: Arnold-Bergstraesser-Institut.

Rüland, Jürgen and M.L. Bhansoon Ladavalya. 1986. "Urbanization, Municipal Government and Development in a Regional City. The Case of Chiang Mai, Thailand." *Vierteljahresberichte* 106: 433-448.

Rungvisai, Suvit. 1983. *The Problems and Effects Caused by the Extension of the Municipal Boundaries of Chiang Mai*. Chiang Mai: Chiang Mai University (in Thai).

_____. 1985. *Voting Behavior of the People of Chiang Mai City*. Bangkok: Social Science Association of Thailand (in Thai).

Samudavanija, Chai-anan. 1987. "Thai Politics at the Cross Roads." Bangkok: *The Nation* Review, 12 April, p. 10.

Simon, Paul. 1987. "Von Buddha bis Marx. Nicht-Regierungsorganisationen in Thailand." *blätter des iz3w*, 142: 23-28.

Singhanetra-Renard, Anchalee. 1981. "Mobility in North Thailand: A View from within," in Gavin W. Jones, and H.V. Richter, eds., *Population Mobility and Development: Southeast Asia and the Pacific*. Pp. 137-166. Canberra: Australian National University.

_____. 1982a. *Commuting and the Fertility of Construction Workers in Chiang Mai City*. Singapore: Institue of Southeast Asian Studies.

_____. 1982b. "Northern Thai Mobility 1870-1977." Ph.D. Thesis, University of Hawaii, Honolulu.

Social Research Institute, Chiang Mai University. 1986. *Proceedings of a Seminar on the Development of Regional Cities in Northern Thailand: Problems, Obstacles and Alternatives to Future Development, April 4-5, Chiang Mai*. Chiang Mai: Social Research Institute, Chiang Mai University (in Thai).

Southeast Asia Development Advisory Group of the Asia Society. 1976. *Ad Hoc Seminar on Development and Finance of Local Government in Thailand, February 2-3, Chiang Mai*.

Suksamram, Somboon. 1982. *Buddhism and Politics in Thailand*. Singapore: Institute of Southeast Asian Studies.

Suriyamongkol, Pisan. 1988. *Institutionalization of Democratic Political Processes in Thailand: A Three-Pronged Democratic Polity*. Bangkok: Thammasat University Press.

Suthandan, S. 1979. "Planning for Small Towns in Thailand: The Role of Public Administration." MA Thesis, Asian Institute of Technology, Bangkok.

Tanrattanakoon, Wilawan. 1984. "Linkage Pattern in Small-Scale Industries in Chiang Mai Province." MA Thesis, Asian Institute of Technology, Bangkok.

Thai University Research Association. 1976. *Urbanization in the Bangkok Central Region*. Bangkok: Thai University Research Association.

Thomas, Ladd M. and Chakrit Noranitipadungkarn. 1975. "Super-Governor of Chiang Mai: Imbalance between Demands and Supports." *Thai Journal of Development Administration* 15: 328-360.

Tongdhamachart, Kramol. 1982. *Toward a Political Party Theory in Thai Perspective*. Singapore: Institute of Southeast Asian Studies.

Tourism Authority of Thailand. 1984. *Annual Statistical Report on Tourism in Thailand 1983*. Bangkok: Tourism Authority of Thailand.

_____. 1987. *Annual Statistical Report on Tourism in Thailand 1986.* Bangkok: Tourism Authority of Thailand.

Technische Universität Berlin. 1983/84. *Umweltfolgen von Dezentralisierungsmaßnahmen am Beispiel Nordthailand.* Berlin: Technische Universität Berlin, Unpublished Report.

Thompson, Virginia. 1955. "Rural and Urban Self-Government in Southeast Asia," in Rupert Emerson, ed., *Representative Government in Southeast Asia.* Pp. 118-150. Cambridge: Harvard University Press.

United Nations. 1979. *UNDP-Project THA-33, Northern Region of Thailand, Regional Planning Study, 7 Vols.* Bangkok: United Nations.

Vatikiotis, Michael R.J. 1984a. *"Ethnic Immigrants from Burma in Northern Thailand: 'Refugees' or 'Displaced Persons'?"* Paper Presented at the International Conference on Thai Studies, 22-24 August, Bangkok.

_____. 1984b. "Ethnic Pluralism, in the Northern Thai City of Chiang Mai." Ph.D. Thesis, St. Catherine's College, Oxford.

Wahnschafft, Ralph. 1984. *Zum Entwicklungspotential des Klein(st)gewerbes. Der "informelle Sektor "in thailändischen Fremdenverkehrsorten.* Saarbrücken and Fort Lauderdale: Breitenbach Publishers.

Wan G'aeo. 1989. "The Nongovernmental Development Movement in Thailand." *Asian Exchange* 6: 59-77.

Wenk, Klaus. 1964. *Die Verfassungen Thailands.* Frankfurt and Berlin: Alfred Metzner Verlag.

World Bank. 1978. *Urban Sector Review.* Washington, D.C.: The World Bank.

_____. 1985. *Thailand. Regional Cities Development Project.* Washington, D.C.: The World Bank, Staff Appraisal Report.

_____. 1986. *Thailand, Country Economic Report.* Washington, D.C.: The World Bank.

Wyatt, David K. 1984. *Thailand: A Short History.* London and Bangkok: Yale University Press and Thai Wattana Panich Co., Ltd.

Xuto, Somsakdi, ed. 1987. *Government and Politics of Thailand.* Singapore, Oxford, and New York: Oxford University Press.

Xuto, Somsakdi, Suchart Prasith-rathsint, Thinapan Nakata, and Twatchai Yongkittikul, eds. 1983. *Strategies and Measures for the Development of Thailand in the 1980s.* Bangkok: Research Institute of the Thai University Research Association and Friedrich-Ebert-Stiftung.

Yanklinfung, P. n.d. *"Chiang Mai: Urbanization of an Intermediate City."* Chiang Mai: Chiang Mai University, Mimeographed Paper.

Yukobol, M. 1984. "Fiscal Structure of Local Government in Thailand." M.A. Thesis, Thammasat University, Bangkok.

Index